≺ ≻

# REALMS OF FREEDOM IN
# MODERN CHINA

# THE MAKING OF MODERN FREEDOM

*General Editor: R. W. Davis*

*Center for the History of Freedom*
*Washington University in St. Louis*

# REALMS OF FREEDOM IN MODERN CHINA

≺ ≻

*Edited by William C. Kirby*

STANFORD UNIVERSITY PRESS
STANFORD, CALIFORNIA

Stanford University Press
Stanford, California
© 2004 by the Board of Trustees of the
Leland Stanford Junior University
Printed in the United States of America

Library of Congress Cataloging-in-Publication Data
Realms of freedom in modern China /edited by William C. Kirby.
    p.   cm. — (The making of modern freedom)
    Includes bibliographical references and index.
    ISBN 0-8047-4878-0 (cloth : alk. paper)
    ISBN 0-8047-5232-X (pbk. : alk. paper)
        1. Human rights—China.   2. China—Politics and government.
3. Social control—China.   4. Liberty.   I. Kirby, William C.
II. Series.
JC599.C6 R43      2004
323'.0951—dc21                                        2003009924

This book is printed on acid-free, archival-quality paper.

Original printing 2004

Last figure below indicates year of this printing:
    13    12    11    10    09    08    07    06    05

Typeset at Stanford University Press in 10/13 Trump Mediaeval

<>

# Acknowledgments

This volume has been generously supported by a grant from the Luce Foundation and from the Lynde and Harry Bradley Foundation. As always, we are also grateful for the support of Washington University.

# Series Foreword

THE STARTLING AND moving events that swept from China to Eastern Europe to Latin America and South Africa at the end of the 1980s, followed closely by similar events and the subsequent dissolution of what used to be the Soviet Union, formed one of those great historic occasions when calls for freedom, rights, and democracy echoed through political upheaval. A clear-eyed look at any of those conjunctions—in 1776 and 1789, in 1848 and 1918, as well as in 1989—reminds us that freedom, liberty, rights, and democracy are words into which many different and conflicting hopes have been read. The language of freedom—or liberty, which is interchangeable with freedom most of the time—is inherently difficult. It carried vastly different meanings in the classical world and in medieval Europe from those of modern understanding, though thinkers in later ages sometimes eagerly assimilated the older meanings to their own circumstances and purposes.

A new kind of freedom, which we have here called modern, gradually disentangles itself from old contexts in Europe, beginning first in England in the early seventeenth century and then, with many confusions, denials, reversals, and cross-purposes, elsewhere in Europe and the world. A large-scale history of this modern, conceptually distinct, idea of freedom is now beyond the ambition of any one scholar, however learned. This collaborative enterprise, tentative though it must be, is an effort to fill the gap.

We could not take into account all the varied meanings that freedom and liberty have carried in the modern world. We have, for example, ruled out extended attention to what some political philosophers have called "positive freedom," in the sense of self-realization of the individual; nor could we, even in a series as large as this, cope with the enormous implications of the four freedoms invoked by Franklin D. Roosevelt in 1941. Freedom of speech and freedom of the press will have their place in the narrative that follows, certainly, but not the boundless calls for freedom from want and freedom from fear.

We use freedom in the traditional and restricted sense of civil and political liberty—freedom of religion, freedom of speech and assembly, freedom of the individual from arbitrary and capricious authority over persons or property, freedom to produce and to exchange goods and services, and the freedom to take part in the political process that shapes people's destiny. In no major part of the world over the past few years have aspirations for those freedoms not been at least powerfully expressed; and in most places where they did not exist, strong measures have been taken—not always successfully—to attain them.

The history we trace was not a steady march toward the present or the fulfillment of some cosmic necessity. Modern freedom had its roots in specific circumstances in early modern Europe, despite the unpromising and even hostile characteristics of the larger society and culture. From these narrow and often selfishly motivated beginnings, modern freedom came to be realized in later times, constrained by old traditions and institutions hard to move, and driven by ambition as well as idealism: everywhere the growth of freedom has been *sui generis*. But to understand these unique developments fully, we must first try to see them against the making of modern freedom as a whole.

This volume, the fifteenth in the series, is also the last. No time is ever likely to be entirely appropriate to stop (at least, we sincerely hope not!). What we have tried to do is to identify a number of issues, events, and periods that we consider vital in the making of what we call modern freedom and examine them in some detail, from what we see as the emergence of the idea of individual freedom in early Stuart England to the subject of this volume, the state of freedom in the modern Chinese world, which no one would claim is as yet exactly flourishing.

Nor, as our second volume shows, was freedom flourishing in later Stuart England; and it remained precarious in Hanoverian Britain. Still, circumstances were bringing a shift in institutions, particularly fiscal crises that favored the growth of representative government. At the same time the flowering of republican ideas reinforced and broadened notions of limited government. The practical effects of these two tendencies are seen in two volumes on establishing liberty after the American Revolution and the implications of the *Declaration of the Rights of Man* for the French Revolution. These are followed by several more thematic volumes, the impacts of revolution and religion respectively on freedom in the nineteenth century, and a volume on the state and freedom of contract in Anglo-American thought. Another study is of the terms of labor, comparing the situations of slaves, serfs, and so-called free labor in the nineteenth century. A volume on the position of women in England in the eighteenth and nineteenth centuries suggests that they had a good deal more actual freedom than has previously been thought. A book on the idea of freedom in Asia and Africa looks both at the origins of the idea and examples of the current state of freedom on these two continents. Our fourteenth volume treats migrations, forced and free, in the Atlantic world and in Russia and their impacts on the societies they touched.

It may be said that this list of topics is not comprehensive. It certainly is not. We never believed that we could cover everything, and there is clearly a great deal of important work yet to be done. That we welcome and look forward to. Indeed, one of the main purposes of this project from its beginning in the early 1980s was to encourage such work. At that time there had never been a dedicated study of one of the most important formative factors in history (though Lord Acton had thought of one). Professor Hexter believed it was time to make a beginning, and this series is the result. Some may wonder whether a volume on China is an appropriate one on which to end. If we wished to argue that freedom is now secure, it would not be. Perhaps, however, that is the very reason it is appropriate. Freedom has never been secure, and it is probably true to say that in this century its security will be profoundly affected by the course China takes.

*The Making of Modern Freedom* grows out of a continuing series of conferences held at the Center for the History of Freedom at Washington University in St. Louis. Professor J. H. Hexter was the founder and, for three years, the resident gadfly of the Center. His contribution is gratefully recalled by all his colleagues.

R.W.D.

≺≻

# Contents

# CONTRIBUTORS

William P. Alford
*Harvard University School of Law*

Irene Bloom
*Barnard College*

Jérôme Bourgon
*Institut d'Asie Orientale, Lyon*

William C. Jones
*Washington University School of Law*

William C. Kirby
*Harvard University*

Arlen Meliksetov
*Moscow State University*

Jean C. Oi
*Stanford University*

Alexander Pantsov
*Capital University*

Elizabeth J. Perry
*Harvard University*

Yuanyuan Shen
*Harvard University School of Law*

Robert P. Weller
*Boston University*

Wen-hsin Yeh
*University of California, Berkeley*

Madeleine Zelin
*Columbia University*

≺ ≻

# REALMS OF FREEDOM IN
MODERN CHINA

<≺ ≻>

# Introduction

WILLIAM C. KIRBY

In the only free societies on earth today, freedom and assemblies of representatives freely elected from constituencies geographically defined have been a symbiotic pair. Of the gifts that that terrifying Magus, the West, has come bearing to mankind they are, though often spurned, among the most benign. They are also purely Western in origin. In the multifold history of man they came into being nowhere else. They have not appeared anywhere else since, except in consequence of Western influence.[1]

By J. H. Hexter's definition of freedom, there should be little purpose in a volume on China in the *Making of Modern Freedom* series of conferences and books that he began to plan in 1986. Indeed, the hopes that Professor Hexter harbored for China early in the heady year of 1989—that "the grip of State and Party has become uncertain, shaky and loose," there as in the Soviet Union, and that for China as elsewhere "the way of freedom and democracy is the only game in town"[2]—all this would be crushed by the tanks of June 4th of that year and by the apparent stabilization of the communist regime in Beijing. Hexter's contention that there were "no serious alternative conceptions" to democracy for human political organization[3] would be challenged by Chinese leaders in the 1990s and beyond, even as they affirmed China's formal commitment to the "universality of human rights."[4]

What, then, are the justifications for a book to search for "Realms of Freedom in the Modern Chinese World"? I believe that there are several. First, the *Making of Modern Freedom* series, as it has evolved under Richard Davis, has found it quite possible to discuss conceptions of "freedom" that do not meet the test of being accompanied by representative institutions of the kind descended, according to Hexter, from the transformative English parliaments between 1529 and 1668.[5] A previous volume in the se-

ries, *The Idea of Freedom in Asia and Africa*, edited by Robert
Taylor, argues persuasively for "collectivist" conceptions of freedom on the part of peoples of those two continents who in the
nineteenth and twentieth centuries were colonized (or feared colonization) by Europeans, who, for their own part, kept their freedoms of speech and assembly, and indeed their representative institutions, mostly for themselves.[6]

Second, to have only one of fifteen volumes of *The Making of
Modern Freedom* explicitly on the non-Western world would seem
to underestimate the importance of discourses of freedom outside
of Europe and the Americas. Not unrelated to conceptions of national and racial freedom toward the end of the imperialist era
were universalistic approaches to "human rights" that would set
alternative international agendas and define debates on human
rights. The Republic of China was one of the early drafters of what
would become the Universal Declaration of Human Rights in
1948, though its initially proposed language on racial equality
would prove too strong for British and American sensibilities.[7] The
People's Republic of China (PRC), while lately voicing "positive
appraisal" of the Universal Declaration,[8] would define human
rights first and foremost as the satisfaction of basic human needs,
such as shelter, food, and health,[9] and would be at loggerheads
with the American and European emphases on civil and political
rights.[10] In China as overseas, there has been now a century of vigorous debate on approaches to civil, collective, and human rights.[11]
The Asia and Africa volume in this series contains an excellent
overview by Andrew J. Nathan of alternative definitions of freedom in twentieth-century China.[12]

However, the Chinese case, with its own universal and historical conceptions of obligations and liberties, surely merits deeper
investigation still. Thus a third and to my mind compelling reason
for this volume is that if the history of freedom—or of its lack—is
to be studied in depth in one non-Western setting, strong arguments can be made for studying the Chinese case, either on its
own terms, in comparison with the modern West, or, preferably,
both.

Before the twentieth century, China had the longest continuous set of political and legal traditions in world history. They defined to a large degree the nature of the political and social orders

that emerged throughout East Asia. (The contemporary caricature of "Asian values" has, after all, some historical foundation.) Two millennia of legal codes and practice established traditions of criminal and—it has recently been argued—civil law under which realms of personal and community autonomy emerged that were different from those of Mediterranean or North European societies, but present nonetheless. We can speak in general terms of meritocracy without political equality; civil governance without civil society; commercial capitalism in the absence of independent urban polities; associational freedoms (for example guilds and trade associations) without personal liberties; a litigious legal culture with but a small legal profession; and anti-tyrannical conventions of dissent and remonstrance in the face of divinely-ordained despotism.

Many of the political, legal, and philosophical structures of imperial China were largely abandoned when the empire fell in 1911, and the decades since then have witnessed an ongoing competition to see what would take their place. In this contest, alternative Western conceptions of liberty, "liberation," democracy, and "people's democracy" have dominated the Chinese political scene. Now, at the beginning of the twenty-first century, the People's Republic of China, still led by a communist party, faces internal and international pressure for political reform; the Republic of China, founded as Asia's first republic in 1912 and now resident on Taiwan, has given offshore birth to the first democratic state in Chinese history; and the PRC's Special Administrative Region of Hong Kong has just "elected" (without an opposition candidate) its chief executive for a new term, a process in which the people of Hong Kong have had about as much say as they did in the naming of British governors before 1997. In short, for the 1.3 billion Chinese in the "Greater China" of the PRC, Taiwan, and Hong Kong, what constitutes "modern freedom" remains in the process of definition.

A fourth reason for this volume is to bring together, in one place, important new work on Chinese legal, ethical, commercial, and political systems and to place these in a historical and, where appropriate, comparative perspective. Our sincere hope is that it will give impetus and direction to much more work in all these areas.

The chapters in this volume have somewhat different concerns but all are consumed with the question of "freedom" in China. The reader will discern several important trends over time. Simply put, they are these. One can speak of very significant realms of freedom, with or without the protection of law, in Chinese personal, social, and economic lives before the twentieth century. This was recognized, and partly codified, under the Republic, whose legal experts initially sought to establish a republic of laws and limits. The process of legal reform would, however, be placed firmly in the service of strengthening the post-imperial Chinese nation-state. The better part of China's twentieth century, particularly under the rule of first the Guomindang and then the Communist Party-States, would witness an ever-increasing level of state control, culminating after 1949 in a despotism that was felt more widely and deeply than any in Chinese history. Yet the last decades of the twentieth century and the first years of our own would witness a slow, steady, but unmistakable re-assertion of realms of personal and communal autonomy, accompanied by experiments in electoral democracy on both sides of the Taiwan Strait that show, even in an era of strong states, at least the prospect of institutionalized freedoms of a kind that Professor Hexter might recognize and applaud.

Was there really a conception of personal freedom in the Confucian tradition? *Yes.* Does China need to "start all over again and become more like the West" in order to realize freedom for its citizens? *Not entirely.* These are the answers found in Irene Bloom's chapter, which begins our volume. She contends that there was a great Chinese humanitarian tradition—a cultural, not national tradition—of the universal dignity of human beings. She chronicles how, as Confucian "protesters" confronted the Imperial state, which became ever more autocratic in late imperial times, they maintained "unfathomable courage" in their willingness to pay a high, often the ultimate, price for their outspokenness. This willingness was not the result of the lack of the freedom of expression: such protesters believed they had the right, as well as the duty, to express their views freely. What they lacked were laws to protect them and their speech. Here is an intriguing argument for an indigenously Chinese concept of natural right—the right to remonstrate being endowed by a Heaven that is superior to any Son of Heaven. The morally autonomous individual of this Confucian ideal—well documented in practice—may be sacrificed for the sake of ideals; but his is a "free personality." Even, and indeed especially, in the most repressive times there are in the Chinese cultural arsenal usable and venerable traditions of historically legitimate protest.

How, however, do Chinese traditions of "freedom from tyranny" compare with those, say, of England and the United States? William Jones describes the difference between "rules" and "contracts." Imperial China could be ruled in part by rules, as codified from the Tang Code to the Qing Code—the regulations or laws promulgated from above that governed the actions of officials—as a means of enforcing self-restraint on the bureaucracy that ruled the realm on behalf of the emperor. To the degree that officials followed these rules, Chinese subjects had that degree of freedom from official abuse, in addition to freedom from the forcible actions of others (murder, kidnapping, and so on) that were forbidden in the code. Beyond this there was a regularity and predictability, if not a formal codification, in commercial affairs. Freedom thus defined was "sufficiently regular and supported by governmental authority that one can say that it was protected by law." That the emperor was himself above the law and any formal restraint was without question, however.

This last point stands in contrast to the case of England, where from the Norman Conquest in the eleventh century one can see contractual (as well as divine) definitions of royal legitimacy. The English political system would over time be defined by a series of what one might call political contracts: legal documents that defined rights as well as responsibilities and loyalties. And in England there developed, as there did not in China, a legal profession and body of law that existed independently of the monarch. Of course revolutions in the name of a natural right to change a social "contract" would be opposed by kings with different ideas. But when successful, as in the case of the thirteen colonies that revolted from Britain and then came together as the United States, a polity was constituted—by a negotiated "constitution"—that was first and last a legal arrangement. In the United States, freedoms would be defined and redefined by law, in courts of law.

How these broadly different historical inheritances affect daily life, even today, can be seen in the distinctive ways in which American and Chinese societies handle injuries suffered by citizens—the stuff of tort law. The Americans are famously litigious; Chinese who suffer injury tend to be handled on the basis of administrative procedure. Those procedures, to be sure, are as likely to be Western as Chinese in origin, such having been the level of legal borrowing in the twentieth century. If freedom is to expand its scope in contemporary China, Professor Jones predicts, it will more likely do so by means of administration, that is, through the state, than through the emergence of a suddenly independent and professional judiciary.

Imperial China, then, was an autocracy with realms of freedom, with indirect protections of certain levels of autonomy. Nowhere was this more true, Madeleine Zelin argues, than in the free economy of late imperial China. China under the Qing dynasty (1644–1911) developed a highly commercialized economy; and Chinese under Qing rule had the freedom to "transact" to a degree that was greater than that of most European states, at least until the nineteenth century. Land was freely alienable. It was bought and sold, rented and worked, all subject to the forces of the market. Late imperial China had its landed elites, to be sure, but no *Junkertum* or similar class of hereditary estate holders. Nor did serfdom exist in any measure like that of Eastern Europe, where it persisted into the second half of the nineteenth century. The population was registered, but it was essentially free to move throughout much of the realm. (Even to areas officially off limits, such as Manchuria, there were enormous migratory flows.) Not just land and people, but goods flowed, largely unimpeded by government regulation. State monopolies all but disappeared. Domestic trade was subject to few administrative barriers and—by any comparative measure—remarkably low taxes. Local and long-distance banking systems grew. In short, as John Schrecker has put it, the economic system of the later empire "rested on a free market and a cash nexus."[13]

Central to all of this was the development and protection of property rights and the *de facto* sanctity of contract. Even without a formal commercial code and in the absence of a system of legal precedents, rights and obligations negotiated in contract were normally upheld in magistrates' courts. This upholding in turn facilitated the growth of more extended forms of private enterprise, such as shareholding partnerships—be they in farming, mining, or commerce. "Corporations" formed around guilds and lineages would be joined by joint-stock business partnerships, several of which developed into very sizable commercial firms long before the writing of the company laws of the twentieth century.[14]

All this developed, Zelin suggests, not because the Qing was "pro-growth" but because it had neither the interest nor means to stop it. The expansion of economic freedom in Qing times came not through struggles between new commercial classes and the state; it came by virtue of common interest, on the part of an increasingly interpenetrated set of economic and political elites, and, at the end of the day, "by default."

It does not seem quite right that the Qing's transformation into a republic (a "people's country," or *minguo*) in 1912 should usher in an age of ever-decreasing liberty for its former subjects, now citizens. That surely was not the intent of the new law codes that aimed to govern this vast Qing realm as a Chinese nation-state, but to some degree they contributed to it. China's modern laws as they developed in the pre-Communist Republican era (1912–49) added modern civil, criminal, and political codes (constitutions), all modeled on international standards. They defined the obligations of citizens with ever-greater precision and, with rather less clarity, set out their rights as well. They did nothing, however, to restrict the power of an ever-more intrusive state apparatus. Rather, they became the legal armature of a state whose ambitions in governance far outdistanced those of the defunct Qing. The new civil code of the Republic, as described by Jérôme Bourgon, is a case in point.

The central assumption of Republican China's new civil laws was the need to codify, and protect more formally, the private relationships and property rights that had received implicit legitimacy under the Qing. At the same time China's civil (especially commercial) and criminal codes would be brought to European standard, in support of Chinese efforts to abolish the special, "extraterritorial" legal rights of foreigners in China. The latter effort would prove more successful than the former. By the end of the Republican era, extraterritoriality had been abolished, and Chinese law applied even to foreigners—a great milestone in the freedom of the Chinese nation from the remnants of imperialism. It would be much more difficult to claim an expansion of the rights and liberties of Chinese citizens over the same period.

The codification was to build self-consciously on what were assumed to be the customary practices of the Qing. This process would prove quite different, however, from the incorporation of customary (often local) rights and privileges in European legal systems. In fact, as Bourgon shows, custom was less revealed than it was interpreted and categorized according to the preferences of the new legal bureaucracy. In other words, to a considerable degree "custom" was whatever the legal experts in Beijing (and later Nanjing) said it was. Thus the great compilations of Chinese customs served as "blueprints for modern regulations allowing state power to permeate local society."[15] And so law, even rights and liberties, would be imposed from above as a means of strengthening the state and "correcting the mores and practices" of its people.[16]

The centralizing approach to law and liberty and their limits that marked the early Republic would be taken further, and then furthest, under the two Party-States that would rule China after 1928. The Party-State, which is the subject of my own chapter in this volume, came into being amid promises of freedom three ways: by nationalism, to free China from colonial powers old and new; by socialism, or forms of it, attending to the people's welfare; and by democracy, ideally embodying in the Party the will of the people. These Three Principles of the People, made so famous by Sun Yat-sen, would be memorized by generations of Chinese, on the mainland and on Taiwan, from the 1920s through the 1980s. They would arguably succeed in two-thirds of their mission. Over the course of the twentieth century a distinct and altogether new sense of Chinese nationality and patriotism would emerge in the Han-dominated parts of the old Qing realm. Socialism would come in alternative, ever more intense, forms, culminating in the Maoist effort to "leap" into communism in the late 1950s. By contrast, the ideal of democracy, which Sun Yat-sen in his more liberal moments had conceived as a popular sovereignty growing from the bottom up, through a progression of elections from the village to the national level, would be honored more in rhetoric (by his National "People's" Party, or Guomindang; or by the "People's" Republic of China) than in reality. At best, this was a promise much delayed. Although they were promised at last in the Republic of China's first formal constitution in 1946, it would take another 40 years for democratic politics to be permitted—under that same constitution—in Guomindang-governed Taiwan.

Institutions, like constitutions, could serve different purposes in different times and circumstances. It is the repeated "inversion" of an institution designed to assist the liberation of workers that is the subject of Elizabeth Perry's chapter. The struggles of workers, especially urban industrial workers, were central to the political narratives of the Nationalist Revolution of 1924–27, and then to the urban civil war, fought—first above then under ground—in Shanghai and elsewhere between loyalists of the Guomindang and the Chinese Communist Party. The dream of proletarian revolution—a Shanghai version of the Paris Commune—captured the imagination of Chinese Communist organizers and their Comintern advisers. Yet no amount of idealism or wishful thinking could make selfless proletarians out of the mercenaries and gangsters who joined the workers' patrols that sought to arm and enforce the revolution. What began, at least for public consumption, as a means to ensure an eventual transition to electoral democracy in China's greatest city quickly took the character of a "terrorist hit squad."[17] After the Guomindang purged the Communists in 1927, their own Industry Defense Corps, modeled on the workers' patrols, would enforce a different kind of order, though with not a few of the same members. And when the Communists returned decades later, in 1949, to "liberate" Shanghai from the outside, a new workers' patrol—composed inevitably of Communists, Nationalists, and the usual ne'er-do-wells—would be called to life, now not to overthrow but to preserve industries and to look for enemies of the incoming regime. Once securely in power, the new PRC would then prove even more wary than its predecessor of the concept of an "armed citizenry." This is not a story of the heroic working class, as once was told by Jean Chesneaux,[18] but of its bullying and buying by two Party-States and of a smartly self-preserving set of urban toughs. So the establishment of the workers' state would prove the last act of a bloody and cynical history of political manipulation in which Chinese workers, caught in the vise between the Guomindang and the Communists, had no choice but to make their institutions their own.

Wen-hsin Yeh returns us to an issue set out by Irene Bloom for much earlier times: how, building upon traditions of dissent in imperial China, but now in the era of the twentieth-century Party-State, did learned Chinese practice dissent? There was already much to draw on: the role of loyal and courageous censors (something that Sun Yat-sen would wish institutionalized, with a Censorate as part of his Five-Power government); exile as a form of punishment with moral rewards; and what one might call the highest form of moral martyrdom—a principled death in dissent. How did all this change once the learned elite lost its automatic connection to authority, after the end of the examination system? How did the growth of urban literacy, a larger "intelligentsia," and political press with a national audience affect government and its critics? Like their predecessors, Republican intellectuals were part of an educated elite; unlike them, they were also citizens of a Republic with at least the formal right, as well as the inherited moral responsibility, to make their views heard.

Yeh offers an illuminating set of case studies of dissent as expressed through modern means of elite communication: writing in the vernacular; writing in journals and newspapers for a national elite; giving public addresses and lectures, which in turn would be published and distributed; and even, as in the case of Wu Han, turning to the ancient technique of writing history in order to critique the present. As repressive as was the Guomindang reaction to public criticism, it never approached the nationalization of opinion that would mark the Communist literary system. Whereas Lu Xun had once criticized a "silent" China that was either too ignorant or too reticent to take national issues to the public arena, in Maoist China silence itself became a sign of dissidence: better to pledge allegiance or to "speak bitterness" than not to speak at all. Before the "voice of the People" came to serve a single author, the self-styled philosopher-king Mao Zedong, Republican China had extended and modernized a set of powerful traditions of political criticism. Censored, harassed, always underpaid and sometimes killed, intellectuals in Republican China were nonetheless a powerful force. As China descended after 1950 into tyranny, the rituals of public criticism were now turned upon the critics.

China in the 1950s was not simply placed under the rule of the Communist Party; it was Stalinized. Mao Zedong's pretenses to ideological originality notwithstanding, he and his comrades remained—as they had been for 30 years—loyal adherents to both the ideals and the discipline of international communism as defined by Moscow Center. It would take a decade of ever-closer association with the Soviet Union to break them of this habit. Before then, however, they gave the new People's Republic an indelibly Soviet genetic imprint.

Arlen Meliksetov and Alexander Pantsov offer fresh perspectives on the formative years of the PRC, on the basis of recently available Soviet and Chinese source material. The new state was born with a promise to usher in an era of "new democracy," of multiple parties and a mixed economy, building on the democratic rhetoric that had become part of the political language of the Republic. Yet by 1953 the new People's Republic had turned down the Stalinist road, which, it turns out, had been Mao Zedong's preferred route from the outset. By 1954 the PRC had its first constitution, plagiarized from the USSR's "Stalin Constitution" of 1936. Even under "new democracy," Meliksetov and Pantsov demonstrate, there had been a steady increase in the "ideological" (and often physical) terror aimed at landholders, businessmen, and intellectuals. In political terms it may be said that a Stalinist regime existed from the outset. China was now part of a broader, young community of socialist states, each of which was similarly emulating the Soviet Union in this, its most exaggerated phase of "High Stalinism."[19] "Stalinism," as Ben Fowkes has written, "meant, first and foremost, uniformity."[20] This meant, everywhere in the Soviet sphere, the absolute rule of the Communist Party, the oligarchic rule of its Politburo, and, inevitably, the emergence of a dominant personality, a "little Stalin." It meant, too, the growth of public security organs, complete economic control by the state, and economic development giving highest priority to heavy industry and armaments. Paradoxically, it was only with Stalin's death—and the willingness of his successors to increase dramatically the USSR's aid to China—that China would also be able to industrialize, collectivize, and otherwise follow the Stalinist path to socialist economic development.

The Stalinist features of the PRC's First Five-Year Plan (1953–57) were "even more pronounced in the Chinese than in the Soviet case," as Alexander Eckstein demonstrated.[21] Even so, it was not ambitious enough for Mao Zedong, who in time would see himself as much larger than a "little Stalin," and would seek to outperform his Soviet tutors. Thus Chinese political and economic development would follow the Maoist offshoot of Stalinism after 1958, leading to disasters as great as, or greater than those Stalin himself had visited upon the Soviet Union: the Great Leap Forward of 1958–60, which would fall into the Great Famine of the early 1960s, at the cost of 30 million Chinese lives; and the Great Proletarian Cultural Revolution, which for a decade (1966–76) would convulse and debase Chinese political and cultural life.

What became, then, of the promises of "liberation" that had accompanied the Communist seizure of power? In no case had they been more publicly celebrated, from the first years of the regime, than as regards the status of women. And in almost no other area, it may be said, were such promises so well kept in the early years of communism. The original PRC Marriage Law of 1950, which legitimized a woman's right to divorce, signaled a legal end to a patriarchal family structure that for Chinese women had become progressively more oppressive over the course of late imperial history. Building on Republican-era campaigns against footbinding, the PRC oversaw the eradication of this longstanding custom among Han Chinese women that, quite literally, had kept them back.[22] Prostitution, which had become endemic in China's great cities, was driven not just underground but out of business in the 1950s.[23] Women may not have been given full credit for holding up "half the sky," despite Mao Zedong's claims, but in the homes, farms, factories, and political cells of People's China they held up more of it, in more formal positions, than ever before, thanks in no small measure to the intervention of the communist state.

The market reforms since 1978 have gradually reintroduced and expanded many of the economic freedoms described by Madeleine Zelin, now supported in law. Yet however successful they may be in promoting economic growth, the reforms have placed at risk the egalitarian social agenda of the early PRC, not least of all in the case of women. What does it mean, in contemporary China, to have "freedom" in marriage? This is the central issue explored in the chapter by William Alford and Yuanyuan Shen.

Alford and Shen recount the history of marriage and family in the PRC and investigate the (counter?)revolution in familial affairs ushered in by market forces and the breakdown of communist systems of social organization such as the "work unit," or *danwei*. The commodification of society that has accompanied economic reform, they suggest, has recommodified women, as the upsurge of prostitution and the sale of women into marriage would indicate. *De facto* property rights for women appear to have declined. Family violence and spousal abuse are widespread, and China suffers from the world's highest rate of suicide among women.

The response of concerned Chinese officials has been to turn to law, with implicit faith in the ultimate rule of law, as a vehicle for protecting the weak. Whereas the Marriage Laws of 1950 and 1980 were meant to benefit women, the law may have increasingly become of use to adulterous men with extra income and, as they wished, extra wives. An historical effort to make marriage a "freer" institution may have done so at considerable cost to poorer women in China's countryside. Alford and Shen's multi-layered analysis of the proposed revisions to the 1980 law takes us into an extraordinarily complex and interrelated set of choices in public policy and public morality in these most private realms of human affairs.

Jean Oi's chapter takes us into the realm of contemporary political change. China may still be under the control of a one-party, Leninist state; dissent is repressed, if need be by force. Yet by any conceivable measure, the average Chinese is freer in matters of daily life, work, travel, and expression and opportunity than at any other time since 1950. Institutions may look the same, but China is undergoing a quiet revolution in political function, if not yet in form. Thus that old Stalinist parliament, the National People's Congress, may appear to be the same, preselected, pliantly reliable rubber stamp for the Party that it has always been; yet debates are more open, on more matters—and the very fact that there *are* debates is a change in itself. In the judicial system, the Party may still select the judges, tell them what to do, and severely constrict the activity of attorneys; but the re-emergence of a national court system together with a significant expansion of litigation, particularly in civil matters, is a sign of both official and popular support for a regularization of legal procedures. In urban society, autonomous workers' unions are still prohibited, and those who seek to found them are dealt with harshly; yet hardly a day passes in today's China when members of the working class, once upon a time the theoretical vanguard of the revolution, do not demonstrate publicly in protest against jobs lost and wages unpaid, and they do so for the most part without official retribution. In rural areas, tax and other protests have become routine, and sometimes violent, on the part of farmers who have developed a strong consciousness of their "rights" vis-à-vis the state.

Beyond all this is the promise of electoral democracy, which dates to the founding of the first Chinese republic. Unlike the Guomindang, which at least claimed to be loyal to Sun Yat-sen's democratic vision for 60 years before actually doing much about it, the Chinese Communist Party has never endorsed the legitimacy of electoral, "bourgeois" democracy. In recent years, however, it has allowed passage of the Organic Law on Villagers' Committees, which gives farmers the right to elect village leaders (though not Party secretaries) by secret ballot. Farmers in Chinese villages may now exercise a right unknown to their ancestors and still unavailable to their urban compatriots. One can dispute the reasons why the PRC has legalized and encouraged village elections (a belief in democracy *an sich* would not appear to be at the top of the list) but the fact remains that elections are in the process of transforming the way China works, politically, at the most basic level of government.

Our final chapter touches on a realm that has historically been marked by both freedom and constraint in China, that of religious association. Robert Weller demonstrates the very sizable room for religious expression and organization that exists today on either side of the Taiwan Strait. Tracing the relationship between religion, society, and polity from the bottom up, Weller shows how great a force—in society, in the economy, and indeed in politics—a religious organization may be when (as in the case in contemporary Taiwan) it is free to develop on its own. This will not be news to historians of Buddhism in Tang China, for example, but it is an important finding for our own era of religious revival and expansion throughout East Asia.

Weller contrasts the explosive growth, from Taiwan outward, of the Buddhist Compassion Relief Merit Association [Ciji gongde hui] with the equally dynamic, indeed equally globalized development of the Falun Gong, emanating from the People's Republic. Their fates, of course, have been quite different: Compassion Relief is rich, powerful, and legitimate on Taiwan; Falun Gong has been branded a "cult" and forced underground on the mainland. This contrast reflects the almost total withdrawal of the state in Taiwan from any serious interference in religious affairs, whereas the PRC, having retreated from the anti-religious policies of the Cultural Revolution, now practices the more traditional policy of imperial China, that of *laisser faire* in religious matters, except when they appear to challenge the authority of the state. After a century of enormous political and social upheaval, religion—either organized or in the form of local popular worship—offers what Weller calls "an alternate civility" for the world of greater China.

Our volume thus ends with evidence of the restoration of historical realms of freedom and the promise of altogether new ones. Before any enduring contact with the West, "freedom" in China might well be defined in terms of indigenous patterns of moral autonomy, political protest, economic opportunity and mobility, and religious belief that were different from those that marked the Western experience but were present nonetheless. These existed in the context of the theoretically unlimited but in fact quite restricted power of an under-institutionalized imperial state.

What seems remarkable, from the vantage point of the early twenty-first century, is the degree to which these freedoms could be so steadily and nearly completely taken away over the course of China's twentieth century, when they were circumscribed by a series of revolutionary republics that promoted first national independence and then social transformation. To be sure, the Guomindang and Communist Party-States fought for power in an international context that set new and often conflicting standards for liberty and "liberation." It was, after all, in search of a communist ideal that China would fall under the totalitarian tyranny of Mao Zedong. But the dismantling of the Maoist project on the Chinese mainland would permit historic realms of autonomy gradually to re-emerge, with the Chinese people now enjoying greater freedom *from* the state, if by no means enjoying the modern freedoms *of* those civil liberties to which even the PRC constitution pays homage. In brief, there would emerge considerable autonomy in practice but not yet freedom in principle. Such realms of freedom as exist in China in the early twenty-first century do so less by "default"—since the Chinese state today is hardly weak—than perhaps *faute de mieux*, tolerated by a state that has learned the lessons of its own over-reaching, and which for its own survival needs to give a freer rein to the productive and creative powers of the Chinese people.

The state-building and socially transformative revolutions of the twentieth century may have been inimical to the making of freedom in their day; but they left legacies that could be placed in the service of later quests. China's legal and later constitutional reforms of the first half of the twentieth century put on paper principles that might later be realized in fact. The founding of the Republic gave public space for movements to assert "human rights." (When the Shanghai bar association was founded in 1912, its stated mission was to "protect the people's rights [*renmin quanli*] and to spread the spirit of the rule of law throughout the country.")[24] The Republican codes are still in force in contemporary Taiwan, and now, under an ever-more independent judiciary, they have contributed significantly to the rule of law on that island. The codes have similarly informed the People's Republic's legal recovery from the lawlessness of high Maoism. In constitutional law, a seemingly endless process of drafting and revision would lead to the Constitution of 1946, which, when much amended, would help to steer Taiwan's democratic transition in the 1990s.

In time, and off shore, electoral democracy would emerge in the Chinese realm through the political reform of the remnant Republic of China on Taiwan from the late 1980s to the early 2000s. There, in what used to be referred to as "Island China,"[25] a raucous, vibrant, open, multi-party political scramble would emerge in the shadow of the Guomindang Party-State and offer an alternative political form to the enduring Party-State on the Chinese mainland. Electoral democracy has not been part of the Chinese historical experience, but who is to say that the deepening of democratic practice on Taiwan and the institutionalization of local elections on the mainland may not, in time, sow the seeds of a new kind of civic culture? This much is clear: as China enters its second Republican century, its pursuit of freedom remains a work in progress, of recovery and of discovery, a process of becoming as much as of being.[26]

# The Moral Autonomy of the Individual in Confucian Tradition

## IRENE BLOOM

WRITING during the 1970s in the closing chapter of the second volume of *The Life of the Mind*, Hannah Arendt characterized "the Occidental tradition" as "the only tradition where freedom has always been the *raison d'être* of all politics."[1] This conclusion, while seemingly uncontroversial on its surface, takes on added depth when it is read against the background of a distinction Arendt had drawn several decades earlier between *political* freedom and *philosophical* freedom. I shall return at the end of this chapter to that distinction and its relevance to our understanding of the history of freedom in China.

Most inquiries into the history of freedom have found its career in China down to and including the twentieth century to have been decidedly, even tragically, limited. If freedom is viewed as a shared political and societal ideal—a priority of Western-style liberal democracy and one promoted through its institutional mechanisms—the traditional Confucian values that are commonly assumed to have guided and sustained the Chinese state are likely to appear deficient, even retrograde, by comparison. Those who are convinced that the Chinese past casts long and ominous shadows are inclined not only to interpret Chinese Communism as a reprise of repressive patterns rooted in the imperial past but to identify those patterns of "unfreedom"[2] as Confucian in origin. And for those who are persuaded that the absolutism of China's imperial past and the totalitarianism of China's Marxist present form a continuum, involving patterns or structures that persist tenaciously over time, the prospects for developing a political culture in which the value of freedom is fully recognized and its expressions are adequately protected may seem remote. Adherents of this view tend to arrive almost ineluctably at the conclusion that the only real solution for China is to start all over again and become more like the West.

The argument of this chapter is based on the alternative view that there are significant differences between the theoretical assumptions underlying the governance of the absolutist state that evolved in China throughout the course of the imperial period from the late third century B.C.E. to the early twentieth century and the conceptual basis of the totalitarian state that came into being in the latter half of the twentieth century. Here I focus on two points in support of this view: first, that the notion of "imperial Confucianism" is misleading if it is taken to imply a compliant Confucianism (and later neo-Confucianism) in supine and self-interested service of absolutist rulers and of the dynastic system; and, second, that in Confucian and in neo-Confucian views of human nature there can be found a metaphysical and psychological perspective on what it means to be human that crucially involves the importance of the moral autonomy of the individual.

On the basis of these two points, I offer a friendly amendment to the argument that freedom was an alien transplant into the Chinese political landscape of the late nineteenth and early twentieth centuries. W. J. F. Jenner has argued, for example, that, "Doctrines of freedom of thought or religion, like doctrines of political or personal rights, never grew on Chinese soil until they came in as exotics."[3] My proposed amendment is intended to suggest that, while it is true that *doctrines* of *political* freedom did not originally grow on Chinese soil, there was a non-doctrinal but discernible sense of *philosophical* freedom—or perhaps it might better be called *psychological* freedom—that was neither exotic nor unfamiliar but indigenous and inextricably intertwined with an identifiably Chinese sense of a free personality. A Western critique of Confucian moral culture (that is, of Confucianism as a "failed" source for conceptions of political freedom) is summarized in Part I; a defense of Confucianism as a support for philosophical or psychological freedom follows in Parts II and III; the Confucian sense of moral autonomy is described in Part IV.

≺ I ≻

*A Western Critique of Confucian Moral Culture*

In a paper presented at a conference on "Confucianism and Human Rights" held in Beijing in June of 1998, Ci Jiwei takes the view that Confucian moral culture, lacking a strong distinction between a conception of "the right" and a conception of "the good," is "seriously flawed" with regard to negative rights—civil and political rights that may be considered essential to the development of a democratic and pluralistic society.[4] His contention is that, owing to this flaw, the Confucian moral tradition has little to offer to the China of the future. Or, put positively, China has important lessons to learn from the West in terms of the "priority of the right." It is worth examining this critique of Confucian moral culture both because it is a particularly articulate version of a common critique of Confucian moral culture and because, although it represents the reflections of a distinguished Chinese political philosopher, it is written from a perspective that can only be characterized as "Western." After almost a century marked by strenuous criticism by Chinese intellectuals of the Confucian moral tradition and its bearing on China's political development, the tendency to deprecate traditional Chinese values as having any useful bearing on modern Chinese realities is still widespread and influential.

The distinction in liberal democratic theory between "the right" and "the good" goes back to the English philosopher Henry Sidgwick who, writing in the late nineteenth century and the early part of the twentieth century, pointed, in *The Method of Ethics*, to a distinction between "the right" (which involves a commitment to certain moral conceptions or demands that are relatively narrowly defined, with compliance being considered *imperative* for all agents) and "the good" (which is more broadly construed, more varied, and perceived by morally sensitive agents as *attractive*). "The right" refers to a well defined sphere of social and political consensus which in a democratic society should be protected by the state. Beyond this protected consensus there is a larger sphere that includes diverse conceptions of "the good," allowing for diversity of values and for individual choice. It is specifically because of the limited scope of "the right" and secure societal support for it, that a space is opened up for "negative freedom" and for diverse conceptions of "the good." The "core morality" based on the "priority of the right" and the negative freedom that allows for diverse conceptions of "the good" are thus correlative: together, according to this liberal model, they are conducive to pluralism, democracy, and human rights.[5]

A point worth noting here is that Sidgwick himself saw the distinction between "the right" and "the good" as marking the difference between *ancient* and *modern* ethics. While the distinction between "the right" and "the good" points in the direction of modernity, the part of the Confucian tradition that occupies Ci Jiwei in his essay is ancient, his chosen primary sources and proof texts being the *Analects* of Confucius and the *Mencius*. He is sensitive to this point, acknowledging that Confucius' understanding of the good is, in general terms, "characteristic of pre-modern ethical thought, not only in China but also in the West."[6] Still, the way the argument actually develops, the comparison that is drawn is between a Western model associated with twentieth-century liberalism and a classical Confucian view grounded in a period more than two thousand years earlier and associated with the evolving concepts of humanity or humaneness [*ren*], rightness [*yi*], and rites or ritual decorum [*li*]. It is in this ancient philosophical milieu that Ci finds what he takes to be a number of "absences" and "obstacles," that foreordain the failure of Confucian moral culture to be conducive to democratic development and the growth of freedom.

Ci suggests that, in the absence of a "core morality" in Confucianism, "morality, or the good, has an all-encompassing scope, such that everything either meets its standard or fails to do so."[7] This "all-encompassing scope" of "morality" becomes so prominent, he argues, that no coloration or shading can be discerned in the way moral actions are portrayed, no ambiguity discovered in the way they are construed. All actions fall into the category of good or evil: "The only distinction that is recognizable is the binary opposition between morality and immorality, good and evil, with no space left for anything that neither conforms to the standard of the good nor calls for condemnation as evil or immoral."[8]

Another alleged "absence" is that of a "'Humean conception' of the circumstances of morality." On this view, the problem with

Confucius is that:

Despite his realistic appraisal of certain human propensities [such as the desire to gain wealth and honor and to avoid poverty and humble station] . . . Confucius does not take the further, "Humean," step of treating such mundane facts [of human nature] as the point of departure for ethics. In Confucianism, selfishness [si] is not something to be tamed or made rational for its *own* good, but something to be eliminated [qiusi] for the common good. As the most telling Confucian formulation goes, *cuntianlu, mierenyu*, that is, human desires must be suppressed in favor of heaven's principles [tianli]. It is thus an extremely important feature of Confucianism that empirical human desires and conflicts do not define the rationale and function of (state-enforced) morality. This helps to explain the absence of a strong distinction between the right and the good and the absence of any full-fledged notion of social contract.[9]

In addition to the "absence" of a "core morality" and of a "Humean conception" of morality, there are, according to Ci, a number of "obstacles" that derive from Confucian values, one of which is "an objective order as the basis for morality." The argument here is that there existed in early Confucianism a conception of a *suprahuman objective order*:

an order that places human beings, both ontologically and morally, in a large cosmic scheme. It is this objective order, in the shape of Heaven [tianming, tianli], that serves as the basis and the point of departure for moral thinking (indeed for every type of thinking). Thus, morality derives its rationale and function not from the empirical circumstances of human beings but from the larger objective order in which they find their place and to which they must conform if they are to achieve their full humanity.[10]

The conception of a cosmic order beyond the human sphere "rules out the idea of morality as answering to empirical human circumstances and issuing from (mere) human agreement"[11]— which, again, works to foredoom any possibility of a social contract. It also "rules out . . . the idea of a plurality of legitimate conceptions of the good"[12] because an objective order must outweigh subjective choices and judgments.

In the conclusion to his paper Ci suggests that there are clear structural parallels between Confucianism and Maoism. In both the Confucian and the Maoist perspective, he says, "the legitimacy of government and of state coercion is based on a monolithic conception of the good,"[13] and the politically dominant conception of the good is based on supposed knowledge of an objective order. He contends further that "Maoism is structurally identical with Confucianism despite the fact that it is substantively distinct from Confucianism."[14] Here "structure" is associated in each case with justifications of state coercion and of concomitant limitations on the expression of individual freedom; "substance," with differing conceptions of "the good" and of the "objective order" per se.

This argument is so carefully constructed and cogently stated that it may gain the ready assent of many readers. My own reservations about it are as follows. First, the notion of a "binary opposition between morality and immorality, good and evil" seems to oversimplify the complex philosophy and subtle psychology that underlie the moral reflection and guidance found in the conversations of Confucius (551–479 B.C.E.) and Mencius (fourth century B.C.E.). The primary Confucian intuition of *ren* or humaneness is, I would suggest, anything but a "monolithic conception of the good." Rather, *ren* can be seen as a flexible, open, and vital concept, involving a fundamental intuition of human relatedness, communicative capacity, and mutual responsibility. One of the ways in which *ren*[15] was understood by Confucius was "not doing to another, what one would not want done to oneself,"[16] often taken as a negative version of the Golden Rule. This idea, ostensibly simple, actually involves not only a complex philosophy but a subtle psychology of sensitivity, forbearance, and, above all, empathy. The idea of *yi* or rightness, especially in the conversations of Mencius, also consistently allows for the need to factor circumstantial variables into moral judgments.[17]

Second, that Confucius took no "Humean step" is undeniable. Neither he nor Mencius had any presentiment of the social contract idea or the distinction between "the right" and "the good" that would assume such importance in the West more than two millennia after their time. However, Confucius' responses to the appeals of disciples for guidance reveal a striking psychological acuity and insight into human nature. Frequently Confucius focuses on attitudes and actions that are deemed conducive both to individual satisfaction and to the benefit of others, an approach not fundamentally different from Hume's. At the same time he seems to judge the utility of those attitudes and actions in much the same way that Hume might have done, in terms of the reactions of others—their predictably human desires and aversions.

Though Mencius, offended as he was by the Mohist use of the term "profit" or "utility" [li], could be acerbic when personal profit was proposed as a motive,[18] his arguments *never* ignore social utility. Had he been in a position to take "the Humean step," he would certainly have been in no way impeded by Hume's understanding that the answer to "why utility pleases" must be found in "the social sympathy in human nature."[19] One who was convinced of the common human experience of "the mind that cannot bear to see the suffering of others," would no doubt have readily understood Hume's note to the effect that

It is needless to push our researches so far as to ask, why we have humanity or a fellow-feeling with others? It is sufficient that this is experienced to be a principle in human nature. We must stop somewhere in our examination of causes; and there are, in every science, some general principles beyond which we cannot hope to find any principle more general. No man is absolutely indifferent to the happiness and misery of others. The first has a natural tendency to give pleasure, the second, pain. This everyone may find in himself.[20]

The view of human nature held by Xunzi (late fourth and third centuries B.C.E.) was, at least in its initial premises, darker than that of Mencius. It is above all through this that he is set apart from Mencius—taking a different view of education, placing greater emphasis on rites as a discipline for sublimating or "beautifying" wayward human emotions, and assigning considerable importance to a societal need for hierarchy. But both resemble Hume in the particular sense that their views of human nature crucially condition their conceptions of morality. Hume, I would suggest, does not find the principles of morals to emerge from "mere human agreement" in the narrow sense, but, like Mencius and Xunzi, has a conception of human nature as a ground—the place where we may, for all practical purposes, stop "in our examination of causes."[21]

Third, to think in terms of an objective order "in the shape of Heaven" that serves as "the basis and the point of departure for moral thinking (indeed for every type of thinking)" would seem to overlook several facts. One is that Confucius, Mencius, and Xunzi held not a single view but significantly different views of Heaven.

What they seem to have shared was a sense that a Heaven that "did not speak" was also extremely difficult to read. In the absence of clear direction from Heaven, one had to make one's own way in the world with relatively minimal guidance save from one's own human nature, understood by Confucius and Mencius to be shared in common with others and by Mencius to be, in addition, a gift from Heaven. For Xunzi, the guidance must come from thorough immersion in a morally edifying culture, especially through ritual practice and attentive dedication to the examples of teachers and sages. Later Neo-Confucian thinkers of the Song, Yuan, and Ming periods were, if anything, even more diverse in their views of Heaven and the moral order. Given this diversity, Confucian ethical thought may not be fairly described as "monolithic." Within the large tent that is sometimes labeled "orthodoxy," there was room for a wide variety of attitudes and opinions.

Finally, the idea of a "structural identity" between Confucian and Maoist thought is based on the assertion that Confucians and Maoists share a fundamental concern with the justification of state coercion and of concomitant limitations on the expression of individual freedom. Ci argues that in the case of the Confucian belief in an "objective order" we immediately come up against "some moral authority such as the Confucian sage or some political authority such as the ruler or a combination thereof"[22] which leads to sage and/or ruler controlling the thinking of others. "The very possession of authority is treated by the rulers and ruled alike as at least prima facie evidence of the rulers' superior knowledge of the objective order and of the good based on that order."[23] According to this argument, Confucianism, like Maoism, was in some fundamental and defining sense conducive to and supportive of authoritarian patterns.

But such an analysis raises the question of whether there is not a crucial epistemological difference between the conception of an objective order associated with Marxist historical determinism and such an order as expressed in classical Confucian ideas of Heaven or Neo-Confucian ideas of *li* [principle] or *tianli* [the principle of Heaven or Nature]. Surely it is significant from the point of view of authority that the laws of history are alleged by Marxists to be fully knowable in the light of "scientific" socialism, while the ways of Heaven are acknowledged by Confucians to be difficult, if not impossible, to apprehend. This would go some way toward explaining why there is in the Confucian tradition a certain circumspection about knowledge and its limits[24] and also an openness with respect to the source from which authoritative or exemplary behavior may derive. In *Analects* 9:26 Confucius is recorded to have observed that "The Three Armies can be deprived of their leader, but a common man cannot be deprived of his will."[25] This saying seems to cast doubt on "the rulers' superior knowledge of the objective order"[26] and to affirm the dignity of an ordinary person—who, we may suspect, must at times have known more than the general.

Politically, there is the issue of how the traditional Chinese state compares to the Leninist state and how traditional Chinese views on government compare with democratic centralism. One obvious difference lies in the differing models of the state—the traditional state having had as its model the family writ large, the modern state being centered around a party writ larger and organized according to Leninist principles (with all of the implications for the family that that entailed). Equally obvious is the difference in the degree of infiltration by the state into the lives and affairs of ordinary people. No matter how many areas of public life were touched by the traditional state, Heaven was still high, as the adage went, and the emperor still far away. Not only would government control become far more pervasive (and invasive) in the totalitarian state, but the entire relation between government and society would be reconceptualized under a form of government the inspiration for which derived from the modern West and which, as in the West, knew no limits between politics and all other spheres of human life. As Hannah Arendt put it,

The rise of totalitarianism, its claim to having subordinated all spheres of life to the demands of politics and its consistent non-recognition of civil rights, above all the rights of privacy and the right to freedom from politics, makes us doubt not only the coincidence of politics and freedom but their very compatibility. We are inclined to believe that freedom begins where politics ends because we have seen that freedom has disappeared when so-called political considerations overruled everything else.[27]

≺ II ≻

### *At Home in History and in a Moral Order*

From the point of view of the larger theme of freedom, perhaps the most basic question—too complex to be simply answered yet too important not to be seriously contemplated—is what bearing Confucian moral culture may have had at any given time in Chinese history on the deepening absolutism of the traditional Chinese state. That absolutism did deepen over time is undeniable; there remains, however, the issue of whether, as Ci Jiwei argues, this was the result of an ancient conceptual pattern inexorably expressing itself over time, determining the dictatorial, rehearsing and reinventing the repressive. If so, was that pattern associated with the Confucian tradition? What were the perspectives of literati grounded in Confucian texts on the power of the state? What were the philosophical and psychological resources that they could bring to bear when they felt obliged, as many often did, either to remonstrate with a ruler over his style of governance or to protest against the malign effects of government policies?

My suggestion is that while, admittedly, there is no term in classical Chinese that precisely expresses the idea of moral autonomy in the modern Western sense of "free will," there are frequent allusions in early Confucian texts to individual behavior that can be recognized as autonomous. These passages tend to have as their major point the demonstration of autonomy—in the sense that they show the exemplar as being in some significant measure morally self-determining.[28] Unlike the discussions of *libero arbitrio* or free will in Western philosophical literature beginning with Augustine, the early Confucian discussions are seldom theoretical. Almost always they are descriptions of the way particular individuals have behaved, and to what effect in terms of their inspiring or encouraging influence on others.[29]

Actions expressive of what we might call moral autonomy may actually have begun very early, perhaps well before the beginnings of the Confucian tradition, with the diviners of the Shang period (c. 1554–1045/1040 B.C.E.). Some of these diviners, as David Keightley now believes, seem to have shown a courageous independence of spirit when recording the outcomes of royal divination.[30] Why some of them—apparently China's earliest historians—should have attached such importance to preserving an accurate historical record is unclear but nonetheless intriguing. What is especially striking is that the verification (confirming or disconfirming the king's prognostication) amounted, in effect, to a judgment on the king's ability to contact the ancestral spirits and to determine—and, in some cases, perhaps, to influence—their intent. We may assume that the kings, like most other people, took little pleasure in being shown to have been wrong, but, unlike most people, were in a strategic position to express their *displeasure*. Diviners who recorded what had actually happened, despite whatever disincentives they may have faced, must have felt some particular affinity for truth-telling or some conviction about the significance of the historian's role and the significance of the divinatory process.

One of the earliest themes in Chinese political thought, and no doubt one of the most influential, was that of the Mandate of Heaven [*tianming*]. This idea seems to have derived originally from early Zhou propaganda that was designed to provide the survivors of the Shang with a justification for their conquest by the Zhou and that at some point found its way in a highly sublimated form into the *Classic of Odes* and the *Classic of Documents*. The word was then out for all time that there is a natural or Heavenly order that holds rulers responsible for the wellbeing of the people and can be relied upon to punish cruel or decadent rulers by withdrawing their mandate to rule and transferring it to successors who are more promising in terms of moral rectitude. It is a notion that is distinctly hortatory yet also ominously admonitory, ostensibly supportive but also potentially subversive. Quite unlike the theory of the "divine right of kings" that would emerge centuries later in early modern Europe, the idea of the Mandate of Heaven served to establish the people's welfare as primary and to provide a justification for rebellion. The "divine right of kings" served to legitimize the *absolute* authority of rulers; centuries earlier, the "Mandate of Heaven" had sought to remind rulers of the *contingency* of their power and to warn them about the possible consequences of failing in their responsibilities to the people.

It is almost a commonplace that, however lofty the idea of the Mandate may have been, however much a conceptual counterweight it may have provided against absolutism, its limitation was

that there was no moral barometer—and no institutional mechanism—by which to determine when the prevailing rule had become so corrupt that a change was indicated. Nor, for that matter,
was there any source of guidance in determining who should take
the initiative in bringing about a change. Thus only a manifestly
*successful* operation, such as the Zhou conquest, could be con-
vincingly interpreted as providing evidence for its own appropri-
ateness. Still, over the course of centuries, the idea of the Mandate
served as a kind of reassurance that there *was* a moral order in the
world and that present wrongs would eventually be righted. Individuals bent on remonstrating with misguided rulers could invoke
Heaven's Mandate as a reminder of that moral order and the risks
of offending against it. Though the idea of the Mandate was pre-
Confucian, it would serve to make it possible for Confucians to be
at home in history and in the moral order.

Ci Jiwei suggests that *tianming* in early Confucianism involves
the idea of a "suprahuman objective order," which by its nature
subverts the idea of a plurality of legitimate conceptions of the
good because an objective order must outweigh subjective choices
and judgments. But there is much to suggest that the "objective
order" associated with Nature or Heaven was not thought of by
Confucius or Mencius as *suprahuman* but, rather, as all-encompassing and indwelling in all living beings. Viewed from this perspective, Ci's suggestion that the notion of *tianming* "rules out
the idea of morality as answering to empirical human circumstances and issuing from (mere) human agreement" seems odd—
odd because the idea of *tianming* can, alternatively, be understood
to *rule in* "the idea of morality as answering to empirical human
circumstances." One might argue, in fact, that a concern for "empirical human circumstances" is at least a part of what *tian* is all
about, as in Mencius' pronouncement that, "Heaven sees as my
people see; Heaven hears as my people hear."[31] Men like Confucius and Mencius, it seems, did not so much theorize about the
moral order as they, like everyone else, lived within it.

From the Eastern Zhou period (771 B.C.E.–256 B.C.E.) on there
are numerous examples of remonstration by officials with errant
rulers. A remarkable example of historians "speaking truth to
power" is recorded in a passage in the *Zuo zhuan* (Zuo Chronicle,
Duke Xiang, 25th year) which records the aftermath of the assas-

sination of Duke Zhuang of Qi (r. 553–48 B.C.E.) by the soldiers of his minister, Cui Shu:

> The grand historian wrote in his records: "Cui Shu assassinated his ruler." Cui Shu had him killed. The historian's younger brother succeeded to the post and wrote the same thing. He too was killed, as was another brother. When a fourth brother came forward to write, Cui Shu finally desisted.
>
> Meanwhile, when the assistant historian living south of the city heard that the grand historians had been killed, he took up his bamboo tablets and set out for the court. Only when he learned that the fact had been recorded did he turn back.[32]

We know nothing of the personalities or the motives of these historians, yet it is clear that they were committed, in the face of certain punishment and possible death, to maintaining an accurate historical record. Comparable situations, often with comparable results, have occurred throughout the course of Chinese history.[33]

Early on there is evidence not only of a commitment to an accurate historical record, but of a conviction that rulers must be open to remonstration and criticism. Another passage in the *Zuo zhuan* (Duke Xiang, 14th year) contains what purports to be a record of a conversation between a famous Music Master Shi Guang and the ruler of the state of Jin:

> Shi Guang was attending the ruler of Jin. The latter said, "The people of Wei have driven out their ruler—what a terrible thing!"
>
> Shi Guang replied, "Perhaps it was the ruler himself who did terrible things. When a good ruler goes about rewarding good and punishing excess, he nurtures his people as though they were his children, shelters them like Heaven, accommodates them like the earth . . . But if he exhausts the people's livelihood, deprives the spirits, skimps in the sacrifices to them and betrays the hopes of the populace, then he ceases to be the host of the state's altars of the soil and grain and what use is he? What can one do but expel him?
>
> Heaven gave birth to the people and set up rulers to superintend and shepherd them and see to it that they do not lose their true nature as human beings. And because there are rulers, it provided helpers for them who would teach and protect them and see that they do not overstep the bounds. Hence the Son of Heaven has his chief officers, the feudal lords have their high ministers, the ministers set up their collateral houses, gentlemen have their friends and companions, and the commoners, artisans, merchants, lackeys, shepherds, and grooms all have their relatives and close associates who help and assist them. If one does good they

praise him, if he errs they correct him, if he is in distress they rescue him, if he is lost they restore him.

Thus from the sovereign on down, each has his father or elder brother, his son or younger brother to assist and scrutinize his ways of management. The historians compile their documents, the blind musicians compose poems, the musicians chant admonitions and remonstrance, the high officials deliver words of correction, the gentlemen pass the word along, the commoners criticize, the merchants voice their opinions in the market and the hundred artisans contribute their skills.

Hence it says in the "Documents of Xia," 'The herald with his wooden-clappered bell goes about the roads saying, "Let the officials and teachers correct the ruler, let the artisans pursue their skills and thereby offer remonstrance . . ."'[34]

Heaven's love for the people is very great. Would it then allow one man to preside over them in an arrogant and willful manner, indulging his excesses and casting aside the nature Heaven and Earth allotted them? Surely it would not![35]

Shi Guang's view no doubt says more about an ideal state than about any actual one, but it is nonetheless interesting that in this ideal state not only were ministers expected to remonstrate with the ruler but the entire society was primed to participate in that task. This assertion of the validity—indeed the practical necessity—of remonstration drew its strength and urgency from the conviction that Heaven, having given birth to the people, loves and cares for them and is unwilling to see a ruler, who is meant to care for and nurture them, act in such a way as to compromise or destroy their nature that has been bestowed by Heaven and Earth [*tiandi zhi xing*].

Mencius, in his conversations with rulers in the fourth century B.C.E., shows no hesitation in invoking the idea of the ruler's responsibility for the people as a challenge for those who are revealed to be oblivious to the people's primacy and neglectful of their welfare. He is acerbic in the challenges he hurls at King Hui of Liang, for example,[36] and unsparing in some of the criticisms he levels at King Xuan of Qi.[37] In the conversation recorded in *Mencius* 1B8,

King Xuan of Qi asked, "Is it true that Tang punished Jie and King Wu assaulted Zhou?"[38] Mencius said, "This is contained in the records."[39]

"For a minister to slay his ruler—can this be countenanced?"

"One who despoils humaneness is called a thief; one who despoils rightness is a robber and a thief and is called a mere fellow. I have heard of the punishment of the fellow Zhou but never of the slaying of a ruler."

Mencius' pronouncement in this exchange, which seems implicitly to justify, or, at least, to explain tyrannicide, is sometimes interpreted to have amounted to a statement of a "right of revolution." Strictly speaking, Mencius says nothing about either "rights" or "revolution," nor was the idea of "rights" in the modern sense known anywhere in the world at this time. However, he does seem to have a clear idea about what in our own time would be called "crimes against humanity" and speaks out as forcefully against them as any contemporary advocate of human rights might do. Like the writer of the *Zuo zhuan* conversation quoted above, in which the Music Master Shi Guang converses with the ruler of Jin, Mencius was a believer in the idea that the nature of the people was endowed by Heaven and that rulers were responsible for ensuring that they did not lose that nature.

In his chapter on "The Way of Ministers" Xunzi goes even further than Mencius in defining the circumstances in which not only "remonstration" but other assertions of authority on the part of ministers were deemed both acceptable and essential for the wellbeing of a state:

When the lord has schemes that transgress and undertakings that err so that one is apprehensive lest the nation be imperiled and the altars of soil and grain be destroyed, and as a great officer or senior advisor one has the capacity to advance to the throne and address the lord concerning these matters, then being agreeable when one's advice is implemented and leaving when it is not is called *remonstrance* [*jian*].

When one has the capacity to advance to the throne and address the lord concerning such matters, then being agreeable when one's advice is used but forcing one's own execution when it is not is called *wrangling* [*zheng*].

To have the capacity to assemble the wise and to collect the strong, to gather all the ministers and the Hundred Officials, to bring together (strong and) martial lords, so that, even though the lord is insecure and incapable and will not listen, the state is saved from the greatest of calamities and delivered from the danger of the greatest injury so that in the end one's lord is shown honor and his country is made secure is called *assistance* [*fu*]. . . .

Thus men who remonstrate, wrangle, assist, and oppose are true ministers of the altars of the soil and grain. They are real treasures to the country and its lord. To an intelligent lord, they deserve the deference and generosity he shows them. But to a benighted lord, they seem to be a threat to himself. Thus,

those whom the intelligent rewards, the benighted punishes; those whom the benighted rewards, the intelligent punishes . . .

A tradition expresses my point:

One should follow the Way and not follow the lord.[40]

With Xunzi, the overriding consideration is not, as with the *Zuo zhuan* author or with the *Mencius* text, preserving the human nature of the people, about which he remained skeptical, but, rather, following the Way and preserving the state. But his intention to stress the validity of remonstration and principled protest is stunningly clear.


<   III   >

*Confucians and the Imperial State*

Beginning with the establishment of a unified state in the aftermath of the Qin conquest of 221 B.C.E., the history of imperial China was marked by a steady process of expansion of the state's powers. Over time, some of the more important initiatives of the state were to keep elaborate records of its population for the purposes of taxation, corvée, and conscription; to monitor agricultural conditions and crop yields throughout the empire; to control population mobility; to institute complex arrangements for mutual responsibility within families and communities as part of the law enforcement system; to control religious organizations and suppress potentially subversive religious movements; to curtail the independent power of an hereditary aristocracy and to exert powerful influence over local elites; to limit the development of competing centers of power in the economy; to prevent cities from becoming centers of autonomous political, social, and economic power; and, at least partly through the medium of the civil service examination, to exert widespread and profound influence over education.[41]

In a strict sense *none* of these policies *per se* had support in classical Confucian thought; in fact, few were even known to the Confucians of the pre-Qin period. Individual Confucians might differ at any given time because, as individuals, they were of distinct persuasions. They differed in various historical contexts because, as participants in an ongoing tradition, they responded variously to changing circumstances. For present purposes the important point is that there were always those whose ideas and ideals were at variance with, if not in outright opposition to, the policies or strategies of the state.

Over the centuries, in every dynasty, even as the Chinese state became more powerful and absolutist, scholars and officials, thinkers and poets (including many who were distinguished in all of these categories), would continue to speak out against what they took to be injustice and cruelty toward the common people on the part of a rapacious state. Their protests included indictments not only of their fellow officials but also of rulers. They protested and remonstrated not only in cases of misfeasance and malfeasance, but also of nonfeasance. Some were subtle and discreet—as in the case of Dong Zhongshu (195?–105? B.C.E.), the leading Confucian of the second century B.C.E., who, with his theory of portents, reflected, for the sake of the ruler, on his enormous power and reminded him, for the sake of the people, of his equally enormous responsibilities. Others were more direct—as in the case of the Confucian scholars who participated in the Debates on Salt and Iron (81 B.C.E.) in the Former Han, protesting the institution by the state of monopolies on salt and iron, the introduction of a system of crop loans, and the adoption of other measures they believed were designed to put the state in a position of reaping a profit at the expense of the people.

Subtle dissent, based on a remarkable awareness of history and a thorough grounding in the earlier tradition, was expressed by some of China's most distinguished poets, among them Du Fu (712–70) in the Tang and Su Shi (1037–1101) and Huang Tingjian (1045–1105) in the Song.[42] The intense sorrow reflected in the poetry of Du Fu had in many cases the character of subtle yet powerful criticism of the emperor Xuanzong (r. 713–55) and of an imperial institution that could not prevent chaos from engulfing the state and devastating its population. In the Song, the eleventh-century commentators on the *Chunqiu* [Spring and Autumn Annals] who were writing about issues of "loyalty to the emperor and expelling the barbarians" were also reflecting on the problem of autocracy.[43] Many of the opponents of the New Policies of Wang Anshi (1021–86) in the eleventh century were forthright in their criticism of what they perceived as statist attitudes and policies.

Not a few of the protesters—including the poet Su Shi—paid a high price for registering their dissent, not only in memorials but subtly, and even more devastatingly, in poetry.[44]

There was an almost unfathomable courage in the refusal of the early Ming scholar-official Fang Xiaoru (1357–1402) to oblige the usurper Zhu Di by writing a rescript announcing his accession in 1402 as the third Ming emperor, Yongle. Fang's refusal was deemed a "crime," a crime for which he was tortured and then executed—not alone, but together with all of his family, associates, friends, neighbors, and students, numbering, according to various accounts, between nine hundred and upward of a thousand persons.[45]

Another example is the sixteenth-century scholar and official Hai Jui (1513–87), famous for displaying his integrity and his defiance by making funeral arrangements and preparing his own coffin before writing a memorial denouncing the notoriously decadent Zhu Houcong, the Jiajing emperor (r. 1521–67), for his failures at every level of private and public life. In 1566 Hai was imprisoned at the emperor's orders and tortured almost to death, escaping that fate only because the emperor himself died the following year before having issued the order for Hai's execution.[46]

In the following century, when the Ming dynasty (1368–1644) was overthrown by the Qing (1644–1911), Huang Zongxi (1610–95) wrote an unsparing critique of dynastic rule in the *Ming-yi dai-fang lu* [Waiting for the Dawn—A Plan for the Prince], published in 1662. Huang was widely acclaimed for his work, but not until more than two centuries later.

Whether subtle or overt in their expressions of criticism, such protesters often paid a high price—sometimes the ultimate price—for their temerity. What is remarkable, and must surely have some profound cultural explanation, is the fact that Chinese have gone on protesting, and paying the price, and are still doing so right down to the present. What motivates them to do so? It is a haunting question.

Of the longstanding tradition of principled protest in China, W. J. F. Jenner has written:

Officials had not rights and freedoms but privileges, which could be withdrawn, without notice, and duties. High officials could discuss matters in their area of responsibility at court conferences, or submit memorials, but only at the monarch's pleasure. Ill-chosen words could lead to disgrace or death. This noble tradition of principled protest was still alive in the second half of the twentieth century, and some of Mao's subordinates paid the price for it—but it was nothing to do with freedom.[47]

Virtually all of this is true. But was it *really* "nothing to do with freedom"?

Considered from another perspective, it seems not only plausible but likely that many of these protesters believed they *had* freedom of expression, even though, in the absence of laws protecting it, it had to be asserted at a price. From a contemporary Western perspective, in which various freedoms (such as freedom of speech and freedom of assembly) are considered to be rights, the very notion of "freedom at a price" may seem oxymoronic. This is particularly so when "the price" goes so far beyond the Jeffersonian "eternal vigilance." But based on Confucian ethics and personality ideals, it is entirely possible that, for those who acted in this way, to have spoken out, to have engaged in remonstration, to have voiced their criticisms, even at a *cost, was* an assertion of freedom. Clearly, it was freedom asserted not with the protection of the state, but, from a Mencian perspective, on the strength of a human nature thought to have been endowed by Heaven or, in a neo-Confucian view, on the belief that human nature was to be understood in terms of that portion of the Principle of Heaven (or Nature, *tianli*) endowed in every person. This was—and is—the freedom to affirm what in the deepest sense one is as a human being—that is, a moral agent—and by affirming this to join a company of principled protesters across the centuries.

≺ IV ≻

*The Confucian Sense of Moral Autonomy*

It is not difficult to discern repeating patterns in the descriptions of morally autonomous individuals—persons whose highest devotion is to their own capacity to be morally self-defining. One finds, for example, a concern with courage or valor, a conscientious commitment to bearing the burdens of the world, and an acceptance of the possibility that, ultimately, one may be called upon to sacrifice oneself—that is, to sacrifice one's life—for others. Taken separately, these values bear some similarity to Greek or Christian values. However, the interesting point is that, in the context of early Confucianism, they tend not to be taken separately or treated analytically but recognized as part of a moral repertoire, as expressions of a free personality.

On the evidence of the *Analects* and the *Mencius*, it would appear that the idea of courage or valor was, like other moral concepts, undergoing transformation in the Warring States period as older, martial virtues came to be questioned or contested among the *ru*—those whose overriding commitment was to the power of learning and culture.[48] Based on several of the discussions of valor or courage [*yong*] in the *Analects* it appears that Confucius must have worried that impetuousness and bravado might all too easily be confused with genuine valor.[49] The contrast is especially clear in *Mencius* 2A2, which contains one of the text's most important discussions of moral psychology. Here Mencius compares three types of valor—the swashbuckling bravado of Bogong You, the ataractic courage of Meng Shishe, and the morally reflective valor that Zengzi claims to have heard about from Confucius. Mencius quotes Zengzi as saying: "Do you admire valor? I once heard this account of great valor (*da yong*) from the Master.[50] 'If, on looking inward, I find that I am not upright, I must be in fear of even a poor fellow in coarse clothing. If, on looking inward, I find that I am upright, I may proceed against thousands and tens of thousands.' "[51]

Three levels of valor are also compared in Xunzi's chapter "Human Nature Is Evil." The highest level of valor, he says, can be achieved when the Mean prevails in the world:

When the Mean prevails in the world, to be daring in holding oneself straight and erect; when the Way of the Ancient Kings prevails, to be bold in carrying its ideals into practice; in a high position not to go along with lords of an age given to anarchy; in a humble position not to acquire the customs of the people of chaotic times; to consider that there is neither poverty nor misery where humane principles are to be found and that there is neither wealth nor eminence where they are absent; when the world recognizes your merits to desire to share in the world's joys; and when the world does not recognize your merits to stand grandly alone in the world yet not be over-awed—such is valor of the highest type [*shang yong*].[52]

"To look inward and find oneself upright [*zifan er so*]," and "to stand grandly alone in the world yet not be over-awed [*kuiran du li tiandi er bu wei]"* suggest the confident mental attitude that distinguishes the morally autonomous individual from those whose courage is not similarly grounded in moral conviction.

The possession of this sort of valor is closely related to the commitment to bearing the weight of responsibility for the world. *Analects* 8:7 attributes to Zengzi the affirmation that, "An officer cannot but be broad and resolute, for his burden is heavy and his road is far. *Ren* (or humaneness) makes up his burden; is that not indeed heavy? Only with death is he done; is that not indeed far?"[53]

Twice in the *Mencius*, Yi Yin, chief minister of the Shang founder, Tang, is quoted as saying:

"Heaven in giving birth to this people causes those who are first to know to awaken those who are later to know and causes those who are first to be awakened to awaken those who are later to be awakened. I am one of Heaven's people who has awakened first; I will take this way and use it to awaken this people."

Of Yi Yin's deep sense of responsibility, Mencius observed:

He thought that if, among the people of the world, there was a common man or woman who did not share in the benefits bestowed by Yao and Shun it was as if he himself had pushed them into a ditch. So it was that he took upon himself the responsibility for the heavy weight of the world.[54]

It might be questioned whether and in what sense a person burdened with such a heavy weight of responsibility is truly free. Still, it is clear that in both of these instances the burden is freely assumed by an individual who recognizes this to be the way of fulfilling his own human nature.

Those who bear such burdens will face occasions when their resolution is challenged. On these occasions it becomes necessary to work hard to preserve one's moral concentration. Such an effort seems to be behind the combative Mencian injunction that:

In advising great men one should regard them with disdain and not take notice of their grandeur. Lofty halls with soaring roofs and projecting rafters—were my wishes to be fulfilled, I would have none of this. Food spread out on vast tables, with hundreds of servants waiting in attendance—were my wishes to be fulfilled, I would have none of this. A whirl of pleasure, a wash of wine, the rush of the chase, with a thousand chariots following along behind—were my wishes to be fulfilled, I would have none of this. What matters to them is of no consequence to me. What matters to me are the standards of the ancients. Why should I be in awe of them?[55]

There are times, too, when one's assessment of the moral circumstances in which one finds oneself calls for the sacrifice of one's life. So, according to Confucius, it may happen that "The determined scholar [*zhi shi*], the person of humaneness, does not pursue life if it injures humaneness. He will even sacrifice his life to fulfill humaneness."[56] A similar sense for the sacrificial possibility is present in Mencius' affirmation that,

I desire fish, and I also desire bear's paws. If I cannot have both of them, I will give up fish and take bear's paws. I desire life, and I also desire rightness. If I cannot have both of them, I will give up life and take rightness. It is true that I desire life, but there is something I desire more than life, and therefore I will not do something dishonorable in order to hold onto it. I detest death, but there is something I detest more than death, and therefore there are some dangers I may not avoid. If among a person's desires there were none greater than life, then why should he not do anything necessary in order to cling to life? If among the things he detested there were none greater than death, why should he not do whatever he had to in order to avoid danger? There is a means by which one may preserve life, and yet one does not employ it; there is a means by which one may avoid danger, and yet one does not adopt it. Thus there are things that we desire more than life and things that we detest more than death. It is not exemplary persons alone who have this mind; *all human beings have it*. It is only that the exemplary ones are able to avoid losing it, that is all.[57]

Xunzi seems to have something similar in mind when he speaks of "keeping resolute from inner power" [*decao*]:

He was born to follow it, and he will die following it: truly this can be called "being resolute from inner power." Keep resolute from inner power because only then can you be firm of purpose [*ding*]. Be firm of purpose because only then can you be responsive to all. One who can be both firm of purpose and responsive to all is truly to be called the "perfected man" [*cheng ren*].[58]

In his note on this passage the translator, John Knoblock, remarks that, "'Firm of purpose' refers to what is within us, whereas 'responsive' refers to what is external."[59] Moral autonomy in Confucian tradition typically has this valence—inner resolution and firmness of purpose, sometimes being defended at the *risk* of one's life—resulting in the capacity to respond to others. Or it may be that one's inner resolution is defended at the *cost* of one's life, in which case the ability to be responsive to others is thought to be achieved not in this life but in a larger life through a characteristically Chinese form of immortality based on the ultimate achievement—that of an enduring reputation.[60]

≺ V ≻

## Coda

The distinction between political freedom and philosophical freedom derives from Hannah Arendt. Once again, her analysis of freedom in the Western context is helpful in highlighting some of the differences between Western and Chinese conceptions of freedom:

This freedom which we take for granted in all political theory and which even those who praise tyranny must still take into account is the very opposite of "inner freedom," the inward space into which men may escape from external coercion and *feel* free. This inner feeling remains without outer manifestations and hence is by definition politically irrelevant. Whatever its legitimacy may be, and however eloquently it may have been described in late antiquity, it is historically a late phenomenon, and it was originally the result of an estrangement from the world in which worldly experiences were transformed into experiences within one's own self. The experiences of inner freedom are derivative in that they always presuppose a retreat from the world, where freedom was denied, into an inwardness to which no other has access. The inward space where the self is sheltered against the world must not be mistaken for the heart or the mind, both of which exist and function only in interrelationship with the world. Not the heart and not the mind, but inwardness as a place of absolute freedom within one's own self was discovered in late antiquity by those who had no place of their own in the world and hence lacked a worldly condition which, from early antiquity to almost the middle of the nineteenth century, was unanimously held to be a prerequisite for freedom.[61]

Perhaps because China knew no comparable separation between church and state, religion and politics, sacred and secular realms, or inner and outer worlds, the phenomenon identified by Arendt as "estrangement from the world" or "retreat from the world" was rare in China, at least among Confucians.[62] For them, retreat was almost invariably non-voluntary, though for the more

fortunate among those who were condemned to exile, the hope
was that such a fate might be only temporary. Their experience
was neither "without outer manifestations" nor "politically irrelevant." Nor was it typically the case that exiles concentrated
their attention on "an inwardness to which no other has access."
In fact, communication among exiled officials and their colleagues
and friends often approached—or quite literally became—an art
form, richly allusive, ingeniously encrypted, and highly civilized.[63]
Often this encoded communication involved a return to the deepest resources of the Chinese tradition as a means of making intel-
ligible or, indeed, bearable, the experiences of exiles. This they accomplished brilliantly by locating their individual experiences in a
larger historical, cultural, and spiritual context. For the poets, the
writing itself was a spiritual consolation not attained through
withdrawal into a sheltered and private inwardness but, rather,
through publication of that inwardness, a reaffirmation of one individual's connectedness with others within and across time.

Such a publication of inwardness is most memorably illustrated by the famous example of the poet Qu Yuan (c. 343–c. 277
B.C.E.), the most consistently celebrated and sympathetically remembered of all Chinese dissidents. Despairing at being relentlessly maligned by those around him at the court of Chu in the
early third century B.C.E., and thwarted in his efforts to achieve
reconciliation with a recalcitrant ruler, Qu Yuan is supposed, finally, to have drowned himself in the river Miluo. In what has
been taken to be his final poem, "Embracing Sand," he left behind
a message intended to survive him:

> I have met my sorrow, but still will be unswerving;
> I wish my resolution to be an example [*yuan zhi zhi yu xiang*].[64]

As these lines from Qu Yuan's last poem suggest, his resolution—
literally, his will [*zhi*]—is bound up with inwardness but not with
solitariness. His exercise of his will suggests what Xunzi called
"firmness of purpose," supported out of the natural resources of a
free personality, while his wish that it should be an example or a
model [*xiang*] for others may be understood as a gesture in the direction of immortality, and, with it, a wish to be capable of "re-
sponsiveness" to others.

Sacrifice—in the case of Qu Yuan, or in the Chinese tradition across time—has a different significance than it has had in the West, particularly in Christianity. Rather than representing, as in the case of Christianity, the central meaning of the faith and a revelation of the relation between God and the human community, sacrifice in Confucianism has consistently represented protest. It has been a movement of protest against repression (of both traditional and contemporary varieties), against denial of human dignity, and against disruption of the moral order of Heaven or Nature. The institutional adversaries of this movement of protest have been numerous and formidable. Still, given its literary and artistic strength, its moral depth, as well as its remarkable historical staying power, it may still be too early to conclude that this movement has "nothing to do with freedom."

# Chinese Law and Liberty in Comparative Historical Perspective

WILLIAM C. JONES

NONE OF the institutions and practices which are regarded as essential to the existence of liberty in the West today, such as an independent judiciary, existed in traditional China. In theory it was a total absolutism. In fact, however, there were some checks on the exercise of absolute power by the Emperor. These were embodied in the way the bureaucracy, which actually governed China, functioned. China is still governed by a bureaucracy, and despite the existence in China on paper of Western institutions, it may be that if liberty should develop in China it will have to be an aspect of the internal administrative control of officials.

◄ I ►

*The Battleground of the Development of Liberty in the Anglo-American Legal System*

Perhaps the most useful definition of liberty in a context like this is freedom from tyranny. That certainly is the burden of both the Declaration of Independence and the United States Constitution, especially the Bill of Rights. In the United States approach to freedom there must also be institutions that permit the individual to assert his "rights"—such as free speech, assembly, habeas corpus, and the like. The most important institution is the judicial system. Judged by these standards, there was no liberty in Imperial China. The Emperor had absolute power. He could do anything he wanted. There was no legal system of the American type. That is, there were, for instance, no independent legally trained judges, and no lawyers in our sense. The only dependable restraint was naked force. If a subject or group of subjects could collect enough military strength to force the Emperor to do or cease doing something, he or they could resist the Emperor, otherwise not.

Or so it appeared, and certainly there were many instances in Chinese history of extreme despotism.[1] Nevertheless there were in fact many restrictions on the powers of emperors, and a certain amount of liberty could be said to have been part of the imperial Chinese legal system. However, as will be explained below, that system was very different from anything we think of as a legal system, and it is difficult for us to recognize it—embedded as it was in an unfamiliar group of institutions and practices. Understanding this system is not just a problem for Americans and Europeans. Very few present-day Chinese know (or care) anything about their own legal history, and they think about law and liberty in American terms. That is, they think about judges and lawyers and law scholars. Law schools teach law that is based on European models, not those of imperial China.

Yet American concepts of liberty are based on institutions which are very special and the product of a long history. It is necessary to understand what these are to see whether any elements of the concepts, as we understand them, existed in China where the political, social, and economic history and institutions of the Anglo-American polity did not.

One of the distinguishing characteristics of Western history has been the importance of law, and the general recognition of this importance. Throughout European history there is reference to charters, agreements, and the like, and rather strained legalistic interpretations were used to justify actions. Even the Church relied on such documents.[2] In England from the justification of the Conqueror's invasion,[3] through the collection of English legal customs in the Domesday Survey, and numerous charters, notably including Magna Carta,[4] there was a constant series of legal documents that defined the English polity. In addition, the feudal state established by William consisted of a series of agreements—one might call them contracts though that is not the usual practice—by means of which vassals held land of their overlords in exchange for services and payments of various types.[5]

There was an additional factor that was very important in the development of the English constitution. This was the existence of an independent legal profession and body of law.[6] English law was studied in special institutions which became the Inns of Court, and eventually all lawyers studied there. Judges were drawn from the ranks of lawyers. The result is that the Common Law had an existence independent of the king and was studied and administered by a distinct body of professionals. This fact has had a permanent effect on the constitutions both of England and, later, the United States.

The way the role of common law affected the development of Anglo-American notions of liberty is quite visible in one of the great set-pieces of English legal history: The Case of Prohibitions del Roy. In this case, in 1607, James I wished to review a decision of the court and decide the case himself. His doing so was resisted by the court under the leadership of Sir Edward Coke, the leading Common Law jurist of the time, perhaps of all time. In the report of the case (written by Coke to be sure) it is stated:

To which it was answered by me, in the presence and with the clear consent of all the Judges of England and Barons of the Exchequer, that the King in his own person cannot adjudge any case, either criminal, as treason, felony, etc., or betwixt party and party, concerning his inheritance, chattels, or goods, etc., but this ought to be determined and adjudged in some court of justice according to the law and custom of England . . . Then the King said that he thought the law was founded upon reason, and that he and others had reason as well as the Judges, To which it was answered by me, that true it was that God had endowed his Majesty with excellent science and great endowments of nature, but his Majesty was not learned in the laws of his realm of England; and causes which concern the life or inheritance or goods or fortunes of his subjects are not to be decided by natural reason but by the artificial reason and judgment of law, which law is an act which required long study and experience before that a man can attain to the cognizance of it; and that the law was the golden metwand and measure to try the causes of the subjects, and which protected his Majesty in safety and peace. With which the King was greatly offended, and said that then he should be under the law, which was treason to affirm, as he said; to which I said that Bracton saith, *quod Rex non debet esse sub homine sed sub Deo et lege* [because the King should not be under man but under God and the law].[7]

This exchange did not conclude the matter. Coke was later deprived of his offices and eventually was sent to the Tower. The power of the Monarchy was only destroyed by great struggles and with much shedding of blood including that of the King. Nevertheless, the idea of the supremacy of law and courts was permanently established, in considerable measure because of the importance of Coke's treatises and reports in legal education.[8] The struggle continued both in and out of courts. Thus slavery—a form of tyranny—was the subject of constant litigation both in England[9] and, to a much greater degree, in the United States. Again, there was bloodshed, notably in the American Civil War, but there were also lawsuits. In a sense, this struggle was brought to an end by a series of lawsuits. The conclusion came in the middle of the twentieth century in the United States when official racial segregation—a form of the denial of liberty—was finally declared to be illegal by the American courts.[10] There was tremendous resistance, including some bloodshed, but the decisions have now been pretty much acceded to by almost everyone. This development represents a recognition of the authority of "law" and courts.[11]

This somewhat mystical notion of "law" as something independent of and superior to ordinary humans was dismissed by Oliver Wendell Holmes, perhaps America's greatest Common Law jurist, as thinking of law as a sort of "brooding omnipresence in the sky." The general—though not universal—tendency of modern American jurists is to agree with another statement by Holmes, in his lecture "The Path of the Law": "The prophecies of what the Courts will do in fact and nothing more pretentious, are what I mean by law."[12] Even so, it is probable that most Americans, including a great many lawyers, do in fact have a lurking affection for Coke's position, particularly as it is embodied in the Massachusetts Constitution:

PREAMBLE
The end of the institution, maintenance, and administration of government, is to secure the existence of the body politic, to protect it, and to furnish the individuals who compose it with the power of enjoying in safety and tranquillity their natural rights, and the blessings of life: and whenever these great objects are not obtained, the people have a right to alter the government, and to take measures necessary for their safety, prosperity and happiness.

The body politic is formed by a voluntary association of individuals: it is a social compact, by which the whole person covenants with each citizen, and each citizen with the whole people, that all shall be governed by certain laws for the common good. It is the duty of the people, therefore, in framing a constitution of government, to provide for an equitable mode of making laws, as well as for an impartial interpretation, and a faithful execution of them; that every man may, at all times, find his security in them.

We, therefore, the people of Massachusetts, acknowledging, with grateful hearts, the goodness of the great Legislator of the universe, in affording us, in the course of His providence, an opportunity, deliberately and peaceably, without fraud, violence or surprise, of entering into an original, explicit, and solemn compact with each other; and of forming a new constitution of civil government, for ourselves and posterity; and devoutly imploring His direction in so interesting a design, do agree upon, ordain and establish the following *Declaration of Rights, and Frame of Government*, as the CONSTITUTION OF THE COMMONWEALTH OF MASSACHUSETTS.

Article XXX states

In the government of this commonwealth, the legislative department shall never exercise the executive and judicial powers, or either of them: the executive shall never exercise the legislative and executive powers, or either of them: the judicial shall never exercise the legislative and executive powers, or either of them: *to the end it may be a government of laws and not of men.* (emphasis supplied)

Statements such as these, and not anything in their own history, are clearly the basis for the demand for the "Rule of Law" so frequently heard in China. In the Anglo-American systems, such abstract ideas are given content by their enforcement in independent courts by aggressive, often greedy, lawyers like Coke. This process is even more pronounced in the United States than in England. The United States is, after all, a legal construct. It exists not as a product of history like England or France, but by virtue of a constitution, a mutual compact. The courts are explicitly made an independent branch of government by the Constitution, and they early developed the power to overturn actions of the other branches of government.[13] Before the middle of the nineteenth century de Tocqueville observed that "scarcely any political question arises in the United States that is not resolved sooner or later, into a judicial question."[14] This tendency toward litigation has only increased in the ensuing century and a half.

To Americans, in consequence, liberty or freedom always means rights that are defined by courts in litigation. This is a point of view that is much more pronounced in the United States than in the rest of the Western world, even England. It is interesting to note, however, that the European Union seems to be employing the American approach. Complaints alleging denial of such rights as privacy are always being made to the European Court of Justice.[15] Moreover, courts of constitutional review are a commonplace in the post-World War II world.[16]

The American institutions that protect liberty are certainly the dominant ones in the world, even when completely divorced from the historical background that governs them. Sun Yat-sen was profoundly influenced by his understanding of them in forming his program for reforming China.[17] The written constitution of the People's Republic of China[18] has an obvious American influence even if the actual policy is quite different.

≺ II ≻

*Elements of Control of Despotism within the*
*Traditional Chinese Legal System*

By this view of liberty or freedom—and law for that matter—of course, there was, as mentioned, no freedom in Imperial China. The basic theory of the Chinese polity was simple. The Emperor had unlimited power. No one had any "rights" that could be asserted against him. However, this was, to a considerable extent, just theory. For one thing, because of China's size, no one man could rule over the whole country, and, at least by the Tang Dynasty, a meritocractic bureaucracy had developed which carried on most of the functions of government most of the time. The Emperor's power accordingly was limited, at least factually. In the first place no absolute ruler wants his subordinates to act independently. They have to be controlled, and the only effective way to do this in a country of any size is by rules. Bodies of rules have a tendency to become permanent. It is more convenient to continue established practice than to start afresh. Moreover they become encrusted with precedent. About 30 to 40 percent of one body of rules, the Qing Code, consisted of rules from the Tang Code. Many more were varied only slightly.[19] The Tang Code was from a period nine hundred years or more before the Qing Code was drafted. An emperor could of course override the bureaucracy, but he could not do this very often if he wanted to retain his system of government.[20]

Moreover, as a practical matter, while any Chinese was the potential object of his sovereign's wrath or whim, very few of them ever had any personal contact, favorable or unfavorable, direct or indirect, with the emperor. Ordinary people were supposed to pay taxes, fix the roads, possibly serve in the military. They should keep out of trouble, and were to be punished if they were involved in disorder. But officials who abused them were also to be punished,[21] in part because such abuse meant they had violated the rules, and absolute monarchs insist on obedience. Moreover this abuse caused unrest and disorder among the people. Hence there were a number of devices, including a system requiring the reporting of actions and decisions to superiors[22] and an inspector-general system (the censorate)[23] to make sure the officials acted properly. Perhaps the most important control factor was the education of officials. They were trained almost from birth in "Confucianism," which emphasized morality and obedience. While it would be naive to assume that training in morality necessarily resulted in a moral man, it would be equally unrealistic to assume that it had no effect.[24]

The result of the existence of this system for the average person's freedom was twofold. To the extent that officials followed the rules, it meant that the subjects were secure in their persons and property. They would not be abused by officials unless they violated the law. They would also not be abused by their more powerful neighbors since such acts as trespass[25] and kidnapping[26] were forbidden.

Of course, the system did not always work. There were certainly instances of corruption, undue influence, incompetence, and the like, though it is impossible to quantify the frequency of such instances. Still it also seems clear that the system was often satisfactory. It functioned for many centuries without inciting serious disorder after all.

In many ways the Chinese polity had a relationship with the legal system that was quite as close as the relationship between the two in England. This closeness is not so apparent because it is not clear to us just what the legal system was. It was not a system that arose out of a method for settling disputes between private individuals—the lawsuit—as Western law, both Roman and English, was. This difference has caused trouble in understanding it, because Westerners expect to find lawsuits or at least dispute-settling devices at the center of legal systems. The problem is analogous to the problems of Westerners dealing with unfamiliar religious traditions. As a commentator on the reactions of judges to claims of Native Americans to the sacredness of certain locations remarked: "In a corner of the minds of many judges is the idea that these just can't be real religion . . . Religion is something you do in a church."[27]

Of course the Chinese had methods for settling private disputes, but the essential element of Chinese society was the totality—in theory—of imperial control. To be sure, China in imperial times was not in fact a totalitarian society as it pretty much became in the Mao years. But this was a matter of lack of means, not of will. Given the methods of communication and transportation available, and the sparseness of available resources, it was simply not possible to control everything. The imperial officials were rather thin on the ground. The lowest official, the District Magistrate, was in charge of a county or *xian*, a unit of several tens of thousands to several hundreds of thousands of people. Most Chinese never saw him. Nevertheless the government—acting through the district magistrate—purported to govern dispute settling, religious activity, education, manufacture, commercial activity, and family and property relations as well as the more obvious governmental functions of defense, tax collection, and the maintenance and construction of public works.[28] The mechanism of control was, primarily, force. But force could not be used too much because of the lack of resources. Consequently there were efforts to use moral exhortation. In addition large areas of life were left uncontrolled in fact. For example, while the central government regarded commerce as clearly subject to its control, it permitted the guilds to exercise a great deal of control.[29] Similarly, every aspect of family life was subject to governmental control, including such matters as the designation of the heir[30] and the management of family property;[31] however, most family matters were resolved inside the family or the clan.[32] The latter could be quite large.

Disputes could be and were settled in both these fora. In addition there were what amounted to arbitration procedures carried on in villages under the supervision of village elders.[33] The Code

provided directly for some matters that were what we would call
matters of civil law to be dealt with by the magistrates under the
Code procedure. The Code provisions that covered these "civil
law" matters included penalties. Thus the redemption of mortgaged property[34] and a breach of promise of marriage.[35] It also provided rather obliquely for the magistrate to settle what we would
call law suits over civil matters such as debt collection and property disputes, without giving him much guidance.[36] Decisions in
these latter cases did not get the regular Code review. Perhaps it
was felt they were less important and hence there was no provision for punishment. Review of offenses under the Code was actually administrative review of the administrative action of the magistrate in recommending a certain punishment. Recently it has
been discovered that there was a great deal of this litigation before
the magistrate, contrary to what had been believed. Some have
drawn the conclusion that this litigation amounted to a system
quite comparable to ours. In my view such a belief is wrong. It ig-
nores the differences in the two systems. The magistrate did not
even make a pretense of being an independent professional who
had undergone special training to practice his profession of dispute
settling.[37] Law was not regarded as a subject for advanced academic
consideration.[38] Law was just something you picked up by doing it.
The legal secretary, who was simply a clerk, not an official, knew
quite a lot about law, but only in the way that clerks in any bureaucratic system know rules.[39] The magistrate was trained as a
generalist and that is the way he functioned. As one leading
scholar wrote:

A magistrate takes charge of the government of a district. He settles legal
cases, metes out punishment, encourages agriculture, extends charity to
the poor, wipes out the wicked and the unlawful, promotes livelihood,
and fosters education. All such matters as recommending scholars [to the
court], reading and elucidating the law and the imperial edicts [to the
public], caring for the aged, and offering sacrifices to the gods, are his
concern.[40]

The magistrate's job was to represent the Emperor at the local
level. There was no separation of powers. Settling cases was an
important part of his job, but so were collecting taxes and taking
care of all of the other administrative tasks that had to be taken
care of. This was true throughout the administrative hierarchy up

to the Emperor himself. The decisions in legal cases were reviewed. Indeed no final action could be taken until they were. But this review was the same for all administrative acts. There were collections of decisions of the Board of Punishment which amounted to precedents. However, there were collections of precedents for all administrative acts such as shipping salt or moving troops.[41] China was a unitary absolutism governed by a meritocractic bureaucracy and the system of governmental control *was* its legal system and vice versa.

While China did not have any institution which resembled a parliament, or that gave the appearance of having a parliamentary function, there were ways in which certain Chinese could let their opinions be known to their rulers. At the local level the magistrate knew members of the local elite and depended on them to enforce imperial policies. If they felt strongly about some issues such as the assessment or remission of taxes (because of natural disasters, for instance) they could frequently influence his actions. At the very top level, there was of course consultation between the Emperor and his high officials. There was even a tradition of dissent.[42] Accordingly, there was the possibility of some checks on executive action. Only by elites to be sure, but in the beginnings of systems of freedom in England and Europe such a system of checks was also the case. The barons at Runnymede were not exactly a representative body after all. For that matter Magna Carta, as originally drafted, was not exactly a charter of liberties.

This is not to say that Qing China had anything like as much freedom as eighteenth century England, to say nothing of the United States. On the other hand it was not a country without some freedom and some of this freedom was sufficiently regular, and supported by governmental authority, that one can say it was protected by law. Moreover the government was often unable in fact to exercise the control it purported to have. For the last half of the Qing, from the end of the eighteenth century, there were a series of uprisings, often connected with religious activities. The most famous is, of course, the Taiping Rebellion, but there were a number of others.[43] If the system of control had been working properly, they would never have got off the ground.

≺ III ≻

*Prospects for Liberty in China*

Was there a loosening of control that might have led to some Chinese version of the freedom that was developing in Europe? No one can say, because these years were about the time of Western intervention in China and the whole system collapsed. Beginning just before the 1911 Revolution, China began establishing a Western legal system on paper. It established law schools, courts, law reviews, and an organized bar. Western ideas of freedom became well known to intellectuals.[44] In 1929–31 a series of European (mostly German) style codes were enacted. These are still in force in Taiwan.[45] The Communists repealed all these laws in 1949[46] and promulgated a series of new constitutions thereafter.[47] These constitutions purport to recognize the freedoms of our Bill of Rights more or less, particularly the most recent one.[48] Since the Third Plenum in 1978, the whole pre-1949 Western legal system has been more or less reestablished on paper.[49]

To be sure, at present, none of this means very much, if anything. Even on paper the courts do not have much independence because the judges are appointed by the legislatures at the local level and do not have life tenure. In fact the courts are not much respected. The judges are not well trained. The legislatures are controlled by the Party and so are the courts.

It is possible, of course, that the Party will permit some free decision-making in the courts as it has permitted some—albeit rather limited—freedom of debate in the legislatures, and some freedom in local elections.[50] One thing that has changed from Qing times is that the intellectuals, the kind of people who would have taken the examinations to be officials in imperial times, are familiar with Western ideas of freedom. Moreover, two Chinese communities—Taiwan and Hong Kong—have a fair degree of freedom, and Taiwan has a democratically elected government. It is conceivable that the People's Republic of China will go through a development similar to that of Taiwan after the repeal of martial law. There are other possibilities as well, however.

The imperial system of government collapsed after the 1911 Revolution and was replaced, first by Sun Yat-sen's version of an American system—at least on paper—and then by the amalgam of that system, the Soviet system, and more direct borrowings from the United States after 1949. A visitor from Qing China would not have been completely surprised, however, at the post-1949 government. China was still a highly centralized absolutism run by a bureaucracy. The bureaucracy was much larger than that of Qing times and not as well educated. At present, it has all the gadgets of the electronic age so that communication is easy. Still the methods of centralized control are very similar. And it is, of course, the same place, with the same provinces and even counties. In many places there are the same crops and methods of cultivation. But most of all, the bureaucracy remains. As mentioned above, during the Qing period (and before), some of the due process protections which are enforced through litigation before courts in our system existed in China, to the extent they did, through the normal methods of bureaucratic control—notably the requirement of full reports and the use of inspectors such as the censorate. The Communist Party absolutism of the People's Republic is just as anxious as the imperial absolutism of the empire to make sure that its rules are observed and that officials do not abuse their powers. This concern is not the result of tender feelings for the downtrodden. The abuse of power causes social unrest, and disobedience on the part of subordinates is very harmful to effective administration.

In view of the secrecy that surrounds every aspect of the activities of the police and the treatment of prisoners, it is impossible to say exactly what is going on in the criminal field. It is possible that the constant effort to punish corruption[51] may be an indication of the center's desire to make officials toe the line. Of course, it may simply be a manifestation of the constant internecine strife that is a feature of all governments. In any event it is clear that in the Maoist period, the behavior of the members of the Security Administration was closely controlled, or at any rate that efforts were made to control it.[52] This meant that the abuse of prisoners was usually according to rule, or, one might say, law.

It may be significant that in at least one area that we would expect to see dominated by private litigation—and is in the West— in China seems to be dominated by administrative procedures. In several areas of tort law, although it is perfectly possible to bring an action in court, most of the cases seem to be handled within the administration by special procedures under special laws and regulations. These include cases of industrial accidents,[53] traffic accidents,[54] medical malpractice,[55] and consumer complaints.[56] Much of this is not unique. Many countries have administrative, as opposed to judicial, devices for dealing with some of these matters, especially industrial accidents.[57] Still, it may be suggestive of special Chinese characteristics, a reminder of imperial practice. In other words, if China develops more freedom, it could be that it will not be solely a matter of having the Western institutions, such as courts, function in the Western way. There may well be some of that. There are certainly many Chinese as well as foreigners who hope for that result. Even if that were to happen, however, it is at least possible that much business that would be handled by courts in this country would be handled by administrative agencies or that bodies called courts would function like administrative agencies. It is not only Communism that can have Chinese characteristics.

≺ IV ≻

*Conclusion*

Imperial China did not have the sorts of institutions that developed into the promoters and protectors of freedom in the West. Nothing similar to courts and parliaments existed in China. China was an absolutism run by a meritocractic bureaucracy. Nevertheless there was significant protection for some of the interests we protect under the concept of due process of law. China remains a centralized absolutism although it now has a plethora of Western institutions on paper. Still, if freedom is to develop there, it may be as much a development within the administration as in the courts and legislatures.

# Economic Freedom
# in Late Imperial China

MADELEINE ZELIN

THE RELATIONSHIP between economic institutions and "free-dom" is a complex one. On the one hand one might examine the degree to which individual economic actors were "free" to engage in transactions of various kinds. Along the same lines, one might examine the freedoms, such as geographical mobility or access to resources and information, that would allow individual actors to engage in other kinds of activities which contribute to their ability to transact. In the literature on modernization, scholars have also focused on what is seen as a complementary relationship between politics and economic institutions. As described by economists such as Douglass North, the existence of certain economic institutions is a necessary [but not sufficient?] condition for the development of certain types of political freedoms and the development of certain political institutions is a necessary [but not sufficient?] condition for the development of a modern industrial economy.[1]

This chapter will look at freedom and the economy in both ways. I will look first at the freedom to transact as it evolved in the late imperial period in China, highlighting those freedoms that are viewed as critical to the development of the modern economy in the West. I will then turn to the broader issue of the relationship between economic institutions and political freedom. This mode of inquiry can, I hope, help us to refine the theoretical literature on the political and cultural environment that facilitated economic growth in the developed world and, equally importantly, force us to readdress some of the widely held assumptions about the relationship between economic development and democratization.

≺ I ≻

## Economic Freedom and Economic Development

When most economic historians talk about the rise of modern
capitalist economies they have in mind a particular transformation of economic institutions which initially took place in a small
number of places; taken together, the transformations are seen to
have provided the conditions necessary for sustained growth of per
capita income. These institutions functioned by approximating
conditions under which private and social rates of return would be
the same for every economic activity and would be equal among
all economic activities. These results would depend on individuals
engaging in profit-maximizing behavior (as opposed to the maxi-
mization of other goods), having the exclusive right to use and
dispose of their factors of production (land, labor, and capital); and
on property rights being defined in such a way that no one else
benefited from or was harmed by an individual's use of his property (reduction of externalities). If these conditions prevailed, land,
labor, and capital would be efficiently utilized, research and innovation would occur, and new knowledge would be applied to economic activities at the right time.[2]

While these conditions have nowhere prevailed in their ideal
formulation, economic historians have drawn our attention to a
number of institutions critical to the rise of the modern economy
in northwestern Europe prior to 1800. Most important among
these are property rights and institutional arrangements that encourage economies of scale, improve market efficiency, reduce
market imperfections, and encourage innovation. In the West,
these conditions have been associated with changes in the relationship between land owners and the tillers of the land, new
methods of utilizing and organizing labor, reductions in barriers to
trade, new ways to pool capital, new fiscal instruments, and the
rise of contract and its enforcement. In the writings of new institutional economists the emergence of these institutions is often
associated with the development of particular political institutions—parliament in England and the merchant oligarchy of early
modern Holland—which encouraged trade by lowering taxes, ending monopolies, and supporting the development of secure property rights. The mutually reinforcing nature of new economic and

political institutions in the fifteenth century makes the determination of the relationship between economic development and democratization particularly difficult. As we shall see, many of the economic institutions that economists point to as critical to the dialectic of modernity in the West can be found in late imperial China. Let us first examine the institutions themselves and then attempt to tackle the more general problem of the interaction between politics and economy as illuminated by the Chinese case.

≺ II ≻

### Economic Institutions in Late Imperial China: Freedoms which Facilitate Market Transactions

The conventional image of pre-modern China is that of an authoritarian state which denigrated commercial activity and realized ideological disdain through market controls and arbitrary taxation of commercial actors. There is no question that the weaknesses of the late imperial fiscal system opened the door to confiscatory practices, in particular the expectation that where statutory revenue did not meet the needs of local government for development of infrastructure and for famine relief, merchant "contributions" would take up the slack. The collection of taxes in the period prior to the tax reforms of the Yongzheng reign period (1722–35) of the last imperial dynasty ran along two interrelated tracks; one consisted of statutory quotas due the central government [the so-called *zhengxiang*]; the other depended on extralegal charges on items within the regular tax schedule as well as a variety of customary fees [*lougui*], some of which fell particularly on members of the merchant class. It was these latter levies that supported the activities of local and provincial government and are generally seen by both scholars and politicians as the tools of an oppressive imperial state blind to the needs of commercial and industrial development.[3]

Particularly prior to the Taiping rebellion (1850–64), state support of guild power was also instrumental in the preservation of monopolies over the manufacture and marketing of certain commodities, including salt, grain, and local specialty items. In addition, the state did attempt to reserve for itself certain strategic resources such as saltpeter, silver, and lead. The state also licensed brokers and set limits on the number of brokers who could operate in particular markets. Doing so, however, was less an attempt to control markets than it was a measure to protect participants in the market from a proliferation of potentially unscrupulous middlemen.

If we think in terms of the two categories of freedoms noted at the beginning of this chapter, freedoms which facilitate transactions by allowing direct participation in the market and those which provide economic actors with choices and access to resources, China's record stacks up surprisingly well in comparison to most countries in northwest Europe in what are generally called the late feudal and early modern periods. Despite periodic government efforts to control residential choice, Chinese in all occupation groups enjoyed considerable geographic mobility in the early modern period.[4] Even in the early Ming dynasty (1358–1644), both government-sponsored and private efforts resulted in the relocation of landless farmers to northern Anhui and the flatlands of Hebei, Shandong, and Henan.[5] The fatal shrinkage of the Ming tax base as farmers evaded taxation by moving away from their legal residences provides dramatic evidence of geographic mobility during the latter part of the dynasty. Over half of the new land added to the tax rolls during the first few decades of the eighteenth century had been abandoned during the seventeenth century or was located in previously unsettled border regions in the provinces of Gansu, Sichuan, Yunnan, Guizhou, Guangxi, Guangdong, and the newly annexed prefecture of Taiwan.[6] Migration continued to serve as an engine of growth throughout the Qing dynasty (1644–1911) as Chinese settlers colonized Manchuria and Taiwan and resettled the Lower Yangzi region following the Taiping rebellion. Overseas trade and migration to Southeast Asia began as early as the late Ming, although the availability of domestic targets of migration probably accounts for the fact that large-scale overseas Chinese migration did not begin until the mid-nineteenth century, aided by the intensification of China's opening to foreign trade and political contacts.

The movement of large numbers of people across the Chinese landscape was not simply a response to growing population and land hunger. Sojourning, both long and short term, was a major factor in the growth of the Chinese economy. It was instrumental in the extension of Chinese economic and political influence along the Chinese frontier. As James Millward has shown, it was merchants, as much as officials and the military, who conquered the far west.[7] They brought Chinese goods to the borderlands in exchange for jade, livestock, and other Central Asian goods and the Qing state relied heavily on them to furnish the state's colonizing enterprise with supplies, to provide loans and cash remittances in times of crisis, and to establish a Chinese presence by settling in the western regions, opening shops and paying taxes.[8]

Migration also played an important role in the survival strategies of Chinese farming families who, throughout the Qing, were able to export seasonal labor to towns and cities to work as peddlers, coolies, and skilled and unskilled craftsworkers.[9] In Furong, Sichuan, men from particular counties came each year to the town to work as salt evaporators and to work in the factories which manufactured evaporation pans. The unfettered movement of merchants during the late imperial period gave rise to a wide range of institutions to meet their economic and social needs, including the well-known *huiguan* or native place associations, established by sojourning merchants and officials throughout China. Long distance merchants such as the celebrated Shanxi remittance merchants facilitated the movement not only of goods, but of commercial and investment capital throughout China's national market. Shanxi merchants not only traded in salt and issued notes which allowed the transfer of payments across vast territories without the transport of bulky silver and copper coins; in Sichuan, for example, they invested commercial profits in the expansion of salt production at Furong, which was critical to the development of that manufacturing complex. The organizational templates developed by these early and wide-ranging Shanxi merchants also served as models for the formation of other business enterprises during the mid- to late-Qing period.

Geographic mobility was accompanied in China by considerable status and occupational mobility as well. The shift from a political system based on inherited position to one based on merit played an important role in opening access to wealth and political influence, a process which began as early as the Tang (618–907) and continued throughout the late imperial period as barriers between degree-holding and other avenues to elite status gradually broke down. While the Ming attempted to perpetuate inherited occupational classifications, artisan households made up only about 3 percent of the Ming population.[10] Hereditary household classification, for the most part defunct by the end of the dynasty, was eliminated by law in the first year of Qing rule. With a few notable exceptions, such as the bound farm laborers of Huizhou, servile labor also disappeared by the early Qing[11] and the unequal status accorded to social groups collectively referred to as mean people [*jianmin*] was eliminated by the 1730s.[12]

Although China never developed institutional mechanisms by which non-aristocrats and non-degree holders were given a formal role to play in the political process, the symbiotic relationship that developed between the state and both the literati and the commercial elite facilitated the expression of the latters' interests in state policy. The right of petition[13] and state recognition of the self-governing authority of merchant organizations provided a regular avenue of access to the bureaucracy. The interpenetration of commercial and scholarly elites,[14] and the manning of the bureaucracy largely by degree holders whose interests as private subjects mirrored that of others of their class, contributed as well to the transmission of elite public opinion.[15] These factors, as much as any professed adherence to Confucian principles, help to explain the policies of low land and commercial taxation,[16] periodic tax amnesty, and protection of property rights that were characteristic of Qing governance. Chinese families of means pursued mixed mobility strategies that often involved grooming sons for both commercial and literati/bureaucratic careers, depending on their individual aptitudes. Indeed, it can be argued that China did not see the development of strong *estates* capable of forcing the institutionalization of power-sharing with the state precisely *because* of the social mobility and interpenetration of elites that prevailed in late imperial China.

The inability of the state to enforce status and occupational classifications was also reflected in the expansion of educational opportunities. Evelyn Rawski has argued that by the mid- to late-nineteenth century between 30 and 45 percent of Chinese men could read and write. A far smaller number of women, perhaps as many as 10 percent, were at least functionally literate.[17] Dorothy

Ko's work on literate women has demonstrated the existence of far-flung networks of women readers and writers, particularly in the more affluent Jiangnan region.[18] While we should not exaggerate the degree to which the average Chinese person had access to education, it is clear that the link between education and political influence (either through degree-holding or through service as a clerk within the government bureaucracy) created considerable incentives to provide educational opportunities at the lowest levels of society. Many scholars have remarked that the sheer volume of printed books and other materials produced during the late Ming and Qing indicated a large market beyond the literati. In addition to a growing output of popular fiction and religious texts[19] were guides for travelers, merchant handbooks, and encyclopedias for daily use. Of greatest interest to us are texts which focused on practical topics such as training apprentices and engaging in specific types of business transactions, as well as on how to write letters, contracts, and other types of documents. Among the late Ming (1368–1644) and early Qing titles examined by Richard Lufrano were *Essential Knowledge for Trade, Essential Reading for Travelers, Guide for Traders and Shopkeepers, Original Edition of the Xin'an Encyclopedia for Gentry and Merchants,* and *Essential Knowledge for the Pawn Trade.* The existence by the nineteenth century of large numbers of crudely produced books of this genre is a clear indication of a mass market.[20] As we shall see, the development of property rights during the early modern period depended in large part on the universal and relatively standardized use of contracts, household division agreements, i.o.u.s and other written agreements, as well as on open and dependable access to the courts and to the market. All of these depended on a social and political system which provided widespread opportunities for basic education of ordinary people.

≺ III ≻

*Economic Institutions in Late Imperial China:*
*Market Freedoms*

Given the mobility enjoyed by residents of late imperial China, it is not surprising that the late imperial period experienced deregulation of the market economy as well. This section examines the markets in land and labor, as well as overall state intervention in trade, leaving a more detailed discussion of the issue of property rights per se to the next section.

The vast majority of cultivated land in China was freely alienable by the late imperial period. While there is disagreement over the existence and extent of manorial farming during the Song (960–1279) and Yuan (1260–1368), it is generally agreed that manorial farming declined dramatically by the Ming and disappeared almost completely by the Qing dynasty.[21] The only remnants of large consolidated estates by the seventeenth century are best viewed as managerial farms, freely alienable and worked with hired labor.[22] Before the seventeenth century, state and aristocratic claims to land removed a considerable acreage from the free market, particularly in parts of the Yangzi delta and north China plain. The practice of forced sales of private delta holdings to the state during the southern Song was continued by the Yuan and maintained into the Ming.[23] The creation of government, palace, and aristocratic estates and pasturelands in north China, particularly after the transfer of the Ming capital to Beijing in the fifteenth century, also removed vast tracts of land from the free market and left a legacy of ambiguous property rights.[24] Nevertheless, despite the state's own role in removing land from private sale, the reliance of the state on land taxes for the majority of its revenues created a powerful incentive for state support for the privatization of land and the clarification of ownership. The Ming state moved in this direction by declaring that all taxable land in the delta henceforth be considered private property. A similar policy was followed by the Qing with regard to the Ming estates in the north.[25] By the eighteenth century most land in China could be freely bought and sold and even land that was legally inalienable became subject to market forces.[26]

From the point of view of the state a relatively sluggish market in land was preferable. Until the eighteenth century, land was the most important target of imperial taxation and revenues from land made up the largest portion of the state budget. State efforts to track land ownership for tax purposes included periodic cadastral surveys and the requirement that all land sales be registered and all land sale contracts be marked with a red government seal. By means of these two mechanisms every county was to maintain fish-scale registers (so named for the resemblance of mapped plots to the scales of a fish) noting the location and owner of every tract of cultivated land under its jurisdiction. Evidence of the liveliness of the land market and the inability of the state to exercise control over an increasingly complex economy may be seen in the difficulties faced by the Qing state in maintaining accurate tax registers, particularly in the Jiangnan region.[27] Fragmentation of holdings was also a product of the free market and reflected both social mobility and the efforts of landowners to evade taxation by scattering their holdings.[28]

The relationship between custom and law is the subject of chapter 4. However, we cannot leave the subject of the factor market for land without addressing the impact of customary practices on the alienability of land. Local customs regarding the sale or transfer of land are numerous. It is well known that the terms for different forms of sale and transfer could vary widely from place to place. Nevertheless, an examination of the *Zhongguo minshangshi xiguan diaocha baogao shu* [Report on a survey of Chinese customs relating to civil and commercial matters], compiled from investigations made by local government legal affairs agencies and by the legal reform bureau of the Beijing government during the 1920s, gives the impression that there was considerable uniformity in practice and standards applied to land.

The effect of customary practices on property rights in land is more difficult to determine. The household as the unit of ownership and the strength of lineage institutions, particularly in the southeast, gave rise to an ideal in which land would not be sold and subsequent generations would benefit from and add to the patrimony. In this regard, two customs in particular are cited by scholars as limiting the free alienation of land. The first was the requirement that land be offered to kin and to owners of contiguous plots before being offered to the general public. The inclusion of clauses to this effect in contracts of sale from every region of China would suggest that the practice was indeed widespread and binding. Nevertheless, Philip Huang, in his study of Jiangnan agriculture, has argued that this requirement was most often applied to subsoil rights (which changed hands infrequently) and not to topsoil (or use) rights.[29] Huang's finding would lead to the conclusion that the market in land as a factor of production, as opposed to land as an artifact of family status, was competitive. In Furong, Sichuan, while land sale contracts and contracts stipulating the contribution of land as an investment share in the opening of a salt well often included the kin/neighbor clause, none of the eight hundred plus contracts preserved from this area indicates that kinship or propinquity played a definitive role in the final sale.[30]

The second oft-cited custom is that of conditional sale [*dian*, *huomai*], whereby the seller of land retained the right to redeem a plot of land or exact a supplemental payment for increased value over time. Conditional sale, which traced its origins to the same belief that it was the responsibility of descendants to protect the inherited patrimony from alienation, clearly contributed to confusion with regard to property rights. The Qing effort to clarify and enforce property rights is discussed below. As we shall see, in most instances custom and statute provided a mutually reinforcing framework within which rights of use, alienation, and transfer of property were clarified and enforced. Therefore, the special problems arising from a tradition of conditional sale should be noted. Efforts to clarify and contain conditional sale were incorporated into the Qing code. Sub-statute 95–3, promulgated in 1730, required that land contracts clearly indicate whether a transaction was a *dian* or an irrevocable sale [*juemai*].

If the contract did not specify the finality of the transaction it was assumed that redemption was possible. Moreover, because the price paid in the case of a *dian* was assumed to be lower than market value, the law clarified the right of the original owner to receive a single supplemental payment if he did not redeem the land and title passed to the *dian*-holder. Likewise, punishments were specified for persons who, following an irrevocable sale, tried to extort additional payments from the buyer. Further efforts to reduce disputes resulting from conditional sale were incorporated into Qing law in 1753.[31] However, it is not clear how successful the state was in enforcing these laws. Even in early nineteenth-century Shanghai, there were contracts requiring successive supplemental payments [here called *jiatan*] from the parties who had previously purchased a particular piece of land or buildings.[32]

Finally, to what extent was the ability to alienate property by bequest limited by custom or law? The issue of the unit of ownership will be discussed below. Dynastic statutes from at least the Tang contained very clear laws governing the rights of kin to succeed to household property.[33] By the Qing the order of succession was male heirs, the sons of deceased male heirs, daughters, and as a final resort, agnatic kin. A woman without sons inherited from her husband but was required to name an heir from among her husband's nephews.[34] The most significant changes in succession laws of the late imperial period appear to have favored the development of private property by limiting the state's power to confiscate land for which no statutory heir survived.[35]

The consonance between custom and law in the area of succession appears to have resulted in little divergence from law in practice. In examining a large number of lawsuits relating to succession, David Wakefield has found that few dispute the distribution of property per se. Most are based on challenges to the status of claimants where there are no surviving sons.[36] Wakefield also notes that while it was highly unusual to bypass the statutory successors to an estate, it was possible to write a will [yizhu] bequeathing an estate to someone else.[37]

Evidence of a free market in labor may by found in a number of sources. By the early Qing, population registration by occupation was abolished and geographic mobility was virtually absolute. Related to this was the withdrawal of the state from production and the increasing reliance of the state on hired labor and the contracting of services. The work of producing the large amounts of porcelain and silk consumed each year by the imperial court was no longer undertaken by state manufactures, but was largely farmed out to private contractors who hired labor.[38] At the same time, the fiscal reforms of the late Ming and early Qing furthered the elimination of corvee labor on state infrastructure projects. By the early eighteenth century the merger of the land and the head tax was largely complete and the state became a major provider of part-time employment in its efforts to build roads, dikes, bridges, and other public works.[39]

Evidence of permanent and seasonal migration in pursuit of economic opportunity is plentiful. In his landmark work on the so-called shed people [pengmin], S. T. Leong demonstrates that, while many migrants to highland areas were pushed by poverty and overpopulation to engage in subsistence farming, a substantial portion came as workers in capitalist enterprises founded by merchant and rich peasant investors. The areas to which they were drawn tended to be close to high-level marketing systems, particularly south of the Yangzi River, and/or to rich mineral, timber, and other natural resources within reach of riverine transport.[40] Anne Osborne has found considerable evidence of hired labor brought in to mine coal and dig lime in the lower Yangzi highlands.[41] Yan Ruyi's early nineteenth-century account of the development of western China tells of merchant investors in timber lands, iron foundries, paper mills, wood ear and fungus plantations, and salt yards who put up the capital and hired managers who oversaw the importation of large numbers of outside laborers, artisans, and transport workers.[42] Robert Gardella's account of the development of the Fujian tea industry likewise documents the movement of large numbers of men into northwest Fujian to work as hired laborers in the region's numerous small and middle-sized tea-processing workshops.[43] The existence of daily labor markets in textile production areas is documented from at least the early Qing.[44] By the late imperial period, longer term relationships between employee and employer were increasingly likely to be established by contract. To aid employers, sample hiring contracts could be found in encyclopedias and specialized merchant manuals.[45] That urbanization progressed slowly in late imperial China appears to be a result of the opportunity structure of employment and not any political or cultural obstacle to the movement of potential workers into cities.[46]

Labor mobility was just one part of the general openness of the market in late imperial China. Beginning in the Tang dynasty (618–907) the Chinese ceased to regulate the location, size, or number of markets. Between the sixteenth and nineteenth centuries the number of markets in China increased by approximately thirty thousand.[47] By the Qing, the establishment and regulation of markets, while technically the responsibility of local government, was largely left to local elites. Borrowing a term from Max Weber, Susan Mann has described this policy of delegating responsibility for the regulation of markets to leading merchants and their organizations, or in their absence, to local gentry, as a form of liturgical governance.[48] Few scholars anymore accept Weber's argument that Chinese economic development was stunted by the dominance of administrative authorities in Chinese cities. Indeed, both Skinner and Rowe have shown that over 95 percent of Chinese urban places were free of any permanent bureaucratic presence as reflected in the location of a government office [yamen] within their territory.[49]

For most of the Qing dynasty, the state's interest in China's domestic commercial sector was largely limited to maintaining an open market as a source of revenue and enforcing conditions that minimized public unrest. Market stability was achieved by regulating and licensing brokers, banning the sale of substandard goods, enforcing "fair price" [defined as market price], and controlling efforts to create monopolies.[50] The state also took a strong interest in the issue of credit and debt. Debt was one of the few civil areas in which the imperial legal code specifically assigned responsibility for adjudication to the state. Likewise, the state specifically took responsibility for punishing those who did not pay their debts. Moreover, whereas the code called for brokers to insure fair prices in the marketplace, the state took responsibility for setting fair interest rates. From the Ming on, a fair interest rate was considered to be around 3 percent per month.[51]

The fact that China was a large continental empire governed by a vertically integrated bureaucracy ensured a minimum of internal administrative barriers to trade. Customs stations were established at key markets throughout the empire. However, even taking account of the fact that officials generally collected surtaxes above the statutory tax, customs revenues came to only about 7 percent of total government revenues in the mid-eighteenth century. A similar percentage was procured in the form of miscellaneous taxes [zashui] such as local taxes on tea, land deed registration fees, and so on.[52] Estimates of the total state claim to GDP in the form of taxes range from 4 to 10 percent during the Qing, which would place the commercial tax share of GDP at about 1.4 percent. Reform of the overall tax system during the Yongzheng reign was extended to commercial taxation as well. On the one hand, the rationalization of the far more important combined land and head tax [diding] reduced the pressure on officials to squeeze revenues from merchants and craftsmen. At the same time, efforts were made to rationalize commercial taxation by instituting uniform tax rates, visible posting of tax rates, and improvements in bookkeeping and monitoring of tax collectors at customs stations.[53] The eighteenth-century elimination of the unloading tax [*luodi shui*], a tax on goods as they moved between markets, further reduced the friction of trade.

The openness of the market was reflected in regional specialization. Regional specialization in the most important crops dated at the latest from the Ming. The expansion of the area of specialized cultivation, serving a growing handicraft-processing sector and supported by cheap grain imports from central and western China, can be traced to the early Qing. The most important cash crops during the Qing period were cotton, mulberry, sugar cane, tobacco, and tea. In addition, small areas specialized in plant dyes, fruit trees, pigs, ducks and eggs, and pond-grown fish. In some areas specialization was quite well advanced. By mid Qing as much as 70 to 80 percent of the land in parts of Songjiang fu, Taicang zhou, Haimen ting, and Tong zhou in Jiangsu were planted in cotton.

Northern cultivation of cotton, especially in Hebei, and in parts of Shaanxi and Shandong, also grew rapidly, accompanied by the growth of handicraft textile manufacture in these provinces. Sichuan, Anhui, Hunan, and Zhejiang also produced considerable amounts of cotton during the early Qing. Cultivation of mulberry, initially concentrated in Zhejiang, Jiangsu, and Guangdong, expanded to Sichuan, Hunan, and Hubei, the main agricultural frontiers of early Qing China. Moreover, the increasingly fine division of labor in the Jiangnan silk industry is underscored by the growing market in mulberry leaves, silkworm eggs, cocoons, and mulberry saplings, as well as reeled silk. Fujian and Guangdong, the main sugarcane-producing areas in Ming China, were joined by Sichuan and Taiwan in the extension of China's sugar industry. And the spread of tobacco production in Jiangsu, Zhejiang, and Jiangxi, and later into Shandong, Shanxi, Shaanxi, and Sichuan, inspired periodic panic on the part of officials who feared the consequences of withdrawing so much land from the cultivation of grain.[54]

Despite the elaboration of Qing market networks, the emergence of new and higher level markets, and the transformation of many periodic markets into permanent markets by the late eighteenth century, the extent of commercialization of basic goods like grain and daily use items is not clear. Wu Chengming estimates that on the eve of the Opium War only 10 percent of all grain produced entered the market.[55] This figure may be low as it does not include the small amounts of surplus grain routinely sold by peasants at periodic markets. By contrast, Dwight Perkins argues that prior to 1900 only 70 to 80 percent of agricultural output was retained for personal consumption.[56] Loren Brandt's estimates for output marketed are even higher, at least for central and eastern China. Although Brandt's analysis is not universally accepted, he makes a strong argument for China's participation in an international market in rice and wheat as early as the nineteenth century.[57]

In analyzing the impact of these market freedoms in the late Qing we should pay particular attention to the role of domestic transit taxes. We have already noted that an early version of these taxes [luodi shui] was eliminated in the early eighteenth century. The reintroduction of domestic transit taxes [lijin] during the Taiping Rebellion injected into the domestic market a level of taxation which inhibited the movement of goods by dramatically increasing their cost as they moved through the market hierarchy. At the same time, lijin, which by the terms of the so-called "unequal treaties" could not be levied on goods of foreign origin, seriously impaired the competitiveness of Chinese goods in domestic markets. The imposition of lijin and the intensification of state extraction of commercial revenues during the last years of the Qing reversed a centuries-long progressive withdrawal of the state from intrusion into the domestic marketplace.[58]

The openness of overseas trade is far more difficult to evaluate. A variety of factors, economic and non-economic, played a role in the formation of state policy. During the Tang period, the state attempted to control what was a lively trade in foreign luxury goods in order to reap the benefits of the high customs taxes this trade could yield. Under later regimes, the state alternately encouraged and tried to control overseas trade, often by restricting overseas access to Chinese markets. The main motivation for such restrictions, which often took the form of setting up special markets for foreign merchants, was state security rather than economic isolationism.[59] However, the Chinese state did little to regulate the movement of Chinese merchants overseas. During the Qing Chinese merchants dominated the Chinese trade with Central Asia and Russia and conducted a lively maritime trade that extended at least as far as Japan, Korea, and Southeast Asia.


≺ IV ≻

*Contract and Property Rights*

Arguably the most important and controversial element in our discussion of freedom and the economy in early modern China is the construction of property rights and their enforcement.[60] The unit of ownership in imperial China was the household [*jia*] and not the individual. During the Qing, and in essentially the same fashion during the entire late imperial period, property passed from a man to his sons either through the establishment of a family division agreement [*fenjia dan*] during his lifetime, or through a will [*yizhu*] if the household property was divided after his death. Household property was divided equally, with some minor exceptions. If a man died without having produced sons his widow inherited the household property, but it was required that an heir be named to succeed to the property upon her death. Over time, the law regarding female inheritance changed somewhat more than that for males. Daughters received a share of the household estate in the form of a dowry. By the Qing, a daughter succeeded to the household property only if she had no brothers and there were no male agnatic cousins out to the fourth degree.[61]

Following household division or the death of both parents, each party succeeding to the household property established a new household. Until the next division, the household head and his sons may be seen as shareholders in the overall estate. The household economy, often diversified and engaged in a variety of employments and investments to which all members contributed and from which all benefited, can fruitfully be thought of as the household firm. Income generated by shareholders was pooled and in the case of rural families and many urban families, common residence and the sharing of a stove (and the taking of meals together) gave physical meaning to the communal economy of the household. The authority to dispose of the household property was vested in the household head [*jiazhang*], the eldest male.[62] Only he had signatory power, although this power could be entrusted to a household manager or *dangjia*. The only exception to the joint ownership of property was a woman's dowry, which became her individual property and by extension the property of the nuclear family created by her and her husband. Dowry, as individual property, was not subject to household division and Wakefield argues that men who worked outside the *jia* firm were sometimes able to sequester their outside income by burying it in their wives' private hoards.[63]

The combination of law and custom requiring the equal partition of household property and religious practices requiring the allocation of resources for burial and sacrifice to ancestors led to the practice of setting aside part of the estate as an indivisible corporation. Income from such corporations could be used for ritual purposes, to support the activities of a constituted lineage organization, and, in the case of corporations with large holdings, to provide income for individual shareholders. In such cases, individual households were the unit of shareholding in the larger corporation, which could include large numbers of households in the case of corporations founded several generations in the past.

The practice of incorporating land for ritual purposes became the template for the development of more complex corporations, often with diverse portfolios. By the eighteenth century such corporations or trusts were becoming the foundation for shareholding partnerships bringing together non-kin investors in productive ventures, commerce, agriculture, and mining.[64] While state policy reflected these popular practices with regard to the distribution of property rights, the state played a critical role in the development of what one could only slightly tongue-in-cheek refer to as strong rights of property with Chinese characteristics. This it did in several ways: by means of specific laws upholding private property, by endorsing the use of written contracts to establish property rights, and by enforcing contracts in its courts.

We have already noted the state clarification of property rights in the statutes on succession. Imperial statutes relating to theft make clear the state's recognition of private property. Among the crimes of theft delineated in the Qing code are sale or alienation of other people's goods, crops, or livestock; sale or retention of real or movable property entrusted to you by others; retention without compensation of items that are the result of the labor of others; and sale of ancestral land or temples by sons or grandsons. The prohibition against retention without compensation of items that are the result of the labor of others contains as illustration the confiscation of grass, kindling, and so on that someone has gathered from an uncultivated area. While easily written off as evidence of China's largely agrarian orientation (along with the separate substatutes against theft of grain, of fruit, and of vegetables) this statute [271] directly addresses the issue of the derivation of property rights. Taken alone it is insufficient evidence of a Lockean theory of property. However, taken together with evidence from other domains it raises some interesting questions. For example, in the case of abandoned land and "virgin land," he who has added value to the land is seen as having established a right in it, although in the case of abandoned land this may only be a right to compensation for value added.[65] In the case of "virgin land" there is strong evidence of a Chinese version of Manifest Destiny which justified the Han occupation of aboriginal lands on the grounds of more productive use.[66]

The state's heavy reliance on land taxes and its equally strong motivation to prevent lawsuits accounts for its interest in establishing clear criteria for determining rights of property in land. According to Qing law, real estate should have been registered with the state, its dimensions and location entered into the county's fish-scale register, and a deed tax paid. Once this was done, a special seal would be affixed to the contract. Such officially sealed contracts were known as "red contracts" [*hongqi*] because of the red color of the seal ink. The statutory establishment of written contracts as the determining evidence in disputes over real estate was the main purpose of most of the substatutes under statute 95 of the Qing code. While substatute 6, promulgated in 1767, attempted to establish *hongqi* as the only accepted proof of ownership in the specific case of burial land, examination of legal cases demonstrates that a signed and witnessed contract, even if it was not officially sealed, was recognized by the state as decisive in most cases.

Other forms of property, including shares, were never dealt with in the Qing statutes. However, by the Qing period written contracts were commonly used to finalize most kinds of transactions, including household division; betrothal; adoption and uxorilocal marriage; purchase of real and personal property; conditional sale and mortgage; purchase of people, loan agreements, promissory notes, and bills of exchange; partnership agreements; employment agreements; agreements to pawn goods; rotating credit agreements; contracts to transport goods; and contracts to pool resources for irrigation, social welfare, group investment, and the creation of lineage trusts. Contracts were even written to establish agreement to accept the decision of a mediator. The significance of written agreements is highlighted not only by the variety of relationships which they confirm, but also by the fact that they are utilized both among strangers and among the closest of blood relatives.[67]

In the absence of a body of commercial law (beyond that just described) and in the absence of a system of courts in which the decisions of the court could operate as precedent for future decisions,[68] the contract itself took on enormous importance in the establishment of property relationships. Drafters made a conscious effort to leave out nothing in delineating the actions to be triggered by the agreement. In more complex business agreements they set out who was responsible for investment, when payments were due, who was responsible for taxes and repairs, how dividends would be distributed, what portion of profits would be reinvested, and so on.

In this regard, contract evidence, much of which is only now becoming available, is fundamentally changing the way we understand Chinese businesses to have worked.[69] For example, it used to be a truism that Chinese companies rarely reinvested profits. We now have contracts from a variety of Qing firms that specifically indicate the proportion of profits to be divided as dividends and that to be reinvested in the firm or in related businesses. For example, the Shanxi merchant firm Dashengkui established the practice of limiting its annual dividend to shareholders to a fixed amount, allowing the firms to spend considerable sums on expansion. As a result, the original trading firm came to include a network of native banks, as well as subsidiaries trading in grain, silk, tea, livestock, wool, and camel hair; and factories producing blankets and rugs for north China nomads and peasants.[70] At the

Zigong salt yard contracts contained a restatement of the industry practice which delayed the distribution of dividends until such time that a newly drilled salt well had reached optimal productivity.[71] Moreover, while there was no state commercial code, it is clear from an examination of business contracts that the customs of individual trades were embodied in the contracts entered into by their members. In deciding contract cases, magistrates were thus guided by local custom, statute, and the customs of the trade.

Not surprisingly, there is a strong tendency toward self-enforcement in late imperial and early Republican contracts. Defective performance appears to have been most often dealt with by means of liquidated damages. For example, in Zigong salt-well contracts it was often stated that if investors ceased drilling, the well would revert to the landowner; or if one member of a partnership failed to pay his monthly share of operating expenses, his shares would be split among the other partners. Nevertheless, the large number of contract disputes brought to the courts is evidence that parties relied on the state to enforce agreements and the rights established within them.

Evidence from disputes in Sichuan and a small sample of disputes elsewhere in China suggests that contracts were indeed routinely upheld in court decisions and that the basis for these decisions was, with a few exceptions, the intent of the parties. While land-related cases were often handled first by informal mediation, business disputes often came directly to the magistrate's courts. During the twentieth century special institutions were given jural recognition or new ones were established within trade associations and chambers of commerce to mediate commercial disputes.[72]

At both the courts and the newly recognized mediation boards, the writing was the most important basis upon which a decision was laid down. Whereas any party had a strong case in arguing for the enforcement of a written contract, in order to break a contract one would for the most part be limited to proving one of five conditions: a) that it is not a real contract, it is forged or the seals of the signatories are forged; b) that the parties who signed the contract did not have the authority to make the agreement contained in the contract (as in the case of sons or grandsons transacting with household property without the authority of the household head); c) that the parties involved were duped through inherent incompetence (usually only with reference to women and minor children and often, I suspect, used as a way to get out of a bad deal); d) that the opposing party failed to perform, most often found in cases of leased property, to which the lessor owed services during the life of the lease; e) that the opposing party perpetrated a fraud, such as passing off damaged goods as whole goods.

Thus, contrary to the received wisdom that Chinese courts routinely allowed ethical considerations and the goals of social engineering to alter the position of the court vis-à-vis "the law," in civil cases, the formal and informal institutions of the state appear to have upheld the rights established by custom and contract and to have provided a predictable venue for the resolution of disputes. In only two types of cases would other considerations override the "intent of the parties": cases in which the contract clearly violated the "customs of the trade"; and debt cases, in which it was common to seek a compromise in which the debtor was spared total ruin, or in which the rights of other creditors were given a hearing, at the expense of strict enforcement of a prior loan agreement.

Contract and state enforcement of privately contracted rights played an important role in the development of new means of pooling capital and the utilization of new fiscal instruments. By the eighteenth century, as noted above, it was common to see non-kin investing in partnerships established by contracts which laid out the investment, purpose, rights, and obligations of each shareholder, including management and governing rules, division of profits, and procedures for entry and exit by investors.[73] The development and widespread use of new fiscal instruments, such as negotiable bills of exchange and notes, negotiable shares, and remittance receipts, all depended on the state's recognition of these documents as contracts to be enforced in the courts.

## ≺ V ≻

### *Economic Freedom and the Realm of Politics*

The above discussion highlights several important characteristics of the late imperial Chinese economy and its associated political and social system, including a high degree of social and geographic mobility; open and competitive factor markets; relatively little state interference in the market; and strong support for private property and withdrawal of the state as a manufacturer and land owner in its own right. These conditions facilitated important changes in the economic institutions during the late imperial period. There were a proliferation of markets and increasing market integration at least to the regional level as well as increased specialization and the development of cash crops. The relationship between landowner and tenant was transformed from one of dependency to one based on contract and increased security of tenure, particularly in the more commercialized areas of southern and southeastern China. There was almost universal recognition of contract as the main evidence of all varieties of property rights. The development of new fiscal instruments accompanied the growth of long distance trade; and new ways to pool capital were particularly evident in the growth of shareholding corporations and business partnerships for both production and marketing.

Freedom in the economic realm has been treated here largely as a matter of the balance of power between society (in the form of individual and collective economic actors) and the state. Observed from this perspective, economic actors in China from at least the tenth century were far freer than their counterparts in medieval Western Europe. Neither political nor ideological organizations in China exercised the limiting power that both church and state exerted in the West. Nor can China be viewed as anti-market. Indeed, at the same time that the church stance against usury posed a major obstacle to the development of commercial institutions in Europe, Chinese lawmakers were defining "fair price" in terms of market rates. Moreover, while the state did maintain control over a small number of strategic commodities such as saltpeter, lead, salt, and so on, the overall trend in the late imperial period was for the state to get out of the business of business. The state that emerges from this investigation is not the barrier to economic development that some studies of the Chinese economy would suggest. Indeed, the recognition that the late imperial state, and particularly the Qing state, gave wide berth to the entrepreneurial impulses of its people suggests that the study of Chinese economic development need look in other realms for an understanding of China's slow growth in the nineteenth and twentieth centuries.[74]

Equally problematic is the relationship between economic freedoms and the development of political freedoms and their supporting institutions. Scholarship in this area is far less advanced than that relating to economic development per se. Therefore, what follows should be viewed as a preliminary foray into this important field. Moreover, the question of sequence complicates analysis of this relationship, as theorists often see economic freedoms as providing the foundation for political freedoms at the same time that political freedoms are viewed as prerequisites for the development of freedom in the economic realm.

At the heart of the contemporary discussion of the relationship between economics and politics has been the role of the "rule of law." In the economic realm, the rule of law is generally held to be alien to Chinese experience for a number of reasons. First is the absence of a civil code in China prior to the early twentieth century. This absence does not mean that economic actors operated in a lawless environment. The state upheld contracts and supported the basic rules of engagement in business. Moreover, while more evidence is needed, it does appear that the circulation of merchants and officials resulted in a relatively uniform understanding of what those basic rules of engagement were. Likewise, Chinese economic actors appear to have operated within a system of customary law that was well understood by judges and those who appeared in their courts.

Second, China is faulted for recourse to community justice. Although there is no way to determine what proportion of civil disputes were sent back to lineage, village, or guild mediators, we do know that doing so could be the first step in a magistrate's treatment of a civil case. Likewise, we can never know what proportion of these cases came back to the magistrate's court, although the survival of large numbers of these cases in county archives indicates that the state certainly did adjudicate contract and other civil disputes. While self-policing communities can dole out justice, it is assumed that the rule of law can exist only where the state imposes an impartial standard on all members of society. In this and other areas, it should be noted, China is often held to a higher standard than that which applied at the same time in Europe. For example, it was not until the eighteenth century that merchant contracts became enforceable in English state courts.[75]

Closely related to assumptions about community justice is the indictment of Chinese courts for basing their decisions on moral criteria rather than "the law." This argument is particularly interesting in that it skirts the basic tension in Western legal theory between law as enacted legislation and notions of a higher law embodied in principles, which were by no means the exclusive purview of Confucian bureaucrats. It also reflects the role of the school of "law and economics" in legal theory today and the faith it places in economic efficiency as the appropriate determinant of good law. Recent work by Chinese legal scholars has demonstrated that while the late imperial codes did embody culturally defined principles, particularly in matters relating to family law, magistrates (and/or their law secretaries) were well versed in the code and referred to it in making their decisions. Moreover, at the risk of overstating this point, in the realm of economic litigation, the state largely based its decisions on the will of the parties to economic transactions.

Clearly, the freedoms that we see in the economic realm were to some extent reflected in the exercise of the rule of law, at least in the narrow sense, during the late imperial period. However, in no case was such an exercise accompanied by a restatement, whether implied or explicit, of the rights of subjects vis-à-vis the state. How, then, should we understand the more general political environment and the apparent failure of an emerging merchant class to wrest greater and more generally applicable political freedoms from the late imperial state?

Chinese dynasties exercised centralized state power long before the consolidation of monarchical authority in the West. By the twelfth century China had a vertically integrated bureaucratic government that collected taxes, issued laws, maintained a national army, and controlled foreign relations. Yet in many ways the power of the central state was limited. The great size and physical diversity of China's landscape made the exercise of central control difficult. The decision to rely on agriculture as the main source of state revenue was a decisive one. It both eliminated the state's motivation to control commerce and assured that the state would never collect sufficient revenues to greatly expand its military or civilian presence. The freedoms examined in the first part of this chapter arose not from a struggle between rising estates and a cen-

tralizing state, but by default. The state could not control a growing population and economy so it ceased to really try.

Nevertheless, the central state did not disappear. Rather, it
came to a number of accommodations which help explain China's
divergence from patterns of political development found in some
Western state systems. Most obvious is the accommodation
reached with Chinese elites. By the Song dynasty the destruction
of a hereditary aristocracy which could challenge the central state
was complete. The position of the new elite was founded on service in the bureaucracy. Recruitment into the elite was merit
based, dependent on success in a state-administered examination
system. Both the content of the academic curriculum and the hierarchical nature of the degree system guaranteed a high level of
homogeneity among degree holders. And while it is true that only
those with means could afford the education necessary to pass the
examinations, the state was not concerned with how those means
were acquired. By the Qing period it was relatively common for
families to pursue mixed strategies, training some sons for state
service and others for commerce or management of family resources. As a result, although a hereditary ruling family headed
the imperial state and had greater or lesser influence over affairs of
state depending on the inclinations of the emperor, in matters of
economic concern there was virtually no status distinction between those who controlled the government and those who held
the major stake in the economy. This fact goes far in explaining
the relative freedom enjoyed in the economic sector and the lack
of incentive to the development of bounded estates competing
with each other and the state for political rights and economic
power.

Despite this apparent homogeneity among the elites who
manned the Chinese state, there existed within the late imperial
political system a significant tension between local and central interests. This tension was manifest both in central government distrust of local officials and local societal efforts to resist the power
of the central state. Key to this struggle was competition over resources. However, at least at the rhetorical level, it was not a
competition between different estates with interests centered at
different levels of the political system. Rather, it was a contest between members of the same elite, some of whom saw the welfare

of society best served by a strong state, and some of whom felt that role was best filled by local elites who understood local conditions.[76] While the chief object of this struggle was taxes, the larger issue was how active the state should be in the management of society and the economy. Examined over the course of the late imperial period, the outcome of this struggle was a stand-off between the two parties, with the alternation between strong state and strong localities being one that ultimately also contributed to the growth of economic freedoms without forcing the redefinition of political rights.

Although other factors also influenced the definition of political rights in the late imperial period, I will end with a little recognized characteristic of the Qing dynasty, the last imperial state. The Qing imperium was both an alien dynasty and an expansionist state. During the 267 years of Qing rule the territory of China doubled in size, not only absorbing present-day Taiwan, Xinjiang, and Manchuria, and parts of Tibet and Mongolia, but also extending Chinese rule to internal frontiers long neglected by previous regimes. A significant characteristic of Qing governance of this vast empire was a policy of differential rule. That is to say, the Qing tailored their style of rule and the laws they applied to the specific group they wished to control. Thus, for example, in areas of present-day Xinjiang, Muslim law was recognized in dealing with native populations.[77] In Tibet and in aboriginal areas of western China, native chiefs held sway while giving nominal allegiance to the Qing state. The ultimate expression of this differential rule was the banner system, which governed the economic, political, and military life of Manchus and their early Mongol and Chinese followers, quite apart from the territorially-based system of governance applicable to all other Qing subjects. At the same time, state efforts to control interaction at these borders, manifest in the regulation of foreign trade and Chinese merchant activity in frontier areas, was undertaken for reasons of state security, not as a matter of economic policy. Rather than an expression of principle, differential rule and frontier regulation were a sign of state weakness, yet another deal with local elites which both diffused opposition to the state and made uniform rule and the uniform application of the law—the ultimate goal of Qing state builders like the emperor Yongzheng—a distant dream.

≺ VI ≻

*Epilogue*

The Chinese case makes it clear that there is no simple relationship between economic freedom and development. Nor is the existence of a relatively laissez-faire economic regime a guarantee of the corresponding growth of future political freedoms. Factors such as China's size, geography, and natural resource base tempered the effects of economic openness; and the existence of a relatively free market at an early stage of development may itself have been a factor inhibiting the growth of an urban industrial regime by diffusing wealth and encouraging rural-based production. China raises even more questions about the dynamics at work in the evolution of political freedoms. Here we find a centralized bureaucratic state which placed few constraints on economic activity. The demise of the landed aristocracy in the early middle ages opened the possibility of entrepreneurship to all levels of society. Likewise, a merit-based bureaucracy promised the possibility of participation in politics to anyone whose economic success could be translated into scholarly achievement. As a result, the challenges faced by the late imperial state were not class based. They were external, in the form of "barbarian" incursion, and internal, in a tug of war between supporters of local autonomy and those of enhanced central power. Both groups were represented by merchants, scholars, and politicians. In neither case were the rights of the individual a factor.

Much changed in the course of the twentieth century. However, several key characteristics of the late imperial regime endure. While the central state in the PRC is far stronger than that of the Qing, a similar trend toward economic liberalism accompanies the interpenetration of elites (now in the form of cadre and businessmen and businesswomen) and tension between local and central power. With the recent declaration by Jiang Zemin that capitalists may join the Communist Party, the interpenetration of elites may be complete. What impact such conditions will have on the development of political freedom remains to be seen.

# Rights, Freedoms, and Customs in the Making of Chinese Civil Law, 1900-1936

### JÉRÔME BOURGON

THE ENTRY of China into the modern world was marked by military defeat, collapse of the empire, the domination of contending warlords over the territory, and an incomplete reunification by the Nationalists after 30 years of turmoil. Yet during this period legal reforms were worked out, so sound as to lay foundations of the Chinese legal system which later developed into a mature rule of law in Taiwan, as well as of the unachieved legal system in the People's Republic of China. This crucial period witnessed decisive breaks with the ancient legal system and ways of government. Admittedly, Western principles were not immediately adopted; rather, a new authoritarianism replaced the ancient autocracy. However, the new forms of power claimed rights and liberty as a foundation of the nation-state.

A major breakthrough was the making of codified civil legislation, which was pursued during almost four decades of legal reform during the late Qing and Republican periods. This codification meant a dramatic change in the legal system, as separate civil laws had never existed in China. Models had therefore to be imported from the West and required that users, to begin with the ruling elite, be familiar with their basic notions. The introduction of a "private law," as civil law is commonly framed, entailed a complete redefinition of social relationships. Civil law holds that society is a collection of individuals entitled to equal rights peculiar to private relationships, with a central place reserved to property rights. Individuals enter into private relationships by contracts, which are the legal expression of their freedom to dispose of their property. The connection between contracts, property rights, and freedom in private relationships replicates general principles of the political macrocosm, according to which state and society are linked by contract. Private freedom and thus rights are the foundations of public liberty and political rights.

This sophisticated construct, elaborated by European Enlightenment scholars, was absent from the Chinese tradition (see chapter 2). However, various forms of contracts and land deeds had long existed in Chinese society, and some were mentioned in the Qing code as well. Modern Chinese lawmakers decided to reemploy parts of Qing laws, and to select a broad set of popular practices as "customary law," to become a complement to and a component of the Chinese civil legislation. Thus, a Western framework would be filled with a Chinese substance.

As pertinent as this general program might seem, it raises many questions, which can range along three main lines. First, were there elements in pre-twentieth century Chinese law or social practice that can be considered as assets for the making of a modern civil law? This is a complex issue. The Chinese system certainly provided for preconditions of liberty, by stressing legal norms in criminal penalties and by assuming general awareness of law by the commoners. Even so, were there in the management of popular customs and in the conception of law some practical or doctrinal equivalents of the "rights and liberties" articulated in European customary laws? Chinese legal reformers in the early twentieth century chose to keep in force sections of the Qing code as a substitute for civil law during the two decades while the civil legislation was being drafted. Does this mean that the Qing code already included "civil laws" prior to the introduction of the Western legislation? Or that Qing magistrates adjudicated local "minor matters" through a distinct "civil procedure," as some recent scholars have contended? In other words, were there any aspects in law or in judicial practices under the Qing that paved the way to a modern civil legislation?

Second, must we accept Chinese law-makers' claim that civil law was sinicized by "customary law"? The question may sound strange, as a generation of Chinese jurists worked on massive collections of customs which would confer historical legitimacy on this claim. Nonetheless, there are serious reasons to doubt that this was an original method invented to match Chinese realities, as customary laws appeared in many colonial countries. Further, the Chinese collections of customs raise questions about their embedding genuine private law and individual rights, ready to be introduced into civil law categories. They even lead to the question: what were the real objectives pursued under cover of customary law?

Third, how, therefore, must we regard the Chinese civil code that was published in the 1930s? How are we to explain that it could remain a reference for the current legislation of Taiwan, as well as for the incomplete civil laws of the PRC? The answer could lie in commonly underrated factors in Chinese legal history: jurisprudence, legal knowledge, and skills of expert jurists. This chapter relies on the assumption that China had not only laws, but Law, a learned discipline with its own categories and techniques of codification. To focus too exclusively on the "customary law" project, with its postulation of a direct contact between Western law and well-formed social customs, might overshadow the deep influence of the Chinese legal tradition on the path of modernization. Instead, a careful examination of the Supreme Court jurisprudence sheds light on Qing jurists' role in the relationship between new laws and traditional remnants.

Ultimately, Chinese law-makers had to decide how to ensure legal continuity between old and new legislation. Was it mainly achieved by enforcing "civil laws" already included in the Qing code? Was it by turning social practices into a customary private law? Or by mixing old and new legal conceptions through jurisprudence? An understanding of the balance among these three devices will give insight on the fate of individual rights and freedoms in the making of the Chinese civil law.

≺ I ≻

*Preconditions for Liberty in the Imperial Legal System*

In the liberal conception now current in Western nations, liberty is a creation of law, while tyranny has been defined as the absence of law.[1] This conception inspired the building of legal and institutional systems in the West from the Enlightenment on and led to comparisons with the Chinese legal tradition. As the opposite of and a foil to the Western rule of law, China became the typical example of Oriental Despotism and Total Power, in which law was but the improper name of the autocratic whim.[2] This opinion is still so widespread that it is necessary to introduce some aspects of the Chinese legal tradition that provided for what can be considered basic requisites for liberty.

According to the outstanding theorist of justice John Rawls, the most basic condition for "justice as regularity" was having a legal system, defined as "a coercive order of public rules addressed to rational persons for the purpose of regulating their conduct and providing the framework for social cooperation. When these rules are just they establish a basis for legitimate expectations. They constitute grounds upon which persons can rely on one another and rightly object when their expectations are not fulfilled. If the bases of these claims are unsure, so are the boundaries of men's liberties."[3]

The imperial legal system satisfied most of these requirements. Arguably, Rawls's requirement of "just rules" might raise questions when applied to imperial China, where criteria of justice and fairness were quite different from our own. However, George Staunton, a well-informed European of the late eighteenth century, who first translated the Qing code in 1801, valued various "political advantages [that] might be found peculiar to the Chinese," when compared to European countries of the same period. Among such "advantages," Staunton highlighted "a system of penal laws, if not the most just and equitable, at least the most comprehensive, uniform, and suited to the genius of the people for whom it is designed, perhaps of any that ever existed."[4] Indeed, conformity to a uniform law, restricting the arbitrary decisions of the judges, underlay the Chinese notion of justice.

Moreover, the Chinese were consistently sympathetic to another aspect stressed by John Rawls: "In any particular case, if the rules are at all complicated and call for interpretations, it may be easy to justify an arbitrary decision." In China, the ideal of simplicity was pursued for centuries. This imperative of simplicity calls for the rule of "no offense without a law" [*nullum crimen sine lege*] stating clearly and explicitly what the offense consists of and how it must be punished, and makes of penal sanctions a gatekeeper of the principle of liberty.[5] In Chinese law, crimes and punishments must be clearly defined. This legal requirement was supported through the circulation of legal handbooks intended not only for professionals, but for a large readership as well, by such means as translations in vernacular languages and compositions in tables and charts, in counting rhymes, or even drawings. The great number of woodblock editions conserved by Asian and Western libraries testify for a mass production, without equivalent in the premodern world.[6] Diffusion of legal knowledge fed a strong feeling of justice among commoners, and ardent expectations of an equal treatment according to law.

Admittedly, modern China has had great difficulties in founding law on rights and liberty defined in a foreign tradition. Moreover, the Chinese legal system entered into its darkest period since the civil wars of the nineteenth century had multiplied illegal punishments. However, it would be a complete mistake to infer that before the twentieth century the Chinese were permanently submitted to a lawless tyranny, or had no notion of law and no sense of justice.

It is ironic that China's precocious legal system tended to become a trap. One major shortcoming was the lack of legal categories to treat popular practices as civil matters. Uniformity and comprehensiveness were pursued at the cost of legal sophistication and doctrinal accuracy. To make the system more cohesive and the legality of the penalties more conspicuous, the Chinese jurists made of the regular penal scale called "the Five Punishments" the general pattern and common denominator of all codified rules. Thus, many notions, rules, and practices used in the management of society that could have developed in civil law were either erased or reduced so as to enter into categories expressed in penal terms. Hence this aspect of the Qing code, where even the laws guaranteeing what would be framed "rights" in a Western legal context are formulated through prohibitions and end with an enumeration of penal sanctions.

≺ II ≻

*The Status of Popular Practices in
the Imperial Legal System*

These basic features of the Chinese legal system help explain why the status of popular practices was so different from the status of customs in the European legal systems. In England, customs were the local rights and liberties of communities acknowledged by the Norman kings and they were progressively formalized and legalized by judges' decisions into a Common law defined as "the general custom of the Kingdom." In France, customs were gradually written down into charters from the eleventh century on, so as to become quasi-civil codes for each particular province in the seventeenth century. This process is closely tied to the "liberties and privileges" granted to particular communities, and can be considered as stages in a slow process of centralization. Meanwhile, private "Civilist" jurists and Church "Canonic law" scholars elaborated doctrinal tools to synthesize the diverse customary charters into a general Civil law, of which the Napoleonic code is the legitimate heir. However, the similarity of the terms must not lead one to believe that rights and liberties proclaimed by the French Revolution and spread in Western Europe by Napoleonic wars were the same as those acknowledged in old customs. Equality before law had become the prevalent rule, whereas old customs were in fact privileges, unequal by nature, which were prohibited by the new civil legislation. Thus, "Customary law" appears as a particular stage in the building of European states. As familiar as the partition law/custom may sound, we must not forget that it resulted from answers given to problems peculiar to the European legal tradition.

Chinese legislation had its own path of change, very different from the European way sketched above. A first difference lay in the bureaucratic management of popular practices. Under the Qing, the territorial administration monitored practices by roughly distributing them into three categories: "good: to be encouraged," "evil: to be repressed," and "indifferent: let people do as they please"; and then measures were appended to address practices according to their label. Once framed in these pro forma bureaucratic categories, local practices became part of a program headed "Corrections of the mores and practices" [*zheng fengsu*]. Though their origins were mentioned incidentally, the itemized practices were not construed as the rights and liberties of a local community, but only as particular cases in an administrative agenda which was basically the same all throughout the empire. They were customs of the bureaucracy, and not of the people.

A second difference from Europe is that this "bureaucratic sieving" was headed by a centralized jurisprudence. Those measures that were deemed to have an empire-wide interest in legal matters were transmitted by the judicial commissioner of each province to the central services of the Board of Punishments. There, they were examined by a specialized Office for Codification [*Lüli guan*]. Then, measures that were deemed applicable to the whole empire were inserted into the code as sub-statutes, appended to a statute, and generally placed under the scale of penalties provided therein. Only by being reduced and reshaped into penal sub-statutes could popular customs and social realities be infused into the code.[7] This process helps explain why no custom was ever enforced by a judicial decision, or written down into a charter as happened in Europe. Hence, when the late Qing and Republican law-givers decided to collect civil customs, they had to start from scratch.

Such hyper-centralized jurisprudence, performed by a very small group of central lawyers, is remote from current judicial activity, and from the real life of the populace. However, only through this narrow window could codified laws be kept in gear with social life and administrative activity. Unlike European customs, practices or rules managed by the Chinese bureaucracy had no legal force before they were reframed at the central level, by the Office of Codification. The legal experts in this office were uniquely skilled in the framing of administrative materials into penal sub-statutes so as to make them cohesive with the whole legislation. Under the late Qing, these specialists acquired an unmatchable virtuosity in the handling, cross-checking, and collation of an amazingly broad number of normative texts of every nature. This legal discipline has its masterwork in the *Persistent doubts when perusing the sub-statutes*, compiled by President of the Board of Punishments Xue Yunsheng (1820–1901).[8] Years before its posthumous publication in 1905, this patient collection of all the contradictions that afflicted the written laws had become the handbook of a new school of legal experts. They used it as a general agenda for legal reforms, which allowed them to ensure continuity during the passage from the ancient to the modern legislation, under its penal as well as civil aspects. The jurisprudence of the Supreme Court that included pieces of social reality into the Nationalist civil code of 1930 was directly inspired by this method.

*Alleged Sprouts of Civil Law in the*
*Imperial Legal System*

Since the 1970s, the progress of Chinese studies has improved our knowledge of local justice under the Qing. Researchers have found that the great bulk of judicial practice dealt with "minor matters" like matrimonial disputes, household divisions between heirs, or land sales.[9] Qing magistrates enjoyed a great liberty for settling "minor cases," which were liable to flogging with bamboo, and which were not submitted to revision by the hierarchy as "serious cases" were. Sensible magistrates were reluctant to inflict corporal penalties on disputants over land property or familial matters. However, court hearings were much the same whether civil or penal matters were being adjudicated; the "flogger" was always present, and at times in action. At any rate, these "minor cases" can be deemed "civil" only through a loose analogy, which must not be pushed too far.[10]

Was a neat separation of civil law more discernable in judicial practice? Philip Huang has contended that magistrates' handbooks, "while confirming the lack of any clear distinction between civil and criminal matters in theory, also indicate a distinct separation between the two in practice."[11] Indeed, magistrate handbooks contain interesting decisions that departed from the letter of the law to rely on different legal sources. For instance, disputes over succession opposing familial interests to ritual obligations grew rapidly in number from the eighteenth century on. In such cases, a skilled judge pointed at a loophole in the imperial code, which he often filled by referring to one of the Confucian Classics.

Is this evidence of a civil law with its substance abstracted from popular practices? No. The same method was used in penal cases, such as the different sorts of "illicit intercourse."[12] Moreover, such decisions were never related to the way of life of a particular community or a given locale. As Philip Huang himself remarks, each case was treated as particular.[13] Such decisions articulated no rights or liberties that other peoples would enjoy thereafter.

Huang's main argument is that the Qing code included sections headed "Family, Marriages, landed properties, money and debts," which made up the "main body of what [he] refers to as Qing civil law."[14] However, the content of these "civil laws" does not square with the "minor cases" as defined above. Far from being limited to "minor offenses," some of these "civil" statutes deal with crimes as serious as "abduction of spouses and daughters of commoners' family." They provide penalties much higher in the penal scale than flogging with bamboo, such as military banishment for a son selling his father's land without authorization.[15] Thus, it would be misleading to believe that the "civil sections" combined with "civil procedure" to produce a cohesive "civil law."

These laws never define any "right." Let us take the example of "property rights" that Jing Junjian reads in prohibitions against "theft," "illegal sale," or "violent seizure" of someone else's land.[16] First, as similar prohibitions are spelled out in purely penal sections of the Qing code, their "civil" specificity is questionable.[17] More importantly, what the Qing code protects in fact is *household possession*, not *individual property rights*. Land use was acknowledged to each household [*renhu*] regularly registered as taxpayer.[18] The household was the real owner, as its individual members could not freely dispose of its wealth: children could settle separately only when parents permitted, but parents were compelled to divide property in due time, in equal shares.[19] Lastly, formal registration did not guarantee absolute, irrevocable rights of property. For instance, families who came back to fields they had temporarily deserted were allowed only the part of them that they were able to put in cultivation; the remaining land could be distributed to other families.[20] Similarly, formal registration was not enough to establish a clear-cut distinction between the rights of the legal owner of a piece of land and the rights of the user of the surface. The same piece of land could be sold or mortgaged by the legal owner and by the user of the surface. Although only sale contracts written by registered owners were legal, confusion prevailed in practice, resulting in a multi-ownership system that jeopardized the fiscal levies.

The Qing code never provided a firm legal background for promoting property rights in rural society. This huge loophole in turn deprived Chinese civil legislation of a firm anchoring in popular practices, as the compilations of customs will show.

In fact, the whole assimilation of Qing code sections with civil law is teleological. It stems from the late Qing reformers' decision to employ the section on "Family, Marriage, land, and debts" as a substitute for civil law until the publication of the new legislation. This modern reemployment of the old technicality of imperial law was dictated by emergency and does not indicate that Qing law evolved by itself toward a modern civil law, or that the former was easily converted into the latter. Thus the civil law enforced during twenty years under the Republic cannot be seen as a mere perpetuation of sections of the Qing code. First, the reformers had previously "de-penalized," or, in other words, "civilized" them, by a general conversion of the penal provisions into fines and damage fees. Second, Qing laws were but a formal framework, the major advantage of which being that the officials and magistrates were familiar with it. Actually, the substance of civil law was abstracted by the Supreme Court from the imperial legislation, through a long confrontation with Western legal principles. Two decades of jurisprudence were needed to express civil excerpts from the Qing laws; meanwhile, the Qing code contained such dubious civil matters that the substance of private law was sought in customary law, to which we turn now.

≺ IV ≻

### Chinese Customary Law: Accommodating Civil Law in a Colonial Context

In 1908, Chinese law-makers launched campaigns for collecting and writing down local customs, as indigenous elements of private law which would complete Western legislation. This move stemmed from a general trend of the Western colonial administration. In many regions of Africa and Asia, customary law was composed by colonial rulers to tighten their grip on local societies.[21] In the Chinese world, this trend had a direct influence only in the British colonies.[22] China was exposed to this influence through the prism of Meiji Japan, which had modernized its legislation just one generation before China. There was an ancient and intimate connection between cultural and legal traditions of these two countries; therefore the Japanese contribution to Chinese customary law goes much further than that of the usual colonial administration. It took place in a general conception of civil law, which included the choice of a type of civil legislation, the framing of a legal terminology, allowing the learning of new doctrines about law and custom, and, finally, the compilation of customs.

The Japanese made a fundamental choice when they adopted a civil code on the German model. In their wake, all Chinese drafts were framed into the characteristic five sections corresponding to great legal categories. These were general principles; obligations (torts and contracts law); rights over things (property law); familial relationships; and succession, inheritance. These general divisions were imposed not only on legislation, but also on the compilations of popular customs.

An additional decisive asset of Japanese scholarship was a glossary of legal terms, which continues to shape Chinese legal language. By way of equivalents to Western notions, the Japanese framed compound expressions of two or three Chinese characters, as was usual in their language for abstract notions. The Chinese then just had to reintroduce these ready-made expressions, the only difference being in their pronunciation.[23] Thus were framed terms for "rights": in Japanese, *kenri*, in Chinese, *quanli*, from two characters meaning respectively "power" and "interest"; or "law" [J. *hōritsu*, Ch. *Falü*], from two characters meaning "law" or "method," in a very broad acceptation of these terms, and "codified statute." As for "custom," an old compound was re-used with a completely new meaning. *Shūkan* in Japanese, *xiguan* in Chinese had been used since antiquity to mark out individual habits, particularly good habits contracted by scholars long familiar with the classics.[24] The term had never been conferred the meaning that the Japanese gave it to produce an equivalent of custom: a practice that a particular community considered as a rule to be abided by. These terms, with many others, made legal, instead of literary, translations of Western legislation, by maintaining their cohesiveness. They also delineated a new configuration of law vis-à-vis society and individuals, by articulating "law," "rights," and "customs." For instance, opposing the compound characters for "law" [*hōritsu/falü*] to those for "custom" [*shūkan/xiguan*] in their ancient sense would have been completely meaningless. In their new meaning, they allowed for the accommodation of new Western theories to the Far Eastern context.

Japanese scholars sent abroad became familiar with the recent trends of European legal debates. Hozumi Nobushige (1856–1926), an outstanding figure in the Japanese codification, brought back from his stay in England and Germany the new conception of customs put forward by the German historical school.[25] This was a reaction against the universal and abstract conception of rights, by virtue of natural law, that the French civil code proclaimed and that Napoleon's conquests had imposed on Western Germany. F. K. von Savigny, the outstanding legal theorist of the historical school, held that written legislation was a mere statement of a pre-existing law, alive in the "spirit of the people." This spirit was embodied in popular customs, which therefore constituted the major source of law. Instead of universal principles of natural law, a legal system was the expression of a national, or even ethnic identity. Savigny's followers speculated on the opportunity to found a new kind of civil codification on collections of popular customs.[26]

The new notion was introduced in China by two figures already famous for their role during the Hundred Days Reform of 1898: Huang Zunxian (1848–1905) and Liang Qichao (1873–1929); both of them had become aware of it through their familiarity with Japanese scholarship. Huang, an official of the Chinese legation in Tokyo, was probably the first Chinese to define customs as local rules cohesive enough to be imposed on a local community.[27] Liang, the famous polygrapher and most influential Chinese intellectual in the first half of the twentieth century, introduced custom into Chinese legal history. In two erudite essays, he demonstrated that the Confucian scholars and imperial magistrates had always respected popular customs and enforced them to complement codified laws.[28] Thus, Chinese customary law matched its European counterpart, the description of which Liang had read in Hozumi Nobushige's book.

Huang and Liang familiarized the Chinese elite with the idea that popular practices were a major source of law. In fact, customary rules were construed as the cultural and sociological identity of a community. Just as in the German and Japanese models, customs were embedded in collective, instead of individual, rights. The liberty they proclaimed was an affirmation of national identity to offset the Western influence. Liang and many other Chinese modernists asserted that law, rights, liberty were tools for a strong state, relying on a more cohesive nation. They all enhanced "the freedom of the group, not the freedom of individual," as Liang put it.[29] In the subordination of individual to national freedom contended by the modernists, the elaboration of a Chinese customary law linked alleged natural communities more closely to the nation-state. This conception of customs and law emulated the colonial experience and construed the making of civil law as an inner frontier for "civilizing" the natives' mores.

The Japanese reformers also showed the Chinese how to put the customary law doctrines into practice. In their homeland, they published two collections of "Customs in civil matters" in the 1880s, which were promptly forgotten as soon as the writing of the Japanese civil code was seriously launched. The idea was, however, resurrected later for the purpose of colonizing Taiwan.[30] The Japanese colonial rulers undertook a general survey of Chinese customs immediately after the 1895 conquest.[31] A big collection titled "Private law of Taiwan," published in 1908, became the classic reference for future students of Chinese customary law.[32] Taiwan was submitted to the Japanese civil law from 1923 on,[33] but in the meantime, the collection had become a model for Chinese lawmakers.

≺ V ≻

*Codifying Customs through Bureaucratic Devices*

The vast program to collect and draft the Chinese customs spanned some 22 years, from the launching of orders to collect customs in 1908 to the publishing of the great collection with the Civil code in 1930. Worthy of notice are the apparent fidelity to the initial project and the obstinacy in carrying it out in the dramatic conditions of the Warlords period. These conditions probably explain why the available documentation is far from complete. Regulations issued by central services to initiate the inquiries as well as the final collection of customs are easy to find and often quoted by scholars, and they lend credence to the project. The local surveys composed during the intermediary stage give quite a different outlook.[34] A confrontation between the intended program and its actual realization raises doubts not only about the final success, but even about the objectives that were actually pursued. Focusing more particularly on the issue of property rights will reveal some discrepancies between the initial project and its actual realization.

The collection of customs was launched in 1908 by a *Regulation in Ten Articles*.[35] It was issued by the bureau in charge of compiling the new codes [*Xiuding falü guan*]. The leading figures of the bureau had been trained in the former Office for Codification, and its head, Shen Jiaben (1840–1901), was the successor-designate of Xue Yunsheng, whose handbook for "perusing the sub-statutes" he had just published. As these imperial jurists knew little of civil law, they were advised by Japanese professors of law and by young Chinese lawyers just back from Japan.[36] Although jurists with a modern training gradually overwhelmed old style officials in the Republican years, the compilation of customs consistently followed the path of the former codification of imperial laws by selecting relevant items from profuse administrative rules.[37]

The first five articles of the *Regulation* display a range of methods characteristic of Qing bureaucratic campaigns. At the provincial level, the judicial commissioner was ordered to supervise the inquiry and transmit its final results to the central Bureau. The provincial authorities appointed investigators, who were required to gain support from the local elite, just as Qing magistrates were used to evaluate relief for victims of natural disasters, or to promote new agricultural methods. However, the new trend urged official investigators to promote activists in the local elite, and to group them into associations for inquiring customs. It is worthy of notice that the recently established judicial courts played no active role in the process. Even when these new courts replaced the judicial commissioner as supervisors of the inquiries under the Republic, judicial decisions remained absent from the surveys. The customs were all along manufactured through bureaucratic, and not judicial, devices.

The last five articles of the *Regulation* deal with the legal side of the process. Article 6 recalls that the German-Japanese code provided categories along which customs were to be distributed, to prepare for their easy insertion in the draft civil code. Meanwhile, the investigators had to respect scrupulously the particularities of local vernacular terms, and to prevent their synthesis with, or translation into, modern legal notions (article 7). While linguistic expression was open to local diversity, the scope of customs was drastically restricted: items were to be collected only "as far as they do not overstep the boundaries of the civil law field" (article 10). That this field had been delineated nowhere in China, except in the mind of the legal experts of the Bureau, will appear clear from the analysis of the replies.

A questionnaire was appended to the Regulation.[38] It was divided into the five parts of the German civil law, without any concession to Chinese local practices or previous official law.[39] This inaccuracy is conspicuous in the questions about "property rights." The second section, headed "Rights over the Things" (property law) starts with a fundamentalist definition of property.[40] The twenty questions appended appear like a set of textbook cases for civil law students, relying on a clear-cut distinction between the "owner" and the "user" of the land (pages 3b–4b). The same orthodoxy permeates the part on "obligations": contracts are formed by the free will of individuals, who are entitled to exclusive rights of property on the thing that they want to sell or rent.

Before examining the local surveys, let us note that the "civil law field" defined by the central Bureau straightaway excluded a wide range of practices from the scope of the inquiries. By way of "property rights," various kinds of sale contracts and land deeds warranted servile bonds, although slavery was officially prohibited in Qing code. In areas of the Pearl Delta in Guangdong, or around Huizhou in Anhui, real estate owned by corporate lineages was tilled by workers temporarily enslaved through contractual forms. Sucheta Mazumdar has suggested that many customary contracts of the Qing period be seen not as sprouts of liberal economy or individual rights, but as charters fixing unequal relationships between dominant and dominated communities.[41] Such contracts were hushed up by the collectors of customs, though they formed a more cohesive "customary law" than many practices included in the compilations.

Although their scope was artificially restricted, the local surveys are extremely wide ranging and include many matters of a dubious utility for civil law. There is an exceptionally accurate response on "property rights" in a manuscript composed for the Wuqing district near Tianjin city around 1915.[42] Under the title "Rights on land surface" [*dimian quan*], a long reply consisted in two opposed paragraphs (headings added):

> *Opinion of the investigators*: According to the "mores and practices" [*fengsu*] of the place, a property belongs entirely to its main owner. A land or a dwelling is the legitimate property of one and only owner. There is nothing like the so-called "rights on land surface." Even though a tenant tills the land and pays a rent, he cannot assume that he enjoys a hereditary right to be transmitted to his heirs.

A sub-statute of the imperial code was appended, to show that the "mores and practices" of Wuqing were in line with the law of the whole empire.

> *Evidence of contrary customs*: However in the customs [*xiguan*], this is entirely different. Two kinds of customs must be distinguished.[43]

And here, the reply engages in a detailed description of two customs. The first amounted to a classic relation between owner and tenant, despite insignificant variations.[44] The second testified to a genuine double property, by distinguishing the rights on the surface from the rights on the subsoil.[45] The investigators stressed in conclusion their willingness to signal the differences between these customs and law, instead of forcefully synthesizing them or confusing them with civil law standards.

The Wuqing investigators were unusually scrupulous in observing the *Regulation* requirement to specify customs that diverged from the civil law standard. In many items of this and other collections, only the opinion of the investigators appears clearly, either to affirm that local customs comply with the law, or to stigmatize diverging practices as "evil mores," with a display of virtuous indignation. Both attitudes evinced officials' effort to avoid troubles, rather than pointing at discrepancies between the official discourse and reality. But the above case highlights a more fundamental problem. The most scrupulous inquirer could only point out the gap between law and practices, and possibly stress the most unruly aspect of the latter. He was not entitled to propose any solution of compromise between the two, as the term "customary law" would lead one to expect. Indeed, no solution of this kind had been prepared by judicial decisions of the local courts, as in the Common law of England, or through the drafting of provincial charters by the French civil jurists. In China, provincial officials had striven to clarify ownership rights since the eighteenth century, but the statutory means they employed had but a poor effect on local society.[46] The customary law project provided for no solution, and the wide gap between multi-ownership and civil law was not filled in the subsequent civil codification.[47]

How did the local surveys contribute to the general collection published in 1930? This is a massive document, of around 2000 pages. Customs fall into the five categories of the German-Japanese model and are ranged therein after their province and district origins.[48] Hence there are tedious repetitions of similar items, in a careless transcription that overshadows the local peculiarities. The minute instructions of the 1908 questionnaire have been ignored by the inquirer, most of the time the local magistrate. When interesting details appear, they are rarely developed enough to give accurate insights on a possible customary rule. But the most problematic issue is the general absence of cohesiveness: one would expect that some common features would appear in the customs of a particular county or province, neatly distinct from those of other regions; and that the preparatory compilations would appear in the general collection as charters of a neatly discernable local identity. But such cohesive sets cannot be found; the local reports have been dismantled, and many of them apparently have been lost. For instance, the minute distinction between topsoil and subsoil rights described in the Wuqing manuscripts can be found nowhere. Instead, there is mention of a local assembly held in 1908 in the neighboring Tianjin district, in which the rights of tenants and landlords are discussed and finally defined in reference to the Japanese "permanent rights of the tenants" [*eikosaku ken*].[49] The local elite of this big city-port, maybe assisted by legal advisors trained in Japan, preferred to consider "civil customs" already manufactured by the Japanese jurists, rather than contending with real practices of the surrounding countryside. Neither a synthesis, nor even a sum of the local surveys, the collection is basically unfaithful to the project it was supposed to serve. For the French jurist and advisor of the Chinese Republic Jean Escarra, who was the most committed supporter of the Chinese customary law, this material was "almost impossible to exploit" as a source of law.[50]

Must we conclude then, that this was a spectacular failure after two decades of patient efforts? Certainly, if we take the project literally, and the general collection for its principal achievement; not so obviously, if we consider that unsaid objectives were pursued under cover of customary law.

Indeed, local compilations contain varied materials on a much wider scope than the "civil law field" defined in central regulations. There are statistics and data on the size of farms, the economic activities, the distribution of wealth among social categories, ordinary food, sanitary conditions of population, local dialects, religious worships.[51] Although not unknown to the Qing administration, such information had never been so systematically researched and drafted, with lists of data and figures appended. In fact, the old bureaucratic agenda and the new program overlap in many ways. For instance, the *Public Archives of the Tile Molder* published in 1911 by a prefect of Huizhou, in Anhui Province, is made on the *gongdu* model, which allowed officials to display a range of their administrative skills in compilations of administrative documents they issued during their careers.[52] But the last section, headed "Legal system," consists of replies to the inquiries about customs of the six districts of the prefecture. Questions and answers fall into three categories: customs on the situation among people; customs on mores and practices; customs on the management of affairs by gentry and scholars. These headings indicate that the content was very different from the civil customs expected by the Bureau of Codification. For instance, "customs of mores and practices" is quite an enigmatic heading, until we remember that, in the Qing administrative agenda, popular practices appeared in the category "Correction of mores and practices."[53] Many "customs observed through the life of the people" of the first section recalled the monitoring of local morals by the magistrate, although their scope is broader and more concerned with social and economic activities than the most complete Qing regulations.[54] Similarly, the third section, on "Management of affairs by the Gentry" is in line with Qing officials' searching of support from the local elite for missions like education or food supplies.

Within this traditional framework, there are signs of new relationships between notables and authorities. Questioning populations on their ways of living and publishing their replies was in itself a significant change in the official attitude. For all that, opinions voiced by the local elite were not particularly favorable to the
vogue of civil law. They rebuked the new language of "rights" that
"young fellows who never managed any affair" were enticed by,
while for those who contributed to raise levies, "no distinction between rights and duties was to be made."[55] Notables were as reluctant to report on common rules they would abide by: "In the customs of Jixi district, when affairs are deliberated, sometimes they
are settled according to a saying, sometimes unanimity is reached
without any articulated word being inferred to as a rule."[56] Not
only "rights," but even "customs" were resented as sources of disharmony.

Nonetheless, the notables had their say about more matter-of-
fact issues. For instance, they wished that their managing of
schools and other contributions to public welfare be acknowledged
as official "responsibilities" [*zeren*], and not mere "self-claimed
duties" [*zicheng yiwu*], and therefore be remunerated. They asked
that their charitable or educational associations be more consistently promoted by the authorities. They also deplored conditions
such as the low ratios of schooled children and the insufficient
data about birth rate.[57] Thus new channels of expression offered to
local society under cover of customary law initiated confused negotiations between the central elite and more traditional notables.
These far exceed the scope of legal reform; the result was to design
a new configuration of society and power at the local level.

Surveys of this kind still are too scarce to follow this process
further. Some implications of a new commitment of the local
elites to state building can be highlighted, thanks to the recent
study that Beatrice David devoted to the "correction of evil habits" of a minority living in Guangxi province. The Zheyuanren, as
they were called, were ethnic Han living among indigenous communities, with whom they shared peculiar matrimonial practices,
like natolocality. This meant that following the marriage cere-
mony, a bride returned to her parents' home, where she was allowed intercourse with one or several lovers, whom she met during ritualized ceremonies. She joined her husband's home only to

give birth to her first child, who, despite his or her having been fathered by a lover, was reputed to be the husband's child and integrated as such in his lineage.[58] Highly interesting from an ethnographic point of view, this practice was no threat to civil law strictly conceived, as the effects of the marriage were just delayed. At any rate, this delay did not preclude the first-born child from enjoying the same inheritance rights as those of the following children.

However, legal reformers saw free intercourse with lovers after wedding as a breach of the principle of monogamistic marriage claimed in new laws. One century before, under the Qing, a local magistrate had attempted to prohibit such practices as "illicit intercourse." While the attitudes of the imperial and republican officials were quite similar, the great difference lay in the attitude of local notables. The Qing magistrate had been completely isolated and asked to "mind his official duty." In the Republican period, the prohibition spelled out in the regulations of the Guangxi province inspired campaigns of local activists grouped in an association for reforming evil popular habits, working in tight collaboration with the investigators of customs. David highlights the continuity between the Republican campaigns and the Communist "movements" that reached a peak during the Cultural Revolution. The latter had a more radical discourse—habits were not only evil, but "backward and feudal"—and, of course, used more expeditious methods. But the two can be seen as stages of the same trend.

In this perspective, the inquiries on customs are no longer the lenient attempt to abstract rights and freedoms from traditional society and arrange them into a civil legal framework. If we take into account the whole documentation conveyed by the compilation of customs, and connect them with "rectification campaigns" that they inspired, we gain insights on a complex process of differentiation and repression amid society that underlies the making of the modern state. A more complete documentation would allow evaluation of how far the acculturation of local elite by new moral and legal standards in Republican China was similar to the "sociogenesis of the state" in a secular "civilizing process" described by Norbert Elias for modern Europe.[59] In the same perspective, this kind of survey is likely to convey a new knowledge, allowing state power to discriminate more accurately the popular habits to be repressed or "disciplined," in Foucault's use of the term.[60] The sources suggest at least that new rights came together with a new moral order, and individual freedoms with internalized prohibitions. Construed this way, the compilation of customs is less important for its contribution to civil law than as a blueprint of modern inquiries and regulations allowing state power to permeate local society.

<< VI >>

### Customs and Jurisprudence in the Republican Civil Code

The poor quality of the materials collected is not a sufficient argument to dismiss the Chinese customary law project, as customs were not supposed to enter into the civil legislation under their primary form. Compilations gathered only the raw material of customary law; the final product was planned to result from a selection through judicial activity. Therefore, the study of civil jurisprudence gives accurate knowledge of the place that was finally reserved to the customs in the Republican civil code.

This jurisprudence was all along an exclusive prerogative of the Supreme Court. The late Qing legal reforms had established a four-tier hierarchy of penal and civil courts, but the inferior jurisdictions had very subordinate functions. When there arose a case not provided by law, the courts could only question the Supreme Court, which replied by "interpretative decisions" formulated in abstract and general terms, so as to be binding for all similar cases.[61] Only these decisions were legal precedents, to be finally included in the civil legislation.

This process is in striking continuity with the centralized jurisprudence that headed the imperial system. The same continuity can be found in the leading personnel of the Court. Among the nine presidents between 1912 and 1923, the scales tip in favor of "old style" jurists trained under the empire. Xu Shiying (1872–1964), the reorganizer of the Court in 1912, was a pure product of the school of jurists that developed within the late Qing Office of Codification, in the wake of Xue Yunsheng and Shen Jiaben. In his memoirs, published posthumously in Taiwan in 1966, this outstanding figure of the Republican judiciaries proudly declared that he had never followed curricula of any foreign law faculty, but owed his amazing career and recognized competence to his training at the Board of Punishments. Dong Kang (1867–1947), who headed the court during half of this period, had the same training in ancient law, completed at best by a superficial initiation to Japanese law.[62] Jurists trained in Western law were not preponderant before the mid-1920s. The foundation of modern Chinese law during the most seminal years was laid by men who were guided by the concepts and techniques of bureaucratic compilation and centralized jurisprudence as much as by legal principles imported from abroad.

It is no wonder that the Supreme Court upheld continuity between the ancient and the new legal system. But did it do so through the codification of customs, as primarily intended? A series of decisions taken from 1912 to 1919 laid out the basic doctrine on customs.[63] Out of almost two thousand decisions on civil matters, less than 5 percent refer to customs. Does this amazingly small proportion conceal a high concentration in quality? Far from it. Of the less than one hundred decisions referring to customs, a small 10 percent (9 decisions) are mere statements of principles, which scholastically reiterate the first article of the draft Civil Code: in the absence of law, a judge must adjudicate according to custom and general principles of law.[64] A more significant 25 percent spell out restrictions or rejections: the judge must ignore customs when they are but an awkward reiteration of a legal disposition; he must forbid them when they are at risk to impede commercial transactions and economic development.[65] Customs were more particularly expelled from fields that one might consider as the core of customary law. Successions and inheritance, for instance, were ruled by "laws of public order, excluding all contrary custom."[66] The same is true with the contracts of all natures: here, law, public order, as well as "the imperative of economic development" reinforce the liberty of the contracting parties: only their will is to be taken into account, and interfering customs are prohibited.

Less than half (44 percent) of the decisions on customs acknowledged them as circumstantial conditions to or as derogation from the law, most of the time through negative forms like "unless a contrary custom exists." This happened more particularly in commercial matters: for instance, the money used for the payment of a contractual obligation is the money currently used at the place, "unless a particular custom provides otherwise." Similarly, the local name given to a manager, the amount due in remuneration of his services, or the various periods of time prescribed in commercial deeds, are all matters on which the Court gave way to local usage. However, this latitude was submitted to restrictive conditions, the most important being that the contracting parties express their will to abide by a particular custom.

Finally, only 17 percent of the decisions mention customs that are local rules significantly distinct from law and endowed with a binding effect. However, these customs can hardly be regarded as a valuable contribution to civil law. These are privileges of the ancient regime, such as the obligation for the Beijing merchants to join one of the local guilds, or for Jilin province farmers to recognize the suzerainty of their Manchu lords on their land.[67] These assuredly were a far cry from seeds of individual rights or liberties.

To summarize, customs made up a very small part of the jurisprudence of the Supreme Court. They had no binding effect, with the exception of some ancient privileges, which later decisions gradually erased. They were statutorily excluded from fundamental matters of civil law such as succession, inheritance, and contracts. They were more frequently tolerated as local variations in the commercial appellations, the moneys or the amount of wages; but this is rather linguistic usage than customary law. Even when paid lip service, customs were subordinate to principles and notions that actually were lethal for them. Equally noticeable was the extensive use of notions like "public order," or "imperatives of economic development," which spelled out a discretionary appreciation by the Court. Such cryptic legal terms in fact covered transactions between the former Qing jurists' conservative doctrine and the political exigencies of the new regime. Thus, the rights spelled out in the Supreme Court decisions were not abstracted from popular practices, and even not significantly influenced by them. Instead of codifying customary law, the Supreme Court framed a series of transactions between the ancient legal system and the general principles of Western law. These transactions were finally included in the civil law, after the articles that they modified or completed.

The Chinese civil code published in 1929 and 1931 consisted of twelve hundred articles distributed along the five parts of the German-Japanese model. References here are to the 1936 edition, which included the Supreme Court jurisprudence.[68] Its presentation is characteristic: quite short, general, and abstract articles, followed by long series of "judgments" [pan] and "explanations" [jie] detailing problems met in their application. This presentation is strikingly reminiscent of the Qing code, in which the general principles and an indicative penal scale were sketched out in the statutes, and detailed rules selected from the administrative and judicial practice were provided in appended sub-statutes. In the amended civil code also "judgments" and "explanations" were living law, while the articles were textual references.

As they were founded on Western legal principles, the articles enumerated individual rights and liberties. For the first time in China, rights were positively defined and guaranteed to any natural person, from birth to death, in full equality, without any distinction of sex, age, or race. Under certain conditions detailed in the opening general principles, any individual was entitled to own property, make contract, or associate in corporate activities. These principles had a particular impact on the two last parts of the code, devoted to "familial relationships" and "inheritance." Marriage was defined as a union formed by the express will of the groom and the bride, and forced marriages arranged by the parents were forbidden. Wife and husband had equal rights and duties; they owned and managed family wealth in common; and both had the right to initiate a divorce procedure, unilateral repudiation by the husband no longer prevailing (article 1049). A major innovation was the equal rights in property inheritance for all children, which Chinese laws had until then reserved only to male heirs (article 1138).

The key point here is how the jurisprudence of the Supreme Court bridged the gap between these legal intentions and the actual practices in Chinese society. The bridging was definitely not done through customary law; the 1930 general collection is not even mentioned; the 1936 code reproduces mainly prohibitions

and restrictions against customs; and the ancient regime privileges
that the Supreme Court had temporarily preserved have disappeared. Instead, these decisions reintroduced in the civil code
pieces of Qing laws that could easily be confused with customs
since the ancient legal system was formally abolished. The Chinese jurists made the difference, however: for instance, they had
categorically expelled popular practices diverging from inheritance
laws by invoking "public order." But they were open to compromises between Qing laws and civil laws about marriage and successions, as the two following examples will show.

The principle of monogamy was upheld in the civil code in
complete disregard of the secondary wives, or concubines, that the
Qing code allowed when the first wife did not give birth to a male
heir. The Supreme Court first applied this principle with utmost
strictness: the concubines as well as their children were deemed
"illegitimate," and therefore deprived of familial status and inheritance rights. In contrast Qing law gave equal rights in inheritance
to concubines and their children.[69] When questioned about pitiful
cases brought to the inferior civil courts, the Supreme Court
turned round so as to consider the concubine as "a member of the
family head's household," with many of the rights and responsibilities that such membership entailed.[70] Therefore, the concubine's children were guaranteed an equal share of family wealth
with other children. Article 985 of the code could affirm monogamy as the only rule in force, while the interpretative decisions of
the Supreme Court appended to the same article maintain the
guarantees offered by Qing law to the concubines and their off-
spring.

Kathryn Bernhardt gives an interesting example of compromise
between old and new succession laws.[71] In Qing law, only male
heirs inherited, while daughters were just given a dowry when
joining their husband's home. The Republican civil code claimed
equality of male and female heirs as an absolute rule. The old
Roman principle that the succession followed the testator's death
was introduced at the same time (article 1147). In China, succession mainly consisted of the equal division among brothers by living parents: this was codified law and popular practice as well.
The Supreme Court first strove to impose the Roman rule and forbid divisions before parents' death,[72] but it finally allowed them

under cover of "pre-mortem gifts."[73] Although an article in the civil code provided that such gifts were prepayments to be counted as part of the recipient's share in future inheritance, still another decision allowed the property owner to declare his will that the gift be not counted against the recipient's statutory portion. This decision allowed parents to divide property at will, without adhering to the principles of equality of daughters and sons. Thus was provided "an easy and perfectly legal way for fathers and brothers to cut daughters off completely."[74] In this case, Qing inheritance laws overruled equal rights of male and female children nominally guaranteed by the civil code.

These examples show that the Republican legal system was not a synthesis between old customs and modern laws. The imperial remnants survived not as popular habits, but as pieces of Qing legislation framed in legal precedents, which were finally included in the civil code. Instead of customary rules, they were laws in force in concurrence with the modern articles. The result was a kind of self-service legal system. The modern articles of the civil code opened new opportunities to the modern social classes of urban society. For instance, women of the big cities widely resorted to mutual consent divorce offered by law more liberal than that in most Western countries of the time.[75] Similarly, decisions of a very modern nature can be found in Shanghai or Beijing judicial archives.

Concurrently, the persistence of old laws offered many ways to sustain ancient social relationships, particularly within the traditional family. In the countryside, family wealth was still transmitted according to old rules, and even urbanized young men who paid lip service to gender equality went on marrying secondary wives. Moreover, the progress of rights proceeded less from the judicial application of the law than from the will of the Nationalist rulers. Although conservative in its basic inspiration, the centralized jurisprudence of the Supreme Court opened more and more to the modernist exigencies of the Nationalist party, as young talents educated in modern law school overwhelmed the old-style imperial jurists. The new generation showed more malleability to political trends and was therefore subject to turns from progressive to reactionary orientations. The making of the civil legislation thus takes place in the shift from an ancient to a new form of authoritarianism and can be seen as a device in the Party-State policy more than a genuine private law shaping the individual rights in the private relationships.

≺ VII ≻

*Conclusion*

The promotion of rights and liberties in Republican civil law asks for a contrasted assessment. These two notions, rights and liberties, were absent from the Chinese legal tradition, and their introduction in the beginning of the twentieth century was a major innovation. Indeed, it amounted to a change in the legal system paradigm. As Philip Huang put it: "The Western language of constitutional government and rights pervaded the political and legal discourse of the day. They came close to standing for universal values that could no more be questioned than industrialization or economic development. That language was what set the context for the rights approach to civil law embodied in all three drafts of the civil code."[76]

From then on, the most authoritarian regime could not but pay lip service to individual rights, as shown by the fact that Communist laws on marriage, for instance, rely on the principle of "equal rights of the wife and husband." Similarly, the recent neo-authoritarian discourse on Asian values is claimed to be a declaration of peculiar "human rights" that the West would ignore and is more evidence that the point of no return has been reached in the making of the civil law.

A long tradition of codified legal system prepared the Republican jurists to draw the consequences of this change of paradigm. On the one hand, they substituted rights for former principles of the Qing code. On the other, they turned formal qualities, techniques, and skills of the ancient system to good account for codifying the new legislation. The jurists of the Supreme Court thus managed a general transaction between the old and the new legal systems, in a centralized jurisprudence that indeed sinicized the Western framework of the civil code. This was enough to ensure legal continuity. After all, this was the main objective to fulfill, and it was achieved with an amazing success considering the chaotic situation in China at that time.

For all that, the Chinese civil legislation does not meet some main requirements of private law. There are inherited as well as newly acquired shortcomings. Loopholes inherited from the imperial legal system were not overcome. The Qing code had failed to respond efficiently to the rising complexity of private relationships since the eighteenth century; and the priority given to the cohesiveness of the legal system had led to conceptual carelessness and practical inefficiency on such crucial matters as land ownership or inheritance. The introduction of Western legislation just provided for abstract general principles. The compilations of customs intended to provide these principles with substance proved useless, partly because of the bureaucratic way the compilation was made, partly because the popular practices themselves were not the precivil customs that they were supposed to be. Only a patient and minute sieving through judicial decisions would have allowed separating the wheat of civil law from the chaff of popular practices. But the imperial legal system had bequeathed no experience for that, and the new legal trend brought no innovation in this direction. The new civil courts were not entitled to settle minute compromises between popular practices and civil law at the local level. Thus, instead of the patient and reasoned arrangements that skilled judges reach case by case in close relationship with the parties, more approximate and compulsory means were employed.

The centralized jurisprudence of the Supreme Court set a series of loose and moving compromises between Qing rules and new civil principles. The result was an ambivalent legal system, in which new rights were just an option at the disposal of the most conscious and self-assertive individuals, while many old rules remained unchanged for the majority. In this context, new rights were more efficiently promoted through political and cultural movements. The campaigns led by modernist associations to "reform evil habits" were obviously not an accurate framework for settling compromises, or a contribution to the evolution of popular customs. They anathematized behaviors "unworthy of a civilized legal system," and thus drove the targeted population to hang onto their practices clandestinely. By way of consequence, the rights they contended for were deprived of historical and societal anchoring that the customary law was designed to provide. Rights and liberties were imposed from above by the new ruling elite, mainly through compulsory means. Under the Nationalist Party-State, law remained basically a device for "correcting the mores and practices," at the hand of a civilizing center, rather than an attempt to reshape rights blooming in the social and economic life. Rights were evoked with the intent to strengthen the state and make the nation more compact, rather than allowing new realms of liberty within the society.

# The Chinese Party-State Under Dictatorship and Democracy on the Mainland and on Taiwan

WILLIAM C. KIRBY

THE THIRD PLENUM of the Central Executive Committee of the Chinese Nationalist Party [Guomindang, or GMD] took place in May 1925, two months after the death of party leader Sun Yat-sen. The plenum decreed that, henceforth, all offices of the party and of the government it controlled would begin each week with a memorial service for the late leader. Everyone would bow three times to his portrait. His last will would be read aloud. "The foundation of discipline," the plenum concluded, "is respect for the character of the President and the teachings he has bequeathed us."[1]

Perhaps no other Chinese has had as many memorial services as Sun Yat-sen. This regimented ritual would be repeated countless times, in countless settings, during the subsequent six decades of Guomindang rule on the mainland and on Taiwan. In its ordered discipline and veneration of leadership, this sacrament embodied, for party and government officials alike, the essence of the Chinese Party-State. Even the Guomindang's opposition could emulate its rites. When Chen Shui-bian was inaugurated as president of the Republic of China on Taiwan on April 20, 2000, ending the Guomindang Party-State's monopoly on power, he, too, bowed formally three times to Sun's portrait after having joined in the singing of the Guomindang hymn that had become the "national" anthem.[2]

The opposition that learned most from the party of Sun Yat-sen was its successor on the Chinese mainland. The Guomindang Party-State was an essential, if unacknowledged, foundation of the Communist Party-State, which inherited concepts, institutions, and policies that had been central to Chinese political life in the decades before the People's Republic of China (PRC) was founded in 1949.

The Party-State stands as the distinguishing, national political structure of post-imperial China. For several Chinese governments, it became the central means of conquering, defending, and developing the country. It debilitated and delayed, almost to the vanishing point, the popular sovereignty that was an implicit promise of the "people's country" [*minguo*], or republic, that had been established in 1912. In the third quarter of the century, it lent legitimacy to one of the greatest tyrannies in world history. Since the 1980s, however, it has relaxed its grip on the society—though not the polity—of the Chinese mainland. In Taiwan it would go further still, first by facilitating and then by giving way to a democratic, multi-party system, even as the politics of a fracturing Party-State remained an important part of the political landscape.

< I >

### *The Promise and Limits of Republics and Constitutions*

Sun Yat-sen was not always a Leninist. The manifesto of his anti-Qing revolutionary society, the *Tongmenghui*, stated in 1905:[3]

All our people are equal and all enjoy equal rights. The president will be publicly chosen by the people of the country. The parliament will be made up of members publicly chosen by the people of the country. A constitution of the Chinese Republic will be enacted, and every person must abide by it. Whoever dares to make himself a monarch shall be attacked by the whole country.

Not all republics are democratic in form or intent, however. The dictionary definition of "republic" that best fit the several Chinese experiences in republicanism is the least decisive: "Any political order that is not a monarchy." That much, at least, the several twentieth-century Chinese republics had in common. (This is not to say that they were without monarchical airs: we may recall President Yuan Shikai's rites at the Temple of Heaven; the Chiang family dynasty on the mainland and on Taiwan; and the self-conscious move of the new communist rulers into the villas of the old imperial city in Beijing.)

Surely the vast majority, even of highly educated Chinese, did not have a clear conception of what a republic would be, once the Qing was overthrown. The republican experiment of 1912 was accompanied by no Federalist papers. Unlike in France, the Chinese enlightenment, if we can still use that term for May Fourth era discourse, followed rather than preceded the establishment of republican government and was in part a reaction against its limitations.

It is perhaps telling that in his 45 days as provisional president of the Republic of China in 1912, Sun Yat-sen was much more concerned about what the Republic would do than what the Republic would be. He issued executive orders on footbinding and opium smoking; he ordered provincial governors to provide charitable relief; and he insisted that clothing be considered a matter of state: he called for the introduction of entirely new designs that were easy to clean, easy to move in, and indeed Republican.[4] To the degree he defined the Republic at all, it was as a socialist republic committed to the tax reforms of Henry George.

It is an unhappy commentary on nine decades of Chinese republicanism that the largest and fairest election to take place on the mainland was held in the Republic's first year, with over 40 million registered voters (some 20 to 25 percent of the adult male population), with debates free and open and reported in the press. As John Fincher has written, they were "the closest thing to general elections ever held in China."[5]

There was a belief in the Republic's early years that, if only the proper constitution were written, republican government would flourish.[6] This view was shared by Western political scientists, who flocked to China to study and advise this great republican experiment—the first in Asia—in a manner not unlike that of the teams of economists who descended on a de-communizing Eastern Europe in the 1990s, often with equally disappointing results.

China's draft and promulgated constitutions have not been few in number: the Provisional Constitution of March 12, 1912; Yuan Shikai's Provisional Constitution of May 1, 1914; the Draft Constitution of the Anfu Parliament of August 12, 1919; the Cao Kun Constitution of October 10, 1923; and the Draft Constitution of Duan Qirui's regime of December 12, 1926.[7] To these one may add the "tutelage" Provisional Constitution of 1931 under the Guomindang; the March 1, 1934, Draft Constitution authored by the Legislative Yuan; the May 5, 1936, draft as revised by the Guomindang Central Executive Committee; the Constitution of December 25, 1946, and the many constitutions of the People's Republic of China. Of these only that of 1946 has had staying power. It has had such power in part because it was a document whose key democratic provisions could be, in the fashion of the century, suspended for large periods of time. Nevertheless it would later prove to be a document capable of surviving the most drastic amendment, so as to legitimize a competitive political system on Taiwan in the 1990s.

Hu Shi, one of the most influential scholars and critics of the Republican era, once observed that the staunchest supporters of constitutionalism were "men out of power."[8] At the same time, Republican constitutions did their part to keep opposition from gaining power. Different as they were in many respects, Chinese constitutions had this in common. They defined China as a unitary, not federal state, and they tended to limit provincial, as distinct from national, rights; in electoral constituencies they favored the urban and educated over the rural and uneducated; and they set parameters of one sort or another on individual rights, which were not "natural," but were conferred by the state.

Constitutional thought generally stressed the collective rights of the people [*minquan*] over the human rights of individuals [*renquan*]. At its first national congress in 1924, the Guomindang declared that the rights of citizenship in the republic should be enjoyed only by those loyal to the republic. An article in the May 5th Draft Constitution of 1936 was slightly more specific: "Every citizen shall have freedom of speech, writing and publication; such freedom shall not be restricted *except in accordance with law*" (emphasis added). Not until the 1946 constitution was this clause omitted from *each* article that guaranteed a right. Even then, article 23 of the 1946 constitution stated that "The Freedoms and rights enumerated in the preceding articles shall not be restricted by law, except in cases where a restriction is necessary . . . for . . . promoting the public interest."[9] As Sun Ke, the son of Sun Yat-sen and a political figure in his own right who had been a vocal proponent of constitutionalism, asserted, "Freedom is a tool . . . so that [the individual] may strive *for society*. . . . It goes without saying that it should be subject to many forms of restriction."[10] Lloyd Eastman, the pioneering American historian of Republican China, summed up the prevailing view: "The people should be sovereign, but should not interfere with the actual governance of the nation."[11]

The greatest disjunction between constitutional theory and political reality would come with the advent of the People's Republic. Mao and his colleagues followed Stalin's suggestions that the PRC needed a "coalition government" as an initial facade for party dictatorship; it needed elections—sham elections to be sure—to the Political Consultative Conference, which served as the PRC's first parliament; and ultimately it had to have (and would have, in 1954, the date recommended by Stalin) a constitution modeled largely on the USSR's "Stalin constitution" of 1936 and on the subsequent one-party constitutions of post-war Eastern Europe. Stalin had described the political purpose of all this bluntly to Liu Shaoqi in 1949:

> Your enemies have two ways to threaten you. First, they can tell the masses that the CCP did not have an election and therefore is not a legitimate government; second, if there is no constitution and if the Political Consultative Conference is not elected, enemies can charge that you have seized power by force. They could say that the government was imposed on the people . . . You should take this weapon away from your enemies.[12]

The twentieth century may have been China's "republican century,"[13] but that definition is incomplete. What form would the republic take? The political scientist Ch'ien Tuan-sheng [Qian Duansheng] wrote at mid-century as if the issue were still open: "Is it to be modeled after the Swiss cantons or after the English-speaking countries? Or is it to be a democracy as envisaged in the 1936 Constitution of the Union of Soviet Socialist Republics? Or is it to be still another form?"[14] By then Ch'ien surely knew that in terms of institutions, if not constitutions, these questions had already been answered, in duplicate.

≺ II ≻

*Political Characteristics of the Chinese Party-State*

The question of post-imperial China's political form was addressed by Sun Yat-sen in 1924, when he reorganized his Guomindang as a Leninist party, including in it the young Communist party, which had been founded in 1921. This he did on the basis of Soviet advice, and in anticipation of assistance from the "General Staff of the World Revolution,"[15] the Soviet-led Communist International, or Comintern. Even before the Comintern catalyzed, energized, and reorganized the Guomindang, it had created the Chinese Communist Party (CCP).[16] But since the CCP was not truly a Leninist organization until 1927,[17] the Guomindang must be considered China's first Leninist party, adapting both the political and the military lessons of the Soviet experience. Indeed nothing was more Bolshevik than the splitting and "purification" of the party in April 1927 as the Guomindang purged its Communist allies and went on to establish China's first ruling Party-State.

Although Sun Yat-sen had died in 1925, his principle of *"yi dang zhi guo"* [government by the Party] meant that China under Nationalist rule would not be a parliamentary republic, like the first, short-lived, republic of 1912–13; nor would it be a presidential regime on the model of Yuan Shikai's reign. It would be a Party-State, that is, a *one*-Party state. The Nationalist Party committed itself to "tutor" both the National Government [Guomin zhengfu] and the nation at large until China was prepared to enter an era of constitutional democracy. A parallel system of party and state organizations was set up nationwide, from the central government down to the provinces, which were organized on similar principles of political hierarchy. Moreover, the party procreated its "cells" within state administrative organs. In theory, the government existed to execute the policies dictated by the party.[18]

The Party-State thus became the central arena of Chinese politics. When the National Government was formally established in 1928 the Guomindang was the ruling party [*zhengdang*]. Other political parties were banned, save for very minor organizations forced into dependency on the Guomindang. "Tutelage" was to last six years. For Chinese under Guomindang rule on the mainland and on Taiwan, it lasted sixty. And when the Guomindang was ousted from the mainland in 1949, it was replaced by the other Chinese Party-State, that of the resurgent Communists, in a continuation, indeed intensification, of the political culture of the Party-State.

The Marxist scholar Su Shaozhi has used non-Marxist terminology to describe this form: "party-cracy with Chinese character-istics." Its main features, he argues, included the centralizing tendency of Leninist political direction (including orchestrated mass-mobilization); the relentless politicization of public life; a high degree of militarization; and a central role for a leading political idol, or leadership cult.[19]

Certainly Guomindang rule presumed centralization: an extraordinary number of Party and government institutions founded after 1927–28 began with the term zhongyang, or "central." The Central Executive Committee managed the Central Party Office [Zhongyang dangbu], which oversaw party and state, communicating to China and the world through the Central Daily News [Zhongyang Ribao]. Students studied at the Central University [Zhongyang daxue] while scholars advised the government from the Central Research Institute [Zhongyang yanjiuyuan], better known abroad as the Academia Sinica. There was a Central Legislative Council, Central Military Academy, Central Organization Department, Central Planning Board, Central Political Academy, Central Statistical Bureau, Central Supervisory Committee, Central Training Corps, and on and on.[20] This was a regime with ambitions for overpowering control.

The ruling party was supposed to be the essential instrument of control. The Guomindang adopted the Leninist principles of "democratic centralism," in which central Party leaders commanded a nationwide hierarchy of party organizations. Political power was concentrated in a small group of one to two dozen figures, normally members of the Political Council of the party Central Executive Committee. The highest-ranking party members served on the standing committees of these bodies and were often in charge of powerful party committees, such as the Organization Department, which controlled party appointments and patronage. Such individuals also held leading government positions. Even the highest organs of the government were subordinate to party rule.

The party existed not only to lead the government, but also to remake the people. The "party-ization" [danghua] of cultural and political life was taken very seriously even before the establishment of the Nanjing government in 1928: the GMD-controlled Sun Yat-sen University in Canton, for example, was "purified" of the politically incorrect by its Office of Political Education as early as 1926.[21] The party exerted an increasing influence over the judiciary that it inherited from earlier Republican governments, and according to Xiaoquan Xu, "made a mockery" of the principle of judicial independence.[22] The party's role in public life extended further in the first decade of Nationalist rule, as evidenced in the growth of press and film censorship, and the ubiquity of weekly political study meetings in schools, businesses, and government offices. As a self-styled "revolutionary" party, the GMD aimed to revolutionize public conduct by a revolution in morality, to give "new life" to an ancient people. Chiang Kai-shek's New Life Movement of the mid-1930s was a nationwide educational campaign that linked the cultural virtues of propriety, justice, integrity, and self-respect with the military discipline it believed was needed in a modern citizenry. The aim of all this was to discipline an undisciplined populace, to give it a sense of obligation to the nation. This was the Chinese Party-State's first (but not last) attempt at cultural revolution.

The Party-State was also a military state. It seized power, and when necessary held it, by force. In 1926–27, the Nationalists conquered China south of the Yangtze and tried to extend military control over the rest. The chairman of the Military Affairs Commission (normally also the party chief), not the head of government, was invariably the most powerful man in the realm. It was thus as "Chairman Chiang" that Chiang Kai-shek wielded *de facto* power during his tenure on the mainland. Military expenditures accounted for at least half of the government budget in every year of Nationalist rule of the mainland. Throughout the Nationalist period, which was marked by a series of wars against enemies internal and external, culminating in the eight-year war against Japan (1937–45) and the subsequent civil war against the communists (1946–49), China became one of the most militarized nations on Earth. And beyond the state, its politics and its finances, those outside the military—the common man rallied to "new life"— were to be militarized as well [*junshihua*] in outlook and deportment.

The Party-State had a Leader. Sun Yat-sen had extracted personal loyalty oaths from his followers from at least 1914, when he took the title of *zongli* or Leader, of the Chinese Revolutionary

Party [Zhongguo kemingdang]. The formal titles given first to Sun, as *zongli*, or later to Chiang Kai-shek, the "Director," or *zongcai*, of the Guomindang, or for that matter to Mao Zedong as CCP party "Chairman" [*zhuxi*], do not capture the depth of their domination over their followers. Slighting the "democratic" aspect of democratic centralism, the Guomindang and the Communist Party were led by a series of leadership cliques that are understood better as conspiratorial brotherhoods than as political factions. Perhaps more accurately, they began as brotherhoods and evolved into bureaucracies of sworn loyalty: thus around 1925 Guomindang members who had addressed each other as *xiong*, or brothers, began to call each other *tongzhi*, or comrades.[23] All were bound to a central individual. As we have seen in the case of Sun Yat-sen's portrait and last will, this was true even after death. To his closest circle, Chiang Kai-shek was known less as *zongcai* than as *lingxiu*, another term for Leader. These were Leaders in a reverential, charismatic, and perhaps fearsome sense, at least to their immediate followers. Whether as a continuation of monarchical political culture or as an example of Soviet and fascist influence, the Chinese Party-State demanded a single head, a *yuanshou*—as the term *Führer* was translated into Chinese.

For all the promotion of unity and central leadership, however, the Party-State has also been prone to factionalism. Particularly under Guomindang rule on the mainland, the theory of the unitary Party-State outpaced its institutional capacities. The Guomindang was never able to realize in fact the centralizing control that it exerted in theory. In an unevenly institutionalized system that would permit no legitimate opposition party, political differences were played out in intraparty factional or clientalist struggles. Factions might be identified with leading individuals as much as, or more than, with distinguishing sets of policies. They could also represent significant interest groups in the regime. Or all the above: the Guomindang's "C.C. Clique," for example, represented, at once, the Party Organization Department, a set of conservative cultural policies, and the two Chen brothers for whom it was named. Factional and patronage relations would remain a political fact of life also in the more tightly organized PRC.[24] But under either regime, the existence of differences within the Party-State could not be formalized or legitimized; and indeed the greater the differences, the stronger the calls for "unity of thought." Chiang Kai-shek put it this way:[25]

Unity of thought is more important than anything. If we want the nation to be strong and to be independent and free, then the first task is to plan for the unity of the Chinese people's thought, and to firmly establish Sun Yat-sen's Three People's Principles as the nation's only thought so they will not again desire a second system of thought to create disorder in China.

The basic traits of the Chinese Party-State would endure in both Nationalist and Communist China. However, none of them automatically defined the policies or priorities of a regime. As Chiang Kai-shek's statement suggests, the Party-State had come into existence with two overriding and interrelated missions: in external relations to defend China's sovereignty and reassert China's importance in an unstable world; and internally not only to *yi dang zhi guo* but also to *yi dang jian guo*, to use the Party literally to build the nation, or as the term was officially translated, to "reconstruct" a powerful, industrial China. Let us look at the Party-State in these two categories, with emphasis on the Guomindang experience on the mainland, before turning to the alternative, postwar Party-States that would face each other across the Taiwan Strait.

## ≺ III ≻

### *The Developmental Party-State*

Sun Yat-sen has often been called the "national father" of the Chinese Republic, though this is not for his brief, provisional presidency in 1912 or his leadership of a united China under the GMD, which he did not live to see. His longest post in any national government was that of Minister of Railways in the autumn of 1912.

Sun believed that the wealth of a nation could be measured in the length of its railway lines (a fact which, if true, would mean that China today would be significantly worse off than it appears to be). He was no economist and certainly no engineer: he argued for the superiority of electricity over coal as a source of power, without seeming to know that electricity was for the most part generated by coal.

Sun was the father of the developmental Party-State: an early, eloquent, persistent, and influential proponent of the idea that the central, defining purpose of the Republic was to "reconstruct" China. In the later workings of Nanjing's many "reconstruction" bureaus, or in the pages of the PRC's pictorial journal, *China Reconstructs*, he found his heirs.

Sun's *minshengzhuyi*, or the principle of the people's livelihood, was not a call, like Deng Xiaoping's in the 1980s or 1990s, to individuals to get rich; it was rather a summons to national economic development. His proposed "second industrial revolution" in which 100,000 miles of rail would be laid, the Yangzi tamed and its Three Gorges dammed, and automobiles manufactured so inexpensively that "everyone who wishes it, may have one," was designed to get the "stagnant race" of Chinese on the move.[26] In short, Sun was both prophet and high priest in China of the secular religion that James Scott has termed "authoritarian high modernism."[27]

First in the Guomindang and then in the Communist years, economic planning and bureaucratic goal-setting became a national obsession. There is a noteworthy continuity among those so obsessed: the engineers, geologists, chemists, and economists who served first Nanjing and then the central planning *apparat* of the PRC. There are distinguished lineages now in nearly a century of the scientific and technical elites: the graduates of Jiaotong and Tongji universities, of MIT and the Techniche Hochschule Berlin, and today of Qinghua and the Hong Kong University of Science and Technology. These scholars and practitioners have fared better in political transitions than have their counterparts in the liberal arts.

Sun was a visionary, not a scientist, economist, or engineer; yet projects of the scale and complexity of those he advocated would bring scientists, economists, and engineers into the center of Chinese governance. The academies, commissions, and ministries created to "reconstruct" China would, in turn, change the mission of the Chinese state. If Sun Yat-sen could admire publicly Lenin's New Economic Policy, praising its promotion of state capitalism and "national socialism,"[28] his successors would lay the foundation for a Stalinist state in China, the economic development of which would become the responsibility of the world's largest bureaucracy.

If the aim of this conception of economic construction was military-industrial security and, in time, self-sufficiency, it can be said to have succeeded within limits. However, the cost of this mission, for the private economic sector and for the economy as a whole, would be high. By mid-century the most important parts of the private sector of the economy had come first under regulation, then outright nationalization, by the Nationalist government, before the entire economy would be the subject of state ownership and planning under communism.

In light industry, such as textiles, but also in a series of financial services, such as banking and insurance, China in the 1910s and 1920s had been one of the world's fastest growing economies. Economic historians have emphasized the vibrancy of at least certain sectors of the new industrial economy before the predations of the state and the destruction of war undid it. As Linsun Cheng has shown, China had developed in the pre-Nationalist years a dynamic and rapidly growing system of private deposit and (at least to some degree) investment banks.[29] It was a system that the Nationalists cut off at its roots in the nationalizations of the 1930s. Banks became not the repository of people's deposits and the source of light industrial/commercial capital, so much as the means of financing, indeed extorting through note issues, the projects of the state. So they remained in Taiwan until the banking reforms of the 1980s; and so they remain today in the catastrophe that is the PRC banking system.

From the perspective of modern Chinese economic history, it seems clear that economic growth has on the whole been highest when government has been weakest and international connections strongest; and growth has been negative only in times of war or of catastrophically inept government intervention, such as in 1948–49 and 1959–62. Perhaps the greatest successes of the Chinese developmental state have come when the government has supplied not the hardware of economic growth—especially through its own industries and monopolies—but the software: the strategic economic guidance and the most fundamental forms of infrastructure, including education.

It is not so much the fact but the nature of China's economic boom in the 1990s, not of producer industries serving an endless domestic market but of light industrial exports to an apparently endlessly consuming West—all mediated by forms of enterprise over which the state had decreasing control—that would have surprised the prophet of Chinese developmentalism, Sun Yat-sen.

≺ IV ≻

*The Militarization of the Party-State*

Military agendas were never far removed from the economic plans of the late Qing and early Republic. In retrospect, it is surprising that they were almost entirely absent as the rationale for Sun Yat-sen's *Industrial Plan* and very understated in the early reconstruction efforts of the Guomindang-led National Government, which governed from Nanjing after 1927. To be sure, programs for road-building, railroad development, and electrification had implicit military dimensions; the concept of a massive hydroelectric power station in the Yangzi Gorges received its first scientific survey under the Defense Planning Commission in 1932. Nonetheless, economic development plans broadly assumed a period free from the incessant warfare and militarization of the early- and mid-1920s.

But in 1932, less than five years after the establishment of the Nanjing government, the Japanese army seized control of China's northeastern provinces and presided over the establishment of the puppet state of "Manzhouguo." From 1933 on, the Nationalist regime carried out a gradual but steady remilitarization. In the five years before full-scale war broke out with Japan, domestic warfare, in the form of attacks on the renewed communist insurgency, actually increased. Only the greater threat of war with Japan brought Chiang and the Communists to a temporary truce, in a "second united front" of the two Party-States.

Foreign relations also became consumed with military matters. China channeled foreign investment toward its own war industries and paid for doing so through the export of strategically important materials. Thus there developed a certain symbiotic relationship between the war economies of China and those of its foreign partners. Above all China's security needs sparked a search for a military alliance with any nation willing to fight Japan. For the first time, China joined the international system as a full participant in the diplomacy of alignments and alliances that would culminate in World War II.

This remilitarization had political consequences. The threat of war strengthened authoritarian tendencies in the Party-State. It ended any thought of a timely end of GMD tutelage and a transition to constitutional rule. The constitutional documents drafted from 1932 to 1935 were each more authoritarian than the last. Authoritarianism was reinforced in the 1930s by the growing international prestige of fascism, which was openly admired by the self-styled "Blue Shirt" organizations within the army, who called on Chiang Kai-shek to act like "China's Hitler." So long as the war lasted, Chiang ruled less as party chief (he would not be anointed *zongcai* until 1938) or as head of government, the position he resigned in late 1931, than as "Chairman" Chiang, that is, as chairman [*weiyuanzhang*] of the Military Affairs Commission. As such he had full military powers and far-reaching civilian authority. It frequently appeared that the seat of power was not Nanking, but Nanchang, Wuchang, Chongqing, or wherever Chairman Chiang had his military headquarters. As the army trained to fight internal and external enemies, its work of internal pacification took place in tandem with the expansion and professionalization of the police and secret services.[30] Unofficially but unmistakably, the military was again the third leg on which the Party-State stood.

The militarization of economic policy expanded the scope of state planning. Developmental efforts were devoted almost entirely to the creation of a "national defense economy," which was to be entirely state-owned and state-managed. It was the first step toward a "controlled" economy in which private and foreign investment would be regulated according to national priorities. Paradoxically, the autonomy of civilian experts managing this economy—cohabiting, as it were, with party and military for the nation's salvation—could be legitimized on patriotic grounds. It was in any event essential if China were to fight and survive a modern war.

Yet victory over Japan in August 1945 signaled no demobilization—political, economic, or military—of the hybrid structure of

the national security state. In postwar politics, the Nationalists finally promulgated a constitution in 1946–47, but one meant to ensure their monopoly on political power. Political opponents could
still be gunned down—in the thousands in Taiwan in the "2–28
Incident" of February 28, 1947—while Chiang Kai-shek assumed,
finally, the constitutional title of President of the Republic. In
economic reconstruction, through relentless expropriation and nationalization, the state's postwar industrial empire included nearly
70 percent of China's total industrial capital. And in military affairs, the Nationalist armies, far from demobilizing, rearmed for
the final showdown with the Communists. In 1946 they started a
civil war that they could not finish.

≺ V ≻

*Alternative Party-States Astride the Taiwan Strait*

Throughout the civil war of 1946–49, the promise of a "new
China" under the leadership of the Chinese Communist Party was
linked to the concept of "New Democracy." Communism, Mao
Zedong and other leaders proclaimed, was a very distant goal. Until it could be realized, the CCP would lead a coalition government of all "democratic" forces. As Mao reported to the CCP party
congress of 1945, "throughout the stage of New Democracy China
cannot possibly have a one-class dictatorship and a one party government, and therefore should not attempt it." The New Democratic system would preside over a mixed economy, setting clear
limits to state power. New Democracy would continue "for a long
time to come."[31]

This was not to be, as Arlen Meliksetov and Alexander Pantsov
show in chapter 8 in this volume. New Democracy was a useful
slogan during the civil war. A few CCP leaders even believed in it.
But for most, and particularly for Mao Zedong, it was not the "real
stuff" for which the Party-State was made.[32] It would be renounced
publicly in 1953, but Mao himself had abandoned the idea by early
1948. As he wrote to Stalin: "[In] the period of the final victory of
the Chinese revolution . . . all political parties except the CCP
should leave the political scene."[33] Ultimately the Chinese civil
war had offered no fundamental choice to the Chinese people, no

alternative to the Party-State. In place of New Democracy there occurred instead an exchange of *zhengdang*, or ruling parties, as first the Nationalist and then the Communist dictatorships ensured that there would be no "third way."[34]

The CCP had already created its Party-State, first in its Jiangxi Soviet Republic in the early 1930s and then in the territories ruled from Yanan from the late 1930s through the mid-1940s. It had all the distinguishing characteristics of "party-cracy" practiced by its Nationalist adversary: the theory of democratic centralism, party tutelage, the centrality of the Leader and the small group of men around him, and the overwhelming militarization of political and economic priorities.

A textbook description of the PRC's formal governing system could just as well be applied to that of Nationalist China.[35] Both parties took directly from the Soviet model, but the commonalities and shared experiences went deeper. The CCP matured under the shadow of the Guomindang Party-State that sought to exterminate it. The CCP did not need to learn only from the Soviet Union to understand the workings of Party dictatorship, organized political murder and terror, censorship, statist economic controls, and the militarization of political and civic life. These features were part of the Chinese scene under the Guomindang Party-State, and many of them would be intensified under the relocated GMD regime on Taiwan in its early years, as it sought, in turn, to learn what had made the Communists such fearsome competitors. What distinguished the Communist Party-State, and indeed ultimately set it apart from it predecessor, was its success in taking all these trends—political, economic, and military—to the most extreme conclusions, before it, like its brother party across the Strait, would begin to retreat.

Let us compare political trends first. As a political form, then, the Chinese Party-State proved powerful and enduring. But beyond continuities there were also important differences between the Guomindang and Communist efforts. The CCP's rule was more than "a postwar refinement of [Guomindang] political tutelage,"[36] for the CCP, unlike the GMD, never promised to end its guardianship. In comparison with the GMD, its political dictatorship was much wider in geographic terms, deeper in its dominance over society, and broader in terms of the powers it arrogated to itself. It was also more relentless in its persecution of its opponents. The terror of the PRC's first years has never been adequately researched, but it is certain that several million landlords and "counterrevolutionaries," real and imagined, lost their lives.

For its first eight years in power, the ruling group in the CCP Party-State was more united internally and even more dependent on its central figure than had been its predecessor. No study of the PRC political system can ignore the overwhelming dominance of Mao Zedong. His position was "the backbone" of the PRC regime. However much his colleagues might disagree with him on policy, they dared not undermine him.[37] Thus his harebrained scheme for sudden economic development, the calamitous "Great Leap Forward" of 1958–60, was allowed to continue even after senior leaders knew it to be ruinous. Thirty million Chinese perished. Even within a leadership group of hardened revolutionaries, the Chinese Communist Party was inconceivable without Mao Zedong. With their help, if often despite their better judgment, Mao became the "great helmsman," the "red sun," whose personality cult knew no bounds: Mao was even written into the PRC constitution. Although after Mao's death in 1976 the Chinese Communist Party would admit of his "mistakes," the PRC's legitimacy had become so entwined with the person of Mao Zedong that even a quarter-century after his death no critical, scholarly inquiry into the disasters of his rule was possible in China.[38]

On Taiwan, Chiang Kai-shek continued his personal rule until his death in 1975, and his family's dominance persisted until his son and successor, Chiang Ching-kuo, died in 1988. The elder Chiang's appreciation for party dictatorship only grew following his expulsion from the mainland, for one of the lessons he took from that "great shame" was that the CCP had proved an even better, tighter organization than his GMD. Reasserting the basic principles of Leninist governance in 1950–52, Chiang carried out a far-reaching reform and purge of the GMD on Taiwan. While he called the new GMD a "democratic" party, because it held local elections, albeit as the only important legal party, above all it was (as the CCP was to Mao) a revolutionary party. As such it "should strengthen the organization, maintain strict discipline, arouse revolutionary spirit, and accumulate revolutionary strength in order to stage a life-and-death struggle with the Communist bandits."[39] Nevertheless the fact that beginning in the 1950s on Taiwan local elections were held in which "non-party" candidates might on occasion embarrass the ruling party was itself a break with the past and kept alive in some form the original democratic promise of the Republic of China.

The younger Chiang would act—where his father had only talked—to move Taiwan toward a more open political system. The toleration of opposition parties that Chiang Ching-kuo permitted in the mid-1980s was an indispensable step on Taiwan's road to democracy, even if it was undertaken in good measure to preserve Guomindang rule. Until then, Chiang Ching-kuo, too, had not been immune from the leadership principle. A graduate of the Soviet Central Tolmatschev Military and Political Institute, he (or his associates) had personal enemies humiliated or assassinated until the early 1980s.[40] It was in his final years that Chiang Ching-kuo demonstrated a toleration of opposition that was pathbreaking for the GMD.

Chiang Ching-kuo's political heir, the Taiwan-born Lee Teng-hui, would inaugurate electoral politics at the highest level, the state presidency, and he presided over the inauguration of a multiparty political system. More than anyone else, Lee Teng-hui can be said to be the father of the first democratic state in Chinese history. Yet during the course of his tenure as president of a newly democratic Republic of China, Lee relinquished none of his power as Guomindang party chief. To be sure, it was a measure of progress in democratization that it was his detractors, not his supporters, who called him *ducai*, or "supreme leader." Lee was undeterred, asserting that his mandate may have come from a source beyond elections, state, or party: "We have now entered a new era in Taiwan. Even Moses and his people suffered, but Moses and his people still were able to leave Egypt. Thus, when we think about the Taiwanese people and their sacrifices . . . I can only conclude that my role is like that in the exodus from Egypt."[41]

Under leaders as different as Mao Zedong, Chiang Kai-shek, and Lee Teng-hui, both Party-States pursued the mission of remaking, culturally, the people under their governance. In the PRC this would culminate, and then decline, with Mao's Cultural Revolution. For the GMD Party-State, ruling as a "national" government of which Taiwan was but one province, the cultural front

was central to its take-over and rule of the island. The first Nationalist governor of Taiwan, Chen Yi, wrote even before the island's return to China in 1945 that the political and linguistic
"reeducation" of the Taiwanese people—the teaching of Sun Yat-
sen's Three People's Principles and the speaking of Mandarin
Chinese—was the "most important area" for postwar Taiwan's
development.[42] Mirroring the Communist domination of society
on the mainland, the GMD in the 1950s "penetrated virtually the
entire social fabric" of Taiwan as it refounded the Party-State on
that island. It penetrated and dominated all important social, educational, and media organizations, ranging from youth groups to
trade unions to farmers' associations.[43] Under Lee Teng-hui, the
GMD would patronize a different cultural remapping of a Taiwanese (as distinct from Chinese) identity. For the Guomindang to
survive the increasingly provincialized politics of Taiwan after the
democratic reforms of the late 1980s and early 1990s, it required
the open discussion of the once-taboo topic of "2–28," the Nationalist suppression of the rebellion in Taiwan of February 1947. In
the process, "2–28" was largely excised as a potentially fatal historical burden for an increasingly Taiwanized Guomindang.[44] It
became instead the name of the public park where the incident
began, in a rewriting of space as well as of history.[45]

   The most basic difference in the political realm between the
two Party-States was that the GMD's political domination had
much greater limits. Under the GMD, one could be part of the
"silent China" that Lu Xun had criticized so trenchantly (see
chapter 7 in this volume). Outright political dissent on Taiwan
was suppressed harshly until the mid-1980s. But unlike the People's Republic, where early on a relentless politicization would
permeate private lives, on Taiwan it was possible to remain apolitical, out of the whirlwinds of political campaigns, even during
the periods of sharpest political repression, such as the so-called
White Terror of the 1950s. As Hu Shih, a leading intellectual who
relocated to Taiwan, told a Nationalist official as he left his Beijing home on the eve of the Communist takeover: "The only reason why liberal elements like us still prefer to string along with
you people is that under your regime we at least enjoy the freedom
of silence."[46]

   That silence would be granted to citizens of the People's Republic only with the death of Mao Zedong in 1976. Thereafter the political world of the Chinese mainland began to look more like that of Taiwan in the era of Chiang Kai-shek. Mao's demise permitted the Communist Party-State to concentrate on its developmental, as distinct from its revolutionary mission. Jean Oi shows that in the 1980s and 1990s the PRC would enter into experiments in political reform, including—as had begun on Taiwan decades earlier—elections at the village level.[47] Open challenges to Party authority could be crushed, as in the suppressions of 1986 and 1989. But a complex and increasingly fragmented structure of political authority[48] would gradually, over the last two decades of the twentieth century, permit ever-greater realms of autonomy for the Chinese people—in their homes, on the streets, and in the economy—so long as the Party's political monopoly was not challenged.

In economics, as in politics, there were initially strong continuities between the Nationalist and Communist Party-States. For much of the first decade after 1950, both Party-States proposed enormous programs of economic development. They continued to link developmental ambitions with national security priorities and skewed state investment to military purposes. Both emphasized central economic planning, the PRC more totalistically than Taiwan. In agriculture, both went well beyond the pre-1949 state in enacting revolutionary land reforms (albeit in quite different ways), in part as a means of financing the state-led, heavy-industrial, import-substituting path to national development that both still favored. As for industry, the Nationalist accumulation of state capital was the foundation for the PRC state sector in the same way that the eighteen state corporations on Taiwan provided the industrial base of Nationalist rule. The Nationalists even bequeathed to their mainland foes a model of industrial organization. This was the *danwei*, the comprehensive "work unit" in state enterprises, in which housing, dining, recreation, and health facilities were provided for engineers and workers alike. Within its first decade, the PRC would apply this model to all urban Chinese.[49]

While Nationalist economic leaders of the 1940s had talked of "following the socialist road,"[50] their successors followed that road to its terminus in Moscow. They engaged in the largest planned transfer of technology in world history. With 250 industrial projects constructed; thousands of industrial designs transferred; 10,000 Soviet specialists visiting China; and over 50,000 Chinese engineers, trainees, and students visiting the Soviet Union, this was at least partial fulfillment of Sun Yat-sen's dream of China's international development.

Where Nationalists and Communists differed fundamentally in the 1950s was in their treatment of the economic, scientific, and technological talent that both inherited. On the mainland as on Taiwan, personnel from the pre-1949 bureaucracy formed the core of early economic planning bodies. On both sides of the Strait, this personnel continuity contributed to the policy continuity that continued to stress defense-related heavy industrial growth until the late 1950s. And both the PRC and Taiwan faced a set of economic decisions in 1958 that would make that year, more than 1949, an important divide in the economic and political history of the Chinese Party-State.

On Taiwan, the economic reorientation of 1958–60 set Taiwan's path toward "export-led" growth and economic "miracle."[51] Small and medium-scale private enterprise emerged from the shadow of the Party-State even if much of it remained, in legal terms, "underground" for a considerable period of time.[52] In time, the great success of these policies and the stable stewardship of Taiwan's economy raised the glass ceiling that had kept the intellectual/technological elite as mere servants of the Party-State. Several of their members would rise to positions of real eminence within it, Premier Y. S. Sun [Sun Yunxuan] and President Lee Teng-hui among them. And the Guomindang, having helped suppress Chinese capitalism earlier in the century, would create its own, vast, business empire to emerge, by the turn of the twenty-first century, as one of the wealthiest political parties on Earth.

Such developments seemed far removed from the mainland, particularly after its own economic turning inward in the late 1950s. The PRC, too, faced the economic limitations of the national security state and concluded in 1957–58 that even with Soviet aid it could not replicate the successes of its first five-year plan (1953–57). At the same time it determined for ideological reasons to dispense with the services of the several hundred thousand intellectuals who were found to harbor "rightist" views. In 1958, as Taiwan began to leap outward for economic growth, Mao Zedong began his Great Leap Forward into communism unencumbered either by Nationalist holdovers or Soviet advice. For the first time since the founding of the Nationalist regime a Chinese government repudiated the services of its most highly trained citizens. The ethos of the early developmental state was now dead, not to be resurrected until Mao's death.

In the 1980s and 1990s, however, what one may call an export-led "Taiwan model" of economic growth took hold on the mainland, with enormous success, fueled not least by massive investment flows from Hong Kong and Taiwan. By the 1990s, the marriage of pre-communist business traditions with socialist political organization seemed one explanation for the emergence of "local state corporatism," in which local governments came to resemble business corporations, "with officials acting as the equivalent of a board of directors."[53] By the end of the twentieth century, the non-state sector of the PRC's economy was growing at a great speed, far outpacing that of state industries, in a manner reminiscent of Taiwan's development in the 1960s and 1970s. While the old state-owned industries came into a state of permanent crisis,[54] and new forms of "bureaucratic capitalism," combining private and political interests, were created, a sizable and dynamic private sector of the economy was emerging for the first time since the early 1950s. In the summer of 2001, the Chinese Communist Party, like the Guomindang before it, would begin formally to recruit businesspeople as members.

The political and economic development of both Party-States after 1950 was inseparable from military affairs. For the CCP as for the GMD, the military remained at the heart of the Chinese Party-State. This is no surprise when one recalls that the first CCP "state," the Jiangxi Soviet Republic of the early 1930s, was based almost completely on its military. Ultimately the CCP would come to national power not by speeches or by majority resolutions, nor on the basis of mass mobilization or popular revolution, but by armed rebellion in which hundreds of thousands died. The new regime ruled through forms of martial law from its founding. Soldier-politicians played central roles in CCP and PRC governance in an "interlocking directorate"; military values crowded out others and became the source of political campaigns.[55] While Chiang Kai-shek had tried to militarize the common man in his New

Life Movement of the 1930s, the CCP really did so, as Chinese farmers engaged in the Great Leap were organized into "brigades" which marched in step to the day's work.

For their part the Nationalists did not demilitarize upon decamping to Taiwan. Nationalist Taiwan, too, had to be pacified militarily in the bloody suppression of 1947 before it could be governed successfully. It too was ruled on the basis of martial law, which was declared when the Nationalist regime retreated to Taiwan in 1949 and which remained formally in effect until July 1987. In the years from 1950 to 1958 its military, like the party, would be purged and reformed to create an efficient, loyal, and formidable force capable of defending the island.

It was on the mainland, however, that militarization, like the other central traits of the Party-State, would be taken furthest. The history of the CCP, Kenneth Lieberthal has argued, witnessed "an almost unique, symbiotic relationship between the party and the military."[56] The Military Affairs Commission through which Chiang Kai-shek ruled in the 1930s and 1940s was a government body; the PRC military was governed by the *Party* Military Affairs Commission that reported to no government authority. Whereas the Nationalist military took oaths to defend the nation, the People's Liberation Army swore to uphold the rule of the Chinese Communist Party. Finally, in the post-Mao PRC, a significant part of the state sector of the economy (no one knows for sure how much) became owned and operated by the military, outside the control of government industrial and planning ministries. Until very recently, the military's independence from governmental authority in the PRC was thus also economic, as the People's Liberation Army, Incorporated, became a state within the Party-State.

Yet here too there would be important changes in the last years of the twentieth century. President Jiang Zemin, whose power was based not the least on his chairmanship of the Party Military Affairs Commission, forced the military to divest itself of its major economic holdings. This large-scale "corporatization" of military-owned industries may have changed more in form than in fact: not a few former PLA industries are now headed by chief executives who happen to be retired military officers. Yet these divestitures may also be seen as a successful assertion of civilian control over the military.

## ≺ VI ≻

### Conclusion

The political culture of the Chinese Party-State defined China's political development in the twentieth century. Both the Nationalists and the Communists came to power on the mainland as military conquest regimes. (That is how the Nationalists came to Taiwan, too.) They had broadly transformational agendas in political, economic, and cultural development. By the early twenty-first century, the CCP Party-State on the mainland had lost the ambition to control all aspects of social life. Pre-communist and indeed pre-Party-State space for areas of cultural and economic autonomy was returning. Only politics remained unchallengeable. Civilians could serve the Party-State, but could not govern separately from it.

The Nationalists for their part developed an ability to cohabit with several generations of technical and managerial elites, from those who dreamed of physically "reconstructing" China in the 1920s to the more sober-minded, authoritarian technocrats who guided Taiwan's economic miracle. However, even these elites never exercised political power independent of the Party-State, and they never fundamentally challenged it. Pressures for Taiwan's eventual democratization would come from other quarters, specifically from Taiwanese resistance to Chinese mainlander control. This, plus a belated but still far-sighted recognition on the part of Chiang Ching-kuo of the need to take the lead in political reform, would move Taiwan from a one-Party-State to a "dominant party" system in the 1990s—when the GMD remained comfortably in control—and ultimately to the multi-party system of today.

To be sure, even after the formal end of Party "tutelage" on Taiwan in 1987, certain habits of the Party-State died hard: in the late 1990s, after a decade of democratic reforms, the Guomindang Central Executive Committee still met every Wednesday to set the agenda for the government Cabinet meetings on Thursday. Although as a state the Republic of China on Taiwan had democratized, presiding over one of the more spirited electoral systems in the world, internally the Guomindang had not. When the GMD lost the March 2000 presidential election, the fury of the Party faithful showed the limits of the new democratic spirit: nothing in their experience could prepare them for the fact that, in an election, they might *lose*.

If the victory of Chen Shui-bian may finally have heralded the end of the Party-State on Taiwan, this was not least because the GMD had divided itself, and its candidates, in an acrimonious split. Yet the victor in this multi-party scramble, Chen's Democratic Progressive Party, owed more than that to the GMD: with its secretary-general, central committee, and central executive committee, the DPP had borrowed its organization liberally from the Guomindang handbook, even if its practice was deliberately less disciplined. For its part, the Guomindang Central Executive Committee continued to meet on Wednesday, bowing to Sun Yat-sen's portrait, listening to his will, and thinking of Thursdays to come. A year after the lost election, an electronic message pulsating on the outside of the Guomindang Central Party Bureau, directly facing Chen Shui-bian's Presidential Office, read: "We shall return!"

That is still a possibility and it is a most important point. Taiwan's Guomindang lost its leading role on Taiwan by democratic means, but now it also had the capacity to regain power by democratic means.[57] In other words, politics in Taiwan had, in a short period of time, legitimized the idea of peaceable regime change, perhaps even on a frequent basis. On the Chinese mainland, the Chinese Communist Party was apparently under no such illusions about its fate in any political reversal. It preferred to talk, haltingly, of reform (and sometimes rectification) within the Party-State, as in the advent of village-level elections; but it still declined to articulate an agenda for national political development. In the realm of high politics, the "politics of transition" chronicled power struggles within a Party-State that sought new legitimacy for its continued rule, now that the original socialist ambitions had atrophied. In the first years of the twenty-first century, the dominant formula appeared to be a combination of internationalist economics and nationalist politics: globalization at the expense of democratization.[58] The Party had indeed become less rigid, but it was still a political monopolist. The military was in its barracks, but it still swore by the Party. The "core leader" was decidedly less dictatorial than his predecessors, but he, like all his predecessor leaders of the Party-State, still had "thought," which all should study. In President Jiang Zemin's "Three Representations" [*sange daibiao*], Mao Zedong's party of workers, peasants, and soldiers was being redefined and, in an important way, regrounded in a more open and more diverse Chinese society. The party would now embody not the iconic social bases of Chinese communism, but the forces of technological modernization, cultural transformation, and—implicitly—the will of the people. The party would represent "the most advanced productive forces, the most advanced culture, and the fundamental interests of the broad masses of the Chinese people."[59] It would do so, however, without any input from the Chinese people themselves.

# Workers' Patrols in the Chinese Revolution: A Case of Institutional Inversion

ELIZABETH J. PERRY

INSTITUTIONS are essential to the attainment and preservation of political freedom. Legislatures, media, courts, as well as police and military forces all play a key part in the functioning of liberal democracies. Of course, as Michel Foucault so vividly demonstrated, the very institutions that underpin modern societies serve also as instruments of crippling repression.[1] By delimiting the "normal" and disciplining the "deviant," they severely restrict the expression and expansion of personal freedom.

The institutionalist turn in contemporary American social science reflects the pivotal role that institutions, for better or worse, have come to occupy in the modern world—particularly in fostering and sustaining market economies.[2] Central to this approach is the concept of "path dependence," which highlights the tendency of institutions to perpetuate previous patterns of behavior through a dynamic of increasing returns.[3] But, as historical institutionalists have noted, institutions also change.[4] Practices that were created for one purpose may even be hijacked to serve a radically different agenda—a phenomenon that I refer to as *institutional inversion*. The precipitants of such a dramatic role reversal are various: divergence between the motives of the leadership and those of rank and file participants, imitation of successful institutional arrangements by rival political entrepreneurs, absorption of revolutionary initiatives by state authorities, bureaucratic competition among state agencies, and others. This chapter traces the process of institutional inversion as it unfolded in one key agency of the Chinese revolution: armed workers' patrols. By examining the patrols from their origins in the 1920s through the early years of the People's Republic of China (PRC), we see how an entity intended to serve as the vanguard of a revolution for human liberation devolved into an instrument of terror and repression. Although a case study of a single institution, the analysis is intended to illuminate the inherent tensions between revolutionary designs and repressive detours in the making of the modern Chinese polity. Institutional inversion has been central to the restriction of political freedom in China—and indeed to modern societies everywhere.

≺ I ≻

### *Ideological and Organizational Origins*

The idea of arming the working class for an epic struggle, whose purpose would be to emancipate humanity as a whole, is of course a cardinal element in Marxist political theory. In reflecting on the Paris Commune of 1871, Marx underscored the importance of the Parisian workers having replaced the French army with a new National Guard.[5] As Marx emphasized, the success of the Commune (transitory though it was) depended directly upon this institutional transformation:

> Paris could resist only because, in consequence of the siege, it had got rid of the army, and replaced it by a National Guard, the bulk of which consisted of working men. This fact was now to be transformed into an institution. The first decree of the Commune, therefore, was the suppression of the standing army, and the substitution for it of the armed people.[6]

According to Marx, arming the proletariat was tantamount to liberating the citizenry at large. As a concentrated (and thus potentially conscious) class, which embodied the extreme effects of exploitation and alienation, the industrial proletariat was in a unique position to act as an emancipatory force. In sundering the shackles of capitalism, workers would militantly complete the promise of a fulfilled humanity—not only for themselves, but for all people.

The Commune experience, as interpreted by Marx, was to serve as a powerful organizational template for subsequent generations of proletarian revolutionaries. Arming the working class came to be seen as the *sine qua non* of revolutionary victory. In the Russian revolution, groups of armed workers formed first spontaneously and then by partisan design. As Rex Wade has written of the Russian workers' militias in the February Revolution of 1917: "The armed bands were a complex combination of spontaneity, voluntaristic action, and initiative from below interacting with ideas derived from outside political ideologies and attempts at control or influence by political parties."[7] After the inauguration of the Petrograd Soviet, the Bolsheviks began systematically to encourage the organization of factory militia in working-class districts across the city. The resultant bands of armed workers, known as Red Guards, were never completely obedient to Bolshevik orders. Wade notes that "though not under firm Bolshevik control, the Red Guards did provide that dependable element of active support for a seizure of power in the name of the Soviet. That was their great significance in the October Revolution."[8]

The Russian exemplar figured prominently in the considerations of young Chinese Communists when they undertook to mobilize a proletarian constituency after the founding of the Chinese Communist Party (CCP) in 1921. During the first major strike inspired by Communist initiatives, the Jing-Han Railway Uprising of February 7, 1923, armed "workers' pickets" [gongren jiuchadui] were formed to carry out the struggle.[9] The term "pickets" [jiuchadui] referred to the familiar practice of posting sentries at factories during strikes to prevent scabs from entering the premises. A spontaneous manifestation of worker militancy that long predated the advent of the CCP, deployment of "pickets" was institutionalized and politicized under Communist auspices.

Although bloodily suppressed by the warlord Wu Peifu in February 1923, armed worker patrols would re-emerge as a principal vehicle of urban insurrection over the course of the Chinese revolution. Shanghai's May Thirtieth Movement of 1925, a nationalistic upsurge that demanded an end to foreign imperialism in China, precipitated a concerted effort by the CCP to sponsor armed working-class organizations of the sort that had been active in the Russian revolution.[10] The newly formed corps—established as a complement to the emerging student movement—kept order among the ranks of marchers at public rallies, carried out factory and neighborhood patrols, blocked strike-breakers from entering factory premises, and conducted searches of suspected counterrevolutionaries.[11]

Shanghai's May Thirtieth experience was quickly replicated

elsewhere around the country. Like their Red Guard forerunners in Moscow and Petrograd, however, workers' patrols in China often displayed a stubborn tendency to defy partisan supervision. Ostensibly responsible for guaranteeing public order, the pickets themselves contributed to disorderly conduct. Michael Tsin writes of a parallel development, with similar complications, during the famous Canton-Hong Kong strike that began in the summer of 1925:

In the words of Governor Cecil Clementi of Hong Kong, the strike organization, with its roving teams of pickets, had become an "imperium in imperio" in Canton shortly after the boycott commenced in early July . . . The problem, insofar as the government was concerned, was that the pickets were not always willing to subject themselves to direction and discipline. Nor were they, in fact, even effectively controlled by the Strike Committee, which was dominated by labor organizers and workers who were members of the Communist Party . . . [A]n internal report of the Communists confirms the complaints voiced in many different quarters about the pickets' activities. The Communists conceded that "illegal activities such as extortion, corruption, misuse and abuse of power were inevitable" on the part of the pickets.[12]

For some months, Canton was under the domination of the two thousand armed pickets who patrolled the city. With individual teams enjoying substantial autonomy over their own operations, the worker patrols degenerated into bands of rowdies who terrorized the local populace. It was in this chaotic situation, according to Tsin, that Chiang Kai-shek triumphed as a strongman able to impose order by sheer military might.[13]

≺ II ≻

## *Revolution Meets Terrorism*

As this unhappy episode unfolded in Canton, a similar scenario—on an even grander scale—was taking shape in Shanghai. As the nation's industrial capital, Shanghai was the obvious focus for a proletarian-based revolution that was expected to pave the road to national liberation. The purported liberators, however, proved to be something of a disappointment. While the Chinese Communist Party planned for its first uprising against warlord rule in the fall of 1926, cadres in Shanghai admitted that the three to five hundred armed workers under their nominal command were actually a "destructive force"—in the same league with the several thousand armed drifters who roamed the city at the behest of gangsters.[14] Undisciplined as the patrols were acknowledged to be, their activities were still deemed essential in spearheading the upcoming insurrection.[15]

The crushing defeat, by warlord and police forces, of the October 26 uprising compelled party leaders to reconsider the role of armed workers. The mercenary calculations of the recruits had been made all too clear at the outset of the insurrection, when dozens of dock workers refused to participate once they discovered that a forty-cent bus fare stood between themselves and their appointed location. Within a day after the defeat of the uprising, disheartened pickets streamed to party offices to demand that new jobs be found for them. When party cadres explained that they were powerless to provide such assistance, the angry workers threatened to seek revenge by enlisting in the rival warlord army. As CCP leaders analyzed the situation, the pickets had been composed largely of unemployed workers who expected to benefit by permanent work with the victory of the armed uprising.[16] This disparity between the motives of leaders and of led would prove to be a continuing problem, pointing the workers' patrols in directions far removed from the idealistic image of the Paris Commune.

Two months later, in preparation for launching a second uprising, the Shanghai party committee—now under the direction of Zhou Enlai—became much more serious about the military preparedness of the pickets. Zhou had developed an interest in proletarian revolution during his studies in France. In 1922, he wrote of the October Revolution that had occurred in Russia just five years before, "The only historically comparable event was the Paris Commune of 1871. Even so, the Paris Commune was a brilliant but short-lived flower in the history of proletarian revolution, whereas Russia's October Revolution laid the revolutionary foundations for the proletarian class of the entire world."[17] In the tradition of the Paris Commune and the October Revolution, Zhou deemed armed workers essential to the success of the Shanghai Uprising.[18]

Although Communist Party leaders were committed in principle to arming the proletariat as a cornerstone of their revolutionary designs, they were also concerned in practice about the problems that such forces generated. Some of the worries were caused by the central involvement of gangsters in the labor movement. In an initiative designed to curb gang inroads, the party cautioned that only gainfully employed workers whose thinking was "very revolutionary" should be issued arms. They must, moreover, undergo high-quality political and military training, conducted in the utmost secrecy.[19]

Despite such proposed remedies, gangster-like behavior continued to mar the pickets' activities. An internal party report on the eve of the second uprising criticized the patrols for transgressions such as arbitrarily arresting workers and merchants, sealing factories and shops, forcing people to join unions, and extorting union dues. They were also condemned for instigating armed feuds [*xiedou*] between rival factions of workers. The pickets were ineffective militarily, with only the appearance of being an armed force of the proletariat; and their arrogation of police prerogatives was said to be giving society a terrible impression of organized labor in general.[20]

When the second uprising was defeated in February 1927, Comintern representatives chided the Shanghai partisans over the issue of arming the proletariat:

The party has done a poor job of arming the workers. Naturally the party can't obtain firearms, but it can call upon the workers to arm themselves . . . The party has, however, actually impeded the arming of the workers—fearing doing so would prove dangerous . . . The party has never seriously addressed the question of mass armed mobilization. The Shanghai party organization didn't educate the Shanghai proletariat in the class spirit of struggle. The Shanghai party organization doesn't understand that what is needed is not the negative resistance of a general strike or boycott in support of the national revolution; but positive promotion of participation in political power.[21]

Within days of the suppression of the second uprising, however, local party leaders were heartened to learn that the pickets had expanded their ranks and were making practical plans for the next attempt at insurrection. Even the fact that pickets were asking for pay in advance was regarded favorably by some party organizers, who concluded that "this shows that they really are planning to do the job."[22] Unlike the first uprising, the second had been accompanied by a general strike. Although the strike came in for criticism from Comintern agents, it was hailed by Chinese cadres as "the first expression of the great revolutionary force of the Shanghai working class since May Thirtieth."[23]

Believing that they were finally getting the knack of engineering a proletarian revolution, the Shanghai Communists turned their attention to grander political ambitions.[24] In preparation for launching a third uprising, they emphasized the significance of popular elections. This commitment to mass representation, the Communists claimed, qualitatively distinguished their aims from those of Chiang Kai-shek's rival Nationalist Party [Guomindang]:

After the Northern Expedition Army arrives, the most important matter will be the issue of city government. We value the masses, whereas they [that is, the Guomindang or GMD] value the exercise of leadership. We want elections, whereas they want appointments. This is an important disagreement. We must quickly carry out elections for representatives. We should change the name to "popularly elected municipal government" so that the people are perfectly clear. Before the Northern Expedition Army arrives, we need to create a very dense atmosphere of popular elections.[25]

With elections as the foundation, the Communists planned to put in place a democratic city government as soon as the warlord forces could be toppled. They envisioned a representative form of municipal governance based in the first instance upon occupational interests:

What is a democratic city government? A government organized by representatives elected by the people themselves. How is a democratic city government organized? The citizens' representative assembly elects an executive committee that organizes the Shanghai city government. How is the citizens' representative assembly organized? First, associations of workers, peasants, students, soldiers, merchants and other types of professions choose representatives (according to the size of their membership) to organize citizens' representative congresses in each district. Then each district congress sends representatives (according to the size of its membership) along with representatives of all political parties, to organize a citizens' representative assembly.[26]

Armed proletarian uprising and the workers' pickets that were to carry out the uprising were merely means to the end of an electoral democracy that would serve the interests of the municipal citizenry as a whole. Even at this extraordinary moment of democratic idealism in the early history of the CCP, however, there were already hints of a more controlled political regime in the making. Popular rule, it was suggested, might be balanced by party oversight inasmuch as "revolutionary parties" would enjoy the right to send representatives to participate in the deliberations of executive committees at all levels.[27]

More ominous still was the fact that the workers' pickets, with party approval, were assuming the role of a terrorist hit squad. If the Shanghai partisans had not fully grasped the Comintern's admonition about the need for "mass armed mobilization," under Zhou Enlai's leadership they certainly had come to appreciate the usefulness of selectively applied terror. Party discussions concluded that, while circumstances might make it impossible for picket terrorists to kill "big running dogs" (major capitalists and their lackeys), they should nevertheless go after smaller fry "in order to bolster worker enthusiasm."[28] Although many of the pickets arrested for killing running dogs had already made confessions to the police, the party still believed that the advantages of this type of activity outweighed the disadvantages because "thanks to the beating to death of running dogs, mass confidence is high." In early March, the party authorized the dispatch of five thousand pickets to hunt down running dogs in the commercial and handicraft sector. To further systematize such initiatives, the (Communist-sponsored) Shanghai General Labor Union established a "special picket department"—responsible for terrorist acts—headed by a former tobacco worker and Green Gang member, Gu Shunzhang. Gu had just returned to Shanghai from Vladivostok, where he had been trained in espionage and armed insurrection.[29]

Party leaders argued (in closed party sessions) that targeted murders were a necessary prelude to a wider proletarian revolution.[30] In preparing for the third armed uprising, Zhou Enlai and his colleagues called for terrorism on a grand scale:

We must actively advance a spiritual and material red terror. In working class districts, since the party committee decided to carry out red terrorism, there have been major results. Many scabs have been killed and workers' self-esteem is very high. Now we should expand the scope of red terror to include all counterrevolutionary elements such as rightist leaders, comprador merchants, student running dogs, etc. At the same time, we should employ terrorist tactics to ensure that counterrevolutionaries dare not reside in Shanghai; this is what we call spiritual red terror.[31]

Buoyed by such encouragement, picket-instigated killings increased dramatically across the city. But as "dog beatings" escalated in the days leading up to the third insurrection, the perpetrators often eluded party control. Foreshadowing bureaucratic rivalries that would plague the institution of the workers' patrols, the party (blaming the union) declared a moratorium:

Beginning today, all dog beating must stop because many comrades have committed many mistakes. Some have openly admitted that the union was beating dogs. This is the secret political work of the party; the union cannot handle this work. When there are assaults to be carried out, they cannot be directed by the union. They must be decided by the party.[32]

Bureaucratic competition was not the only problem facing the Shanghai revolutionaries on the eve of the third uprising. In moving beyond terrorism to armed rebellion, the procurement of additional weaponry was essential. Whereas the various merchant-sponsored defense leagues scattered across the city were generally quite well armed, the same could not be said for the Communist forces. Aware of this disparity, Zhou Enlai made a fateful proposal that the pickets should infiltrate the opposition. When pickets expressed reluctance to go along with the idea, Zhou met personally with the workers to solicit their compliance:

Zhou asked the workers, "What do we lack?" Replied the workers, "We lack guns and ammunition." Zhou continued, "Right! If we infiltrate the defense league, won't everyone have guns and ammunition? Not only that, but we can take advantage of the defense league's legal status to carry out military training, as a cover to prepare for our uprising."[33]

Zhou Enlai's strategy proved efficacious in facilitating the victorious third armed uprising. However, the practice of infiltrating enemy ranks set a dangerous precedent. Here, in embryonic expression, was a form of institutional inversion with profound and enduring consequences. Revolutionaries and counterrevolutionaries would become partners in a shadow dance destined to define the contours of the modern Chinese state.

The victory of the third uprising in March of 1927 ushered in a brief period of euphoria and experimentation. For the moment, the Communists felt sufficiently relaxed to take the extraordinary step of offering party membership to anyone who wished to join. All pickets were automatically awarded membership. Registration tables were set up just outside picket headquarters (at the Huzhou

Guild Hall) where any interested Shanghai resident could freely enlist in the Communist Party. Equally surprising, party branch meetings were conducted openly so that ordinary citizens might attend and lend their voices to the deliberations.[34]

As the Communists grew concerned about a counterrevolutionary backlash, however, these remarkable open-door initiatives rapidly receded in favor of a more secretive *modus operandi*. The CCP's mounting suspicions were well founded, of course. On April 12, in a bloody assault that Harold Isaacs considered "the tragedy of the Chinese revolution," Chiang Kai-shek and his allies turned on the pickets.[35]

≺ III ≻

### *Revolution Meets Counterrevolution*

The April 12 massacre and its aftermath have been recorded as a milestone in the annals of modern Chinese history. From this point forward, the textbooks tell us, the Chinese Communists abandoned the cities in favor of a peasant-based revolution. Less often noted is the continuing interplay between GMD and CCP initiatives in the cities, particularly in the realm of labor control. Standard histories emphasize the hostility with which the GMD treated the labor movement, viewing it as the handmaiden of Communist political ambition. Generally unnoticed, however, are the many ways in which GMD policy actually perpetuated and perfected CCP strategies. State-labor relations, as they emerged out of competition between the two rival parties, left a definitive imprint on the modern Chinese state and its intolerance for basic political freedoms.

While the CCP had justified its arming of the proletariat by reference to Karl Marx's observations on the Paris Commune, the GMD—at least after its bloody break with the Communists—could plead no such ideological excuse.[36] But lack of doctrinal rationale did not deter the Nationalists from imitating, and "improving" upon, the brutal tactics of their adversaries. The innovations of the GMD, in turn, were instantly appreciated and incorporated by Communist spies and strategists. As William Kirby explains in chapter 5 in this volume, the basic features of the Chinese Party-State developed out of just such interactive borrowing.

One important area of mutual emulation was in the matter of an armed workers' militia, where the GMD proved itself a master of institutional inversion. Within weeks of the Nationalist take-over in the spring of 1927, an Industry Defense Department [*hugong bu*] was established. The Department was responsible for co-ordinating the operations of an Industry Defense Corps [*hugong dui*], whose activities directly mirrored—and enlarged upon—those of their picket forerunners. Working in close cooperation with military intelligence forces, the Defense Corps played a key role in investigating factories and unions to ferret out suspected Communists.[37]

Exactly who joined the Industry Defense Corps is unclear, but there apparently was considerable overlap with the Communist-sponsored pickets. In Shanghai, the Industry Defense Department complained that the Commercial Press, a hotbed of Communist picket activity only a few weeks before, was now "falsely using the name of the Industry Defense Corps."[38] Officers in the Defense Corps were often "converted" Communists.[39] To what extent this continuity between pickets and Corps represented purposeful in-filtration, as opposed to simple opportunism on the part of work-ers desperate for some form of gainful employment, is uncertain. In any event, the disciplinary problems characteristic of the pick-ets continued to plague their successors. Department archives re-veal that public criticism of the Corps was widespread.[40]

In June of 1927, an educational program for new recruits to the Corps was instituted. The curriculum included instruction in military commands and etiquette as well as in the meaning of Sun Yat-sen's Three Principles of the People. Guns for the Corps were purchased in Nanjing. Uniforms, made of domestic cloth to reflect national pride, were grey in color and cut in the "Sun Yat-sen style" (later known in the West as the "Mao jacket"). The training evidently bore results. Soon the Corps was deemed capable of as-suming key duties that previously had been shouldered by mili-tary intelligence forces.[41]

Trusted Corps members were dispatched to every Shanghai fac-tory to "secretly investigate the situation of each worker." At union meetings, Corps members were supposed to be on tap "to lecture about the benefits of the Three Principles of the People and the dis-astrous consequences of Communism." For the Communist pickets, fomenting strikes (often through terrorist tactics) had been a key focus; for the GMD's Corps, strike-breaking (often through coercive means) was an important aspect of the job. To end a silk filature strike in Hongkou, Corps members forcibly escorted women workers back to their factories. When the Shanghai pole-carriers union reported that armed Communists were blocking their movements, Corps members moved in to provide protection. A report from the Jianchang machinery factory, complaining that arms had been hidden on the premises as part of an attempt to foment a strike, was met by a quick deployment of Corps members to the scene. The Corps also maintained order at large public meetings and demonstrations by posting sentries around the perimeter of assembly halls and alongside marchers. On numerous occasions, Corps members detained suspected Communists who were then handed over to military or police authorities.[42]

Ironically, in Shanghai the Industry Defense Corps (and its sponsoring union, the notorious Unification Committee) was headquartered at the very same Huzhou guild hall that the Communist pickets (and their General Labor Union) had once occupied. A petition from tramway workers in July 1927 complained about the abuses of the new occupants:

The "wolf-like" Industry Defense Corps beat up women silk workers in Hongkou, injuring many. They also act as watchmen for factory management, spying on the workers and serving happily as the capitalists' running dogs. This organization has become completely gangsterized and bureaucratized. To enter the Huzhou Guild Hall is to enter the devil's gate. Going there is like going to a dictator's yamen. It takes forever for a worker to get a hearing. The staff are all gangsters. Some smoke opium. This angers the workers, who ask "with this crew running the union, how can the national revolution be completed?"[43]

While the Nationalists fashioned their "new" urban order, remnant Communists persevered in efforts to mobilize an armed picket force capable of completing the revolutionary enterprise. Although most Communists who survived the April 12 blood bath fled to the relative safety of the countryside, a few intrepid organizers—many of whom would later be accused of Trotskyist tendencies—stayed behind to brave the hostility of the GMD. Seemingly undaunted by the grim realities of the day, these diehards continued to press for a proletarian uprising. Year after year, they disseminated handbills calling for the reestablishment of armed workers' patrols.[44]

Considering the inhospitable political environment, it is hardly surprising that the remnant Shanghai Communists did not score major victories in these initiatives. The little response that they did evoke was concentrated in the western part of the city, in the mill district where the May Thirtieth Movement had originated and where leftist unions were still in place. In July 1930, a new workers' picket unit was established at the union of the West Shanghai cotton mills. The founding manifesto extolled the victories of the Red Army and called for greater emphasis on "dog beating." Such activities, it was claimed, would increase the success rate of strikes and prepare the ground for a fourth armed uprising. In fact, however, Communist-instigated subversion was severely constrained by the political climate of the day. Cadres complained that efforts to carry out sabotage at the British Tramway Company repeatedly failed because the head of the workers' pickets there enjoyed close relations with a "running dog."[45]

The Japanese take-over of much of urban China during World War II necessitated an abrupt change in strategy on the part of GMD and CCP alike. As soon as the war was over, however, both parties scrambled to re-occupy the cities. Once again, workers' patrols figured centrally in their designs. Even before the Japanese defeat, GMD labor movement czar Lu Jingshi had begun to arm his followers in the Shanghai factories (with weapons from secret police chief Dai Li). Lu's "Workers' Loyal National Salvation Army" helped to derail Communist plans and facilitate the Nationalists' recovery of the city in 1945.[46]

Although Lu Jingshi's "workers' army" was demobilized once the Japanese military had retreated, his ambitions of directing a loyal proletarian force did not diminish. In June of 1946, Lu established a new organization known euphemistically as the Shanghai Workers' Welfare Committee [gongren fuli weiyuanhui], the primary purpose of which was to recruit GMD members in each factory who would provide intelligence on the labor movement to government authorities. Finances for the Welfare Committee came from a combination of workers' dues and contributions from both government and capital.[47] That August, under the auspices of the Welfare Committee, training sessions were held for cadres of all the major unions in the city. Underground Communists who were serving as union cadres also participated. Publicly, the training sessions were advertised as a means of promoting production and fostering harmony between labor and management. Privately, they were intended to cultivate special agents who would then ferret out Communist activists within the labor movement. At the end of the one-week session (which included political instruction as well as military exercises), all trainees were collectively inducted into the GMD. Under explicit instructions from higher party authorities, Communists also enrolled as GMD members so as not to attract attention to themselves. In November, a second and more rigorous round of training was held during which military uniforms were issued and instruction was offered in techniques of surveillance, arrest, and the like.[48]

Communist infiltration was an occasional embarrassment to the authorities. When Generalissimo Chiang Kai-shek journeyed to Shanghai to review a citizens' parade at the race course, a large contingent of protesters suddenly emerged from among the ranks of marching workers. Wearing red and white armbands on which were written the characters for "pickets," they pulled out pieces of chalk from their pockets to scribble slogans on the cement or on parked vehicles: "Oppose dictatorship!" "Eliminate special agents!" "Down with capitalists!" "Help unemployed workers!" "Labor is sacred!" "Thoroughly implement democracy!"[49]

Frustrated in his efforts to eliminate the Communist challenge, Lu Jingshi officially revived the para-military cadre of workers (again supplied and trained by military intelligence and the secret police) known as the Industry Defense Corps. In keeping with its pre-war namesake, this was an armed unit whose raison d'etre was to combat Communist influence among the Shanghai proletariat. The Corps operated under the auspices of the Welfare Committee and reported directly to Lu Jingshi. The training and overtime wages of Corps members were supposed to be covered by their factories, on grounds that keeping one or two dozen armed informers on the payroll was a small price to pay for countering leftist influences among one's workforce. In fact the Industry Defense Corps was a costly enterprise, however. To support its 20 big brigades, 100 middle-sized units, and 300 branch units, the reincarnated Corps required a budget of 26.4 million yuan in its initial year of operation for routine operations, wages, travel expenses, and the like. Employers often refused to help defray the cost.[50]

Communist labor organizer Zhang Qi learned of the Industry Defense Corps two months before its formal inauguration. According to his memoirs, Zhang decided against trying to forestall this development, unwelcome as it was. He reasoned that any effort to block Lu Jingshi's initiative would prove to be a fruitless struggle in which Communist identities would be revealed needlessly. Instead, following in the footsteps of Zhou Enlai some twenty years earlier, Zhang recommended that his fellow Communists attempt to infiltrate the Industry Defense Corps and use it as a cover for pursuing their own revolutionary exploits.[51]

At the China Textile Company, which was targeted by the GMD for development of an Industry Defense Corps chapter, the 54 members who enlisted included 10 underground Communists. The director was a Communist, as was the training instructor. Many of the other members, moreover, were labor movement activists with a progressive orientation. As a result, the chapter proved often more of a hindrance than a help in carrying out GMD directives. When the unit was ordered to suppress strikes at nearby mills, for example, the director demurred on grounds that all the Corps members were skilled mechanics whose services were sorely needed on the job.[52]

Nevertheless, taken as a whole, the activities of the Industry Defense Corps amounted to more than a minor annoyance for the CCP underground. The Corps posed real challenges to the Communists, not least because the styles of the two groups were remarkably congruent. Tellingly, government reports often used the terms "Industry Defense Corps" and "pickets" interchangeably. Application forms for the Industry Defense Corps read like carbon copies of those for workers' pickets. And just as pickets were to serve as an appendage of the Communist Party, so Corps members were pledged strictly to obey the dictates of the GMD. The handbook for Industry Defense Corps members, while stressing the anti-Communist mission of their organization, nevertheless reveals numerous similarities to their ostensible enemies. Corps members swore personal fealty to the supreme leader, "pledging to serve as loyal and courageous warriors for their revolutionary commander, Chairman Jiang." They also promised to act as "capable cadres" for their personal patron, "Mr. Lu Jingshi."[53]

Members of the Defense Corps, like their Communist counterparts, were subjected to periodic political and military training sessions that sometimes raised concern on the part of employers, particularly when factory management was asked to finance these exercises. In August 1946, the printing house of the Yizhong Tobacco Company (a branch of the British American Tobacco Company) balked at the idea of paying full wages to two Defense Corps workers sent to Nanjing for "summer camp"—despite repeated prodding from the Bureau of Social Affairs. Ironically, that same month Lu Jingshi wrote to the chief of the Bureau objecting to Communist training sessions for workers at the same Yizhong Tobacco Company. According to Lu's complaint, the Communists were also planning to send two workers off somewhere—probably to an army camp in Subei, he surmised—for two months of military and political instruction.[54]

Despite their training, members of the Industry Defense Corps were not immune to misbehavior. The Bureau of Social Affairs was frequently forced to investigate allegations of illegal arrests, assaults, and extortions instigated by the unruly Defense Corps. It was common practice for Corps members, brandishing weapons, to board public buses without tickets. When told to buy a ticket, they would flash their Defense Corps identification cards, claiming to be military personnel.[55] Even Lu Jingshi admitted that discipline was lax and that grassroots leaders were using their positions to enrich themselves through extortion. Sounding a good deal like his Communist counterparts, Lu complained that "Shanghai is an environment filled with evil, while ours is a revolutionary organization that must be committed to reforming society. We must tighten checks on cadres at all levels."[56]

In an effort to promote discipline among its unruly membership, the Industry Defense Corps issued new uniforms—the cost of which was to be borne equally by workers and their employers. Men were given military-style hats and white gloves to wear with their blue uniforms. Women were issued blue *qipao* (or *cheong-sam*) along with the white gloves. All were required to wear numbered badges as well. At some enterprises, the number of Defense Corps volunteers more than doubled when the new uniforms and badges were introduced.[57] The distribution of uniforms marked the evolution of the Industry Defense Corps from a secret to a semi-public organization.[58] Guns were to be better controlled through a licensing procedure overseen by the Garrison Command. To add more of a martial flair, trumpets were purchased for every Corps unit. But such efforts did not necessarily improve the situation. Uniformed Corps members waltzed brazenly into dance halls and theaters, creating public disturbances.[59]

To further complicate matters, the Three People's Principles Youth League—a rival GMD organization—was severely criticized by Lu's Welfare Committee for issuing its own armbands and identification cards to armed workers, "thereby confusing the workers and creating an opportunity for Communists to seize the advantage."[60] Communists were indeed gaining the upper hand; a planned May Day display of Industry Defense Corps prowess, scheduled to be held at the Shanghai race course, had to be canceled for fear that Communists would disrupt the festivities.[61]

In a campaign that eerily foreshadowed the Suppression of Counterrevolutionaries Campaign of the early 1950s, in which Communist workers' pickets would play a critical role, trained members of the Industry Defense Corps in 1948 spearheaded a Liquidate Traitors Campaign [xiaojian yundong] to smoke out workers suspected of Communist ties. A light sentence for those targeted in this movement was job dismissal; a heavy sentence could mean the death penalty.[62]

In early 1949, underground Communist organizers in Shanghai sponsored the formation of their own Factory Defense Corps [huchang dui] to serve as a direct counterweight to Lu Jingshi's Industry Defense Corps. The Factory Corps was charged with fingering GMD agents and preventing the removal of factory equipment in anticipation of a Communist victory. As the New Fourth Army approached the city, armbands were issued to members of the Factory Defense Corps—who began to call themselves Factory Defense *Pickets* in deference to their forebears of two decades before. Their efforts would prove crucial in the Communist takeover of the industrial sector.[63]

≺ IV ≻

## Revolution Meets Regime Consolidation

With the Communist advance on the cities gaining momentum in the spring of 1949, the CCP's interest in arming a loyal force among the urban proletariat escalated in tandem. Before long the diverse array of pro-Communist factory corps and pickets that had sprung up in various cities around the country were (at least nominally) unified under the name of People's Peace Preservation Corps (PPPC) [*renmin baoandui*]. Sporting white armbands emblazoned with red characters, members of the PPPC served as a paramilitary force to assist the People's Liberation Army in its remarkably swift and successful urban campaign.[64]

By the time of Shanghai's "liberation" in late May, the city's PPPC numbered more than 60,000 workers. Corps members were assigned to patrol duties in factories as well as public spaces, charged with uncovering enemy agents, confiscating their weaponry, and maintaining order.[65] Smooth as these activities appear in retrospect, at least in the Shanghai case, they did not proceed unopposed. According to Communist estimates, more than six thousand GMD secret agents were active in Shanghai on the eve of liberation. Many of these individuals remained in the city after the Communist takeover, engaging in surreptitious initiatives of various sorts.[66]

Despite the notable achievements of the Shanghai PPPC, the force was disbanded on orders from the Military Commission within two days of the New Fourth Army's assuming effective control of the city. In a reversal of the pattern extolled by Karl Marx in his observations on the Paris Commune, in Shanghai workers' patrols were being replaced by a professional army— rather than the other way around.

The military's initiatives were not always welcomed by labor activists, however. A Shanghai union report in the summer of 1949 bemoaned the hasty demobilization of the PPPC, noting that GMD secret agents were still active in instigating labor strife and spreading rumors.[67] To improve factory security, the union decided to resurrect the workers' pickets, who would be assigned to assist public security agencies in capturing spies.[68] In the summer of 1949 the pickets were reinstated in major urban centers across the country. In Beijing, for example, more than two thousand pickets—drawn from the ranks of railway and factory workers—were mobilized.[69] In Shanghai, a much larger cohort was quickly assembled.[70]

A major turning point in the union's efforts to reinstate the institution of workers' pickets came with the bombing of Shanghai on February 6, 1950, by Guomindang planes. Although there had been a few smaller raids prior to this date, the February 6 attack marked the first instance of sustained industrial damage.[71] The raid, which took place during the meetings of the city's first workers' representative congress, triggered an emergency bulletin that called upon all unions in the city to organize workers' pickets as soon as possible in order to strengthen defenses against air attacks.[72]

In the aftermath of the February Sixth Incident, as it was soon known, a Pickets' Office [jiucha chu] was set up under the auspices of the municipal trade union, assisted by the students' federation and public security bureau. Under the direction of this office, more than 20,000 pickets were mobilized in Shanghai within the space of two weeks. Rifles and bullets were issued to these recruits, who received a brief stint of military training from People's Liberation Army instructors.[73]

The course manual for training sessions took care to distinguish the "revolutionary" workers' pickets from the "reactionary" Industry Defense Corps of an earlier era:

In the past, the reactionaries set up the Industry Defense Corps to oppress the workers. That organization was staffed by gangsters and backward elements. The workers' pickets of today are entirely different. They are part of a glorious history of more than twenty years that included countless underground struggles. In the 1923 Jing-Han railway strike, workers' pickets—under the general union of the railroad—led opposition to the warlords. In 1927 in Shanghai's three armed uprisings the workers' pickets—under the leadership of the Communist Party—initiated military struggle and confiscated the warlords' weapons. On the eve of Liberation, the Shanghai workers' pickets (whether called Factory Defense Corps or People's Peace Preservation Corps), under Communist Party direction, defeated Chiang Kai-shek and helped the People's Liberation Army seize enemy weapons. In the February 6, 1950 bombing, under the leadership of the air defense command, they continued to play a very positive role.[74]

Although the training sessions for new recruits were lengthened to three months, the quality and motivation of the volunteers was of growing concern. Once again, leaders and led subscribed to very different conceptions about the purpose of the institution. With factory shut-downs having generated a severe unemployment problem, the union decided to target laid-off workers for picket recruitment. The idea was that after their factories reopened, these individuals could return as activists in union, youth league, production, and picket work. Hundreds of young new pickets were mobilized in this drive, but many of them proved less than committed to the enterprise. A number of them were loath to undergo military training, afraid that they would be sent off to invade Taiwan as soon as they had acquired some soldierly skills. Others were more favorably inclined toward the training session, but only because they saw it as a chance to enjoy free room and board for a few weeks. With both men and women encouraged to join the pickets, many of the recruits reportedly viewed their induction as an opportunity to find a marriage partner. Even more worrisome to the union was the discovery that a substantial number of the young men were "dandies" [*afei fenzi*] who applied liberal doses of cologne and sported "airplane" hairdos. These flamboyant individuals insisted on interrupting their training several times a day to wash up and change clothes.[75]

Problems with the quality of new recruits notwithstanding, the pickets constituted a sizable force to buttress the power and legitimacy of the new regime. On May 1, 1950, Mayor Chen Yi and other municipal cadres gathered triumphantly at the Shanghai race course to review their armed pickets, who now numbered nearly 30,000.[76] If the organization of the post-liberation pickets was in the first instance a reaction to enemy air bombardment, the institution was soon reassigned to less lofty challenges. In preparation for the Suppression of Counterrevolutionaries Campaign, the Shanghai union expanded the ranks of the pickets to some 45,000 by the spring of 1951.[77]

Despite continuing efforts to distinguish the pickets from the "oppressive" Industry Defense Corps of the GMD era, during the Suppression Campaign the similarities became glaringly obvious. As part of the unfolding campaign, the pickets' department of the union entered into a collaborative arrangement with the economic security office of the city's public security bureau—not unlike the cooperation that the Industry Defense Corps had enjoyed with military intelligence. According to the agreement, the head of the pickets' department served concurrently as deputy director of the economic security office. This collaboration allowed the pickets to intensify their constabulary operations within the factories.[78]

The application form for new pickets—like that of the bygone Industry Defense Corps—included on one side a loyalty oath, to be signed by the applicant and by his or her sponsors. On the other side of the form was a resume of the political and work history of the applicant. It was not uncommon for applicants to refer to compromising episodes in their past; for example, "In October 1948 an underground Party member introduced me to the Industry Defense Corps."[79]

The overlap between erstwhile members of GMD-sponsored "reactionary organizations" and newly recruited pickets created special complications during the Suppression of Counterrevolutionaries Campaign (which would resurface with a vengeance during the Cultural Revolution). Former members of Lu Jingshi's Industry Defense Corps and Workers' Welfare Committee were frequently targeted for mass struggle, and sometimes for public execution, during the course of the campaign. However, a number of these "counterrevolutionaries" were actively serving in the very picket forces that were charged with ferreting them out. In one notorious case of industrial sabotage at the Great Southeast Tobacco Factory, it turned out that the culprit—a "secret agent" of the GMD—was none other than the director of the factory's pickets.[80]

Union leaders headed a special task force to oversee Shanghai's Suppression of Counterrevolutionaries Campaign. In conjunction with the campaign, thousands of pickets underwent special training in how to capture and forcibly restrain victims. Equipped with flashlights, handcuffs, ropes, and the like, they were a formidable element in carrying out the operation. Instead of declaring martial law before launching the assault on alleged enemies, the government decided to adopt more "flexible" methods. Victims would be seized by surprise when they went to work, and then handed over to the police station. Thanks in large part to the efforts of the pickets, nearly 8,500 alleged counterrevolutionaries were rounded up in a single night on April 27, of whom approximately one-third were apprehended on the premises of industrial enterprises.[81]

The Suppression of Counterrevolutionaries Campaign was a turning point in the consolidation of power by the new Communist regime. The workers' pickets played a starring, if less than heroic, role in this vicious drama. But when they had completed their assigned part, there arose the question of what to do with them. The party committee of the Shanghai union suggested it was now time to wean the pickets from the task of suppressing enemy agents to the equally critical job of safeguarding production.[82]

Redirecting the energies of the pickets was easier said than done, however. Having once mounted the political stage, many of them were reluctant to withdraw from active engagement. The familiar catalog of picket excesses was now cited as a reason for curtailing their activities.[83] The question of links to their GMD predecessors was particularly problematic. A confidential report on an investigation of the Number Ten Cotton Mill revealed that "the masses are not happy that so many former Guomindang types are in the pickets. Some of them behave arrogantly toward the ordinary workers."[84] Although Lu Jingshi's Industry Defense Corps had been an important target of the Suppression of Counterrevolutionaries Campaign, with many of its members sentenced to execution or labor reform as a result of the movement, by no means were all former participants eliminated. At the Number Ten Cotton Mill, for example, the post-Campaign investigation found that 45 of the 95 pickets serving at the factory had once enjoyed close connections to the GMD; of these, 13 had been members of the Industry Defense Corps.[85] Drawing clear lines between Communists and Guomindang was no simple matter. A worker who was accused of reactionary connections put it well: "There was nothing unusual about participating in the Industry Defense Corps or the Workers' Welfare Association. Didn't the Communist underground comrades also participate? I joined some of those reactionary organizations in order to protect workers' interests. In the past, the GMD said I was Communist; today the Communists say I'm GMD."[86]

In October of 1951, a registration of the more than 50,000 pickets in the city was carried out to establish a distinction between those with redeemable and those with irredeemable records. Confessed Industry Defense Corps members were investigated with an eye toward smoking out former colleagues who had been less forthcoming in registering with the authorities. The reorganization effort was linked to the union's resumption of complete control over the pickets following a complicated agreement that returned authority from the economic security office of the public security bureau to the federation of trade unions.[87]

Once the registration effort was completed, and the pickets had been properly "purified," the question remained of how best to utilize their talents.[88] Considerable confusion surrounded the issue, as various agencies jockeyed for control. With public security forces having gained increased power in the course of the Three Antis Campaign (an anti-corruption initiative), the capacity of the union to retain an armed para-military organization was called into question. Although the union had stopped making and distributing armbands during the Three Antis, the pickets still controlled thousands of guns which needed to be turned over to the police. Moreover, a large number of workers—energized by the experience of the Three Antis and unaware of the reorganization effort—were applying to enlist in the pickets. The union noted that, while there was a pressing need for factory security, disciplinary problems among the pickets remained chronic. Corruption and other forms of illegal behavior were legion.[89]

By the fall of 1952, the municipal union's exasperation with the situation was palpable:

Despite our countless reports about the pickets, we've received no guidance. We don't yet know whether our municipal-level pickets department has actually been abolished or not . . . What is to be done with the more than 50,000 pickets? In the past, when leadership was unclear the masses wavered. What happens now? The basic picket members are grumbling, "When the leadership has problems they call on us; when they don't have problems they forget about us." . . . We need clear and immediate guidance on whether or not to announce dissolution. We don't believe this is really an occasion for secrecy. Certainly the morale of the pickets cannot be sustained through secrecy.[90]

The following year the union received its answer. After three and a half years of service under the PRC regime, workers' pickets were dissolved. Those members deemed politically reliable and morally upright were absorbed into factory security committees or appointed as union cadres.[91]

## ≺ V ≻
### Conclusion

The concept of an armed citizenry, whether justified as a vehicle of class revolution (a la Marx) or as a guarantee against tyranny (a la the Federalists), has occupied a central place in modern political theory. The practical consequences of these conceptions, however, have often strayed far from the ideals of those who recommended them in the first place. Institutional inversion is an instance of unintended consequences, born of the gap between political theory and historical reality. Just as we grapple in the United States with the appalling crime rates attendant upon our revolutionary right to bear arms,[92] so the Chinese have seen their proletarian patrols devolve into instruments of terror in service to one political faction or another.

Historical circumstances alter the operations of institutional arrangements, no matter how laudable their initial aims, presenting unforeseen challenges to later generations. Joyce Lee Malcolm, in her study of the origins of the Anglo-American right to keep and bear arms, shows how the exigencies of the English Civil War transformed the king's militia such that the new post-war institution "was not limited to the role of its predecessor, the suppression of occasional riots and defence against invasion. Rather, it was used as a police force whose primary function was the prevention of subversion . . . an instrument for surveillance and disarmament of its political enemies."[93]

In tracing the evolution of China's workers' pickets, we witness the impact not only of conscious political design, but also of pressing social and economic problems as well as bureaucratic priorities and rivalries. Yet, at each turn in the road, pre-existing institutions pose opportunities as well as constraints for leaders with alternative political agendas. The history of China's armed workers' patrols did not end in 1953 with the dissolution of the pickets. During the Cultural Revolution, urban militias [*chengshi minbing*] were developed under the sponsorship of the "Gang of Four." These militias, composed overwhelmingly of workers, were also justified by reference to the Paris Commune—particularly when they prepared for an armed uprising in Shanghai following the arrest of their radical patrons in October 1976.[94] Then in the early 1980s, workers' pickets were resurrected by the municipal trade unions to combat the urban crime wave that accompanied the return of millions of sent-down youths to the cities. But the pickets of the post-Cultural Revolution era did not confine their contributions to the relatively apolitical function of crime control. In an ironic twist of fate, an institution that had developed under Communist supervision back in the 1920s to complement the student movement was deployed by the Communist Party in 1989 to crush the student movement. On June 9, a reported 100,000 workers' pickets were called up to clear away barricades and restore order to the city of Shanghai.[95] Institutional inversion had come full circle.

The mobilization of workers' pickets to combat the student movement of 1989 was a national phenomenon. An internal-circulation party report noted that "in Beijing, Shanghai, Tianjin, Liaoning and other urban areas, workers' pickets were formed to protect factories and preserve social order. They assisted the party and government in suppressing the turmoil and quieting the counter-revolutionary chaos."[96] Reflecting upon such contributions, President Jiang Zemin asserted at the eleventh congress of the All-China Federation of Trade Unions that "The working class is completely trustworthy."[97]

As the active involvement of labor in the protests that spring had indicated, however, the Chinese working class also harbored deep-seated grievances against the government. This was perhaps clearest in the case of the Workers' Autonomous Federation in Beijing, but it was not limited to that one organization or city.[98] In Shanghai, the official trade union donated a considerable sum of money to support the hunger-striking students.[99] In Nanjing, protesting workers even dubbed their rebel organization "workers' pickets."[100]

Institutional inversion is after all an uncertain and ironic process, ever open to surprising reversals. As Valerie Bunce has written of formerly Communist countries elsewhere in the world, "Over time and certainly by accident, the institutional framework of socialism functioned to deregulate the party's monopoly and to undermine economic growth. This set the stage for crisis and reform—and, ultimately, for the collapse of all of these regimes."[101] If the history of Chinese workers' patrols demonstrates the danger that purported means of liberation may devolve into powerful mechanisms of repression, a more hopeful outcome is also within the realm of future possibility.

# Discourses of Dissent in
# Post-Imperial China

WEN-HSIN YEH

THIS CHAPTER examines practices of dissent in the public arena in early twentieth-century Chinese political life. To put it quite simply, the argument draws on a combination of historical research and critical analyses to make three principal points.

First, despite the presumed authoritarianism and repression in its political system, dissent was a central feature in Chinese politics under the emperors as well as the republics. The fall of the Qing in 1911, to be sure, put an end to the monarchical system. The new Republic of China failed, however, to deliver its promise, whether phrased in terms of rule by the people or as social justice to all; and Chinese intellectuals continued their dissenting practices under the successive Republican regimes. Post-imperial discourses of dissent were as rich and complex as before.

This brings us to the second point, about the seeming continuity in dissenting practice against the backdrop of significant institutional changes over the course of the twentieth century. Two sets of historical developments are of special relevance. The new Republic, as explicated elsewhere in this volume, witnessed the rise of the Party-State even though it did not see the destruction of the old imperial bureaucracy. The Chinese Party-States of the twentieth century not only set in motion a thorough overhaul of the Chinese political system but also put in place new sets of political ideology. Additionally, the early decades of the twentieth century witnessed the birth of the Chinese public intellectual, or of figures of culture or learning using words to exercise authority through the printed medium. The rise of modern printing, publishing, mass media, and higher education in the cities provided the institutional backdrop for the rise of these men. These intellectuals' public criticism of the Party-State redefined the practice of dissent in post-imperial China.

To elaborate on the above point, let us consider for a moment the late imperial institution of bureaucratic censorship. Confucian critics of the court had sometimes functioned in their capacity as appointed censors of the imperial bureaucracy. It was a much-cherished Confucian ideal that, in attempts to save the regime from its own mistakes, loyal ministers should speak the truth while challenging the powerful. Censorial critics functioned, in this sense, within the bureaucratic system and voiced dissenting comments for the purpose of saving the regime. Such loyalist opposition critiqued policies and individuals but rarely questioned the underlying assumptions of governance. As in the past, twentieth-century Chinese states institutionalized the equivalents of such official censors and used them to monitor the misconduct of government officials and Party members. Sun Yat-sen, the "founding father" of the Republic, had envisioned a five-power constitution that contained a branch of "inspection" [*jiancha*] to police the conduct of the state. This branch would presumably tighten the administrative discipline of the state bureaucracy without challenging its ruling authority.

But in contrast to an earlier time, the self-policing of the state in the Republican period took place in the context of new developments in the public arena. The Chinese political press had come into being at the turn of the century, when members of the educated elite acquired the publicizing capacities of missionary publicists and commercial booksellers. There was, at the same time, a rise in urban literacy, a proliferation of civic associations, and the birth of the nation as opposed to the state as an imagined community. Dissenting intellectuals sometimes mounted ideological challenges against the regime and raised questions that went beyond loyal opposition. Commerce, industry, and urbanization, furthermore, had produced a more complex society to break down the shared cultural outlook and political consensus that used to spread across a wide spectrum of Chinese society. Rising ideological imperatives, meanwhile, steadily reduced the regime's capacity to tolerate internal as well as external dissension. How the new Party-State set limits on the public expression of dissent thus defined the terms of political freedom in China's twentieth century.

The third point of this chapter concerns the connections between institutions and practices as well as continuities or discon-
tinuities between the past and the present. Twentieth-century
Chinese Party-States resorted to a variety of institutional means,
legal ones in particular, to set limits on public discussions of public affairs. Over the course of the century there also emerged a political ideology centered upon the sovereign rights of the people
and their civic participation. The state's capacity to make use of
legal means and to assert its presence in the public arena, as chapters 4 and 5 have shown, has significantly outstripped that of the
civil society to project its will and to protect itself from the power
of the state. Social divisions have arisen, meanwhile, in the process of industrialization. Just as the Party-States sought to legitimize political authority on the basis of the representation of all
people, in other words, fissures and oppositions have developed
from within the ranks of the people to challenge the imagined integration of the national community. Post-imperial discourse of
dissent thus must be examined against the transformation of both
the modernizing state and the expanding civil society.

≺ I ≻

### Dissent in Imperial China

Dissent in imperial China came in many forms and drew upon
multiple systems of symbolic resources. There were Confucian
acts of moral protests. There were also Daoist renunciations of
power and an aesthetic embrace of the rustic. And, when combined with sectarian beliefs, mainstream intellectual values sometimes fueled popular protests that exploded into peasant uprisings
with millenarian aspirations.

Most scholars agree that, since the formation of the first imperial academies in the Western Han dynasty, there has long been a
convention of political protest in China.[1] High-profile protests and
principled stands of dissent that invoked Confucian classics had led
repeatedly to the formation of elite factions in the Eastern Han, in
the Song, and in the Ming. There had been so many instances of
such occurrences in Chinese dynastic records that political protests
risked becoming an exalted convention by late imperial times.[2]

This is not to say that there had been a convention without differentiation. New forms of social criticism, aimed at social injustice, official corruption, tax levies, or bureaucratic extortion, gained in scope, intensity, and frequency with the rise of urban wealth and the spread of popular literacy in the late Ming and early Qing. Paul Ropp, in his study of dissent in vernacular literature, saw the seventeenth century as a new moment charged with a new spirit of protest. Social criticism in this context was fueled both by the iconoclastically egalitarian fervor in the Taizhou School of Wang Yang-ming philosophy and by Huang Zongxi's post-mortem critique of Ming autocracy. Ropp believes that the rise of vernacular literature, whether in the form of literary realism as in the case of *Jinpingmei* or in the social satire of *Rulin waishi*, contributed significantly to the circulation of dissenting views among the reading public.[3] There were, in short, plenty of instances of social criticism and intellectual dissent in a culture of public reading that could be tied to the "sprouts of capitalism" in seventeenth-century urban economy. When late-Qing fiction writers used the vernacular to satirize the bureaucracy and to expose high-place corruption, they were not taking a modern departure from the past but following a well-established convention, which in turn reached back to a well-entrenched romantic tradition of martial arts justice and knights-errant chivalry.[4]

Social criticisms in late imperial days rarely aimed at the system as such. They attacked, instead, the failings of individuals in positions of power. When Confucian ministers asserted their moral autonomy against figures of authority, they at the same time conducted themselves as guardians of principles that buttressed the system. The price of their autonomy, as Frederic Wakeman has argued, was precisely their unquestioned bond to the principles behind the system.[5] Late imperial dissent was thus hardly "progressive" in intent despite the radical potential. It was aimed not at changing the ground rules but at rectifying political practices via a return to an enduring moral vision—a vision, in the words of Philip Kuhn, that amounted to a text-based constitutional rhetoric grounded in the Confucian Classics and speaking to general truths about public life.[6]

It is useful for us to remember that, more often than not, traditional political debates and literati criticisms were framed in the conservative language of ritual propriety and dynastic precedents. Many critics were actually successful in having their day in court.[7] As the critics and the targets of their criticisms shared so much in basic beliefs, dissent was a result of impasse or failure to arrive at mutual political accommodation. But the cost of dissent to the dissenting individual could be high, as Wakeman shows, and tales of martyrdom did fill the pages of historical records. Officials who threw themselves in the paths of the powerful ran the risk of jeopardizing their careers and losing their lives. One might argue, nonetheless, that it was a function of the rules of good storytelling that only the spectacularly unsuccessful cases of dissent would receive the fullest benefit of narrative dramatization in historical annals.

Death or dismissal in the case of failed criticism, meanwhile, was not totally devoid of rewards. A failed protest by the subject was almost by definition a bungled management by the ruler of the rhetoric and drama of dissent. Those who lost their fights in political struggles were thus paradoxically assured of an honored spot in literary or poetic justice. Above and beyond the power of the ruler there was always a higher realm of authority, whether in the principles of the *dao* [the way] or in the judgment of history. Political martyrs became venerated figures in popular lore or historical narratives. Their integrity was certified by the hardship they endured or the blood that they had shed.

Exile was another fate that awaited the dissidents. It, too, was a form of punishment with its reward. In the lore of Qu Yuan, the loyal minister of third century B.C. who had spoken the unflattering truth was sent away [*fang*] on exile. His subsequent roaming and wandering in the wilderness provided the backdrop for reflections on the human fate as well as dialogues with deities. Immortalized in the rhymed verses of *Chuci* [The Song of the South], the poet's divine communications directed attention away from the political to the aesthetic, from the fortune of the moment to the everlasting in history.

In the annals of Neo-Confucian masters, the classicist Han Yu (768–824) denounced as an act of sheer folly the emperor's lavish worship of a piece of ossified bone allegedly from the Buddha's little finger. No sooner had the denunciation been submitted than Han was banished to the diseased land of the malarial south.

Thanks to the emperor's intemperate rejection of Han Yu's argument, his memorial was canonized as a classic at a critical juncture in medieval intellectual history.

Exile similarly was the fate awaiting Lin Zexu, the governor general of Guangdong and Guangxi, in the aftermath of the first rounds of the Opium War (1839–42). Lin's banishment to China's Muslim region in the Central Asian desert put an end to a distinguished career. The downfall paradoxically secured for him a reputation as a staunch patriot in anti-British popular lore.

Exile as a form of punishment was thus of dubious value for the rulers who imposed it. The "wilderness" [ye], to which the offenders were banished, was no mere place of discomfort or barbarity. So long as ye could be opposed to the chao [court] as an alternative realm of significance, it lay beyond the reach of the court and underscored the limit of the state. There was open space on the margins of the state, which made possible the inscription of alternative systems of meaning. There were local temples, county gazetteers, popular drama, vernacular stories, and so forth to provide the institutional underpinning and cultural infrastructure for a life in this space.

Confucian canons and Daoist aestheticism both applaud the strategy of yin or yi [to become invisible, to disengage]. Both schools placed value on a principled renunciation of power. Exemplary hermits and recluses in periods of dynastic transition can be found in the Analects as well as in the Five Classics. A man of virtue must serve only rulers worthy of that virtue. It is a ruler's task, meanwhile, to recruit the able and talented [xian] from all four corners of the realm. In times of disorder, mountaintops and riverbanks become sites of purity and integrity and an ethical counterweight to the moral compromise or corruption at the center. Under the Southern Song and the Yuan, centers of private Confucian classical learning in places such as Jinhua and Yongjia in Zhejiang produced a disproportionately large number of scholars who had withdrawn from court politics and poured their energy, instead, into the moral ordering of the lineage and the locale. The academies and the ancestral halls that they built were tangible institutional expressions of a cultural space that was both public and local, that had been set apart from the power of the state in vocal as well as quiet disapproval.[8] It is significant, however, that when a new dynasty came to power, these paragons of local virtue found themselves enshrined as sages in state Confucian temples first under the Ming and then under the Qing. The Song withdrawal was thus to a realm of purity away from the court of corruption. It was not a move toward a stand of opposition nor the affirmation of an alternative to the center.

Literary idealizations of recluse abound, meanwhile, in the records. There was Tao Qian in the Six Dynasties and his Daoist celebration, in poetry and rhymed prose, of the freedom of withdrawal. A thousand years later, the prologue to the seventeenth-century novel *Rulin waishi* features the tale of Wang Mian, a man of natural integrity and wisdom whose exemplary conduct put to shame a whole host of self-promoting individuals who sought offices and curried favors.

Prominent intellectual leaders, meanwhile, were often believed to be able to live up to this ideal of withdrawal during periods of turmoil and transition. The Ming-Qing transition provided the backdrop for the withdrawal of Huang Zongxi, who retired into the mountains of Zhejiang; of Gu Yanwu, who became a wandering traveler; and of Wang Fuzhi, hermit in the remote cave terrain of Hunan. These men rejected repeated attempts by the new dynasty to lure them to the court in Beijing. They turned the sites of their self-imposed exile into centers of vision and cultivation. Daoist aestheticism, in particular, places high ethical value on nature as a source of beauty and meaning. The imperial court had at its disposal the service of official historians and offices of dynastic histories. But it was those in the "wilderness" who recounted tales that commanded public imagination. Failed cases of dissent and exiled dissidents of late imperial China, in short, did not end up in oblivion. Instead these became materials of symbolic representation charged with political potency.

≺ II ≻

### *The End of Imperial Discourse*

In April 1895, Kang Youwei and some twelve hundred provincial examination degree-holders [*juren*] of sixteen provinces assembled at the gates of government offices in Beijing to submit a "ten-thousand-character letter" that protested the signing of the Treaty of Shimonoseki. By doing so, these examination candidates acted against the convention of the dynasty that banned non-officials from interfering with the affairs of the state. Kang and his compatriots, driven by concern over the court's handling of China's humiliating military defeat at the hands of the Japanese, were interested not in adopting a grand gesture but in forcing upon the court a particular course of action. Rejected by the dynasty, Kang and his student Liang Qichao went on to organize a study society to agitate for reform and to stir up educated opinion.

In his study of Chinese democracy, Andrew Nathan named Kang and Liang the pioneering figures "who laid the foundation for the ideas of both the democracy activists and the party reformers of the late 1970s."[9] One may wish to quibble with Nathan's construction of historical genealogy, but the 1895 events were of watershed significance in modern Chinese political history. The protestors of the turn of the century not only submitted memorials to the throne but also published news articles and founded a political press. They presented their case not simply by citing sacred canons and ancestral precedents but also by noting developments in foreign countries—the Meiji Constitution in Japan, for example—and around the world.[10] They agitated not only for the court's adoption of their position but also for its recognition of their right to take part in such decisions. The events of the decade called into being a politicized public and an expanding political nation, which in turn set the stage for a new kind of political dissent in the following century.

In a recent collection of essays, Philip Kuhn pinpoints Spring 1895 as a major turning point in the long history of Chinese political history. Kuhn identifies a paradigmatic shift in intellectual understanding of the norms of Chinese "constitutional agenda" and political participation. For over two thousand years Chinese elite had subscribed to a hierarchical conception of the political state in which virtue and initiatives emanated from the top and spread to the bottom. In the 1890s political elites turned to a style of thinking that signaled a radical departure from this classical conception. The educated Chinese began to think in terms of local self-government and citizenship participation instead of mere bureaucratic service.[11] These new lines of thinking, Kuhn suggests, guided Chinese elites to issues such as the negotiated allocation of resources among competing interest groups and the political representation of status and power that had been earned outside the bureaucratic system. Dissent thereafter was not just a matter of bottom-up critique of a top-down exercise of political power, but also the challenge of old-style bureaucratic privileges by an extra-bureaucratic constituency. It was no longer bureaucrats against bureaucrats, or gentry officials prominent in the provinces critiquing gentry officials serving in court. It was the people against the state, and the state claiming to represent all people.

Institutionally, in 1905 the Qing abolished the civil service examinations that for over ten centuries had functioned as a key instrument to recruit the educated into bureaucratic service.[12] This action spelled the end of scholar officials as a distinct social group and altered their standing vis-à-vis the Chinese state. By the 1920s the elite of the modern educated had become graduates of Western-style schools based in the cities. From the turn of the century onward there had also been a steady fragmentation of the formal system of education at all levels. While some schools were founded and operated by Protestant or Catholic missions, others were supported by private or public Chinese sources. These schools offered different sets of curricula and by the 1920s it became difficult to speak of a cultural consensus about what it meant to be an educated Chinese. While some had persisted in the study of Chinese classics with little attention to new branches of knowledge, others had concentrated instead on foreign languages and "new learning" at the expense of the "old learning." New-style schools, first founded in coastal cities, only gradually made their appearance in hinterland provincial towns and county seats. But to be modern and educated, it was also essential to leave behind one's old-style hometowns.

Government service and political parties continued to employ a significant number of the educated. But the new century witnessed the rise of private enterprises and urban professions in the cities. There were professional writers, professors, journalists, translators, artists, editors, and publishers who earned their livings in the marketplace. A growing number of individuals also made their living on the basis of systematic knowledge of pragmatic subjects such as accounting, finance, law, medicine, and so forth.

Compared with their imperial predecessors, China's modern educated no longer depended exclusively on the officialdom for their careers.

Reform and revolution in the early decades of the century had meanwhile contributed to significant changes in governing assumptions about the relationship between the individual and the state. In the apt words of Joseph Levenson, the "1912 Republic, while a failure, was not a mistake."[13] Beyond the symbolic changes in matters such as clothing, hairstyle, calendar, national anthem, political rituals, and official titles, there were distinct ideological and linguistic shifts that marked the birth of the republic and the end of the empire.[14] The first president of the Republic shared his power, albeit reluctantly, with a parliament of elected representatives and political parties. Despite incessant civil conflicts, the 1920s witnessed Sun Yat-sen's systematic elaboration of the *Three Principles of the People*. The Nationalist Government (1927–49) of Chiang Kai-shek was a military regime aided by the secret service. It nonetheless grounded its legitimacy in terms of service to the nation and the people and adopted, in 1947, a constitution that remained in effect on Taiwan after 1949. Compared with their imperial predecessors, Republican intellectuals were not only members of an educated elite but also citizens of a republic. In theory if not in practice, it was their right rather than privilege as members of the "nation" and the "people" to be heard and represented in public.

Apart from the state and the schools, a third area of change had to do with the birth of the political press, the affordability of printed materials, the creation of a postal system, and a steady rise in the urban literacy rate. The early decades of the twentieth century had witnessed, furthermore, the invention of the vernacular, the proliferation of vernacular forms of communication, the rise of radio broadcasting and film making, the spread of photo studios, and the birth of the popular press along with the advertising industry. Andrew Nathan and Leo Lee estimated that in a city like Shanghai in the early twentieth century, the literacy rate was over 80 percent among men and over 60 percent among women.[15] These urbanites were not only consumers of popular fiction—the "Mandarin Ducks and Butterflies" that Perry Link has studied, the courtesan tales that Gail Hershatter has examined, the martial arts stories that Jeffrey Kinkley and Christopher Hamm have researched; they were also audiences of popular theaters, story-telling, radio commentaries, movies, operas, and amusement shows.[16] By the mid-1930s films, plays, songs, cartoons, paintings, woodblock prints, and other forms of visual images had all become vehicles of political expression and targets of censorship action.

The expansion of this literate audience—and the diversification of the textual medium of communication—was accompanied, meanwhile, by the rise of public speech and the organization of propaganda campaigns for civic education. Sun Yat-sen and his revolutionary comrades of the 1890s were perhaps among the first ones to deliver rousing speeches as a way to mobilize followers. During the May Fourth movement in 1919 student activists organized themselves into lecture corps to explain patriotism to the people on the street. This new emphasis on verbal communication, which departed from an old bureaucratic emphasis on the written text, went hand in hand with the political discovery of the power of the people. Banners, posters, flyers, handbills, flags, and pamphlets all became ubiquitous in Republican political culture. These changes pointed to the rise of an urban public on city streets and a media in a broad sense, both of which were features of emerging cultural practices with major institutional ramifications.

Socioeconomically as well as institutionally, elite Chinese intellectuals saw their circumstances changing significantly in the first decades of the twentieth century. With the rise of the city and the emergence of the culture industry, the educated gained in autonomy with both their enhanced access to the means of public communication and their relative financial independence from the Chinese state. The 1920s and 1930s saw the formation of civic associations of all sorts. In the city of Shanghai alone no fewer than three thousand journals and magazines were in circulation on the eve of the War of Resistance in 1937. As citizens of the Republic, Chinese intellectuals spoke up on behalf of themselves as well as the people. Dissent became a mainstream activity and intellectual leadership often entailed a critical stance. Broadly speaking, each decade in the first half of the century confronted a unique set of issues and produced its high point of dissent. This record in turn underscored the institutionalized capacities and the discursive richness of intellectual dissent prior to the founding of the People's Republic in 1949.

## ≺ III ≻

### Lu Xun and the Cultural Critique of Public Speech

Old-style dissent involved Confucian officials speaking out of order yet within the bounds of the imperial bureaucracy. A weakened ruler deserved to hear what his minor officials had to say. One way to shore up support, meanwhile, was precisely to allow all the ones otherwise excluded to speak their minds. Among their first demands, nineteenth-century Chinese reformers had called for changes in the means of communication within the political system. The *yan lu* or the "path of words" simply must be broadened in order to permit the unobstructed flow of ideas and information up and down the corridors of power.

But the Qing *yan lu* proved to be blocked in many ways. Sun Yat-sen's lengthy memorial to Governor-General Li Hongzhang in 1884 was a call for the provincial authorities to open their minds to the newly emergent merchant elite in maritime trade.[17] Yet the document succeeded neither in changing views nor in stimulating discussions. Even as the court gravitated toward constitutional monarchy in the 1900s, imperial bureaucracy remained restrictive in its willingness to entertain different ideas.

With the gentry-elite spearheading a constitutional movement, leading reformers turned their attention to issues of communication in a different direction. Intellectual leaders of the 1890s believed that a nation's wealth and power rested upon the virtue, intelligence, and physical strength of its people.[18] A new mission was born to transform imperial subjects into citizens of the nation. Inspired by what he had seen in Meiji Japan, Liang Qichao was among the first to elaborate upon how popular fiction and drama could serve as vehicles of civic instruction. A leader of the constitutional movement and a founder of several influential political journals, Liang Qichao single-handedly fashioned a new prose style that was noted for its capacity to stir as well as to move. His political commentaries freely borrowed concepts and phrases from foreign languages. When Chen Duxiu and Hu Shih launched a campaign for vernacular literature in the pages of *New Youth* in 1917, their attack on the eight-legged essay in classical Chinese was in some sense but an extension of a movement that had begun with Liang.

The May Fourth movement of new culture in 1919–20 witnessed a mushrooming of vernacular journals on school campuses all across the country. In the newspaper language of their day, student activists denounced the "darkness" and "feudalism" of Chinese social customs and called for the "awakening" of the reading public to the new light of a new era. In speaking the new social "truth," these progressive youth settled upon a literary voice that supposedly allowed them to communicate directly with the people on the street. The vernacular, in short, was the medium for intellectual awakening as well as for social communication. With their vernacular revolution, their journal publications, their liberation from the bureaucratic conventions of the past, and their access to new political ideas from the West, New Culture elite of the May Fourth movement believed that they had come upon a vehicle that was at once public and transparent. The vernacular in print was not only a tool of intellectual self-emancipation; it was also an instrument for social liberation.

Against the euphoria in favor of this emerging cultural ideology, the writer Lu Xun pointed to the seeming transparency of the new language and the pitfalls in the discursive field. He was skeptical, first of all, whether the vernacular would permit meaningful mass communication, let alone the communication of "truth." He was deeply suspicious, furthermore, both of the nature of public speech and the possibilities for open exchanges in the public arena.

In his famous speech "Silent China," Lu Xun presented the picture of a public domain in which speech was the privilege of those with special access.[19] He noted that for decades there had been warfare, revolution, famine, and flood devastating many parts of China. The Chinese people presumably were suffering. Yet they had been remarkably silent about their feelings. Few had ever given voice, according to Lu Xun, to their joys or sorrow, sufferings or delight. This was, first, because only a privileged minority among the educated had acquired the ability of self-expression in writing, which had been made deliberately difficult by centuries of bureaucratic obfuscation of the Chinese language in its written form. Most common folks simply used the spoken form. But there were hundreds of spoken dialects in China, and people were simply isolated into mutually incommunicative communities. When they spoke, their plain expressions rarely went beyond the face-to-face interactions in their villages.

But the deafening silence of China had even deeper roots. For centuries, the Chinese had lived under the harsh discipline of the censorship and punishment of their rulers. This condition had deprived them, over time, of their habit of public speech. As a result, even when the Chinese of modern days have been shown the use of the vernacular that presumably emulated the spoken language, it has remained a problem for people to find their own voice. To break the deep silence of China, Lu Xun suggested, it was imperative that the people recognize their subject position in public discourse and regain their power, as citizens of the nation, to speak.

The discursive domain—the journals, newspapers, public addresses and lectures—of the new era was also a politicized arena, according to Lu Xun. Expressions in the vernacular might have appeared direct and transparent. But the modern vernacular served as a vehicle for lies, distortions, half-truths, and misinformation just as readily as for messages of value. The mediation of the publishing industry inevitably meant a separation between what an author might be preaching and what the same person was practicing. Little could be true, in fact, in this very system of communication that produced the "public." A "revolutionary cafe," for instance, was a hotbed of radical ideas for revolutionary intellectuals who produced words that incited others to action. It was also a place where the authors themselves sipped coffee and enjoyed their book proceeds.[20] Similarly, a personal diary was presumably valuable because it recorded inner truth. But a published diary must never be accepted on those same terms, because a diarist writing for a public could never be quite true to the self. Intrinsic in the process of publishing, in other words, was both the objectification of the author and the manipulation of the reader. Far from being an instrument of full communication, the print medium and the publishing industry functioned just as readily to conceal and distort the truth.

Even if an author spoke nothing but the full truth, Lu Xun went on, there remained the problem with audience. No utterance guaranteed its own audience or reception.[21] A lone protestor might wish to raise his javelin to the sky and let out a cry. But this cry might be met with total indifference. Sheer opposition often would not crush a protestor's spirit. It was the deep silence from the unfathomable indifference that annihilated the significance of his endeavor.[22]

Lu Xun's profound skepticism toward the vernacular stemmed, in the final analysis, from a distrust of public speech, especially when the development of such speech was driven by a search for influence or power. The author of hundreds of *zawen* [miscellaneous essays], he was a master of literary satire and subversion. He placed himself consistently on the sideline vis-à-vis the leaders of the contemporary intellectual scene and, with an unrelenting skepticism, scrutinized those who wielded their influence in the limelight. He was no friend, as left-wing critics were delighted to note, of the Nationalist authorities of his day. Nor, as Leo Lee shows, was he much of a follower of the Communists and their agenda.[23] His powerful presence and strong views on literature sowed the seeds, according to Merle Goldman, of factional struggles and literary dissent in China in the 1950s.[24] Whether his pessimism derived ultimately from his perception of human conditions in the age of modernity, Lu Xun projected the image of an uprooted individual in isolation who did not believe in the possibility of meaningful communication. By the logic of Lu Xun's cultural criticism, the rise of the modern publishing industry and the means of mass communication simply enhanced the capacity for those in positions of power to distort and to deceive.

≺ IV ≻

*Hu Shih and the Quest for Constitutional Government*

In the first decade of the Republic, a new generation of educated Chinese returned home from Europe and America. Unlike those who had picked up professional subjects in Japan, these were students who were drawn to the constitutional law and political philosophy in the Anglo-American system. Many of them achieved considerable scholarly reputation and held distinguished academic positions. Although small in number, they spoke with a distinct voice and wielded intellectual influence disproportionate to their numbers.

The most influential figure among them was undoubtedly the

intellectual historian and philosopher Hu Shih.[25] While still a student at Columbia University in 1918, Hu Shih earned a large reputation with his call for literary revolution in the pages of the journal *New Youth*. Upon joining the faculty of Beijing University, Hu Shih emerged, in 1919, to become one of the leading spokespersons for the New Culture Movement. Hu Shih believed in the public role of a modern intellectual and consistently maintained an active interest in current events. To create a forum, Hu Shih and fellow intellectuals launched a series of periodicals from the early 1920s on. These journals—*Endeavor*, *Crescent Moon*, *Weekly Review*, and *Independent Review*—were devoted to political commentaries in a broad sense. They argued—whether during the turmoil of the Warlord era, under the heavy-handed censorship by the Nationalist government, or at a time of growing Japanese military presence in China—in favor of principles of constitutional governance and the rule of law. The tireless advocacy and fearless criticism of these intellectuals testified to their steadfast insistence on the freedom of speech.[26]

On April 20, 1928, the new Nationalist government, which had just conducted a bloody purge of Communists from its ranks, issued an order [*mingling*] to protect human rights:

Human rights are protected by law in all nations of this world. At this time as this government takes charge, it is of urgent necessity that it establishes its foundation in law. Within the entire domain under the legal jurisdiction of the Republic of China, whether persons or organized entities, without any exception, must not invade or do harm to the body, freedom, and property of any others through unlawful practice. Those who disobey this order will be punished swiftly and severely according to law and without mercy. The Executive *Yuan* and the Jurisprudence *Yuan* are hereby ordered to generally announce this order so that all may obey in unity. This is the order.[27]

In response to the announcement, Hu Shih published two sharply worded essays: "Constitution and Human Rights" and "When May We Have a Constitution?" He called the government's proclamation on human rights "remarkable" and made three points. What did the Nationalists mean by the protection of the "body, freedom, and property" of the people, Hu asked, and what seemed to be the definition of these terms? Second, the order banned "persons" [*geren*] and "organized entities" [*tuanti*] from doing harm to others; yet why did it not mention the government and the ruling Nationalist Party? Third, the order threatened the violators with severe punishment "according to law." But what law was to apply or had such a law been adopted? Contrary to the protection of human rights that it had ordered, Hu Shih argued, the Nationalist Party-State had blatantly acted against the rights of the people and had departed from the teaching of Sun Yat-sen! Hu Shih offered several examples to describe the arbitrary punishment and arrests that had been made by the Nationalists. He urged that the new government adopt a set of constitutional guidelines as soon as possible. He warned that without them the Nationalists would be no more than a military dictatorship. Hu concluded his essays by urging the Nationalist government to draft a constitution and to place the power of the state under a basic law.[28]

In the context of its own day, a case can be made that the Nationalist government, in seizing the "human rights" initiative, was attempting to attain a monopoly in the use of violence—a monopoly that had distinguished all modern states from their feudal predecessors. The "persons" and "organized entities" targeted by the new order ranged from north China warlord regimes and the soviets of the Chinese Communist Party to village heads, clan elders, gentry leaders, large landlords, guild masters, heads of extended households, and so forth. All of these persons or entities possessed a certain capacity either to tax, to coerce, or both, whether in accordance with well-entrenched customs or newly instituted practices. They had also functioned to shield individuals from the immediate reach of the state. Nationalist authorities, in their pursuit of a state-centered vision of modernity, did not hesitate to devise legal means to aid their use of coercive force in order to achieve the leveling of all citizens under the state. Nor did they refrain from placing the Party-State above the law.

In response to Hu Shih's criticism, Nationalist authorities reacted in ways that showed little tolerance for either liberal viewpoints or public statement. The Party propaganda department pressured all newspapers not to print any of Hu Shih's essays or responses. The military police acted as if they were about to put Hu in jail. The Ministry of Education held up the certification application of China College, of which Hu Shih was the president. Irate, Hu mailed a full set of his journal essays to the deputy minister of education, Chen Bulei. Insisting that his reasonableness had been misread, Hu demanded that the latter personally examine the materials and not delegate the investigation to "some ignorant Party followers."

Hu's colleagues at the offending journal, *Crescent Moon*, determined that they were not to be silenced, printed more articles on human rights. The Nationalists banned the distribution of the magazine and forced it out of existence. The authors then collected their essays and printed a volume on human rights.[29] The accreditation application for China College meanwhile continued to stall. Heated debates erupted on the college's board of directors over what to do. Hu Shih resigned from the presidency and left Shanghai for Beijing. But not even this departure was sufficient to restore the college to the good graces of the Nationalists. The school was forced out of existence in 1932.

From the mid-1920s onward, the Nationalist Party introduced measures that were to result in the "Partification" of education and culture. A key element of this campaign was the indoctrination of students at all levels of schools, including colleges and universities, in aspects of Sun Yat-sen's social and political teachings as interpreted by Chiang Kai-shek's trusted Nationalist ideologue Dai Jitao. As part of this push to transform campus culture across the country, faculty and students were organized into groups to study these writings and to take part in public rituals that required bowing to the portraits of national leaders and saluting the national and Party flags. Students were required to pledge their allegiance to the Party and were issued uniforms to attend semi-military training. The Ministry of Education, through a variety of accreditation and certification requirements, tightened its control of the various aspects of institutional life by actively inserting itself into critical educational decisions. Ministry decisions ranged from the selection of textbooks, the establishment of curricular requirements, the hiring of faculty members, the certification of degrees, and the determination of admissions quota and criteria to the allocation of funding within each institution. Schools that failed to comply were punished severely: the degrees that they had conferred were no longer recognized, and their graduates were banned from government service—measures of major economic consequences in the context of the Republican decades.[30]

Along with fellow academics and intellectuals, Hu Shih fought these measures of control and resisted the spread of the Party's influence into the intellectual arena.[31] He treated Sun Yat-sen's writings as yet another corpus of materials for close reading and critical analysis. He offered measured endorsement for Sun's vision of a Republic with a five-power constitution. He was however quick to denounce the Nationalist authorities for departing from Sun's intent. And he was furiously opposed to the Nationalist campaign to produce blind followers of the words of Sun Yat-sen. In a day and age when even the words of God could be called into question, Hu asked, on what ground did the Nationalists stand when the authorities insisted that words of Sun and its government should be placed beyond questioning?

Instead of a Party-State with an all-powerful military leader, Hu insisted upon a civilian government in which all men, rational and thinking, stood equal before the law. In the aftermath of the Manchurian Incident in 1931, as Japanese troops took Manchuria, the Nationalists moved toward a policy of accommodation with leaders of the intellectual community. Chiang Kai-shek summoned Hu Shih for personal meetings and showered attention upon him. Hu Shih made famous his advice to the generalisimo by presenting to him a copy of *Xunzi*. Master Xunzi, Hu explained, produced disciples who became legalists rather than moralists and laid the foundation of a philosophy that placed law before ethics. So long as it was a matter beyond the bounds of law, Hu believed, a responsible ruler must refrain not only from doing evil but also from doing good. It was the integrity of the law rather than the intention of the ruler that would ultimately guarantee the common good.

Scholarly friends advised Hu Shih to spend more time on ancient texts rather than current events. Hu responded by quoting an ancient tale about a parrot. Once there was a parrot atop a mountain tree, the tale went. The branches afforded shelter and the forest his sustenance. The bird called the treetop his home. One day the forest caught fire. The bird rushed to the rescue by dipping its wings in the ocean and sprinkling drops of water over the mountain. To the parched bird the deity asked: "Why do you not see the futility of this effort and why do you not desist?" The bird replied: "It is not that I do not see the futility. This mountain was once my homeland and I just cannot bear to see it burn."[32]

"Even in ashes," wrote Hu Shih, "we remain Chinese. And our forest is burning." It was with the pathos of "burning forest" that Hu Shih, professor, journal editor, college president, and foundation chairman, spoke up on public issues in the voice of a common citizen.

≺ V ≻

*Zou Taofen and the Critique of Patriotism*

In the 1930s, Japanese military stepped up pressure against the Chinese. Within the span of three years, large parts of north China came under Japanese control. The occupation of Manchuria in September 1931 cut off from the rest of the country a major source of raw materials and tax revenue. This was followed in the next year by the creation of an autonomous region in Inner Mongolia, and, after that, by the removal of Chinese troops from north China.[33] Beijing intellectuals and their students now found their campuses directly exposed to the enemy's line of fire. On more than one occasion, college students poured unto Beijing streets and demonstrated in favor of armed resistance against the approaching enemy. Their calls for patriotic mobilization and their criticism of the Nationalist government were heard nationally. Students in Shanghai, Tianjin, Xi'an, Wuhan, Guangzhou, and elsewhere also left their classrooms. Many boarded trains and headed toward the seat of the government in Nanjing. During the height of student protests in the December Ninth Movement in 1935, tens of thousands poured into the capital to submit petitions and to demand a reversal in government policy.[34]

But the Nationalist Military Council, under the chairmanship of Chiang Kai-shek, was gaining momentum in its military campaign against Chinese Communist forces, which in 1935 had just withdrawn to China's northwest. In response to student activism, the Ministry of Education, under the firm hand of Chen Lifu, stepped up its "Partification" measures in schools and imposed additional accreditation examinations. Political instructors on college campuses were placed in charge of military training for men and nursing classes for women. College administrations were encouraged to build programs in sciences and technology to help save the nation. Programs in liberal arts and legal studies were denied admissions quota as these studies were viewed as hotbeds of anti-government agitation.

Critical sentiments against the Nationalists, however, had spilled onto the streets and could no longer be contained within college campuses. Modern means of mass communication, journals and radios included, had spread words to a much larger sector of the population in cities and towns. The use of pictorial images—films, photographs, posters, cartoons, prints, and so forth—had sent messages even to those who were not fluently literate, or had difficulty devoting time to news and books. Critics of the government found a receptive audience in the 1930s as the effects of economic recession took hold and many in industries and commerce experienced hardship. Against this backdrop the editor Zou Taofen emerged as one of the most vigorous advocates of a national policy of resistance and patriotism.

Zou Taofen's career as an editor began in the mid-1920s, upon his graduation from Shanghai's St. John's University.[35] He worked as an English secretary for Shanghai's Cotton Exchange and also for its Vocational Education Association. The Association, with the support of a group of Shanghai industrialists and education reformers, was the publisher of a weekly magazine for Shanghai's "vocational youth." The latter included shop clerks and apprentices in finance, commerce, and industry, who had attended middle schools and yet were unable to continue with their education. There were tens of thousands of these white-collar workers all over the city. They worked long hours, lived in dormitories or on shop floors, rented penny-press fiction series, and gambled if they could. The mission of the Association was to teach morality and to impart knowledge. The Association's well-intentioned yet humdrum and lackluster magazine preached in vain to a dwindling audience until Zou Taofen took over the editorship in 1926. In the next few years he turned the journal, *Shenghuo*, into one of the liveliest and most widely circulated publications in the city.

Zou Taofen's secret to success combined elements of content with those of style. The journal engaged in intimate discussions of personal life choices on matters ranging from romance, study, health, and career to money and family. It also developed an essay style that was simple, accessible, and straightforward. Zou person-

ally authored a majority of these articles, each a few hundred
characters in length. He wrote for people with jobs to do and he
saw them as reading on the run. His essays convey simple messages with clarity. They mixed preaching with storytelling, the
prescriptive with the dramatic or even the graphic. *Shenghuo* articles, furthermore, addressed issues of pragmatic utility. The journal sold not just by telling people why they were discontented, but
by giving advice about how to find feasible remedies. It cajoled,
aroused, entertained, and sympathized all at once, speaking in an
avuncular voice that sent warnings as well as assurances, earning
confidence while giving directions. A journal that sought to capture an audience on the move, *Shenghuo* came into its own when
successfully capturing the chaotic dynamism of the commercial
hub. Zou Taofen in that sense was among the very first to land
upon a literary formula that permitted effective communication
with a mass audience with short attention span and limited sophistication.

The dissenting potential of Zou Taofen's enterprise was realized in the early 1930s, when, after the creation of Japan's puppet
state Manchukuo in the former Manchuria in 1931, Zou turned
his publishing activities into crusades against the Japanese as well
as the Nationalists. The war drove home a sense of doom among a
population already struggling with the woes of recession. Left-
wing journals gained popularity in the city, presenting images of
flood, famine, rural bankruptcy, and displaced provincials. It was a
widely accepted notion among Shanghai intellectuals in the foreign concessions that the government of Chiang Kai-shek had not
only ignored the founding doctrines of Sun Yat-sen but was also
about to betray the interest of the Chinese people. In addition to
essays, *Shenghuo* turned to the use of photographed images to help
portray the humiliation of defeat and the incompetence of the Nationalist authorities. The journal's circulation hit a record high in
the aftermath of war between Japanese and Chinese troops in
Shanghai in early 1932, selling more than 150,000 copies each issue. It ran special editions on the war, with page after page of pic-
tures accompanied by simple captions. It called for an end to
power struggle and an immediate cease-fire between the government and its domestic rivals. It urged the creation of a broad and
firm alliance in a war of resistance against the real enemy. *Shen-*

*ghuo* was banned from further publication in the spring of 1932. Zou Taofen's plan to launch a daily newspaper was also canceled despite popular support. For nearly a whole year Zou was forced to travel away from China, yet he launched new journals almost as soon as he returned to Shanghai and persisted in his critique throughout the rest of his career.

In 1934, in the aftermath of the pullout of Chinese troops from the Beijing area, Zou and six other public figures organized a National Salvation Association in Shanghai. Dubbed the "Seven Gentlemen," these men who led the association included lawyers, bankers, publishers, and educational reformers. The Association called upon the support of white-collar employees working in the city's financial, professional, and commercial sectors. These employees formed vocational associations by firms and by trade. They built social networks through the organization of cultural activities ranging from song festivals, drama groups, literacy classes, and night schools to reading clubs and correspondence societies. They staged street rallies and held public gatherings. Some of these song festivals, held at sports stadia and featuring songs of patriotism, drew crowds of tens of thousands of people. Pamphlets and biweeklies calling for war and national salvation were widely distributed. Plays were written satirizing Chinese officials bending to the will of foreign powers.

Zou and his colleagues led the Association under the banner of two slogans: the "emancipation of the Chinese people" from Japanese and all colonial powers, and "the democratic reconstruction of Chinese polity" against all dictatorial regimes including the Nationalists. During the December Ninth Movement of student patriotic protests in late 1935, the National Salvation Association was at the center of the mass demonstrations in Shanghai calling for the Nationalists to reform and to reverse policies. Zou and his colleagues represented themselves as the "voice of the people" and showed a growing empathy with the Chinese Communist movement. Nationalist authorities banned the activities of the Association, placed all seven leaders under arrest, put them on trial, and sentenced them all to jail. It was not until after the release of Chiang Kai-shek by his military abductors in the Xi'an Incident in December 1936,[36] when the Nationalist government, under pressure, reversed its policies on war, that the Seven Gentlemen were allowed to go free. The civic associations that they had fostered, with all their institutionalized cultural activities, meanwhile became strongholds for left-wing patriotic mobilization once the War of Resistance broke out.

≺ VI ≻

### *Wu Han and the Use of History*

With the outbreak of the War of Resistance in the summer of 1937, significant changes took place in the Chinese intellectual arena. That September returning students of Beijing's leading public universities were asked to report to temporary campus locations in Changsha. Military developments soon made it necessary that the universities relocate even further into China's southwest. After a few more moves, a group of college seniors, predominantly male and escorted by a dozen or so faculty members, embarked upon a thousand-mile journey on foot that took them, after three months, to Kunming.[37] Displaced and isolated, these intellectuals found themselves dependent upon the state for support. The Ministry of Education issued clothing and shoes in addition to stipends. Tuition was free, as was room and board. Still, as the war dragged on, rampant inflation eroded income and crippled the economy. To make ends meet, Chen Yinke, Qinghua's most distinguished historian and classicist, sold whole collections of books and reference works in exchange for hard currency. Wen Yiduo, a poet and literary scholar, took orders cutting seals to support his large family. Others resorted to what impoverished scholars traditionally did, selling calligraphy and looking for editorial assignments. Economic hardship spelled the end of urban civic associations if not also the pursuit of scholarship.

Censorship control intensified meanwhile as the state now had at its disposal one of the largest military intelligence apparatus that had ever been built in China's long history.[38] The special service was created to fight the Japanese yet the machinery was just as often turned toward internal surveillance. Almost as soon as the war broke out, meanwhile, long lists of goods came under the control of special economic agencies armed with new regulations and laws. The supply of paper, for instance, became a matter of rationing. Travel, telecommunication, transportation, and postal service were matters that drew attention from the secret service. The growing power of the military and the rise of the bureaucracy in the everyday life of the ordinary people afforded many opportunities for abuse as well as corruption.

A group of historians turned their scholarship into biting criticisms of the circumstances of their time. The leading figure among them was the Qinghua historian Wu Han, a specialist of Ming (1368–1644) dynastic history. Wu Han's work of this period included a biography of the dynasty's founder, Zhu Yuanzhang.[39] Wu depicted the Ming founder as an autocrat who built a reign of terror through the spying on his subjects, the torture and imprisonment of college students, the execution of able ministers, and the suppression of the freedom of public speech. In Wu's judgment the first emperor of Ming had put in place one of the most repressive regimes in Chinese history. It was only natural, as depicted in the late Ming fiction *Jingpingmei* [Golden Plum] that the dynasty should preside, at the height of its material affluence, over a society rotten to the core, and it was only a matter of time before the regime would crumble.[40]

Wu Han delved into historical materials not only for scholarly essays but also for the *zawen*, commentaries on current events that covered a whole range of miscellaneous topics. Was there tyranny in China's past, he asked rhetorically. The tyrants and despots of the past were far more constrained, he concluded, than the ones of the present, for the former empowered censors and controlled themselves. How did dynastic rulers contend with issues of official corruption? During the Song, by paying its officials well and thus buying their integrity; during the Ming, by swift and cruel punishment, thus intimidating them into integrity. But neither approach produced long-lasting effects over time, and corrupt officials inevitably brought down dynasties. Dynastic rulers, in short, heeded the voice of their critics and curbed the abuse of power. It was modern rulers who had broken all rules of decency.

Wu Han and his colleagues believed that given time, all truth would come out on its own accord, and that the judgment of the "people" contained no error. Powerholders might succeed in silencing the voice of the people in the short run. But there was no escape from the judgment of history. If any further proof was necessary, the sort of work that he produced—the kind of historical judgment he passed—attested to the rising voice of the people in history.

With his twin emphases on "history" and the "people," Wu Han established his reputation as a leading progressive intellectual of the 1940s. A notable figure in the democratic league, he also offered his sympathy to the Chinese Communist movement. More than anyone among his contemporaries, Wu Han pioneered the technique of "shadowy history" [yingshe lishi], that is, the use of historical parallels to deliver a critical point on current events. A strategy devised to circumvent obstacles in an environment in which government censorship suppressed the open expression of dissenting views, "shadowy history" amounted to an encoded language that depended upon the participation of an initiated audience to infer and to interpret the message. The discrepancy between the surface and the hidden texts opened up an interpretive space. Authors were enrolled not only to elude the censors but also to ridicule the presumably literal-minded authorities. The text, in other words, functioned as a vehicle of dissent not for what had been stated in the open but for the interpretive readings that it elicited—readings that took place surreptitiously as well as subversively.

Wu Han escaped the fate of other critics of the Nationalist regime—Li Gongpu and Wen Yiduo, for example, prominent public intellectuals who were gunned down in 1946 by military intelligence agents. After the founding of the People's Republic, Wu received appointments to high-ranking Party positions, including the deputy mayoralty of Beijing. He continued to enjoy eminence and visibility in the printed pages in the public arena, just as momentous changes were taking place to transform the structure of intellectual life under the new Republic.

≺ VII ≻

*The Communist Literary System and Dissenting Practice*

In their relationship with the political authorities, Chinese intellectuals continued to "advise and dissent" throughout the course of the twentieth century.[41] The founding of the People's Republic in 1949, however, marked the rise to power of a Party-State under the self-proclaimed philosopher/historian Mao Zedong.[42] State management of "differences within the people" entered a new era and the ramifications were broad and profound.[43]

Printing and publishing industries, for instance, underwent socialization in the 1950s. The reorganization closed the book market and brought to an end commercial publishing. As the decade wore on the printed medium also came under intensified ideological scrutiny. Writers, artists, journalists, and intellectuals now became registered members in organized work units or associations and received compensations by rank. The bureaucratization of writing and publishing amounted to a socialization of literary, artistic, and scholarly production under the watch of the Party-State.[44]

The 1950s meanwhile witnessed education campaigns that changed scholarly vocabularies and reoriented the educated to a framework of reference centered upon studies of Marxism-Leninism and of the Soviet Union. Major political campaigns took place from time to time to weed out class enemies and to eradicate misguided lines of thinking. The campaign against Hu Feng and Feng Xuefeng in the second half of the 1950s resulted in the long incarceration of prominent writers and literary theorists of the 1930s and 1940s. In the cultural arena a "system" had been put in place that not only restricted intellectual options but also restructured the intellectuals' relationship with the Party-State.[45] Post-1949 dissent, in comparison with the Republican period, took on a different character. For the purpose of this discussion we will briefly note the following points.

There was, first, a subtle but important shift in the dynamics of compliance and defiance between individuals and the state. Dissenting practice became more problematic than ever, and this was because Party political culture now placed a high premium not on mere compliance but on an active performance of positive consent. One might observe that decades of political mobilization, under the Nationalists as well as the Communists, had produced a mass culture of the streets as well as the squares that was a complex theater of slogans, rallies, marches, protests, speeches, posters, and more. Under the Communists, the dynamics of Party-orchestrated mass campaigns further fashioned a culture of fervent pursuits, instant results, ardent talks, and relentless activism. Under the PRC the Chinese were no longer a nation mired in mute ignorance as in the "silent China" of the 1920s, but a people accustomed to an abundance of rehearsed and staged public speeches. Silence among the stylized voluble was no mere silence; it was either the result of enforced expulsion from the comradeship of speech or a gesture of withdrawal from an unreserved manifestation of solidarity. Public space was not where differences were articulated but where uniformity was performed. As no rightful disagreement was logically plausible, dissent was tantamount to deviation. And the very ambiguity of silence, as it implied a deliberate withholding of active consent, made it a punishable act of dissension.

A second point had to do with the disappearance of the wilderness and the expanded reach of the state beyond the traditional range of its institutional capacity. The combined use of print, media, statistics, and maps had produced a system of administrative knowledge that placed every single village evenly under the grasp of the state. In the new republic of three quarters of a million production brigades and many more commune cadres, furthermore, tractor factories and fertilizer quota were often the most tangible returns and rewards for hard-line Party allegiance. In the 1930s and 1940s, the Nationalist leader Chiang Kai-shek was able to permit himself, in the heat of a political struggle, the grand gesture of "going into wilderness" [xiaye] by withdrawing to his countryside home. Chiang's Communist successors, by contrast, could only be "sent down" [xiafang] without being sent "away." Thanks to the steady intensification of state institutional development, there was simply no room left for the existence of Buddhist caves or Daoist gardens for recluses and mystics. The "out" had been tamed to become merely the "low" or "base," from where thousands of villagers looked up to the sky to welcome the sight of crop-dusting helicopters dispensing pesticides.

≺ VIII ≻

*Conclusion*

From Lu Xun's dark skepticism to Hu Shih's measured reasoning, from Zou Taofen's impassioned plea to Wu Han's submerged anger, there was a rich and vibrant tradition of political criticism in the first half of China's twentieth century. Against the backdrop of profound institutional and ideological changes, intellectuals from a broad spectrum of political opinions spoke up on matters of public concern. Their criticisms covered a whole range of issues from culture, language, social justice, and state policies to the national polity. Their critical voice persisted despite the intensification of the state's power to control.

Those who spoke up under the Nationalists often found themselves targets of violence or suppression. Some were jailed and others lost their lives. But the power of intellectuals in modern Chinese society was not to be underestimated after all. Republican intellectuals played a crucial role setting the tone of public discussion. The disaffection of progressive intellectuals, Zou Taofen and Wu Han included, corroded the legitimacy of the Nationalist government and contributed to its ultimate downfall in 1949.[46]

Through the modern publishing industry, the press, and academic institutions, Republican Chinese intellectuals maintained the elite standing of their Confucian predecessors and found new ways to turn their words into power. After the founding of the People's Republic in 1949, institutional and ideological changes continued to transform the conditions under which Chinese intellectuals worked. The bureaucratization of culture and the "work unit" system put in place an intricate set of relationships that bound the intellectuals and their lifetime prospects to the new state. Chinese intellectuals became cultural workers under the People's Republic. This did not, however, spell the decline of their importance. When de-collectivization occurred in the 1980s, the creation of the "velvet prison" underscored the centrality of the intellectuals to the socialist political system that had functioned both to enhance and to reduce their standing.

In the early decades of the People's Republic, critique and criticisms became central features in intellectual life. Post-1949 criticisms followed the directions of Party ideologues rather than dissenting instincts. No longer a loner's javelin pointed to the sky or a muted cry drowned in the silence of wilderness, these critiques were publicized and promoted in either the Party press or political rituals. Major journals, newspapers, and publishing houses closely observed the ideological guidelines handed down by the propaganda department of the Party's Central Committee. Critiques and debates on the ideological front, meanwhile, were inextricably bound up with the Party's internal differences over policy issues.

In 1957 Mao Zedong mounted a massive campaign to collectivize Chinese agriculture and to induce a Great Leap Forward in production. The campaign turned out to be a leap into a major economic disaster that resulted in the worst famine in recorded human history.[47] During these years the historian Wu Han published a series of articles on Hai Rui, a minor Ming official who crossed his superiors and sacrificed his career in order to protect the lawful rights of the people. In 1961 Wu Han finished a play, "Hai Rui's Dismissal from Office."[48] It dramatized the official's popularity with the people. It also ended on a high note celebrating Hai Rui's audacious confrontation with the emperor.

Wu's play came on the heels of a charged Central Committee meeting on Lushan in the summer of 1959, when Defense Minister Peng Denghuai attacked Mao Zedong for policy failings with regard to the Great Leap Forward. Wu Han in the 1960s might not have intended to use late Ming events as shadow history to critique the Communist Party Chairman as he did in the 1940s with the Nationalist Generalissimo. But the interpretive space that had once existed under the Nationalists between the surface and the hidden structures of the text, between writing in the open and reading in private, had now been compressed under the new regime. The realm of personal practices, in effect, had been appropriated by the public regime. In 1965, amidst deepening divisions over the Party's economic policies, Mao chose to read Wu's play as a veiled attack on himself, the "emperor," and a show of sympathy for the disgraced Minister of Defense, Peng Dehuai. The play, so it went, projected Peng as a modern Hai Rui pleading for the people and against the policies of the Leap.[49] Orchestrated critiques of Wu Han's play in Party press began with the publication, in the Shanghai newspaper *Wenhui Daily*, of an essay entitled "A Critique of the New Historical Play, 'Hai Rui's Dismissal from Office'," by Yao Wenyuan, an editor and a seasoned Party "stick." The critique, which appeared on November 10, 1965, declared that the historian's play was a "poisonous weed" aimed at the Communist Party and socialism. The essay mounted the ideological campaign that was to claim the lives of Wu and his family as the first victims of the Cultural Revolution (1966–76).[50]

It was both a paradox and an irony that public criticisms, which early twentieth-century intellectuals had mounted against political authorities, should have become, half a century later, tools in the hands of the authorities against the intellectuals. The May Fourth generation, in launching the vernacular revolution, had invested much hope in a new language that, by giving voice to the voiceless, promised to unleash the power of the people. In those heady days of youthful optimism, few seemed to heed Lu Xun's dark warnings that it was a potent formula of unpredictable consequences if words were to become power and vice versa. As the century progressed, the "Voice of the People" became institutionalized in the commands of the Central Committee of the Chinese Communist Party. The power of this voice was only for those who had been declared a target of the "democratic dictatorship of the people" to know.

In the post-Mao era many Chinese gained renown, in the pages of *The New York Times* and *The New York Review of Books* as well as other mainstream Western media, as leading advocates of human rights, freedom, Western-style liberal and democratic ideals, and other forms of autonomy. Debates among Chinese intellectuals unfolded with intensity. Major dimensions of Chinese intellectual life regained vitality.

Against this search for resistance heroes of liberal conscience, Geremie Barme argues that post-Mao policies of marketization have given rise to "commodified socialism" instead of market capitalism in China. Thought control had not been relaxed in the 1990s. Instead, the Communist Party had been able to advance its position by availing itself of market techniques of advertising and image manipulation. "Many of the possibilities of critical public cultures in China have themselves been subverted," Barme suggests. Communist symbolism now reached into realms opened up by commercial mechanisms.[51]

Barme recognizes the impact of market incentives and the outside world on Chinese intellectual activities in the Deng era. But instead of liberalizing Chinese intellectuals to speak their minds and work in ways of their own choice, outside (Taiwan, Hong

Kong, and the West) interest in Communist China had turned signs of dissent into images and stories for consumption. A non-event, Barme suggests, could be turned into a cause celebre if there were signs of Party suppression. To the extent that the world at large expected the Communist system to be totalitarian, Chinese artists enhanced their marketable value if they performed the part of persecuted dissidents under Party tyranny.[52] The disappointment of the Deng era was the corruption of dissent, however authentically intended, by its systematic appropriation by the forces of commercialization.

Barme's comments draw attention to the corrupting impact of both the market and the limelight on the individuals. It also brings this discussion full circle back to the earlier point in the century, when Lu Xun voiced his skepticism about the public space as a forum for truthful communication on significant subjects. What, then, do we learn from a history of the discourses of dissent over the course of China's twentieth century? Is it mainly and inescapably a tale about the triumph of state power over intellectual autonomy? Is it principally a chronicle of demise, whether that of the dissidents under Party dictatorship or that of dissent itself in a system of market economy?

Post-imperial Chinese discourses of dissent, as this chapter shows, have been fashioned through vigorous encounters with the growing power of the state. For decades in the twentieth century, Chinese intellectuals claimed the right though they did not enjoy the security of speech in public. This condition did not detract from the ideas that the intellectuals sought to advance. Talks of rights, citizenship, the power of the people, and the judgment of history gained expanding currency in Chinese politics. Slowly but surely, a new constitutional rhetoric, centered upon the sovereignty of the people, took hold.

On the basis of the performed and the articulated, post-imperial China has produced a complex and variegated tradition of intellectual dissent. There has developed, over time, a rich repertoire of symbolic acts. There has also emerged a growing consensus of a political language that is centered upon the people. The consensus alone is no small accomplishment. It provides the basis, in the days after the eclipse of the canonical authority of Confucian classics, of a common language that enables the discussion of public affairs across a wide spectrum of Chinese society.

But the social practice and cultural politics of public speech remained problematic, despite the emergence of a unifying rhetoric that at times promised democratizing possibilities. One might take the view that issues with autonomy, integrity, courage, and authenticity, implied in Lu Xun's pessimism and amplified in Barme's critique, might not be unique to the Chinese intellectual scene. But Chinese history of the past century produced particular circumstances that placed Chinese dissenting discourses on a different base.

It is over a century since Liang Qichao, in search of a post-Confucian Chinese nation, turned to the notion of a political community of the Chinese people. The history of dissent since Liang's time has been a history of contestations between the state and the intellectuals over the representation of the people. A sovereign people in solidarity are seen as the legitimate source of all power. Both in state ideology and in dissenting discourse, much energy has been invested in the construction of such solidarity. Yet the people's voices are many. Their unison, more often than not, turns out to be elusive and fictitious at best.

In the 1990s the discursive context of Chinese dissent again significantly changed. Debates over human rights and democratic freedom were no mere domestic issues but an intricate part of international politics. Western liberals debated Western socialists over Chinese human rights records and Chinese prospects for democracy. Internal and external audiences overlapped and intersected with each other, meanwhile, when Chinese intellectuals spoke in public. Local and global issues converged, and as a result late twentieth-century Chinese discourses of dissent were often not just about dissent. They had become, in addition, part of an international discourse of dissent that was more concerned with China's place in the world than other issues. Some in China welcomed this departure while others resisted it. Whichever position one might have chosen, it was difficult to reject the emerging consensus: to retain their voice in this internationalized context, Chinese intellectuals, whether dissenting or not, must now learn to speak in a new language that had not been their own.

# The Stalinization of the People's Republic of China

ARLEN MELIKSETOV AND ALEXANDER PANTSOV

T HE CONVENTIONAL VIEW of the early years of the People's Republic of China, shared by Chinese, Western, and Russian historiography, is that these years can be divided into two very distinctive periods—that of so-called "new democracy" or "bourgeois-
democratic revolution" (1949–53) and that of "socialist construction along the Soviet lines" (1953–58). The division implies that until 1953, Mao and the Maoists tried their best to implement their
own tactics and strategy, which were different from the Soviet ones.
They took into account the fact that China was more backward
than Russia and therefore was not ready for Socialism. The process
of Stalinization—the implementation of the Stalinist totalitarian
model of political, social, and economic transition—began in China
sometime in 1953.[1] Some scholars argue that the rapid end of the
new democratic phase was "unexpected."[2] Others point out that it
is still difficult to understand "exactly why" the Chinese in 1953
chose the Soviet model.[3]

At first sight this understanding appears to conform to the historical facts. The Chinese Communist Party (CCP) indeed came to
power not under the banner of Socialism, Communism, or Stalinism. The party appealed to national, rather than social, concerns of
its countrymen. During the Anti-Japanese War of 1937–45 and the
so-called Third Civil War of 1946–49, which the CCP waged
against its historic opponent, the Chinese Nationalist Party [Guo-
mindang, or GMD], the CCP abandoned its image of a political organization based on the principles of the "class struggle" and "proletarian internationalism." It did not seek a radical proletarian
revolution, but rather social reforms along the lines of the late
Chinese President Sun Yat-sen's Three Principles of the People:

Nationalism, Democracy, and People's Livelihood (the latter indicating various social and economic programs that would benefit the majority of people). The CCP gave a liberal interpretation of Sun Yat-sen's ideas, promising to guarantee private ownership and to stimulate national private business, to protect the domestic market and to attract foreign investments only under strict state control, to lower taxes and to develop a multi-party system, to organize a coalition government and to maintain democratic freedoms.

This doctrine of the "new democracy," as Mao Zedong himself claimed, differed from the "old Western democracy" since it was carried out under the leadership of the Communist Party.[4] Mao set forth the new line in December 1939 in his article "The Chinese Revolution and the Chinese Communist Party" and then in January 1940 in his brochure *On New Democracy*.[5] He then developed it in a number of subsequent writings as well as in his famous speech at the Seventh Party Congress, April–June 1945, *On Coalition Government*.[6]

In their struggle against the Guomindang the Communists relied on the Chinese democratic tradition. It would be a great mistake to suppose that in the first half of the twentieth century China was a country without a democratic tradition. Many factors stimulated the substantial renovation of Chinese political culture. Among them were the victory of the anti-monarchical Xinhai revolution of 1911–12; the promulgation of the Republic on January 1, 1912; the adoption of the 1912 Constitution; the election to the first Parliament and the parliamentary debates; the opposition to Sun Yat-sen's successor, President Yuan Shikai, and Yuan's plans for monarchical restoration; the collaboration and competition between the CCP and the GMD within the first united front of 1924–27; the student and labor movements; and, finally, the declaration of the "new democracy." The New Culture movement of 1915, the anti-imperialist May Fourth movement of 1919, the "debate about Socialism" of 1918–22, and the anti-Japanese December 9th movement of 1935 also strengthened the democratic inclination of the Chinese intelligentsia. Many of the intellectuals were extremely active in the political and ideological struggle, and it was this part of the population that enthusiastically followed Mao Zedong's "new democracy."

In sharp contrast, during the Anti-Japanese War the GMD leader Chiang Kai-shek adhered to a tough *étatist* interpretation of Sun Yat-sen's ideas. He declared it necessary to assert state control over the economy and over private ownership, to promote the collectivization of agriculture, to strengthen the GMD political monopoly, and to persecute dissidents.[7] These views alienated the liberals, and the GMD ultimately found itself isolated.

The CCP managed to take advantage of the situation and unite all non-GMD liberal forces. During the civil war the GMD was totally defeated, and by the end of 1949 the CCP had taken over mainland China. On September 30, 1949, the Communists organized a multi-party Coalition Government, and on October 1 Mao Zedong proclaimed the People's Republic of China. For the next three years the PRC remained a "new democratic" state. It is true that it maintained especially friendly relations with the Soviet Union and its satellites; it vigorously opposed Western imperialism and fought against United Nation troops in Korea during the war of 1950–53. But it is also true that in this period, at least formally, the PRC did not copy the Stalinist economic and political model which implied priority in the development of heavy industry, strong centralized economic planning, huge spending on national defense, elimination of private property, collectivization of the peasantry, and one-party rigid control over the political and intellectual life of the citizens. The Chinese Communists officially proclaimed the onset of the Socialist construction only in 1953 and then successfully went on Stalinizing China until the Great Leap Forward of 1958.

These are all well-known facts. The question of the Stalinization of the PRC, however, is not as simple as it may have seemed. Important documents found in Soviet and Chinese archives shed new light on this issue.[8]

≺ I ≻

*Stalin, Mao, and the "New Democratic"*
*Revolution in China*

The available documents demonstrate conclusively that Mao's "new democratic" policy in no way contradicted the general course of the world Communist movement directed by Stalin himself. The "new democratic" policy of the CCP was in total agreement with the "people's democratic" shift of international Communism as a whole.

This shift took place during and after the Seventh Comintern Congress of 1935. It was then that Stalin began to anticipate a real Nazi menace to the Soviet Union. This anticipation was the primary reason he started to change Communist tactics as he sought allies among the democratic nations. Needless to say, in his armchair calculations he was far from abandoning his strategic goal of the ultimate Communist conquest of the world.[9] He was simply engaging in maneuvers that, in essence, were aimed at trying to deceive the West. During World War II Stalin even dissolved the Comintern. According to Yugoslavian Communist Milovan Djilas's memoirs, the idea of dissolving the Comintern first arose "around the time the Baltic states were joining the Soviet Union,"[10] that is, around 1940. Here is what Stalin himself revealed in 1944: "The situation with the Comintern was becoming more and more abnormal . . . the Comintern was pulling in its own direction—and the discord grew worse."[11] It was deception that constituted the foundation of Stalin's "people's democracy," and in his private talks with his comrades-in-arms the Bolshevik leader made no secret of it. As Djilas recalled,

The substance of his suggestions was, on the one hand, that we ought not to "frighten" the English, by which he meant that we ought to avoid anything that might alarm them into thinking that a revolution was going on in Yugoslavia or an attempt at Communist control. "What do you want with red stars on your caps? The form is not important but what is gained, and you—red stars! By God, stars aren't necessary!" Stalin exclaimed angrily.[12]

This policy would also facilitate the Communists' takeover of their own countries after the war. In their capacity as national "democratic" parties the Communist organizations could most likely establish their hegemony over a relatively broad coalition of nationalist forces. After all, Stalin would only benefit from the triumph of his satellites.

While seeking victory he could be quite cautious regarding its results. As a Russian National Communist, Stalin must have worried about the future emergence of new mighty centers of Communist power. A Communist Yugoslavia or even more plausibly a Communist China, which would accomplish the same Soviet model of a short-cut economic modernization by dictatorial means, might create a challenge to his hegemony over the Communist world. Limiting the ambitions of foreign Communists to the "democratic" tasks of their own indigenous revolutions, Stalin bound them to himself and subordinated their policy to his.

Stalin's worries about a mighty China could have been aggravated by his steady suspicion that Mao Zedong was more a "peasant Nationalist" than a Communist. The rise of the Chinese revolution in the countryside led by Mao seemed to refute the ideas of Marx, Lenin, and Stalin himself in regard to the "historical role" of the working class. Mao had never traveled to Moscow, and Stalin did not know him personally. But the Kremlin constantly received letters from Soviet informers both inside and outside the CCP accusing Mao of being an "anti-Leninist" and a "Trotskyite." One of these informers was an ex-leader of the CCP delegation to the Comintern, Wang Ming, Mao's most aggressive antagonist. Wang sent his information to Stalin in 1942–45 via the Soviet representatives to the CCP Central Committee A. Ya. Orlov (Terebin) and Peter P. Vladimirov (Vlasov).[13] Vladimirov had also provided Moscow with unpleasant characteristics of the Chinese Communist leader.[14] It is not surprising that Stalin, according to Nikita S. Khrushchev's recollections, called Mao "a primitive Marxist."[15]

We cannot underestimate Stalin's dogmatic approach to Marxist historical materialism. According to Stalin's views,[16] the length of a path to Socialism depended on a level of socio-economic development of a particular country after the Communist takeover. The less economically advanced countries would have to go through a much longer preliminary period than would Russia before getting to Socialism. This period would resemble that of the Soviet New Economic Policy (NEP) of the 1920s. Even if Stalin himself and also his close confederates were indeed much more radical in their practices than they were in theory, they still fanatically observed some kind of sacramental religious ritual while preaching how to achieve Socialism.

When World War II ended in 1945 the first factor that determined Stalin's shift—the existence of the anti-fascist coalition—

no longer prevailed. The Communist takeovers in a number of countries in subsequent years also invalidated the second factor—the Communists had no longer to play a role of national "democratic" parties to facilitate their revolutions. Stalin's fear of a multi-polar Communist world, however, and his adherence to theoretical dogmas did not disappear, but rather actually increased. So did his suspicions of Mao, especially after the 1948 "Yugoslavian shock"—the break with the Yugoslavian Communist Joseph Broz Tito, who had been considered by Moscow as one of its closest satellites but had unexpectedly demonstrated no obedience. Shortly after the "Tito affair," Stalin in his private talks to his confidants began to look increasingly puzzled by a new possible threat—now from China: "What kind of a man is Mao Zedong? He has some special, peasant views, he seems to be afraid of workers and isolates his army from the urban population."[17]

In 1945–49, in his geopolitical strategy Stalin also had to take into account the newly emerged monopoly of the United States on nuclear weapons. Being unprepared to counteract a plausible American nuclear attack, he was obliged to try his best not to provoke Washington. The Yalta secret agreement among the Great Powers (February 1945) and the Soviet-GMD Treaty of Friendship and Alliance (August 1945) limited his initiative as well. They both benefited the Soviet Union, providing Moscow with some economic, political, and territorial concessions in the Far East. Needless to say, Stalin did not want to jeopardize these benefits by actively supporting the CCP. Thus shortly after World War II the Kremlin leader began to display his doubts about the Chinese Communists' abilities to take power. In the fall of 1945, he even advised Mao Zedong "to come to a temporary agreement" with Chiang Kai-shek.[18] However, he overcame this "deviation" quite quickly when Mao Zedong assured him that the CCP would contend with all difficulties.[19] Still, until the successful test of a Soviet atom bomb in August 1949, his policy in the Chinese Civil War was cautious.[20]

All the factors that conditioned Stalin's moderate approach to the Socialist revolution in China affected the CCP. It is noteworthy that Mao Zedong began to expound his "new democratic" ideas right at the time when the idea of dissolving the Comintern first occurred to Stalin. Was this a mere coincidence? Apparently not. Mao might have not had "much good feeling" about Stalin,[21] but he perfectly understood that his own struggle for power in China could be successful only if the CCP had Soviet military and economic support. Therefore, it was necessary that he be extremely loyal to Stalin, in particular as he was aware of Stalin's suspicious nature. That is why, for example, in his telegram of August 28, 1948, while describing to Stalin the issues he would like to discuss with him during his future visit to the Soviet Union, Mao declared: "We should come to agreement in order to make our political course totally in line with that of the USSR."[22] As he did with the Yugoslavian Communist leaders in 1944, Stalin also periodically cooled Mao's true Communist excitement. Strange as it may seem, documentary evidence indicates that during the official struggle for New Democracy, Mao Zedong was more rigid than Stalin. With respect to New Democracy, he was even reluctant or negative but continued to follow its course in order to placate the Moscow leader.[23]

It was Stalin rather than Mao who tried to show that the CCP had allegedly distanced itself from the Bolshevik party. Moscow refused to receive the head of the CCP until the People's Republic of China was proclaimed. From late 1947 Mao constantly expressed his yearning to meet Stalin but Stalin did not want to welcome him and give the West a pretext to declare Mao "a Soviet agent." Instead in January 1949 he sent the Politburo member Anastas I. Mikoyan on a secret mission to the Chinese Communist headquarters in Xibaipo in Hebei, to discuss the most important issues. Among these issues there was one that dealt with the nature of the future New Democratic power in China. Here is what Mao Zedong wrote about it in his November 30, 1947, telegram to Stalin: "In the period of the final victory of the Chinese revolution, following the example of the USSR and Yugoslavia, all political parties except the CCP should leave the political scene, which will significantly strengthen the Chinese revolution."[24] This thesis apparently contradicted what Mao himself wrote in his *On Coalition Government*. Moreover, it opposed the entire course of New Democracy, which aimed at creating a multi-party system in China.

Stalin responded in a telegram of April 20, 1948, in which he said,

We do not agree with this. We think that the various opposition parties in China which represent the middle strata of the Chinese population and are opposing the Guomindang clique will exist for a long time. And the CCP will have to involve them for cooperation against the Chinese reactionary forces and imperialist powers, while keeping hegemony, i.e., the leading position, in its hands. It is possible that some representatives of these parties will have to be included in the Chinese people's democratic government and the government itself has to be proclaimed a coalition government in order to widen the base of this government among the population and to isolate imperialists and their Guomindang agents. It is necessary to keep in mind that the Chinese government in its policy will be a national revolutionary-democratic government, not a Communist one, after the victory of the People's Liberation Armies in China, at any rate in the period immediately after the victory, the length of which is difficult to define now.[25]

Stalin then further elaborated this idea, pointing out that

[t]his means that nationalization of all land and abolition of private ownership of land, confiscation of the property of all industrial and trade bourgeoisie from petty to big, confiscation of property belonging not only to big landowners but to middle and small holders exploiting hired labor, will not be fulfilled for the present. These reforms have to wait for some time.[26]

Mao seemed to accept Stalin's point of view without reservation and in his April 26, 1948, telegram to Stalin put the whole responsibility for "leftist tendencies" on local CCP leaders, informing Stalin that these tendencies "have already been thoroughly corrected."[27]

Nevertheless, as early as September 1948 Mao Zedong tried to revise the CCP's political course. Now he looked at the matter from an economic point of view. At the meeting of the Politburo he maintained that Socialism would occupy a leading position in China's economy even during the period of New Democracy. After the revolution, he continued, the Communist state would expropriate the so-called bureaucratic capital of the GMD officials and would nationalize all other big industrial, commercial, and banking enterprises, thereby establishing the socialist economy.[28] The Politburo members seemed to support this idea, and Liu Shaoqi, who was the second in command, even elaborated on it, making a statement that "in the new democratic economy the main contradiction is that between Capitalism (capitalists and rich peasants) and Socialism." At the same time it was Liu who noted that the

CCP could not "adopt a political course toward Socialism too early."[29]

In January–February 1949, during his meetings with Mao, Mikoyan again made the Soviet position clear to the CCP leader. Mao formally affirmed his acceptance,[30] but shortly after that, while anticipating the inevitable triumph of the Communist Party in its fight with the Guomindang, he tried to get back to his radical premise. At the time Mao once again inclined to abandoning the notion of a New Democratic revolution in light of how the situation in China would likely develop after the CCP's military and political victories of 1948 and 1949. He was about to do so in order to stimulate the revolutionary process and transcend what he saw as the limited scope of New Democracy. Characteristically, in his report to the Central Committee second plenary session in March 1949, Mao Zedong almost completely avoided mention of the New Democratic revolution, using the phrase "popular democratic revolution" instead. The resolution of the second plenary session indicates what difference Mao could imply while contrasting these terms. It contended that in countries of Eastern Europe, which at the time were considered to be "people's or popular democracies," "the existence and development of Capitalism . . . the existence and development of free trade and competition . . . are limited and cramped."[31] As for the notion of a New Democratic revolution, it meant more economic democracy.[32] The concept of New Democracy virtually disappeared from the texts of Mao's speeches and articles of the time[33] and his new programmatic text, which he would publish on June 30, 1949, would be titled "On the People's Democratic Dictatorship."[34]

Stalin again intervened. His personal conversations with Mao Zedong during the Chinese leader's visit to Moscow in December 1949–February 1950 are particularly germane here.[35] During these talks Stalin emphasized that "the Chinese Communists must take the national bourgeoisie into consideration." He also softened Mao's harsh position in regard to the Western world, pointing out that "there is no need for you [the Chinese] to create conflicts with the British . . . The main point is not to rush and to avoid conflicts." Mao had to reassure Stalin that they would not touch the national bourgeoisie and foreign enterprises "so far."[36]

Stalin's tactical maneuvers were skillfully covered by the Soviet media and most of the Soviet social scientists, notably Sinolo-gists.[37] They finally helped the CCP establish its own dictatorship. The Chinese Communist Party's course aimed at creating New Democracy turned out to be an integral part of the initial Stalini-zation of China.

≺ II ≻

## Contradictions of "New Democracy"

The further Stalinization of the PRC, that is, the construction of Soviet-type Socialism, was, however, restrained by a number of factors. Stalin's dubious China policy of 1949–53 was one of the most significant. With the creation of the People's Republic Sta-lin's fears of a mighty industrialized China as a threat to his he-gemony seemed to begin dominating his mind. During the Mos-cow summit Mao himself, according to his personal interpreter Shi Zhe, sensed Stalin's "Pan-Russianism" very clearly, since Sta-lin expressed it "even more strongly than the Russian people."[38]

It is no secret that Stalin's policy toward his Chinese com-rades-in-arms was, in essence, imperialistic. Stalin, for example, did not want to conclude a formal treaty with the new China as he felt comfortable with the one signed with the GMD regime.[39] Spe-cial agreements accompanying this treaty gave the Soviets rights to keep their troops in the Lüshun military naval base in China's northeast, to run the Dalian port, and to co-own the Chinese Changchun Railway for 30 years.[40] Stalin changed his position and agreed to a new treaty—it was signed on February 14, 1950—only when he learned, in early January of that year, that the British had decided to recognize the PRC.

The Chinese Communists' joy regarding the formal treaty be-tween the USSR and the PRC was soured by Stalin's consistent aspirations to control not only Mao's politics, but also the new China's economy. Secret additional agreements signed by Soviet and Chinese representatives in the wake of the official 1950 Treaty of Friendship, Alliance, and Mutual Assistance reveal Sta-lin's true intentions. The first of the agreements allowed the Rus-sians to maintain their privileges in China's northeast and Xinji-ang, excluding all non-Soviet foreigners from these regions. Stalin

even wanted to sign separate trade agreements with these periph-
eral Chinese areas that would thereby strengthen Soviet control,
but faced strong objections from Mao Zedong and Zhou Enlai.[41]
Two other agreements established four joint ventures that served
Soviet interests in exploiting China's economic resources.[42] A new
agreement on the Chinese Changchun Railway, which supplemented the treaty,[43] further distressed the Chinese.

The more Stalin interfered in Chinese affairs, the more he desired. His suspicions of Mao grew correspondingly. He could not
hide his mistrust. As Khrushchev later recalled, after meetings
with Mao Stalin spoke of him with no great appreciation. "One
sensed some kind of arrogance he demonstrated with reference to
Mao," noted Khrushchev.[44] Once Stalin even challenged Mao
openly by contending: "[I]n China Communism is Nationalist,
and albeit Mao Zedong is a Communist, he has Nationalist
moods." Stalin also said that there was a danger of the appearance
of "its own Tito" in China. According to Mao, he replied to Stalin
with only one phrase: "All that was said here does not accord with
reality."[45] However, trying to clear away Stalin's doubts, Mao
asked Stalin to send "a Soviet comrade" to China to review and
edit his writings.[46] His real intention was to get somebody whom
Stalin trusted to China to see with his own eyes whether China
was truly practicing Marxism.[47] Mao would later say more than
once, that only after the PRC entry into the Korean War (that is,
after October 19, 1950) did Stalin finally remove "the tag of half-
hearted Tito" from Mao's head and begin to believe that "the Chinese Communists were not pro-Americans, [and] the Chinese
revolution did not represent 'National Communism'."[48] This contention may not be true, however. Stalin sent the Soviet expert in
Marxist philosophy, Pavel F. Yudin, to China to check Mao's cre-
dentials in 1951. Upon his return Yudin was questioned by Stalin
in the presence of several members of the Politburo: "Well, and
what about them? Are they Marxists?" (Stalin made a stress on
the last word.) Yudin, of course, replied: "Marxists, Comrade Stalin!"[49] Then, according to Yudin, the Kremlin boss summed up:
"That's good! We can be calm. They've grown up themselves,
without our help."[50]

Mao would later recall Stalin's mistrust on numerous occasions.[51] Intertwined with Stalin's hegemonic and dogmatic stand,

it compelled the Moscow leader to limit Soviet aid to the PRC in its early years in order to slow China's transition to Socialism. The state of the post-war Soviet economy probably would not have allowed him to render a bigger amount of help to the PRC even if he really wanted to. However, all available documentary sources support the view that it was more political than economic motives that prevailed behind Stalin's decisions to limit help to China. Stalin simply did not let the Chinese accelerate constructing Socialism. The recollections of the former Soviet deputy minister of foreign trade Konstantin I. Koval of Stalin's negotiations with Zhou Enlai are quite revealing in this regard.[52] During the negotiations that took place in August–September 1952[53] Stalin did not support Zhou when the latter suggested, "You will help us construct Socialism and we will help you construct a Communist Soviet Union."[54]

Neither did Stalin endorse the Chinese yearnings to work out the first five-year plan for the period 1951–55, considering them unrealistic.[55] His financial aid to the People's Republic, as specified in an agreement signed on February 14, 1950, did not exceed three hundred million dollars (United States) in loans over five years at a favorable one percent per annum interest.[56] It is true that Mao himself requested this sum during his meetings with Mikoyan at Xibaipo.[57] He believed it would be "better for us to borrow less than to borrow more at present and for several years."[58] But it is also true that Stalin on his part did not offer more, and during the period of the Korean War the Chinese had to use the Soviet loan to purchase military supplies from the Soviet Union. This use looked unjust to them because the loan had been aimed initially at solving China's domestic economic problems and in Korea, as the Chinese believed, they were fulfilling their "international duty."[59]

By the time of Stalin's death, in early March 1953, the Soviet government had formally agreed to assist China in building and reconstructing only 50 out of 147 enterprises that China projected[60] and was in no hurry to implement these agreements. The realization of the projects drowned in bureaucratic discussions.[61] In fact Stalin turned down all Chinese requests to accelerate Soviet assistance, persistently advising the CCP leaders not to hasten their modernization. During his meeting with Zhou Enlai on

September 3, 1952, while discussing a draft of the PRC five-year plan for the period 1953–57 Stalin expressed his dissatisfaction with the Chinese Communists' yearning to set the yearly industrial growth at 20 percent. He could not accept this pace because the Soviet economy itself, according to official statistics, grew 18.5 percent per annum during the Soviet first five-year plan.[62] Stalin advised Zhou to slow the overall growth rate to up to 15 percent and agreed to consider a number of 20 percent for yearly plans only as a reserve margin.[63] In early February 1953, the USSR State Planning Committee chairman Maxim Z. Saburov passed remarks by Soviet experts on the Chinese five-year plan to the PRC vice-chairman of the Finance and Economic Commission, Li Fuchun, who at that time was in Moscow. (Li remained there for about ten months, from August 1952 through June 1953, participating in economic negotiations with the Soviets.) Following Stalin's considerations, he suggested the Chinese comrades fix a yearly industrial growth at an even lower rate, of 13.5 to 15.0 percent.[64] The Chinese government was obliged to accept it and on February 23 Zhou Enlai, Chen Yun, Deng Xiaoping, Bo Yibo, Deng Zihui, and Gao Gang informed Li Fuchun of this decision.[65] Finally, the yearly industrial growth set the plan at 14.7 percent.[66]

Stalin's meetings with the Chinese Politburo member and Mao's deputy Liu Shaoqi in October 1952, when the Nineteenth Congress of the Soviet Communist Party (CPSU) was in progress, also showed Moscow's caution about construction of Socialism in China. At the time Stalin expressed his resolute opposition to the idea of accomplishing cooperation and collectivization of the Chinese peasantry in ten to fifteen years. This idea had been shaped by Mao Zedong a month before Liu Shaoqi's visit to Moscow, at a meeting of the CCP Central Committee Secretariat,[67] and was submitted to Stalin by Liu Shaoqi in his report on the Committee's current policy.[68] Soviet Ambassador Vasilii V. Kuznetsov recorded in his diary that in early November 1953 Liu Shaoqi had recalled to him that "Comrade Stalin advised him not to hurry over the setting up of agricultural cooperatives and collective farms, as the PRC was in a more favorable condition than the USSR during collectivization."[69] Liu conveyed Stalin's message back to Beijing.

However, Mao Zedong did not blindly follow all of Stalin's advice. During the period of 1949–53 Mao on his own responsibility tried his best to intensify the Stalinization of his country. After the establishment of the PRC, a bitter civil war continued and did not end even with the expulsion of the remnants of the GMD army to Taiwan, which took place concurrently with the installation in power of Communist local authorities during the land reform movement in 1950 and after. The peasantry remained passive, and the CCP leadership sent special Party activists' brigades to the rural areas. These brigades, numbering annually about 300,000 people, set up peasants' associations, installed a new power elite, and harshly persecuted the "landlords" and "wealthy peasants." Mass public trials with simplified judicial procedure were held in numerous villages. Death sentences were the typical outcome. Hundreds of thousands were executed or sent to labor camps. Regardless of what policy the party officially proclaimed, the number of well-to-do peasants was reduced radically. Power in the countryside along with substantial economic privileges was transferred to the new Communist elite.

The urban rich shared the fate of their rural counterparts. In December 1951, the CCP initiated repressive campaigns against the bourgeoisie: the *Sanfan* ["three anti"] campaign against bureaucratic corruption and the *Wufan* ["five anti"] campaign against private business. Following these campaigns, mass public trials were convened in a number of instances.

The intelligentsia also became an object of the ideological struggle. In 1951, on the CCP's initiative, a campaign of Marxist indoctrination began. The controversy over the film *Life of Wu Xun* was used as a pretext. Starting with an intellectual discussion, it turned into an ideological condemnation of dissident views that launched the thought reform movement. This very first campaign demonstrated the methods of ideological terror, which would play an ominous role in the intellectual life of the People's Republic. According to some estimates, in the early years of the PRC more than four million "counterrevolutionaries" were executed.[70] Even the ruling party was affected by the intensification of the class struggle. By 1953, 10 percent of the Party members had been purged.

During the period of New Democracy, however, not all Chinese leaders wholly accepted the political course drawn by Mao.

Some top Party officials preferred to view New Democracy differently. The most prominent among them was Liu Shaoqi. From the recollections of Ivan V. Kovalev, the Bolshevik representative to the CCP Central Committee, we know that as early as 1949 Stalin received confidential information on Liu Shaoqi from another CCP Politburo member, Gao Gang, chairman of the northeast regional government. Gao accused Liu of "right-wing deviation" and of "overestimation of the Chinese bourgeoisie." Stalin, nevertheless, rejected this denunciation and during his meeting with Mao Zedong at the end of December 1949 even handed Gao's report over to Mao. Kovalev learned about it from Mao's personal interpreter Shi Zhe, who attended the meeting.[71]

Mao Zedong considered the Stalin act a demonstration of the same "mistrust and suspicions" of the CCP Central Committee.[72] However, Stalin might have done this for other reasons. First, he actually might not have believed in the truth of such accusations. Gao Gang had previously provided him so many denunciations of the Chinese Communist leadership that his information itself could look suspicious. Among those who had been denounced by Gao were, in addition to Liu, Mao and some other CCP leaders. At the end of July 1949, for example, Gao, via Kovalev, informed Stalin about the anti-Soviet, "rightist-Trotskyite" tendencies of Mao Zedong and his allies in the Chinese Communist Party.[73] Stalin seemed to consider all the denunciations by Gao as a manifestation of the CCP's intra-Party struggle and simply ignored them.

Second, from the summer of 1949 Stalin was deeply dissatisfied with Gao, who in Stalin's eyes behaved foolishly at one of his meetings with the Chinese delegation led by Liu Shaoqi. Obviously trying to be more "Catholic than the Pope," Gao in front of members of the Chinese delegation made a far-reaching proposal for Manchuria to become the seventeenth republic of the Soviet Union.[74] Stalin angrily interrupted him by calling Gao "Comrade Zhang Zuolin"[75] (a Chinese warlord who had ruled Manchuria as an independent region up to 1928).

Third, Stalin, if he trusted the information, could consider Liu's "deviation" quite favorable to his own policy of "containing" Mao Zedong's radicalism.

Finally, Gao was not Stalin's only ace in the hole among the Chinese Communist leaders. Liu Shaoqi himself seemed to be another. As the former MGB (Ministry of State Security) official Peter S. Deriabin recalls, Liu Shaoqi was recruited in the 1930s while he worked in Moscow as a Chinese representative to the Profintern (the Red International of Labor Unions). Liu continued to act as Stalin's informer through the 1940s.[76] If Deriabin's information is true, then one might assume that Liu should have been a more valuable source for Stalin than Gao due to his high-ranking position—he was just below Mao Zedong in the CCP hierarchy. By his willingness to sacrifice Gao Gang, Stalin could strengthen the position of his most important ace.

However, Gao's apprehensions seemed to have some grounds. The Chinese Communist leadership was not united. Contrary to Mao Zedong, some other leading CCP members continued to use freely at the time the notion of a New Democratic revolution. Notably, Liu Shaoqi and Zhou Enlai spoke about a "New Democratic state," "New Democratic construction," and the "New Democracy trend in literature and art."[77] It was these leaders who at the time formed the opposition to Mao's radical interpretation of New Democracy.

During this time the CCP policy thus was quite contradictory. The democratic approach was recorded in the Common Program of the Chinese People's Political Consultative Conference (CPPCC) and other documents that determined China's development during the early years of the PRC. The CPPCC was convened by the Communists in September 1949. A variety of non-Communist political and social groups participated in its meetings. This type of organization was known in China as early as 1946. It could be viewed by the Chinese as a traditional democratic form of organization of the new authority. The CPPCC as an organization of the united front exercised the prerogatives of a constituent assembly. It was on behalf of the Consultative Conference that the Communists formed their new ruling bodies. The Common Program, accepted by the Communists on behalf of the CPPCC, had the appearance of a constitution. The program proclaimed democratic rights but emphasized the CCP's leading role. A multi-party system was established, and eight non-Communist political parties that acknowledged the CCP's leading role received legal status. The program encouraged private ownership, endorsed national entrepreneurs, and spoke about mutually beneficial regulation of labor-capital relations. The document formulated the course to the democratic development of the country. It eschewed the idea of a socialist transition. Even the word "Socialism" was not used in the program.[78] The Land Reform Law in the PRC passed by the government on June 28, 1950, was likewise officially in the spirit of New Democracy.[79] The new regime in 1950 passed a new marriage law that gave women rights and drew attention to the equal status of women.[80]

In the period 1949–53, not only Liu Shaoqi and Zhou Enlai, but also Chen Yun, Deng Xiaoping, Dong Biwu, Bo Yibo, and some other leading CCP members expressed moderate views in regard to Chinese New Democracy even in their unofficial talks with other Communist parties' activists.[81] In their opposition to Mao these CCP leaders used Stalin's authority, referring to his advice not to hasten Socialist construction. This kind of political backing by Stalin regardless of his true intentions was tremendously important for the Chinese "moderates" as it helped them lay a foundation for their practices. Stalin's stand also had an impact on the "radicals" who were obliged to take into account the opinion of the "big brother." It is noteworthy that Liu Shaoqi appealed to Stalin's prestige during a talk with the Soviet ambassador even after Liu was already defeated by Mao, in November 1953. He was still trying to solidify his opposition to Mao's attempts to speed up the pace of the agricultural cooperative movement.

Mao Zedong and his opponents did not differ in their interpretation of socialist ideals, but they did differ in their comprehension of how to promote their achievement. Here are just a few examples. In the spring of 1951, Shanxi provincial leaders proposed speeding up cooperation in villages. Liu Shaoqi did not confine himself to mere criticism of these ideas at a propagandists' conference, but actually prepared and sent out in July 1951 a document on behalf of the CCP Central Committee, in which this provincial obsession was branded "an erroneous, dangerous and utopian notion of agrarian socialism." However, Mao Zedong rose to the local activists' defense and two months later disavowed Liu Shaoqi's document.[82] In December 1952, a cabinet meeting chaired by Zhou Enlai discussed and approved the draft of the new tax system prepared by Finance Minister Bo Yibo. The basic difference of the bill from the old practice was in the uniformity of taxation for all forms of ownership. Thus state and cooperative enterprises were going to lose their tax benefits, while the private sector was placed in favorable competitive conditions. It is important to note also that the bill, as it turned out eventually, had not been approved by the CCP Central Committee, and Mao Zedong had not seen the text. Soon afterward, on January 15, 1953, Mao Zedong sent an angry letter to the top people in the government (State Administrative Council)—Zhou Enlai, Chen Yun, Deng Xiaoping, and Bo Yibo—in which he said that he saw no reason behind the government's desire to stimulate private enterprise.[83] The Tax Law, a mistake in the opinion of Mao Zedong, became an excuse for a vigorous ideological and political campaign against the "moderates" and generally anyone opposed to Mao Zedong's policy.

By the summer of 1953, this campaign had become particularly sharp. It culminated in the All-China Conference on Financial and Economic Work that took place in Beijing from June 14 through August 12. Liu Shaoqi, Deng Xiaoping, and Bo Yibo had to engage in self-criticism.[84] Zhou Enlai backed Mao. Thus, Mao Zedong imposed his views on the CCP. "Socialist construction along the Soviet lines" commenced officially.

≺ III ≻

### *On the Way to Socialist Industrialization*

The developments that conditioned Mao's triumph at the All-China Conference had been influenced by the death of Stalin on March 5, 1953. Mao, who should have seen Stalin as a political rival jealous of the PRC's successes in economic construction and at times a hindrance to his own attempts at speeding up the revolutionary transformation, that is, ultimate and total Stalinization of China, could breathe more easily now. An additional factor of tremendous impact was Zhou Enlai's success at his negotiations on economic aid with the new Soviet leadership led by Georgii M. Malenkov and Khrushchev.[85] The negotiations first resulted in signing, on March 21, 1953, a new trade agreement between the USSR and the PRC and an agreement on Soviet assistance in building and reconstructing power stations in China.[86] They then led to concluding, on May 15, agreement that the Soviets would provide technology and complete sets of equipment in building 91 large industrial projects in China by the end of 1959.[87] In addition, the negotiations accelerated the Soviet work over construction of 50 other plants which the Soviet side had previously promised to undertake.

The March negotiations marked a sharp turn in the Soviet approach to the Chinese plans of socialist industrialization. It is hard to say what exactly made the new Soviet leaders amend Stalin's cautious policy so radically. It is plausible that they sought Mao's political support in the post-Stalin period fearing that Mao could take advantage of the situation and liberate himself from the Soviet tutelage. They could sense the danger and tried to please Mao in order to keep him off Marshal Tito's path. Moreover, at least Khrushchev in the Soviet leadership understood that the China policy of the late dictator had been imperialistic. He was eager to change it.[88] It is likely that Malenkov had the same feeling: unlike Stalin, Molotov, or Mikoyan, he and Khrushchev had never been engaged in determining the Soviet China policy and had not been responsible for humiliating Mao.

The new position of Moscow had tremendous significance for Mao Zedong. From now on he could use the Soviet extensive aid in his pursuit to build a great industrialized and socialist power. And only now, with Soviet political and economic backing, could he finally crush the intra-Party opposition to his plans of repudiating the New Democracy. The discussions and decisions of the summer 1953 Conference on Financial and Economic Work reflected this new ideological and political situation.

The debates were followed by new bureaucratic campaigns inside and outside the Party aimed at wiping out those labeled as "hidden" counterrevolutionaries, that is, all waverers who had doubts concerning the correctness of Mao's course toward Socialist construction. In two years some 80 thousand "counterrevolutionaries" were repressed. An atmosphere of fear was so unbearable that many Party members became frightened of being accused. Within one year starting from the second half of 1955, more than 190 thousand lost their nerve and came to the offices of Public Security to make false confessions.[89]

Finally, Mao managed to carry the day. He was so thrilled that in 1954 he even included a contention about the significance of the Soviet model for China in the Constitution of the People's Republic. He made the suggestion while correcting the text of Liu Shaoqi's report on the draft of the Constitution.[90]

Some credit for Mao's victory goes to economic successes demonstrated by the Communist regime in the first half of the 1950s with the help of the Soviet Union. The implementation of the first five-year plan (1953–57) embodied the CCP course to industrialization and socialist transformation. The plan assumed constructing 694 major industrial units, which were to lay a foundation for a fast-growing heavy and military industry. It also called for development of a cooperative movement in the countryside, the aim of which was that by the end of 1957 about 33 percent of peasant households would be organized into "semi-socialist" or "lower-stage" agricultural producer cooperatives. In these co-ops peasants would pool their resources while retaining their private allotments and would divide their crops in accordance with their labor input and the amount of property pooled. In addition, a cooperation movement was to extend to about two million craftsmen in the cities. Most privately owned factories and merchant shops would be transformed into state governed or controlled units.[91]

Having assumed the post of the first secretary of the Soviet Central Committee in September 1953, Khrushchev began to play a decisive role in determining the Russian China policy. The aid to China acquired "high priority"[92] and was placed under his direct supervision.[93] In early 1954, Khrushchev made a new, much more important, concession to Mao Zedong. Having received a Chinese request for accelerating the Soviet aid in constructing heavy industrial projects, he took it so enthusiastically that he ordered the proper Soviet ministries to work out a plan on an unprecedented scale. He offered Mao a new long-term credit and rendered great economic assistance in various spheres. At the same time Khrushchev chose to clear the Sino-Soviet relations of all inconsistencies, making them truly equal. "We will live with the Chinese like brothers," he stated. "If necessary, we will divide a piece of bread in half."[94] He increasingly needed Mao's whole-hearted recognition of himself as Stalin's successor and as the authoritative leader not only of the Communist Party of the Soviet Union, but also of the international Communist movement.

In late September 1954 Khrushchev convened a special meeting of the Central Committee Presidium to persuade all members of the Soviet leadership to accept his China policy. He maintained that "[w]e will lose a historic chance to build and strengthen friendship with China if . . . in the next five years we fail to render assistance in implementing the most important steps of socialist industrialization of China."[95] It was his enthusiasm that made other leaders of the Soviet Union refrain from making any objections.

Shortly after the meeting, from September 29 to October 12, Khrushchev led a top-level Party and government delegation to Beijing to participate in celebrating the fifth anniversary of the People's Republic. During the summit the Soviets signed a series of agreements with the Chinese, providing them with a 520-million ruble (in export prices) long-term loan, enlarging by 400 million rubles the technical support in constructing 141 industrial units, and offering help in initiating an additional 15 industrial projects. Moreover, Khrushchev gave up the Soviet share in four joint ventures.[96] He also canceled the secret agreements that determined the Soviet privileges in China's Northeast and in Xinjiang. Finally, he agreed to help China with nuclear materials to train Chinese specialists.[97]

Mao was pleased: as he later conceded, "the first time I met with Comrade Khrushchev, we had very pleasant conversations . . . and established mutual trust."[98] However, Khrushchev seemed to go too far in his generosity. His ostentatious internationalism as well as excessive gifts confused the chairman. The very fact that it was Khrushchev who was the first to visit Mao, not the other way around, added to Mao's confusion. A true disciple of Stalin, Mao could respect only force. He was not able to stomach Khrushchev's gregarious style and seemed to take it as a sign of weakness. This feeling was aggravated by his awareness that Khrushchev needed his moral support.[99] During the summit Mao and Zhou tested Khrushchev by bombarding him with requests. Mao even asked the visitor to disclose the secret of an atom bomb and build a submarine fleet for China.[100] Although Khrushchev declined most demands, his image as a weak partner prevailed. The summit, therefore, marked the onset of Mao's self-emancipation. In this regard, Khrushchev gained results directly opposite from what he had expected. For the time being, however, Mao's feelings did not surface: it was not so easy even for him to get rid of esteem of the "big brothers" overnight. In addition, China's need for Soviet aid in constructing Socialism was now greater than ever before. At that time, industrialization had been already under way and it was generally anticipated that with Soviet aid China could successfully achieve rates of growth set in the plan.

The results, however, surpassed all buoyant expectations. Chinese industry grew at a more rapid pace than had been anticipated. According to different estimates, the actual per annum increase was between 16 and 18 percent. Total industrial output for five years more than doubled, while pig iron and rolled steel production increased more than threefold.[101] Although direct Russian financial aid was not too high—the amount of Soviet credit available for new investment (1.57 billion yuan) accounted for merely 3 percent of the total Chinese investment (49.3 billion yuan)[102]—the significance of Soviet help can be hardly overestimated. Not only did the Soviets provide the Chinese with some funds, but they also gave them an immense amount of technological information that on the world market would cost hundreds of millions of United States dollars. While helping China in constructing a substantial part of its key industrial enterprises, the Soviets also greatly assisted their Far Eastern neighbor in training scientific and technical cadres. In the 1950s, according to some information, the People's Republic sent more than six thousand students and some seven thousand workers to the Soviet Union. China also received more than twelve thousand Russian and East European specialists and advisers.[103]

However considerable was the Soviet aid to China, the rapid growth of Chinese industry was ensured foremost by huge state investment for economic modernization. It accounted for 97 percent of the investment in basic development. The source of the primary accumulation of capital to finance urban industrialization was predetermined: it was the countryside. In building Socialism the Chinese still relied totally on the Soviet experience that in spite of its shocking brutality had demonstrated great economic effectiveness.

≺ IV ≻

*Toward Socialism in the Countryside*

It is not surprising that the realization of the first five-year plan for agriculture was at the center of the Party's work. The completion of the 1950–53 land reform had radically changed a social and economic situation in the Chinese countryside. Most peasants became individual "lower-middle-class" proprietors and felt more independent economically than ever before. However, the post-reform agricultural economy turned out to be incapable of supplying society with enough foodstuff and raw materials. The basic reasons were rooted in the low development of China's productive forces, overpopulation, a lack of fertile land and, hence, the existence of meager farms, a non-sophisticated rural infrastructure, and archaic social relations. The consequences of land reform, first of all the emergence of "lower-middle-class" peasantry as the basic class in the Chinese countryside, made the economic crisis much sharper. It happened because the level of peasants' consumption went up, but commercialization of their economy decreased. It is noteworthy that after the reform Liu Shaoqi, in his talk with Soviet Ambassador Kuznetsov on November 9, 1953, had to admit that "if peasants eat well, they will consume all grain produced in the country, and the town will be out of grain . . . Under these circumstances, we still cannot let the peasants eat as much as they wish."[104]

The Party began a search for new forms of collaboration with the peasantry. By that time, to be sure, market solutions for economic problems already had been ruled out. A socialist utopia had begun to determine the policy. In the fall of 1953, Mao Zedong launched an attack on the New Democratic social relations in the countryside. On October 16, the Central Committee passed a resolution to establish total grain monopoly by the state from November 25, 1953, on. The next year the state monopoly extended to raw cotton and cotton fabric merchandise as well as vegetable oil and its products.

The powerful state repressive machine tried to control all major commercial streams, but it did not improve the situation. In fact, more than half of the rural population was on the verge of starvation and tens of millions of families could not survive without direct support from the state.[105] The situation was paradoxical. On the one side, the state extracted from the countryside a huge portion of agricultural surplus through the collection of taxes and purchases of grain and other commodities at the low controlled price, thereby creating an illusion of its economic mightiness. On the other side, it had to send back to the countryside more than two thirds of the purchased grain in order to save millions of poor peasants from starvation. The real ability of the state to stimulate rural economic development was getting more and more limited. The amount of agricultural products peasants were compelled to sell constantly increased and made them lose any motive to boost production. Thus, the number of those who needed state aid continued to grow rapidly. In essence, the anti-market policy trapped Mao and his confidants in a cul-de-sac. It was this situation that encouraged the acceleration of the cooperative movement.

As early as the autumn of 1953 Mao Zedong held meetings with the staff of the CCP Central Committee Countryside Work Department.[106] What followed was the CCP Central Committee's decision of December 16, 1953, on "Development of Agricultural Producer Cooperation," that became a program for socialist transformation of the Chinese countryside.[107] To be sure, it still called for gradual and steady cooperation of peasant households: in the Party leadership there were people who still attempted to contest Mao's radical intentions. Head of the Central Committee Countryside Work Department Deng Zihui, for instance, insisted on realizing the cooperation program in accordance with the five-year plan.[108] His position was supported by Liu Shaoqi, Chen Yun, Deng Xiaoping, Bo Yibo, Li Fuchun, and in particular Zhou Enlai. The issue was presented to the Politburo, which after careful consideration spoke in favor of Deng Zihui's position.[109]

In this situation Mao Zedong appealed to the local cadres at large. On July 31, 1955, he convened a meeting of secretaries of provincial, city, and regional Party committees and called upon them directly to support his plans. His report "On the Co-operative Transformation of Agriculture" was aimed at persuading the Party middle-rank bureaucrats to accelerate the timetable of the rural socialization. Contrary to the five-year plan that had been adopted by the National People's Congress a day before, Mao insisted that not 33, but 50 percent of the peasant households

should be organized into cooperatives by the end of 1957. As for
co-ops, the number 650 thousand should be doubled by the fall of
1956.[110] His speech contained the traditional praise for the Soviet
practice. Mao declared that "Soviet experience tells us that it is
entirely possible" to accomplish large-scale collectivization of agriculture in a short period.[111]

At the same time one could notice that the chairman, though
still much inspired by the Soviet model, began envisioning a pace
of the Socialist construction that would surpass the Soviet tempo.
He severely condemned "some comrades" who emphasized Stalin's well-known criticism of "impetuosity" and "rashness" made
during the Soviet collectivization campaign.[112] (Later, in September
1956, Mao would confess that Stalin's work "Dizzy With Success," containing criticism of "impetuosity" and "rashness," was
among those that he disliked.[113]) When Khrushchev asked Mao not
to hasten the pace of cooperation, Mao refused to listen.[114] In the
new political atmosphere, whereas the Soviets continued to demonstrate equality in the relationships between the two countries,
Mao felt increasingly independent in his actions. He optimisti-
cally spoke of a great rise in the cooperative movement. His position was received sympathetically by Party cadres; it flattered
them.

The July meeting was of great significance. For the first time in
the history of the Party Mao overrode the Politburo, and he openly
revealed disagreements within the Party leadership to the local
cadres. Overall, his maneuver turned out to be successful. Having
received the political support from "below," the chairman could
now force the Party leadership to accept his program of accelerated
Stalinization. In October 1955, he convened the Sixth Plenum of
the Central Committee in order to ratify his political course. It is
noteworthy that the number of middle- and lower-rank *ganbu*
[bureaucrats] invited to attend the sessions exceeded that of CC
members by tenfold. These numbers helped Mao to be sure of the
plenum's proper decision. The Party forum supported Mao's accelerated program totally. Deng Zihui, Bo Yibo, and Li Fuchun were
attacked for their "right-wing" deviation and had to engage in self-
criticism. Zhou Enlai spoke, entirely backing Mao.[115]

By early 1956, Mao Zedong and his confidants had managed to
speed up the pace of cooperation tremendously. A new stage—that

of rapid collectivization—was essentially completed in the first half of 1956. The local Party cadres skillfully manipulated the egalitarian zeal of the poor peasants who still constituted a majority of the "lower-middle" proprietors of meager farms. As a result, agrarian socialism triumphed. By the end of 1956, 756,000 cooperatives made up more than 96 percent of all peasant households in China. Almost 89 percent of the households belonged to "higher-stage" cooperative farms, that is, fully "socialist" collectives.[116]

Needless to say, Mao had achieved a great political victory. However, according to Soviet information the social tension that had begun developing after the introduction of compulsory grain deliveries did not lessen. "[China's] agrarian collectivization has encountered peasants' opposition," stated the Soviet Far East Economic Committee in early 1957.[117] Discontent arose among members of some newly organized cooperatives. The scale of the peasant resistance, however, was not as impressive as it had been during collectivization in the Soviet Union. In essence, Socialism came to the Chinese countryside peacefully.

≺ V ≻

*From Stalinization Toward Maoization*

The year 1956 brought about an event that deeply shocked China as well as the whole world. The news came from Moscow, where on February 25 at a secret session of the Twentieth Congress of the Soviet Communist Party Khrushchev delivered a speech denouncing Stalin. Nothing, to be sure, was said about Stalin's distrust of Mao Zedong, but Khrushchev talked a lot about Stalin's errors in relation to Tito.[118]

The first reaction of Mao was positive. The condemnation of the Kremlin ex-dictator emancipated the Chinese leader totally and ultimately. The process started by Khrushchev's 1954 visit to China came to an end. Henceforward, Mao could no longer look back at the Soviets and feel indebted to their experience. If in late 1955 and early 1956 he had only spoken in favor of accelerating the tempo of Stalin's collectivization of agriculture, now he could really try his own way in making China a great industrial power. He might even attempt to catch up with the USSR and surpass it.

Shortly after familiarizing himself with Khrushchev's report, on March 31, 1956, Mao met with Soviet Ambassador Yudin to discuss the Twentieth Congress results. Although the chairman "without a doubt" continued to regard his former mentor as "a great Marxist, a good and honest revolutionary," he, as Yudin recorded, "stressed that the materials from the [Twentieth] Congress made a strong impression on him." Mao declared that "the spirit of criticism and self-criticism and the atmosphere which was created after the Congress will help us . . . to express our thoughts more freely on a range of issues. It is good that the CPSU has posed all these issues. For us . . . it would be difficult to take the initiative on this matter."[119] Mao also shared with the ambassador his grievances toward Stalin's erroneous China policy and informed Yudin about a forthcoming lead article of *Renmin ribao* dedicated to the Stalin issue.

The article, written by Mao's confederate Chen Boda[120] and corrected by Mao and some other Politburo and non-Politburo members,[121] appeared on April 5. It was intended for the general public and hence did not contain much criticism of the former Communist idol. The CCP leaders and first of all Mao did not want to let anybody use an anti-Stalin banner against their own dictatorship.[122] Neither did Mao intend so far to disclose his secret feelings concerning his quest for the new ways. The article summed up Stalin's deeds and mistakes generally in a ratio 70 to 30. Nevertheless, it praised the Soviets for their "courageous self-criticism of . . . past errors."[123] The next day Mao expounded these ideas before Khrushchev's personal messenger, Mikoyan.[124]

Mao's presentation to the four-day enlarged meeting of the Politburo in late April 1956 marked, in essence, a new great shift in his world outlook. The speech, presented on April 25 and entitled "On the Ten Great Relationships," outlined the new course of the Party in the construction of Socialism that differed from the Soviet model. For the first time the chairman placed the Soviet practice under harsh criticism and openly called for a different path.[125] Mao did not present a detailed program, but elaborated some points of strategy aimed at development of "Chinese-style" Socialism.[126] Among other things were substantial increase of investment in light industry and agriculture, rapid growth of inland and interior areas, and decrease of direct investment in defense along with accelerated growth in economic construction. Also proposed were stimulating moral incentives, such as initiative and activity, rather than material ones; reducing economic spheres under centralized bureaucratic direction; and developing relatively autonomous units of production and labor-intensive projects. Mao Zedong did not keep secret the divergence of his new strategy from the Soviet one.[127]

Mao's speech was not published at the time, which is hardly surprising. Not only did it openly challenge the Soviets, but it also ran counter to economic views of many other Chinese leaders. Among them were Liu Shaoqi, Zhou Enlai, Chen Yun, and Deng Xiaoping. At the enlarged Politburo meeting Zhou Enlai, for example, openly opposed Mao when the latter spoke in favor of increasing construction investment by two billion yuan. Zhou said that it would cause tension in commodity supply as well as the overgrowth of the urban population.

Mao felt deeply offended.[128] On May 2, 1956, he elaborated most of his new ideas at the session of the Supreme State Conference.[129] In this situation the Central Committee had to distribute the text of Mao's speech of April 25, but only to the high and middle-rank Party cadres.[130] At that time Zhou Enlai, Chen Yun, and other Chinese economists were engaged in preparation of the second five-year plan, and Mao's unorthodox ideas were confusing. Moreover, in 1956 the CCP launched a move to complete the socialist transformation of industry and commerce that needed the whole Party's attention. The leading members of the Communist leadership had no time for the further discussion of Mao's proposals, so they largely ignored them.

The socialist transformation in the Chinese cities continued the previous Party campaigns against the bourgeoisie (the *Sanfan* and *Wufan*), which had been conducted in 1951–52. In the wake of these movements, in 1953–54, the CCP imposed state control over the sale of all major commodities, further limiting the market economy. State industrial and commercial companies began to oust the private enterprises. The Communists used various forms of the so-called "lower-stage" state capitalism in order to pursue their policy. In 1955, the government put under state control over 80 percent of small and middle private enterprises. Large units that employed more than 500 workers were transformed into

joint—state-private—ventures. By the end of 1956, private property
had been abolished in the entire country.[131]

The CCP changed Chinese society in an historically short
time. The Party tactics were quite effective and as in the countryside did not rouse much opposition among the rich in the cities.
The resistance of the bourgeoisie was weakened by the decision of
the Chinese government to pay former owners 5 percent of the ex-
propriated capital per annum for seven years.[132] More serious opposition came from another social group—the working class. The socialist transformation brought about lowering of workers' income.
The workers also lost some privileges that the system of workers'
control over employers had guaranteed. This system had been introduced to private enterprises after the 1949 Communist victory
and had indeed protected interests of workers. State labor unions,
which replaced workers' control after the socialization, defended
the government, not employers. The workers began expressing
their discontent by going on strike, and the local administration
managed to suppress the "riots," not without great difficulties.
According to official data, in the period from August 1956 though
January 1957 in the country at large there were over ten thousand
big and small strikes and more than ten thousand student sit-
ins.[133]

In this situation the Eighth Party Congress took place, on September 15–27, 1956, in Beijing. The formal sessions were preceded
by secret meetings held from August 29 through September 12.
These meetings actually predetermined all major decisions of the
forum. Behind closed doors the delegates discussed and adopted
drafts of all the resolutions and texts of the main reports and presentations. They also coordinated cadre decisions. In the wake of
Khrushchev's denunciation of the cult of personality and Mao's
own defeat at the enlarged Politburo meeting of late April 1956,
Mao Zedong at the Congress was quite cautious. He did not preside over the sessions and did not make the main reports. He addressed the audience with only two short speeches, in which he
did not return to the ideas outlined in "The Ten Great Relationships."[134] Liu Shaoqi, Zhou Enlai, and Deng Xiaoping were the
most active.

Mao, however, had not given up. He tried to push his ideas
while amending a draft of the Political Report of the Central

Committee, which Liu Shaoqi was to deliver. On August 29, for example, he added the following sentences to the draft:

It should be clear that the Chinese revolution and the Chinese construction are mainly based on the development of the forces of the Chinese people itself. The aspiration for foreign aid is supplementary. It is completely wrong to lose faith, think that you cannot do anything, believe that China's destiny is not in the hands of the Chinese themselves, and totally rely on foreign aid.[135]

Deliberately demonstrating his disagreement with Soviet paternalism, Mao even refused to attend the session at which Khrushchev's envoy Mikoyan spoke.[136]

The main tone of the Congress was different, however. The delegates paid homage to the Soviet model and supported only those social experiments of Mao Zedong that had led to the rapid fulfillment of the Chinese Stalinization. The Congress officially proclaimed that the "Proletarian Socialist Revolution" in China had achieved basic victory. All the speakers enthusiastically acclaimed the results of the socialist transformation in the countryside and in the cities.

Some decisions of the Congress were particularly disturbing for Mao. In the new atmosphere, he had to accept deletion from the Party Constitution of a reference to "Mao Zedong Thought" as "a guiding line" of the CCP. The Mao formula had been adopted by the Seventh Congress of the Chinese Communists in June 1945; now it was replaced with a more vague phrase: "The Communist Party of China takes Marxism-Leninism as its guide to action."[137] In addition, in his "Report on the Revision of the Constitution of the Communist Party of China," Deng Xiaoping emphasized the necessity to struggle "against the exaggeration of a personality, against its glorification."[138] The reestablishment of the post of the Party General Secretary was also meaningful. Although the revival of the post was proposed by no one but Mao,[139] it was Liu Shaoqi's man, Deng Xiaoping, who received it. Hence, direct control over cadres fell into the hands of the Party's "moderates."

The cult of personality issue was among the most distressing issues and Mao decided to counterattack. Right after the Congress, while talking to a Yugoslavian Communist Union delegation, he noted, in passing, that "[f]ew people in China have ever openly criticized me. The people are tolerant of my shortcomings and mistakes. It is because we always want to serve the people and do good things for the people." These words sounded like a warning to his opponents, especially as Mao explained that "bossism" was not a real problem in China. He also added, "[W]hen some people criticize me, others would oppose them and accuse them of disregarding the leader."[140]

The 1956 anti-Soviet movements in Poland and Hungary helped Mao solidify his position. In October 1956, a new Polish Communist leader, a former prisoner of Stalin, Wladyslaw Gomulka, who assumed power in the wake of the suppression four months earlier of a workers' uprising, expelled Stalinist members of the Polish Politburo. Anti-Communist moods spread very quickly among the Poles. In the meantime, new democratic leaders came to power in Hungary as a result of an anti-Communist revolt. The events were clearly caused by Khrushchev's denunciation of Stalin. At the Soviets' request the Chinese actively participated in resolving the crisis.[141] Although both crises were finally solved and Communism remained on its feet, Mao Zedong and other leaders of China seemed to be deeply shocked. On October 1, 1956, Zhou Enlai stated the common views of the Chinese leadership to the Soviet Central Committee member Boris N. Ponomarev. Zhou began criticizing the CPSU for "making mistakes" in denouncing Stalin: first, "no preliminary consultation was carried out with fraternal parties"; second, "an all-round historical analysis was completely lacking"; last, the leading comrades from the Soviet Party "lacked self-criticism." At the end of October, Liu Shaoqi conveyed these revised views of the Chinese leadership directly to Khrushchev.[142] On October 23, 1956, Mao Zedong in the conversation with Yudin abruptly noticed that the Russians had completely renounced and thrown away such a sword as Stalin. As a result, he added, enemies had seized it in order to kill the Communists. That is the same, as if, having picked up a stone, one were to throw it at one's own feet.[143]

The chairman elaborated the ideas about "the thrown sword" at the Second Plenum of the Eighth Central Committee in November 1956. His attacks on the Soviets were unprecedented. Mao even contended that some Soviet leaders have discarded "the sword of Lenin . . . to a considerable extent." Moreover, he shaped a new sphere of disagreements with Moscow, starting to criticize

Khrushchev's thesis about the possibility of the so-called peaceful transition from Capitalism to Socialism. The Soviet leader had raised this possibility in his main report at the Twentieth Congress.[144] "[T]hat is to say," said Mao, "it is no longer necessary for all countries to learn from the October Revolution. Once the gate is opened, by and large Leninism is thrown away."[145] According to Mao, the fundamental problem with some East European countries was that their Communists had not waged a genuine class struggle and had left many counterrevolutionaries at large.

Mao took advantage of the situation to promote a new acceleration in the economic construction, resuming attacks on the "moderates." In this connection he called for a new "rectification" campaign in the CCP in the next year.[146] He did not name the main "moderates," but the delegates understood that he aimed at Liu Shaoqi, Zhou Enlai, and Chen Yun, who had made the main reports at the plenum.[147] Mao's dissatisfaction was caused by the fact that at the time Liu, Zhou, and Chen tried to set forth a course for a "temporary retreat" in China's industrial development, fearing the "overheating of the economy."[148] What was the most challenging was that Liu and Zhou had connected the events in Eastern Europe with previous economic policies of the Polish and Hungarian leaders, particularly with their insistence on the rapid pace of industrialization and collectivization.[149] It is noteworthy that the day the plenum opened, on November 10, *Renmin ribao* published an article that in accordance with Liu and Zhou's ideas stated that the Hungarian leaders had erroneously pushed forward the 1951–53 industrialization of their countries and had collectivized their peasants by force. Although all the speakers at the plenum, including the "moderates," shared Mao's anger in regard to the Soviet "mistakes," the chairman still was upset.

In December 1956, the Chinese Politburo ordered the editorial board of *Renmin ribao* to prepare a new lead article on the Stalin issue. Six drafts were prepared. They were discussed at the enlarged meetings of the Politburo. Mao made some revisions, of which the most meaningful was the deletion of the following phrase from the sixth draft: "The rapid progress in the course of the Chinese Socialist construction to a large extent is a result of the study of the Soviet experience." At the same time he wrote in the margin: "The future will show whether the course of the Chi-

nese construction is correct. Here no [one] will say."[150] The article
was published on December 29, 1956.[151]

Having sensed a danger, Khrushchev tried to soften the Soviet
position on Stalin. On January 17, 1957, while greeting Zhou Enlai
at the party in the Chinese embassy in Moscow, he pointed out
that the Soviet Communists are still "Stalinists." He said that
"we had criticized Stalin not for having been a bad Communist . . .
The name of Stalin is inseparable from Marxism-Leninism."[152] Regardless of this, in early 1957, Mao expounded his accusations of
the Soviets in several internal speeches.[153]

At the same time the chairman made a new attempt at promoting an accelerated program of modernization. Making an open
speech at the enlarged session of the Supreme State Conference on
February 27, he again appealed to the middle-rank cadres—the
kind of functionaries who attended the Conference. However, he
expressed his doubts that the Party would be able to transform the
country into a great military and economic power within a short
time. In order to renovate the Party spirit he invited non-Party
members, in particular members of "democratic" parties and other
intellectuals, to criticize Marxism and the CCP cadres, bravely
and honestly evaluating the Party policy. He agitated for a broad
ideological movement that would serve antibureaucratic purposes.
Indeed, he probably hoped to channel criticism from the masses
against his opponents in the Communist leadership; Mao's appeals to the people to attack the leaders resemble his future calls
during the Cultural Revolution. The campaign was supposed to be
unleashed under the slogan "Let a Hundred Flowers Blossom, Let
a Hundred Schools of Thought Contend."[154]

In May 1957, a Hundred Flowers campaign was officially
launched. The CCP leadership seemed to offer the people full freedom of speech as if acknowledging ideological and political pluralism. From early May 1957, for about a month, all Chinese newspapers and other media welcomed critical views on political issues. Many critics, however, began to attack not "separate errors"
but rather the whole system of the Communist dictatorship. In
early June Mao stopped the campaign. Freedom of speech was
abolished and the Communists turned back to their traditional
methods of political terror.

A new repressive campaign against intellectuals exceeded the previous ones. For the first time in the history of the People's Republic millions of educated people were labeled "right bourgeois elements" and became objects of persecution. About half a million were sent to "labor reeducation camps."[155] Not all of them were true critics of the regime; many were loyal citizens.

The atmosphere of fear helped Mao avenge himself on his main opponents, first of all on Zhou Enlai. As Chinese historian Li Ping reports, in late summer 1957 Mao challenged Zhou, claiming that the premier had made serious mistakes in trying to balance an economic development of China. The chairman declared that he himself "favored adventurism" and that he was not afraid of breaking up the balance to accelerate China's transition to Socialism and Communism. Mao even considered replacing Zhou with Ke Qingshi. Zhou agreed to resign, but other members of the Politburo opposed it.[156]

The Third Plenum of the Central Committee in early October 1957 summarized the results of the ideological and political movements. It considered them quite effective. Even Mao was satisfied and by the end of the plenum decided to soften the rectification campaign. Now he could address the Party with a symbolic question: "Can't we avoid the Soviet Union's detours and do things faster and better?" The answer was presupposed: "We should of course strive for this."[157]

Mao returned to the ideas set forth in "The Ten Great Relationships," thinking more and more closely over the possibilities of the Great Leap Forward—a new model of the accelerated economic construction under Communist political auspices, based primarily on China's advantages, first of all on extensive use of her major resource, human labor. The new way would lead to further worsening China's links with the Kremlin traditionalists.

In January 1958, at the Hangzhou and Nanning conferences, Mao intensified his criticism of those who opposed "impetuosity and rashness" and those who still followed the Soviet model.[158] In Nanning, on January 18, he warned the Party cadres that the struggle against "rashness" would damage "enthusiasm of 600 million people."[159] He further alerted Zhou Enlai that the distance between him and a rightist was "only 550 meters."[160] The *ganbu* supported the chairman, and the premier had to undertake a self-criticism.

Mao triumphed again. On January 31, he summarized the results of both conferences in an important document, "Sixty Articles on Work Methods," that in essence finally set forth the new cause of the Great Leap Forward. Thus, Stalin's model of the Socialist transition that had inspired Mao Zedong exhausted itself.

≺ VI ≻

## Conclusion

The era of Stalinization of the People's Republic covered a longer period than has been conventionally assumed. It lasted from the very foundation of a New China in 1949 through early 1958. It was during this time that the Chinese Communists tried to impose the Soviet model of Socialist construction on the Chinese people. Their objectives were clear for them: the suppression of the counterrevolution, the reconstruction of the national economy damaged by war, and later the industrialization of the economically backward country, the collectivization of the peasantry, and the nationalization of private property. To carry these out they were to impose tough bureaucratic control over the economic development as well as the political and ideological life of the citizens. No one in the Chinese leadership had any doubts on that. Neither did their Soviet mentors.

Their divergences concerned the timetable, but not Stalinization itself. In this respect, the Kremlin position was of particular importance as at the time the CCP deeply depended on Moscow's political, economic, and military aid. The views of the "big brother," however, were inconsistent. A crucial difference existed between the approaches of Stalin's and Khrushchev's administrations. It sounds ironic, but the available documents suggest that it was Stalin who in reality had always endeavored to moderate the Stalinization of China. Khrushchev, who acquired a worldwide recognition as an anti-Stalinist, did exactly the opposite. It was he who, indeed, facilitated China's transition to Stalin's Socialism.

Within the Chinese Communist elite there were at least two major factions, and the struggle between them determined a balance of power in the Party. From the very beginning a group under Mao occupied a leftist position. It was this group that constantly but cautiously opposed Stalin and intra-Party conservatives. The New Democratic China began a Stalinization movement right after the Communist takeover. Mao, however, formally had to adhere to new democratic slogans through 1953, but only to keep close relations with Moscow. A faction of "moderates" led by Liu Shaoqi, Zhou Enlai, Chen Yun, Deng Xiaoping, and Bo Yibo pursued a different policy: they took Stalin's advice seriously and followed it strictly. In a vigorous struggle Mao finally, after the death of Stalin, managed to make them accept his views. Nevertheless, the subsequent years of 1953 to early 1958 demonstrated that the shift in the outlook of the "moderates" was formal. Having reluctantly commenced industrializing and collectivizing China, they attempted to slow it down as much as possible. Mao soon began feeling dissatisfied and resumed his fight with the "moderates"—this time trying to accelerate the pace of Stalinization.

At the highest point of Mao's struggle, however, when the goals seemed to be very close, he abruptly began to change strategy. From the spring of 1956 on, he embarked on reviewing the Stalin model, considering it not so radical and the Soviet pace of economic construction not too fast.

His ideas of "Chinese-style" Socialism and of the Chinese way to construct the ideal society could have been born only in the post-Stalinist atmosphere created in the worldwide Communist movement by Khrushchev as well. Hence, Khrushchev stimulated Mao not only to a rapid Stalinization, but also—contrary to his true intentions—to the final abandonment of the Soviet path. Stalinism in China had come to an end, and one could speak not about Stalinization, but rather about the Maoization of the People's Republic. At the same time one should bear in mind that Maoism itself was no more than a Chinese form of Stalinism; and while Soviet Stalinization of China was at the end, the influence of Stalinism as a totalitarian political and economic system was by no means over. It would in many ways define the evolution of the PRC from that time until today.

# Have You Eaten? Have You Divorced?
# Debating the Meaning of Freedom
# in Marriage in China

WILLIAM P. ALFORD AND YUANYUAN SHEN

A GREAT DEAL of discussion about freedom in the People's Republic of China has proceeded on certain assumptions about the role of the state and about law's place in helping define it. At the heart of these assumptions is the idea that the cause of freedom in China will best be advanced through the state's retrenchment and a concomitant ceding of power to non-state actors, particularly with respect to economic and social matters. This notion is perhaps most obvious in calls for the promotion of greater economic freedom via both the "privatization" of state-owned enterprise and an increasing reliance on market forces, but it also informs the view that such measures are or soon will be leading to a marked growth in political freedom. And it undergirds the conviction of most observers that what is termed the rise of civil society will perforce enhance personal freedom in China. As the noted Chinese scholar Liu Junning observed in a recent essay extolling Friedrich Hayek, "almost all of those who shape public opinion in China are liberals [as] classical liberalism now dominates China's intellectual landscape."[1]

Law occupies a prominent position in this vision, being increasingly seen in both academic and policy circles as critical to the attainment for Chinese of fuller economic, political, and social freedoms. In part, the prominence accorded law is attributable to its perceived potential, however imperfectly realized to date in the PRC, to facilitate the above described transfer of power from state to society by limiting the spheres of life over which the former has authority and providing constraints as to the manner in which such authority is to be exercised. No less importantly, law is extolled for the vital role it has to play, once the state has receded, in establishing the proverbial "level playing field" on which a new society is to be grounded.[2] In contrast to the avowedly political and highly particularistic manner in which the Chinese state historically reached into citizens' lives,[3] law is commended for being facilitative, rather than determinative, providing a neutral framework through which citizens, each endowed with the same rights and each entitled to invoke the uniform procedural protection that formal adjudication is intended to provide, may work things out for themselves.[4]

There are, to be sure, highly compelling reasons why one might so approach the study of contemporary China. At the most obvious level, the horrors of the period immediately following the Great Leap Forward (in which perhaps as many as 20 to 30 million people died) or of the Great Proletarian Cultural Revolution (in which untold millions suffered)—not to mention on-going abuses of basic human rights—provide powerful support for the notion of a sharply circumscribed state. But the rationale for such an approach transcends the 50-year history of the PRC. The manner, for example, in which the Chinese state, over thousands of years, has distinguished among individuals on the basis of characteristics (such as gender, age, familial relationship, and class background) beyond their control enhances the attractiveness of seemingly clear-cut rules that in aspiring to apply uniformly to all, by definition, limit the state's capacity to distinguish among citizens. And the broader temper of the era in which we live, especially since the collapse of Communism as an ideology, would seem to buttress the claims of those inclined to believe that the "end of history" is or should be bringing with it the deserved withering away of a state that as a matter of course would intervene in the lives of its citizens.[5]

Compelling though the rationale for a drastically circumscribed role for the Chinese state may be, it does not provide us with a sufficiently nuanced metric for thinking about freedom in the PRC. Without slighting the values to which this vision speaks, we need soberly to confront difficult questions regarding our definition of freedom, the place of even a scaled-back state in ensuring basic freedoms, the interplay between different types of freedom, trade-offs between freedom and other fundamental values, and the

ways in which even the most seemingly neutral of rules intended
to do no more than structure autonomous decision-making may
shape outcomes and have an impact on freedom. This chapter uses
debates leading up to the revision of China's Marriage Law on
April 28, 2001, to examine the complexity of freedom in the PRC;
a comparable inquiry might well be conducted regarding the role
of the state and place of law in constructing a market economy or
in establishing civil society.[6]

The debates surrounding the revision of China's Marriage Law
provide an intriguing vehicle through which to examine the "making of modern freedom" in China for a number of reasons. Most
significantly, in addressing such issues as the ease with which divorce is to be granted and the legal foundation for outlawing extramarital relations, they raise vexing questions of a very fundamental nature about the meaning of freedom. How, for instance,
are we to assess the impact on freedom of a tightening of divorce
requirements that are intended to protect the interests of some of
the weakest actors in Chinese society (women, especially from the
countryside, of limited economic means and often minimal literacy or less)[7] but that by definition limit the choices of others while
increasing the involvement of the state in the most intimate of relations? Is individual freedom better enhanced through a conception of marriage principally as a bond between two individuals or
as situated in a broader societal setting? And how germane to such
deliberations is either the manner in which marriage was thought
of historically or the profound social dislocation and the thorough-
going recasting of the state's role in the provision of basic social
services that mark the PRC today? What are the implications for
freedom of the growing tendency to anchor citizen participation
and avenues of redress in a rhetoric of individual rights and formal
legal processes, rather than group interests and administrative solutions as articulated through quasi-governmental bodies such as
the All China Women's Federation? And how, in weighing any of
these alternatives, is one fully to account for the staggering corruption, monetary and otherwise, that seemingly pervades all PRC
institutions?[8]

Beyond their significance with respect to the marital context,
the foregoing questions raise yet broader themes pertinent to our
consideration of freedom in China more generally. They push us,

for example, to think about matters such as tensions between state paternalism and individual choice (and with it the value of participation, however inexpert); the interplay between community (however defined) and individual autonomy in the realization of freedom; the relationship between the generality to which "modern" law is said to aspire and particularity (of the type *guanxi* is said to embody); and the implications of a society such as China, with thousands of years of history, experiencing in less than a generation industrialization and associated changes that took a century in Europe.

That issues surrounding marriage illuminate yet larger systemic inquiries regarding China is fitting when one considers the central role that family has long played in Chinese life. It was, as the Confucian *Analects* recognized, not only the prime social institution itself, but also both the principal nexus through which individuals might define and cultivate their own virtue at the micro level and the foundation of and organizing metaphor for the world at the macro level. This centrality was mirrored in the *li*, the ethical precepts/rules intended to structure life, as well as in imperial law (from at least the Han dynasty onward) with its intense focus on reinforcing family both internally and vis-à-vis others through a variety of differential penalties and privileges. And it has been well appreciated by those who, in more recent times, have sought to transform China more generally, as evidenced by the ways in which the leaders of the *Taiping Tianguo*,[9] the May Fourth movement,[10] and the early Chinese Communist Party[11] all saw a reconception of family as interwoven with the broader political changes they sought. Indeed, it was not coincidental that the first major law promulgated by the PRC was the Marriage Law of 1950[12] and that many of the PRC's most epochal undertakings of its first half century (of which it has had more than its share)— such as land reform, communization, the one child policy, the Cultural Revolution, and Dengist rural economic reform—have demonstrated the centrality of family to politics and vice versa.

The debates regarding revision of the Marriage Law also warrant our attention for a seeming paradox they present. At one level, they represent the most open and extensive public conversation in the history of the PRC, engaging citizens across the nation who had in most instances not previously been involved in deliberations concerning freedom. And yet, as vigorous and candid as these debates have been, the platforms from which the chief protagonists spoke and the range of alternatives envisioned in them suggest the ways in which constraints on fundamental political freedoms continue to limit the ways in which other forms of freedom are considered.

This chapter has four sections. Part I briefly sketches profound changes underway in Chinese society from the conclusion of the Cultural Revolution in order to provide the background from which the debates commencing in the mid-1990s regarding revision of the Marriage Law emerged. The next section turns to the debates themselves, tracing both the more sweeping concerns they have evoked and the more seemingly technical legal issues on which attention has principally been centered. Part III offers an overview of changes enacted in the Law by the Standing Committee of the National People's Congress (NPC) on April 28, 2001, while the concluding section seeks to illuminate lessons that these debates may suggest about freedom in modern China and law's role therein.

≺ I ≻

## *The Context*

No institution has experienced the vicissitudes of the political, economic, and social changes that have marked the PRC's first half century more sharply than the family. This may have been most dramatically obvious with respect to the direct challenges posed to "traditional" family life at the time of the foundation of a "new China" on October 1, 1949, in the aftermath of which millions of rural marriages were dissolved, often at the initiative of women.[13] The communization movement of the 1950s strove to recast the role of rural families, while the Cultural Revolution of the late 1960s and early 1970s tore asunder many an urban household. And although the transformations that China has been undergoing since the downfall of the Gang of Four in the mid-1970s have been focused principally on economic development, international engagement, and other areas seemingly at a remove from the family, their impact on that institution has in its own way been no less consequential.

At the heart of these changes has been the accelerating breakdown, in the face of the market-oriented liberalization of the past two decades, of the so-called *danwei suoyouzhi* [unit based system] in China's cities and of its rough rural counterpart, the commune system, in the countryside. Although never as uniformly administered as ideology or mystique would have it, the *danwei* system not only functioned as the "basic organisational form of State-run modern industry" throughout much of the early history of the PRC, but as well "is like one's parents and one's family," wrote one Chinese observer in 1996, in that "it fulfills a range of responsibilities such as arranging work, food, accommodation, entertainment, political study, pensions [leaving Chinese dependent on it] even in death."[14] As such, during its heyday, it gave considerable definition to marriage and other dimensions of family life literally from their inception onward through, for example, circumscribing the social (and, to some degree, physical) space within which one was likely to find a spouse and subsequently reside, ensuring that the quality of one's marriage and any extra-marital involvements were likely to be known to those with whom work and residence were shared, limiting exposure to heterodox or even particularly novel ideas (be they regarding gender, pornography, or politics more broadly), and providing the means through which any marital or other familial disputes might be addressed.

The changes ensuing from or associated with the ongoing demise of the *danwei* system are so many and variegated as to defy more than summary treatment here. In some respects, they would appear to pull in distinct, if not contradictory, directions, on the one hand facilitating a re-assertion of practices with pre-Communist historical roots while on the other fostering an embrace of what might be described as market-oriented modernity (for lack of a better term)—even as each of these trends shapes the other. So, for example, as communes were dissolved and collective enterprises have faded in importance, the family (albeit chiefly in nuclear form) has re-emerged as the principal unit of economic organization in the countryside, even as the allure of economic opportunity in China's cities and newly emergent industrial zones has drawn over 100 million Chinese from their rural homes, often leaving behind other family members.[15]

The impact of such changes on the family, as well as on the status of women both within and beyond it, has been considerable. At least in aggregated national terms, the reform era's prosperity has eased economic burdens, facilitated an increase in life expectancy, and promoted literacy and educational opportunity more generally, even if many such gains have been realized by men and women in differing measure.[16] Together with heightened mobility and substantially greater access to new ideas (regarding, *inter alia*, gender),[17] these gains have led to what some studies suggest is a greater degree of choice in marital partners (and, to a much lesser extent, in the very decision as to whether or not to enter into the institution of marriage)[18] and what all observers agree has been a growing incidence of divorce.[19]

At the same time, the past quarter century has also witnessed a marked increase in social problems having serious consequences for family and a particularly deleterious impact on women. So it is, for instance, that with a loosening of formerly tight societal strictures and the growing commodification of society, such phenomena as the abduction and sale of women (both for forced marriages and into prostitution), the taking of mistresses, and the coarser side of what Mayfair Yang terms "consumer sexuality"[20] have, once again,[21] become significant dilemmas, as acknowledged through arrest statistics, legislative efforts, and growing public discussion.[22] This increase in social problems is also tragically evident in what many suggest is a high and perhaps escalating incidence of spousal abuse and family violence[23] and in the PRC's extraordinary suicide rates, which are not only "about three times the global average" but also mark China as "the *only* country in the world that reports higher rates of suicide in women than in men" (italics in the original) and are especially prevalent among rural women.[24]

Many women and families have also suffered in other ways. Empowered by economic reform to undertake more of their own personnel decisions, many employers have responded by discriminating against women, often quite explicitly and in open contravention of the law. Government agencies have been among the most notorious offenders, with, for example, 27 of the 42 ministries under the State Council in 1996 indicating that they would not entertain applications for various positions from women, although academic institutions have not been without shortcomings of their own.[25] Wages and promotion for women have typically lagged those of men, who have generally been allowed to work longer and receive more extensive retirement benefits than their female colleagues.[26] Women typically have been among the first laid off as state-owned enterprises have contracted and have often been the ones evicted from company-owned housing in the event of divorce, irrespective of who initiated it.[27] Juvenile delinquency seems especially pronounced among broken families.[28] And, at least in some parts of rural China, women who married outside their local villages have to a startling degree found themselves dispossessed upon divorce, with the families into which they married reclaiming the land on which they had been working and living, even in instances where the husband is the one to have sought termination of the marriage.[29]

## ≺ II ≻

### *The Debates*

The social problems ensuing from these changes have been the subject of substantial and growing concern on the part of official, quasi-official, and other parties, although the solutions proposed—and, indeed, the very definitions of what is problematic and of root causes thereof—have, not surprisingly, varied radically. National leaders have delivered much publicized addresses; the State Council has launched a master plan regarding the development of the PRC's female citizenry; relatively "traditional" political campaigns have been launched against prostitution, trafficking, and spiritual pollution; international agreements have been ratified and foreign assistance garnered; and experimentation has been conducted as to ways in which programs with potentially deleterious effects might be altered,[30] even as the state has continued to embrace developmental and other policies that arguably have contributed to the very difficulties at issue. And throughout a small but vibrant collection of scholars and activists have endeavored to make their voices (and alternative perspectives) heard.[31]

Law, typically operating in conjunction with campaigns, has come increasingly to be seen by many in and beyond official cir-

cles as a promising instrument through which to address these
concerns, although, as will be discussed below, it too, arguably, is
not without considerable infirmities. At the national level, the
most prominent measures following the passage of the 1980 Marriage Law included the affirmation of the equality of men and
women in the 1982 Constitution; the articulation in the 1986
General Principles of the Civil Law of the importance of marital
autonomy; the passage in 1992 of the Law on the Protection of
Women's Rights and Interests[32]; the promulgation of an inheritance law intended to protect the interests of women[33]; and the is-
suance of an array of laws, regulations, circulars, decisions, and
other formal administrative pronouncements focused on the registration of marriages, abductions, and, to a lesser degree, sexual violence.[34] These have spawned complementary measures at the sub-
national level, including the enactment of provincial and municipal provisions regarding domestic violence, in addition to making
their impact felt in *laojiao* [re-education through labor] and other
informal administrative practices that have continued to play a
role in China's definition and handling of deviance.[35]

Notwithstanding these steps, however, by the mid-1990s a
number of actors, prominent and otherwise, had come to believe
that much of the energy therein expended had been directed toward behaviors that, though important, were more symptomatic
than causative. It was necessary, they suggested, to confront the
institution of marriage itself more directly. And doing so, in turn,
it was further contended, could be accomplished only by undertak-
ing thoroughly to revise the Marriage Law of 1980. The debate that
ensued was one as much about the broader questions implicated—
the meaning of freedom in the marital union, the balancing of
state and individual interest in that relationship, and the relative
domains of law and morality—as it was about the specific legal issues around which discussion coalesced, namely, the appropriate
standard for divorce and the legal foundation for punishing third
parties and securing financial redress.

For Wu Changzhen,[36] one of the principal figures in the debate
and a professor of law at the China University of Politics and Law
long known as an advocate for the interests of women and children, and for many other critics[37] of the Marriage Law of 1980, the
tale of the reform era was as much about burgeoning social tur-

moil as about material development. For all the obvious benefits of prosperity, it was accompanied by a sharp rise in divorce, spousal abuse, child neglect, and an array of other social problems. Without being overly simplistic about causation, at the heart of these problems, wrote Wu, was a failure of Chinese society properly to understand the meaning of freedom in the marital relationship, if not more generally—which failure was both mirrored in and perpetuated by the 1980 Law.

Both society and the Law misunderstood freedom, argued another critic, Wu Hong,[38] viewing it principally in absolute terms as a matter of individual preference, as evidenced by the ease with which one spouse might unilaterally obtain a divorce. Freedom ought instead to be seen in more relative terms, given the implications of a decision to terminate a marriage both for weaker parties (typically women and children) and for social stability more generally. The fact, wrote Wu Changzhen, that women accounted for some 70 percent of suicides in China and that among these one half could be tied to problems associated with marriage was chilling both in and of itself and for what it suggested about the condition of Chinese society. The vulnerability of children, suggested Professor Tong Man of the People's University, provided a powerful example that freedom was relative and needed to be weighed against responsibility.[39] And beyond the family itself, the laxity that had been allowed to creep into marital matters was contributing to the broader decline of social order, some suggested, referring to the fact that officials, particularly in Guangdong, had turned to corruption to support mistresses and second households.[40] It was, therefore, critical that the terms in the 1980 Law pursuant to which divorce might be granted be revised so that law could do its part in promoting the basic dignity, fundamental morality, and social order upon which freedom and civilization itself rested.

Others also expressed concerns about the tenor and implications of the Marriage Law, even if they did not counsel revisions of the law explicitly intended to constrict party autonomy in matters such as divorce. Chinese intellectuals since the May Fourth movement, wrote Professor Zhu Suli of Beijing University's law faculty, have mistakenly assumed, based on a stereotypic understanding of the West, that the more freedom a society allows in the decision to marry or divorce, the more progressive it is and the more it can be understood as promoting happiness.[41] Actually, argued Zhu, who had spent almost a decade in the United States, Western history is a good deal more complicated, by no means suggesting so clear a correlation. The real question for China, instead, is one of how to use freedom responsibly, particularly in view of the likelihood that the profound changes China has been undergoing as it moves from a socialist to a more market-oriented nation have left women more vulnerable to exploitation. In such a context, the possibility of divorce becoming more difficult to obtain could, suggested Zhu, have the salutary effect of making those contemplating marriage more serious about the step they were considering and those already wed more committed to their union. Although less reflective than Zhu, others in the law world mirrored such concerns in contending that society had changed so during the reform era that the 1980 Law no longer was sufficient for the challenges presented by contemporary China.

The efforts of Wu Changzhen and others to advance a conception of the law that they thought protective of the interests of women and of society more broadly did not, however, find universal acclaim. It is simply wrong, argued one group of activists, to situate considerations of freedom with regard to matters such as divorce within a broader societal context. Indeed, in their mind, the 1980 Law really was more one on family than marriage as such, given the inclusion in it of provisions regarding adoption, the child policy, support for elderly parents, and other topics going well beyond the marital unit itself. Law, some argued, ought to be used to protect the rights of individuals, rather than to sublimate them to maintain social stability. It was the discovery and nurturing of the individual, after all, that was responsible for so much of the progress that the West has enjoyed, compared to China, since medieval times.[42] To constrict freedom through steps such as making divorce harder would be to turn back the wheel of history [*kai lishi daoche*].[43]

Others echoed this opposition to the position advanced by Wu Changzhen and her colleagues. Professor He Weifang of Beijing University's law faculty chided Wu's concern with "third parties" [*di san zhe*] interfering with marriages by asking rhetorically whether China would be better off if the third party interposing itself between a husband and wife were the government?[44] "Restricting freedom of divorce," observed Chen Xinxin of the Chinese Academy of Social Science, "not only violates one's right of freedom of marriage, but also sends the wrong message, for people will not know whether marriage is meant to be one's private matter or 'a matter of consequence for the state'" [*guojia dashi*]. At a time when economy and society were moving in the direction of greater self-reliance, how could such "protection," asked Chen rhetorically, be beneficial for the liberation and development of women? Women (and, for that matter, even men) would be better served if the law instead encouraged people to take responsibility for their own affairs.[45] Moreover, continued Chen, while law undoubtedly possesses the capacity to make divorce harder, was there any reason to believe that it can bring happiness to those stuck within an unhappy marriage? Is there not, wrote Professor Deng Weizhi of Shanghai, a danger in overemphasizing the problems some have in marriage and so altering the law in ways that would produce difficulties for many more?[46]

Still others took a more sociological focus. Li Yinhe, a prominent United States–trained sociologist heading the Marriage and Family Research Office at the Chinese Academy of Social Science, argued that far from always being something to be dreaded, divorce might in some situations be desirable, not only freeing unhappy individuals from an unfortunate union but sparing their children the prospect of growing up in acrimonious households.[47] Others suggested that, contrary to the fears expressed by Wu Changzhen and company, China was not, in fact, experiencing a wave of divorce that was aberrant on an international standard, but was simply responding as had other societies as they underwent industrialization and urbanization.[48] Yet others took issue even with the basic link between familial and social stability, suggesting that whatever problems China might be facing in the latter regard had yet additional rationale. And, although less caught up in reform of the marriage law itself, still others used the occasion of these debates to raise even more fundamental questions. So, for instance, they wondered about the capacity of a state so set, consciously or otherwise, in patriarchal values and practices to produce and sustain marital or other social institutions—or even conceptions of gender—that could foster genuine respect and a rich and full sense of equality.[49]

Beyond these general considerations, the debate centered around a number of more concrete issues. Two of the more noteworthy concerned the question of the legal foundation of marriage itself and the appropriate standard for divorce.[50]

Controversy over the legal foundation of marriage came into particular focus with respect to the question of the basis for punishing extramarital relationships and for providing compensation for abandoned spouses. To advocates of revision, the need for action in this area was starkly apparent. Not only was the nation's divorce rate growing, but increasingly, extramarital involvement, which could take the form of so-called "second wives" [*bao er nai*] or more casual relations, was implicated as a prime cause.[51] An extensive study by Beijing University's Research Center for Women and Law concluded that extramarital affairs were responsible for at least one in ten of all divorces, while less academically oriented surveys suggested that adultery might be a factor in as many as one half of all divorces.[52] And there was evidence of husbands simply refusing to reach appropriate pecuniary settlements with abandoned spouses, particularly in instances where the wife had remained in the family's rural home while the husband had achieved some measure of financial success elsewhere or taken on an entire new family or in situations where the husband had taken a new wife to avail himself of a loophole in the one child policy (which permitted someone remarrying to have a second child).[53]

Monogamy had, for the most part, been a core principle for the Chinese Communist Party from the first laws promulgated in the revolutionary base areas well prior to the foundation of the PRC onward, and one might, therefore, reasonably have assumed that this principle would have precluded polygamous relations of all types.[54] The Marriage Law of 1980, however, unlike its predecessor (and earlier relevant laws) did not state an explicit bar on concubinage [*naiqie*] or bigamy—perhaps because by 1980, unlike 1950, concubinage had supposedly been eradicated, while more conventional bigamy was forbidden under the criminal law. By the 1990s, some observers found this omission problematic in view of the social phenomena described above and what they thought to be the excessively narrow parameters of the criminal law (which provided that bigamy would only obtain if the relationship with the third party were registered as an official marriage).[55] Accordingly, they thought it critical that the Marriage Law be amended regarding both bigamy and marital rights and duties more generally. In the former regard, they urged that the Marriage Law contain an expansive definition of bigamy that would include married individuals engaged in on-going sexual relations with someone other than their spouse, even if the second relationship was not officially registered.[56] In the latter, they argued that the Marriage Law should be amended to provide a sharp direct statement of spousal rights and duties that all could understand.

"Morality," argued Ma Jijun of Beijing University, "in our current society no longer adequately restrains behavior," with the result that reliance on it alone may have the ironic result of "actually encouraging bad conduct and a neglect of the harm that victims are suffering."[57] Law is needed, suggested Wu Changzhen, to buttress morality, as well as complement administrative sanctions and Communist Party discipline.[58] Law may not be able to infuse a marriage with genuine affection, but law certainly had the capacity to foster "sincerity in the husband-wife relationship" by establishing minimum requirements of "equality and mutual respect" and by explicitly outlawing "infidelity."[59] Toward that end, Wu Changzhen, Yang Dawen, and others of like mind produced a 157-article draft revised law.[60]

Revising the 1980 Law along these lines, suggested advocates, would provide dual benefits. In a positive vein, it would crystallize the rights and duties spouses owed one another, thereby exerting what Wu Changzhen terms a "directional influence" in the sense of promoting sounder behavior and serving as a deterrent to those who might otherwise easily be swayed.[61] And for those not so amenable to the high road, it would provide a strong legal foundation for injured parties seeking compensation from those whose actions caused harm ending in divorce. This would be in keeping with the tenor of China's broader economic reforms in its emphasis on individual economic responsibility.[62] After all, if the civil law could call on parties entering contracts to act in "good faith," noted Professor Long Yifei of the People's University, why not include a right to and duty of "faithfulness" in the marriage law.[63] Or as Lu Chunhua put it rather more succinctly, "if we can have laws dealing with things like garbage disposal and traffic violations," surely it is not unreasonable to have rules that would deal with extramarital affairs and the devastating impact they have on families.[64]

Li Yinhe and others greeted these proposals with something close to derision, offering both philosophical and more practical arguments. In the former vein, the sociologist Qiu Renzhong argued that "law is not a tool to promote particular moral standards. Legal scholars and legislators who want to use the law to punish extramarital relations have fundamentally blurred two distinct spheres—law and morality—and so created [what might be called] legal moralism." "Legal moralists," Qiu continued, "do not understand how important the existence of private space is to a modern society. Creativity requires the state to be less involved."

Indeed, further contended Zhou Xiaozheng, "law is not capable of regulating and therefore should not regulate people's thoughts and feelings [including] love and sex. Fidelity, extramarital affairs, and the like are issues of one's belief system and should be resolved by those norms. We should not make a fetish of law, misuse the rule of law, or try to use laws to regulate a domain law is incapable of regulating and so should not regulate!"[65] The case could even be made, suggested Zhou and Wang Jianxun, that sexuality was so fundamental a human freedom that it ought not necessarily to be abridged even by the institution of marriage itself.[66]

The effort to draw the state into the regulation of personal life through the outlawing of extramarital affairs and the establishment of a right of compensation also would not work at a practical level, argued Li Yinhe. This, after all, was not exactly something new in Chinese life. Chinese authorities had, for instance, involved themselves in a range of intimate matters during the Cultural Revolution with dreadful results. At present, adultery and associated activities were so prevalent that it was simply not realistic to assume that law could restrain them, she further contended, quoting a Chinese proverb to the effect that law cannot punish if too many people are involved [*fa bu ze zhong*]. Moreover, even if such a law could be enforced, it might well have a number of unintended undesirable consequences. One, for example, might be to make people more reluctant to get married in the first place, given the heavy legal responsibilities marriage would carry. A second might be to increase the anxiety levels of people once married by encouraging the collection of "evidence" about possible misbehavior (much as lawyers might build a case). A third might be, ironically, to accentuate China's growing inequality and commercialization in the sense that an obligation to pay compensation would be far less daunting to the wealthy than to others. And a fourth might be to divert attention from genuine problems in Chinese society, while leaving China yet further behind the modern world.[67]

Relative to the drama surrounding questions of second wives and the relative spheres of morality and law, the issue of the appropriate legal standard for divorce might seem a rather technical one, of interest primarily to lawyers; but as with so many matters that arose during these debates, it, too, was infused with far broader political and social import. To appreciate this, it is necessary first briefly to review the treatment of this issue over the PRC's first four decades.

The PRC's original Marriage Law, a mere twenty-odd articles cast in the most general of terms, did not specify a substantive standard for determining whether a divorce should (or should not) be granted. Instead, it only provided a procedural requirement that mediation precede any application for divorce—which had the practical effect of either requiring both parties to agree to the marriage's termination or, if they did not agree, leaving it to the state (whether through local political authorities or, less often, the local judiciary[68]) to determine at its discretion whether the marriage should continue. The state, in turn, freely exercised this discretion. First encouraging divorce in what all major observers have termed an extraordinary break with the past, the leadership then sought sharply to discourage it "in the wake of the 1953 marriage law reform campaign,"[69] with the result that the more than one million divorces that year would prove to be "a number that we would not see again until 1997."[70] But whether seeking to promote or to constrain divorce, Beijing was driven by the imperatives of building a new Chinese state, concerned in the former instance with uprooting traditional hierarchies and freeing women from oppressive marriages (generally not formed of free will) and in the latter with halting what came to be seen (correctly or not) as an undue erosion of social stability.

The sharp turns in the state's early policy toward divorce

prompted an energetic debate among Chinese experts over the course of the 1950s, culminating during the One Hundred Flowers Movement and subsequent Anti-Rightist Movement, as to the degree to which the basis for divorce (and, indeed, marriage itself) should be understood in material, rather than more personal, terms. Some experts, such as the scholar Han Youtong, acknowledged the importance of broader structural concerns such as the elimination of vestigial feudalism but also argued that emotions mattered and that it should therefore be possible for parties to secure a divorce in the event of a mutual alienation of affection.[71] Others, such as Liu Yunxiang, countered that taking affection into account only served to accentuate lingering bourgeois tendencies and urged that in a Marxist state divorce should only be granted on material grounds if, for example, "one party . . . seriously violates communist ethics . . . or commits other crimes."[72] This tension is poignantly portrayed in the novel *Waiting*, in which the protagonist, the army doctor Lin Kong, returns to his native village annually over an eighteen-year period in the hope of securing an end to his arranged marriage to Shuyu so that he might marry a nurse with whom he had fallen in love, only to be rebuffed by the local authorities who tell him "you are a revolutionary officer [who] should be a model. What kind of model have you become? A man who doesn't care for his family and loves the new and loathes the old . . . Do you deserve your green uniform and the red star on your cap?"[73]

The frustrations engendered by the materialist approach, together with the baleful impact of the Cultural Revolution on marriage,[74] spurred efforts in the late 1970s to revise the Marriage Law in a manner that might take fuller account of matters of the heart in divorce. One major consequence was the elimination of the requirement that mediation precede divorce and its replacement in the 1980 Law with Article 25 which provided that the courts "should" [*yinggai*] grant a divorce upon finding that a marriage had "broken down emotionally" [*ganqing que yi polie*]. The article was designed both to establish a new substantive standard for divorce and, as a procedural matter, to empower either party to assert that the marriage no longer was tenable.

The 1980 Law was, indeed, followed by a marked increase in divorce, although so much has been in flux in Chinese life gener-

ally since that time that there may be some artificiality in attrib-
uting this upward spiral principally to this Law. The very vague-
ness of the standard contained in the Law, however, soon proved
troubling to some members of the judiciary, many of whom had
assumed their posts during Beijing's rapid expansion of the legal
system with little formal legal training and no experience in dealing with contentious family matters. What, after all, constituted a
breakdown of emotions, especially if the two parties disagreed as
to the condition of and prospects for their marriage? To resolve
such questions, the Supreme People's Court exercised its authority to issue judicial interpretations, promulgating a number of rul-
ings, including, most notably, a 1989 "opinion" [*yijian*] identifying
fourteen different situations in which a breakdown of emotion
might be said to have occurred.[75]

These efforts did not, however, resolve lingering questions regarding the standard for divorce embodied in the 1980 Law. Concerned observers argued that the focus on "emotion" encouraged
too casual an attitude toward marriage, accentuating, as it did, the
feelings of the husband and, less often, the wife, to the neglect of
broader familial and societal responsibilities. Divorce on the
grounds of unilateral intentional alienation of affection, some
concluded, should be strictly restricted.[76] In the words of the moral
philosopher Ding Qiong, "divorce should be the last resort in handling bad marriages instead of a sorry escape from marital responsibility."[77] Some further contended that "the breakdown of emotion" constituted an oddly inappropriate standard by which to determine whether to terminate a marriage, given the relative unim-
portance of emotional considerations in the decisions of many
Chinese to marry. And some, such as Professor Yang Dawen of
the People's University law faculty, one of the few men to have
long worked on questions of marriage law, took a more formally
legalistic bent. They suggested that whatever the independent
merits of Article 25 as originally drafted and of the Supreme
Court's subsequent efforts at clarification, the two were simply
incompatible, as many of the fourteen illustrations cited by the
court in its 1989 opinion, such as "physical inability to consum-
mate the marriage" and the prolonged, unexplained absence of
one's spouse, dealt chiefly with concerns other than the emotional. In the end, Yang and many others in law circles argued,

China would be better served were the standard converted from that of the "breakdown of emotion" to one of the "breakdown of the marital relationship [*hunyin guanxi polie*]."[78]

The reaction against this proposal was strong. Perhaps as few as three out of every ten Chinese marriages, conceded Xia Zhen of the Shanxi People's Congress Standing Committee, were love unions [*aiqing hunyin*], but it was for that very reason that Article 25 of the 1980 Law had been adopted.[79] The "breakdown of emotion" standard, Xia suggested, provided women who had been coerced into unfree, loveless marriage with a legitimate rationale for escape and it affirmed freedom of marriage, as well as of divorce. And whatever difficulties law professors might say they had with the standard, the *laobaixing*—the common people—argued Li Zhongfang and others, clearly had come over the twenty years since its adoption to understand and accept it.[80] Indeed, some observers said, rumors that the standard might be toughened were responsible for generating a modest upsurge in divorces, for fear that the opportunity to end a marriage might subsequently be narrowed.[81]

Others suggested what they saw as powerful additional reasons to retain the standard set forth in the 1980 Law. The re-emergence during the 1990s of such "feudal" practices as the buying of brides made it all the more imperative to re-affirm the place of the free will represented in the idea of emotion.[82] Moreover, even if undertaken principally to clarify the Law, detailed criteria of the type represented in the Supreme Court's fourteen-point opinion of 1989 had the effect of re-introducing ideas of fault into divorce decisions and so, unwittingly or otherwise, shifting the balance of decision-making power away from citizens and toward the state. This shift not only represented a diminution of freedom, but ran contrary to the lessons of world history, whether one's principal focus was the West or the former Soviet Union. In the words of Li Yinhe, it was simply "regressive."

≺ III ≻

*The Law*

The events culminating in the revision of the 1980 Marriage Law illustrate well the difficulty of efforts to characterize the lawmaking process in the PRC as one largely driven by society or as one predominantly dictated by the state. Given the depth and breadth of feeling that discussion of possible revisions of the Law evoked and given the way in which that passion helped move it to the fore notwithstanding its initial placement in the second tier of proposals in the NPC's 1998–2003 five-year legislative plan,[83] it would be misleading to see the particular Law that did finally emerge as pre-ordained by China's leadership. At the same time, however, given the central role played in framing these issues by intellectuals affiliated with the Party-State[84] and by the All China Women's Federation, the officially authorized vehicle for matters concerning women,[85] and given the ways in which the state apparatus did eventually come legislatively to cabin the energies unleashed by this debate, it would also be erroneous to treat the Marriage Law as a pure expression of civil society. In the end, as with so much else in Chinese law-making, this Law bears the imprint of a complex interplay of the Party-State, governmentally organized non-governmental organizations, a state-sanctioned elite speaking on behalf of society, and society itself more broadly working through institutions that bear some, but by no means all, of the key indicia of legislative processes of liberal democratic states.[86]

If China's senior leadership was initially relatively inattentive to possible revision of the Marriage Law, by virtue of being focused upon more avowedly political and economic concerns (and, one suspects, because it may have been inclined to see the topic as principally concerning women's issues), that was to change as controversies of the type discussed here grew in national prominence during the late 1990s. The political leadership, which had not previously displayed any particular concern about the Law's revision, ultimately sought to play a role in the shaping of the All China Women's Federation's final position. It may have been urged on by the fact that Peng Peiyun,[87] deputy head of the Federation and a long-term high-level cadre, was married to Wang Hanbin, who had previously been vice-chair of the NPC's Standing Committee and who remains important in Party circles.[88] And so it was that Li Peng, head of the NPC and former premier, chose personally to preside over Standing Committee discussions of proposed amendments to the Law. These included an unusual, joint

convening of six panels of NPC members who were not on the
Standing Committee but had potentially relevant expertise and an
invitation to the general public to express its views that resulted
in some 4,000 letters regarding the draft legislation.[89]

Perhaps not surprisingly, given the controversy that marked
the foregoing debates and that also found expression in its own deliberations, the Standing Committee endeavored to effect compromise or leave issues open where possible. Further commending
this posture was the Committee's awareness that the Supreme
People's Court, through the vehicle of judicial interpretations, and
the NPC, through its ongoing work on an overall civil code, might
in the future be able to fill in any gaps that compromise might
leave. So it was that a revised law, adopted by a vote of 127 to 1
with some 7 abstentions, emerged.[90]

With respect to the marital relationship, the Committee turned
aside the 157-article draft prepared by Wu Changzhen and her colleagues that would have vested spouses with a detailed panoply of
rights even as it moved to amend the law more substantially than
was desired by Li Yinhe and others concerned about encroach-
ments on individual autonomy. The result is a mixture of general,
almost hortatory language regarding the marital relationship with
a more modest number of legally actionable measures, not all of
which are fully spelled out. So, for example, as urged by Wu and
others, the Law added the specific requirement that "husband and
wife shall be faithful to and respect each other" but fails to indicate whether less dramatic though widespread behavior short of
bigamy and the like (such as extended or serial adultery) might
suffice as grounds for divorce (save for whatever implication one
might read into the drafters' decision to reject the proposal that
such adultery be equated with bigamy).[91]

Similarly, the revised Law stakes out new ground in becoming
the first piece of national legislation to address domestic violence,
going so far as to provide a right for its victims to seek compensation. It does not, however, define critical terms such as "domestic
violence," "cohabitation," or "bad habits."[92] Additionally, it seems
to suggest that a person being abused should first request that her
neighborhood committee or work unit seek to dissuade the abuser
or conduct mediation with him and should turn to public security
organs only in the event of "ongoing domestic violence."[93]

Or, to take another example, the revised Law goes well beyond its predecessors in identifying property and associated rights but states these in quite general terms. It calls, for example, for a recognition of the rights of both spouses in "household-based lands,"[94] and indicates that the "greater duties that [a spouse] has fulfilled in the past in bringing up children, waiting on elders, and assisting the work of the other party" may result in a right to compensation.[95] And it speaks of the possibility of a variety of other payments between divorcing parties—including "appropriate assistance if one party meets difficulties in life," alimony, support, and compensation for losses occasioned by desertion, among other actions[96]—but provides no real guidance as to the particular circumstances in which different types of payments might be required.

The treatment of the issue of the standard for divorce also reflects the Committee's desire to find a middle ground. Divorce, indicates Article 19, "shall be granted if it is both the man and the woman's own free will [to do so]." Indeed, the importance of free will is underscored, no doubt because of the resurgence in the countryside of involuntary wedlock (objectionable to both sides of the debates recounted in this chapter), with new measures that spare the need in such situations even to reach the issue of divorce by treating such marriages as "invalid from the very beginning." Yet to the disappointment of Wu Changzhen, Yang Dawen, and others, the Committee chose to retain the much criticized "breakdown of emotion" [ganqing polie] standard, rejecting the opportunity to embrace the more concrete "breakdown of marriage" standard. As if addressing those concerned that the former standard was so vague and subjective as to pose a threat to marital stability, the Committee simultaneously sought to identify, without limiting, prime instances of what might constitute a breakdown of emotion. Thus, in the same Article (32) reiterating the *ganqing polie* standard, the Committee incorporated four of the thirteen illustrations of such a breakdown that the Supreme People's Court had identified in its 1989 interpretation of this term while also leaving open the possibility that there might be "other circumstances."[97]

≺ IV ≻

*The Implications*

It is too soon to know to what extent the positions advanced in the debates leading up to the Marriage Law's revision will be vindicated. Early commentary from involved individuals such as Wu Changzhen has been cautious, acknowledging both victories won and areas in which progress remains to be made, but counseling that firm conclusions are not yet in order.[98] The NPC continues to debate the contents of what would be the PRC's first civil code.[99] And the Supreme People's Court has issued an interpretation that helps flesh out elements of the revised Law—by giving some content to the term "domestic violence," indicating that cohabitation is not to be equated with the criminal offense of bigamy, providing that compensation may be warranted for both material and emotional harm, and underscoring the importance of registering marriages.[100]

Lower level courts have accepted a growing number of cases—including some that are wonderfully dramatic.[101] In one much publicized early case, an urban businesswoman was ordered to provide compensation to the husband she was divorcing. In another, the court sentenced a man to six months in jail for cohabitation in violation of the marriage law without explaining how imprisonment was possible under a civil statute, while in yet another, the court rebuffed a wife's attempts to introduce her husband's pet parrot's utterance as evidence of his infidelity.[102] There does not yet, however, appear to be a clear pattern to cases brought or judgments rendered and, even if such emerges, Chinese courts are, of course, not formally obligated to follow precedent. That it is as yet premature to know the full implications of the amendments made to the PRC's Marriage Law in late April of 2001, however, ought not to deter us from considering larger lessons regarding the meaning of freedom suggested by the debates that led up to those revisions.

Consider, for instance, the question of the role of the state. As suggested in the introduction to this chapter, the idea that the ceding by the state of power to non-state actors in the economic and social spheres in itself advances freedom in China undergirds much pertinent scholarship, both Chinese and Western. The controversies surrounding revision of the 1980 Marriage Law usefully expand the horizons of those discussions by highlighting tensions that may exist between various forms or conceptions of freedom and between freedom and other values, such as equality and dignity, that are not only important themselves, but are also arguably crucial to the attainment of freedom itself. For example, few would dispute that China has made substantial strides over the past twenty years toward greater economic, social, and even (to a modest degree) political freedom, at least in a classically liberal sense. The argument could, however, be made that these gains have had significant attendant costs in terms of the more societally oriented definition of freedom advanced by persons such as Wu Changzhen or, if one were to eschew Wu's definition, in terms of the degree of more conventionally understood freedoms enjoyed by many citizens, including, in particular, women and children. But even if one were here loathe to employ the language of freedom to describe the cost side of the equation (for fear of using the term so capaciously as to diminish its utility), fairness dictates that we take account of the baleful, as well as the positive, consequences of the reform era, again especially as concerns the more vulnerable members of society.

This is not to deny that there is an appeal to the arguments by Li Yinhe and her allies. Their profound distrust of a patriarchal Party-State that long exercised a heavy, if not brutal, shaping hand in procreative and other vital decisions is hard to gainsay, especially for those of us who have not had to live with such constraints. We would do well, however, to heed the concerns that other Chinese feminists have raised, directly or otherwise, about assumptions of society's benevolence and from this, to be mindful of the perhaps singular capacity of the state to curb private abuses of power and structure an environment in which freedom might be widely enjoyed.[103] This point may be relatively readily apparent when one considers practices such as trafficking in human beings or, less dramatically, widespread gender discrimination that not only have re-emerged but, imbued with the rampant commercialism of the age, have gathered considerable force and for which Chinese society, at least so far, has yet to generate any answers. It also, however, has analogues beyond marriage, family, and gender. There is, for instance, little evidence that the rampantly corrupt doling out of state assets will be stemmed or that the economic freedoms of the vast majority of the Chinese people (including labor which is not free to organize in any meaningful way) will be advanced through reliance on the market and civil society alone, as these are now structured in China.

There has been a tendency on the part of many, particularly in the West, to see law as offering a way around such dilemmas for China—in the sense of providing rules through which citizens might bind both the state and society. The more pronounced proponents of such views have gone so far as to argue that legal reform is now the lynchpin to the realization of fuller political and economic freedom.[104] At one level, the debates around which this chapter revolves would seem to offer confirmation for propositions regarding law's potential—why, otherwise, would intelligent people have waged so intense a struggle over possible revision of the marriage law? And yet the same debates are also suggestive of how the very nature of law poses serious questions about its capacity to fill the full role that many would have it play in China's transformation.

Those who advocated significantly amending the Marriage Law, for example, appear not to have appreciated fully the tension between their larger objectives and the methods they sought to deploy to attain those ends. Their call, when addressing the issue of the appropriate standard for divorce, for a shift in emphasis from marriage as primarily a matter for two people, either as individuals or as a unit, toward a fuller consideration of its broader societal ramifications, seems difficult to reconcile with their campaign sharply to remake marriage in terms of legal rights and duties. After all, even if intended chiefly to serve broader societal ends, the articulation of rights—particularly to the detailed degree stressed by Wu Changzhen—tends to accentuate the individual, rather than the collective, as rights holder.

The emphasis on formal rights also seems likely to feed into the PRC government's more general efforts to emphasize the official legal system and in particular courts, at the expense of quasi-official or even less formal means for redressing problems (such as those employed by the All China Women's Federation).[105] Lawyers, particularly outside large cities, have not been much involved in divorce litigation.[106] Nor does it seem likely that they soon will be, especially for cases involving poorer people in the countryside. Indeed, even if they were inclined to take such cases, it is hard to imagine country practitioners (of whom there are not many, given the concentration of China's legal profession in the cities) bringing successful actions against husbands resident in China's cities (given the strong element of local protectionism in Chinese courts and the difficulty of securing enforcement of judgments by courts from other jurisdictions). In the meantime, there is a risk that the Federation—for all its limitations, being poised between state and society, and lacking major political clout and large numbers of highly trained professionals—may find its role as a readily available and highly familiar outlet for both the collective and individual problems of rural women diminished by virtue of this new emphasis on formal rights.

To be sure, the Federation has responded to this shift in direction by moving to build up its legal advice section. Considering, however, that these fledgling efforts do not compare with the way in which the Federation has, in its more traditional social service role, blanketed the country and considering also the sharp limits on American-style impact litigation in China, there seems little prospect of the Federation through more formal legal means being able to reach the numbers it now serves as an informal advocate. And even should women gain greater access to the formal legal process, be it via the Federation or otherwise, there is the need to be cognizant of the ways in which the language of rights has the potential to be captured by the powerful, particularly when the political and judicial institutions that will be administering those rights suffer from problems of the very type that the law is meant to address (as would appear to be the case in China, where the vast majority of judges who will be applying it are men, few of whom have any special training with respect to these issues). None of this is to argue for enshrining the institutions of the status quo, but rather simply to caution against abandoning them without thinking through the consequences thereof and of the proposed alternatives.

The views of those opposed to revising the Marriage Law are not without their own seeming inconsistencies that also are informative about the role law more generally might play. Their oft-voiced argument—that law and morality are and should remain

distinct—seems at best disingenuous and at worst to reflect a na-
iveté about the character of law and legal institutions that remains
fairly widespread in the PRC (occasioned in part, one fears, by the
suggestion both of the PRC government and of foreign legal advisors that the "rule of law" is neutral and transcends particular political choices).[107] The 1980 Law itself represents a very clear set of
state-sanctioned choices about the nature of the marital relationship—embedding it, for example, in a set of rules concerning one's
responsibilities regarding parents, children, family planning, and
the state that make it seem more a set of state policies regarding
the family and the role of women than simply a law concerning
marriage. The faith in the substantive law's neutrality that seems
to inform those opposing revision also appears to slight the ways
in which run-of-the-mill procedural requirements necessary for
citizens to avail themselves of legal protection may, in fact, be bi-
ased, consciously or otherwise, against those with limited education or financial means (who are disproportionately women). It
further appears to slight the ways in which the morality of those
charged with administering the law shapes its application, even in
states with a rather longer and deeper commitment to the rule of
law than the PRC. Indeed, in their opposition to efforts to recast
the many vague general provisions of the 1980 Law in more pre-
cise terms, Li and other opponents of revision seem largely oblivious to the possibility of the Law's opacity leaving considerable discretion in the hands of officialdom that might one day once again
be utilized to limit the very freedom in marital matters they extol.

To highlight the tensions that mark the major positions staked
out in this debate is not to deride the principal protagonists in a
national controversy of near epic proportions for their lack of theoretical elegance. Rather, it is to use the debates to underscore the
interdependence of different forms of freedom in contemporary
China. As one PRC commentator on the marriage law debates
noted, "in the 50 years since the founding of the New China, there
has not been any law that has caused such a widespread concern
from ordinary people."[108] And yet the constraints that continue to
shape political discourse within China also took their toll here,
limiting who played a role in these debates, their analysis of the
problems at hand, and the solutions potentially available to them.

The debates surrounding revision of China's Marriage Law

were, indeed, widespread and candid. Over their course, national media devoted considerable attention to them, by all appearances engaging the citizenry and, in particular, a segment thereof— women—whose views on public affairs have not typically been regularly solicited.[109] Somewhat unusually, a draft of the Law was published. And some of the criticisms voiced by leading players were as sharply critical as any that have been expressed in a sustained fashion at the national level since the Cultural Revolution. Think, for instance, of Wu Changzhen's depiction of a China in decline, failing its families (and especially their most vulnerable members), or Li Yinhe's attack upon state meddling into private affairs as grossly harming the citizenry while being responsible for China lagging far behind the West.

The state's indifference, if not condescension, toward women helps explain how these debates were able to achieve such public prominence and take on the character they did. Notwithstanding the significance of family and marital issues historically, central authorities did not initially view the matter of the revision of the marriage law as politically sensitive (at least in the sense of posing a challenge to the Party's exercise of power) or even as particularly important, as evidenced by the decision to accord it a second tier status on the NPC's agenda. Hence, with the regime's attention focused principally on issues more seemingly directly political or economic, these debates were able to take on something of a life of their own—further fueled, it would seem, by what might be described as the tendency of female cadres to have a greater appreciation than their male counterparts of the gap between the state's stated ideals and its performance.

To be fair, by the late 1990s, the regime had come to have a keener sense of the implications of marriage law reform. This sense was illustrated by the high-level attention accorded during the revision's final stages and by the regime's acceptance of the provisions in the amended law concerning domestic violence and of the financial responsibility of the wealthier party to a divorce to support the less well-off party (which was, no doubt, appealing to a government confronting a massive social welfare burden). Nonetheless, it is, we would suggest, revealing that the authorities assigned the task of publicizing and promoting implementation of the revised Law to the All China Women's Federation, as if it were essentially a woman's issue, rather than enlisting the joint efforts of the Party, the State Council, the NPC, the Supreme People's Court, and other major agencies, as has been the case with some other major measures.[110]

As much of a landmark of openness as the Marriage Law debates may have been in PRC history, we can still see in them the constraints imposed by the circumscribed nature of political discourse there. Wu and Li are sincere and articulate figures—they succeeded, after all, in goading the NPC to focus more readily than it had intended to on marriage law reform—but the fact is that they are a part of a highly urbanized state-approved elite and, most likely, would have been unable to retain the national public forum from which they spoke had they not been. Stated differently, it is hard to imagine poor rural women being represented by spokespersons appreciably closer to their own profile, given the degree to which the Party-State continues both to exert its influence in all manner of social organizations and to determine centrally who will speak nationally for whom on major issues.[111] It should, therefore, not come as a surprise that for all of Wu's heart-felt concern for those left behind by economic reform and mass internal migration and for all of Li's interest in women's autonomy, neither side seemed as attuned as it might have been to the implications of the legal positions it advocated for tens of millions of their fellow citizens, especially in the countryside.[112]

These constraints also show up, albeit more subtly, in the extent to which the proposed solutions to the problems afflicting Chinese women identified in the debates centered on law. Most observers tend to take the emphasis on law as a solution to these and other societal problems in China as a sign of progress, and yet one cannot help but wonder whether Wu and others have placed so much weight on legal change because so many other avenues remain closed. Baldly stated, it simply is not possible to advocate structural political change in the sense of arguing for the establishment of multiple political parties able to compete equally with the Communist Party for the vote of women or for direct elections through which senior officials might be held accountable at the ballot box for policies that consistently subordinated the interests of women to economic development. Nor is it possible to articulate solutions anchored in a rich conception of civil society, calling, *inter alia*, for more genuinely autonomous women's groups or labor unions, or for a media consistently able to publish whatever it wants. Indeed, it remains enormously difficult even for those proposing use of the law as a prime vehicle for reform to speak frankly about the limitations that the Communist Party's intimate on-going involvement in the judiciary poses for these very proposals.

More open and democratic political institutions in themselves are no guarantee of effective answers to the problems of spousal abandonment, domestic violence, and social disintegration—any more than law as such is a panacea. The history of marriage in the United States as insightfully sketched by the historian Nancy Cott,[113] the political theorist Michael Sandel,[114] and the legal philosopher Martha Minow clearly illustrates that such problems are too complex and the interests at play too variegated to be so readily soluble.[115] Nonetheless, given the forces unleashed in China by the changes described in this chapter, one hopes that China's citizenry will soon have before it the institutions that would enable it to have even fuller discussions both of the many possible meanings of freedom in the familial context and of the daunting task of reconciling different conceptions of freedom and their interplay with other core values.

# Realms of Freedom in Post-Mao China

JEAN C. OI

OVER THE last two decades China has enjoyed dramatic economic growth, yet the political system exhibits many of the Leninist characteristics exhibited when the reforms began. China continues to be ruled by the Chinese Communist Party (CCP), the standing committee of the Politburo still sets policy, and the bureaucratic organization still allows for mobilization. The Party remains almost identical to the state. Perhaps most importantly for those interested in political openness, China continues to arrest dissidents and those who try to establish opposition parties, or those who are perceived to present a challenge, such as the Falun Gong. These repressive acts reinforce the impression left by the 1989 brutal crackdown on demonstrators in Tiananmen that there exists little in the way of "freedom" as many would understand it in the West.

At the same time that abuses of human rights remain serious and the CCP retains firm authoritarian control, significant changes have taken place in China's political system in the past two decades that have expanded the autonomy available to the majority of its citizens. In spite of repression toward selected groups within society, a case can be made that realms of freedom have expanded under post-Mao CCP rule. Overt institutional changes, such as the adoption of popular elections for top leaders or the right to form opposition parties, are not the only or even the best measures of political reform. In transitional systems such as China an alternative and perhaps more useful gauge is the existence of new articulations of interests, including collective action by citizens in the form of demonstrations, marches, petition drives, and remonstrations to higher levels of government.

There is no inherent reason why the existence of collective action in a transitional system need necessarily be a sign of weakness in regime control. This chapter considers the possibility that certain types of collective action in post-Mao China are allowed as part of a strategic loosening by the CCP regime for its own political ends. Rather than a sign of decay, the existence of such overt political expressions may be a sign of adaptation in an authoritarian system intent on maintaining one-party rule. Political change can occur under the cover of institutional continuity.

This chapter will first elaborate an alternative research agenda for studying political change. It will then identify the emergence of new realms of freedom that exist and analyze why they exist and what they say about change in China's still Leninist system.

≺ I ≻

*Level of Analysis in the Search for Political Change*

The amount of political change one sees in a political system may vary depending on where one looks and what one includes as examples of "political change," "autonomy," or "freedom." In seeking to assess political change in a reforming Leninist system such as China, many observers tend to focus on the national level. Some national-level political changes have occurred in China, ranging from the institution of open civil service exams, to new roles for mass organizations and people's congresses, to a rejuvenated leadership,[1] to the passage of legislation such as the Administrative Litigation Law and other measures that suggest movement toward the rule of law.[2]

The consensus is that these political reforms are far from complete in China. For many analysts of democracy, the obvious failing is the inability of citizens to elect national leaders. Developments at the national level are the most observable and generally set the overall tone of the political system, but they may mask meaningful changes within the larger political system, especially those occurring at the lower levels. If one uses a micro rather than macro level approach to study political change, if one looks beyond the lack of popular national elections and the regime's treatment of dissidents to study modes of interest articulation and pursuit of interests at the grass roots, in cities and villages, one finds a very different picture of political activity in China. Citizens still lack the right to elect their national leaders, but a range of *other* activities and channels never before possible in China has become open to citizens to articulate and pursue their interests. Shi Tianjian's work provides useful insights into the nature of political participation in Beijing.[3] This chapter continues that line of inquiry but it uses cases of more radical and disruptive forms of political activity to assess whether there are increasing realms of freedom for political action. These include overt expressions of discontent in both urban and rural areas, which range from peasants using laws to combat cadre abuse to demonstrations, strikes, and attacks on government offices. It also considers the impact of the passage of legislative measures such as the Organic Law on Villagers Committees, which gave villages the right to hold democratic elections.

≺ II ≻

### New Forms of Political Expression

Of the new forms of political expression, the most worrisome for the leadership but perhaps the most significant for assessing political change and realms of freedom is the overt expression of discontent that has been occurring in both rural and urban areas.

Peasant grievances against state policies are nothing new. What is new are the ways that peasants manifest this discontent and pursue their interests. During the Mao period peasants pursued their interests mostly through covert channels, often through the *non*-articulation of interests, and sometimes in collusion with their local-level cadres, to evade exactions by the upper-level state.[4] The post-Mao countryside has witnessed an array of overt, sometimes violent, expressions of peasant discontent.

The more informed and peacefully inclined peasants use published laws to obtain their rights and to punish their cadres—this is the "rightful resistance" that Lianjiang Li and Kevin O'Brien have described.[5] David Zweig observes along similar lines that "villagers are developing a strong 'rights consciousness' and using the law to their own advantage."[6] Other peasants take action into their own hands and beat their cadres, burn their houses, or march on the upper levels of government. Sometimes, whole villages or even groups of villages have marched to county or higher levels of government, sometimes peacefully, to petition higher-level authorities to come to their aid in resolving disputes. Sometimes the marches turn violent, such as the Renshou riots in Sichuan in the first part of the 1990s. In such cases, there may be serious destruction of property, injuries, and sometimes even deaths. In the case of Renshou, troops were called to quell the disturbances.[7]

The number of such incidents and how many participate are difficult to know. Thomas Bernstein notes that in "the fall, winter, and early spring of 1996–1997, confrontations in the form of demonstrations . . . as well as petitioning . . . erupted in nine provinces in thirty-six counties. Two hundred thirty cases were labeled cases of turmoil or rebellion [*dongluan, saoluan, baodong*]."[8] In another example Bernstein states that between mid-May and mid-June 1997 half a million peasants took part in demonstrations in the four provinces of Hunan, Hubei, Anhui, and Jiangxi.[9] Accounts of peasant disturbances continue to be commonly reported in both the Chinese and Western press.

Workers also have always had ways to pursue their interests, but as with their rural counterparts, most of their strategies were likely to be covert, often using personal connections.[10] Again, what is new is the degree to which workers are willing to articulate their grievances through overt channels.[11] What is most surprising is that the government has allowed workers to engage in what can be considered collective action to demonstrate their demands. Workers not only have visited government offices as individuals or small groups of people, but also have participated in group demonstrations and processions, work slowdowns, strikes, and attacks on government offices and officials.[12]

Another feature of worker unrest that departs from the pre-reform period is the action of workers independent of their work unit. The cohesion and tight control of workers in the unit system are well known.[13] A common strategy of workers to get ahead was to curry favor with their shop floor and factory leaders. This strategy no doubt still exists, but now one also finds that workers complain and demonstrate openly against their factory leaders. Sometimes angry workers take matters directly into their own hands and march their factory directors in the streets, sometimes in Cultural Revolution style, forcing them to assume the "airplane" position, roughing them up along the way.[14]

As in rural areas, it is difficult to know how many workers are taking part in collective action. The number of laid-off workers grew from 3 million in 1993 to 11.51 million in 1997;[15] by the end of the decade it was more than 17 million. But those numbers tell us little about how many of these are discontented or how many would take political action. We have reports of various incidents of unrest, but the national picture is unclear. Dorothy Solinger cites a report stating that in 1995, 11 incidents nationwide involved more than 10,000 workers.[16] Ching Kwan Lee, citing a different source, reports protests involving more than 20 people rose to a record high of 1,620, involving more than 1.1 million people and occurring in more than 30 cities, in 1995.[17] More recent research found that in Shandong province in 1998, the party committee and the government at the county level and above received close to 15,000 visits, an increase of over 40 percent from the previous year; the numbers participating also increased over 40 percent. In Liaoning, between January and May of 1998, there were more than 1,100 collective visits to the government that involved more than 50 participants.[18] Most of the time, the actions are contained within a factory, although there are examples of strikes and protests spreading beyond a factory's gates. Solinger, for example, cites sources that indicate that one strike spread to involve 40 enterprises.[19] When workers in one factory marched their director in the streets, there were reportedly 20,000 people involved throughout the city by the end of the day.[20]

≺ III ≻

### Sources of Discontent and Expanded Autonomy

The demonstrations and other forms of public expressions described above, while not examples of legislated political reform, represent political change. The question is what kind of political change? Are these disturbances indicators of an authoritarian system losing control?[21] That is possible. However, there is an alternative explanation. The existence of overt expressions of interest and discontent may also be indicators of the adaptation of the

CCP to the new realities that have been created by earlier reforms, mostly economic. While there remains a lack of change at the top, while high profile dissidents continue to be arrested and groups like the Falun Gong relentlessly pursued, the communist regime may concurrently and strategically choose to be more tolerant in certain other realms. One cannot rule out the explanation that the regime is *allowing* certain expressions of discontent to take place.

To begin to unpack this question let us first ask why workers and peasants are now willing to take overt action, to take to the streets, and to openly go to upper levels of government. One possible reason is that peasants and workers have come to the end of their patience. Their situations simply have gotten too bad. By extension, such an explanation might also conclude that the regime is unable to stop such protests and thus may be on the brink of collapse.

When one examines the sources of peasant and worker discontent there is ample evidence to support the idea that the situation for workers and peasants has deteriorated to the point where they have little recourse. Peasants and workers are protesting against the injustices of the system and against cadre corruption that have made their lives unbearable. The questions are whether such discontent is sufficient to prompt political action and whether the regime is allowing such action to take place.

Much of the peasant discontent stems from the unintended consequences of economic reform, namely the decollectivization of agriculture. It is widely known that decollectivization changed the organization of production and increased the incentives for peasant production under the household responsibility system. Less understood is the link between decollectivization and increasing peasant burdens. The return to household farming deprived village officials of the right to income needed for village administrative expenses that earlier had come from the sale of the collective harvest. With the demise of the communes, if a village has no sources of collective income, such as village enterprises, it is dependent largely on the village-retained fees [*tiliu*] for its operating budget.[22] Because villages are not considered an official level of government, they receive no budget allocation from the upper levels, unlike the township level and above. The only right village officials have to household income is a surcharge, the *tiliu* as-

sessment, a charge that villages levy above and beyond the national agricultural tax on each household. The central government
legislated rules that forbid these fees to exceed 5 percent of peasant income. The problem is that this limit is routinely exceeded as
local cadres raise these levies to meet local needs. The poorer the
village, the greater is the need to press peasants for more fees.

Peasant burdens are further aggravated when local officials
falsely report production and income. Such problems are especially
prominent in the less developed areas, where officials try to increase their bonuses and chances of promotions by inflating their
economic performance. Often such problems are portrayed as
cadre corruption. However, not all cadres who engage in such
practices are driven by corruption. Some are pressured by their superiors at the township or county level, who themselves are subject to the same economic and political pressures, to report higher
levels of development than actually exist.[23]

Another practice that has sparked peasant protest is local officials issuing IOUs instead of cash when peasants sell their harvest
to the state. Central funds are earmarked for procurement. The
problem is what happens to these funds once they come down to
the county and township levels. Cadres misappropriate funds designated for state procurements and then force peasants to wait for
payment until more funds can be secured. *Nuoyong*—the misap-
propriation of funds—has been an ongoing problem between the
local and central state since at least the 1980s.[24]

An additional area of discontent is the increasing costs of production, which reportedly went up 15 percent a year between 1984
and 1996.[25] The problems are aggravated when corrupt local cadres
skim off the low-priced state-supplied goods and sell them ille-
gally on the open market at much higher prices.

So too in the cities, recent research suggests that the sources of
discontent are a familiar mix of the consequences of economic reform and cadre corruption. The disaffected include laid-off workers
[*xiagang gongren*], workers in factories that have been declared
bankrupt and closed, workers in unprofitable but not yet bankrupt
factories who are owed back wages because their factories lack
funds and cannot get loans, and retired workers who are not receiving their pensions.[26] The degree of dissatisfaction among these
individuals, however, is a complex issue. Contrary to what one

might expect, it cannot be assumed that all laid-off workers are discontent. New research finds that at least a portion of them are actually enjoying a higher standard of living than before they were laid off. Some have since found higher paying jobs in the private sector. Obviously, this is not true in a large number of cases. There are many families whose standard of living has declined dramatically as the result of layoffs, sometimes with the husband and wife both being the victims.[27]

Workers are not just upset with being laid off or that their factories are not paying owed wages. As in the countryside, the financial difficulties of factories are made worse by the corruption that exists or that workers perceive to exist. Workers are upset by the closure of factories and the layoffs, but in some cases the protests are aimed at specific instances of corruption or the failure of their factories to carry out provisions instituted by the state to protect the welfare of the laid-off workers, such as payment of a portion of a worker's wages during the period when he or she is laid off. In other instances, the anger is specifically directed at a factory director who is thought to be skimming off funds, stripping assets, wasting scarce funds on frivolous expenses, or falsely reporting high profits to the higher levels in order to earn personal bonuses while workers go unpaid, sometimes for years.

While frustration and discontent are well-known motivators of collective action, they may be necessary but not sufficient conditions for collective action. One must remember that workers and peasants, particularly those in China who have lived under a tightly controlled system, are likely to calculate the costs that their actions probably will bring upon themselves and their families. It is this second aspect of the equation that requires that we examine the power of the state and its response to collective action.[28]

After decollectivization, most production teams became the village small groups [xiaozu], subordinate organizations under the village retaining little economic power. The village became the lowest level of administration. But like the production team, the village as a collective lost much of its direct control of agriculture; the ability of cadres to distribute collectively owned goods and resources was decreased. In the early years, village officials still retained control over the allocation of some key inputs, such as fer-

tilizer, farm services, and land. But as input and service markets
have gradually matured in China, this control has waned in importance. The major exception is land, which is still allocated and
redistributed by village leaders.

The ability of the Chinese state to penalize the peasants is
much reduced from the Mao period. Institutional changes, namely
decollectivization and the reopening of markets, gutted the Maoist
control system that kept peasants compliant and tied to the farms.
After the reorganization of the commune system in the early
1960s, after the Great Leap Forward, the production team was the
legal owner of the land and the harvest, and the unit to which individual households belonged and in which they worked and from
which they received compensation.[29] In that system, the hierarchy
of power was clear. The key decision-maker was the production
team leader, who almost always was a Communist Party member—there was no separate party cell or officially designated leading party cadre (or secretary).[30] There were elections, but there was
no choice. The slate of one candidate per office was pre-selected by
the brigade and commune officials.

Individual peasants were dependent on the production team
and its leader for their entire livelihood. The team leader managed
production, guided the work effort of team members, and carried
out other productive and non-productive tasks assigned to him by
the production brigade and commune. The team leader allocated
work assignments and work points, which determined peasant
cash and food grain distributions. By virtue of holding office, all
team leaders were in a position to be the gatekeepers of opportunities and resources for their production team and all its members.
Moreover, the power of the team leader, while underpinned by the
Communist Party and the local commune government (its work
teams, police force, and other organizations), was amplified by
Mao's development strategy that bound farmers to the land and
the countryside.[31] Appointed officials could exercise power and get
villagers to comply by offering to grant them access to goods and
opportunities (for example, income, leisure, or social services) or
by threatening to deprive them of these resources.[32]

After decollectivization and the shift to household production,
local officials no longer had monopoly control over economic opportunities and resources. No longer can the state at any level ef-

fectively use the household registration and rationing system to control migration. Permits are technically still required, but with the reopening of free markets and the availability of rooms for rent in the urban areas peasants now travel at will, knowing that with money they can secure both food and shelter. Peasants are no longer dependent on the collective for their food or income. This new independence from the collective means decreased cadre power. This decrease in dependence in turn makes it *less costly* for peasants to express their discontent with their local cadres. In this sense the state, both at the central and local levels, has become weaker and less effective.

This change in authority relations, however, is masked by the continuity in political institutions. The same dual power structure—a party secretary and a village head[33]—still exists in all villages. The difference is that after the reforms, only some who hold these offices have power. In some villages, the power of these bodies has been eviscerated. The most obvious example is the "paralyzed villages" that are reported in the Chinese press, where peasants are poor and cadres do nothing.[34] In such villages, the costs for peasants who protest are relatively low. Peasants not only do not fear their cadres, but there is little that cadres can do to those who refuse to cooperate.[35] Such peasants have little to lose but maybe something to gain by exposing the corruption and incompetence of their local cadres.

Control over workers has similarly been loosened, as they have become less dependent on their work unit, their factory. The bonds are increasingly weakened when factories fail to live up to their commitments as the "iron rice bowl" cracks more and more. Not only are workers laid off, but even those who are not find that their factories have run out of funds and are no longer able to provide them with their basic wages, not to mention welfare services such as health care or pensions.

While the effectiveness of state controls has decreased, that in itself is an insufficient explanation for the increase in overt political activity. Despite those who pointed with alarm to the increasing fiscal power of the localities and declining fiscal revenues of the center,[36] if one looks more broadly at the overall political and economic system, at the levers the central state still does control, the case for a weakened state on the verge of collapse is dramatically overdrawn and misleading. This caveat is particularly needed in the face of theories that predict a "market transition" and the emergence of "civil society" or a "societal takeover." Many civic associations have emerged in China, but few are political. The crackdown on the Renshou riots in Sichuan[37] and the continuing repression of the Falun Gong suggest that the Communist Chinese State still has the coercive power to quell social unrest and disband unapproved organizations. This continued repressive power is publicized to deter others from similar courses of action.

Because we do not know how many times the regime has cracked down compared to the total number of demonstrations that have taken place in the rural and urban areas, the mere existence of demonstrations tells us little about state strength or weakness. We do know, however, that there are many examples of demonstrations in which the state has purposely not intervened to stop the protestors or arrest those who participated. If the total number of demonstrations is much higher than arrests, then we must look for an alternative explanation for the regime's non-repressive response.

If the state is strong enough to have the choice of whether to use force, then an alternative explanation of the large number of incidents of social unrest is that the state has made a conscious decision to withhold its full coercive apparatus to stop such demonstrations. In this alternative explanation, the airing of peasant and worker grievances has become an accepted part of local politics.[38] This explanation thus posits that an added reason why peasants and workers are more willing to take to the streets is that they feel that it is now *allowed* by the higher-level authorities, as long as they stay within certain bounds. Some might stress that this is still strictly state-defined participation, but the fact remains that this realm of freedom in China has expanded.

In this interpretation, the state over the course of the reforms has consciously adopted a complex strategy that includes the political changes that allow for more political participation, on the one hand, but that, on the other hand, also serve to strengthen the regime's own position. The latter is crucial. This logic can be seen in a number of policies that the state has adopted in the last number of years to alleviate problems, especially in the countryside.

≺ IV ≻

*Defusing Discontent, Redirecting Blame, and*
*Legislating Institutional Protections*

As with other aspects of reform, the Chinese state shows two
faces. It still periodically relies on the stick to ensure stability, but
increasingly it has been offering carrots to relieve the pressures
and defuse the discontent in order to shore up its legitimacy. It is
these carrots that suggest the regime is willing to bend to deal
with societal demands. The carrots include providing funds to factories so that they can pay demonstrating workers their back pay
and funds to pay peasants holding IOUs. In other instances, the
state has abolished certain fees in the aftermath of particularly severe peasant unrest, such as occurred in Renshou in 1993, when
37 fees and fund-raising programs were abolished and limits were
placed on 17 others.[39] More recently, the state attempted to change
the system of ad hoc and variable fees into a system of standardized taxes that will reduce the arbitrariness of local officials to increase the peasants' burden.[40]

In addition to short-term ameliorative action, the state has also
legislated new political institutions that will provide longer-term
protection against the type of problems that have been fueling discontent. Perhaps because the state-owned enterprise (SOE) reforms
have just gotten under way, most of these legislative actions have
been with regard to the rural areas.

The best example of the degree to which the regime has been
willing to allow increased political participation in the face of potential unrest is the promulgation of the highly publicized Organic
Law on Villagers' Committees. This law gives peasants the right
to hold free and competitive elections for the village committee
and establish legislative assemblies, thus creating a new basis of
village power—popular election. Through various methods, some
more democratic than others, villagers can nominate candidates
for village committee head and the other four to six members of
the committee that is designated the governing body of a village.
Candidates give campaign speeches, often on voting day. Voting is
by secret ballot and the votes are counted openly in front of the
electorate. Candidates and winners need not be party members. In
some villages, non-CCP private entrepreneurs have been elected

over party members as peasants look to economically successful individuals to lead them to prosperity. In some areas the enthusiasm for these elections has gotten to the point that there is vote buying.

It is estimated that as of the mid- to late 1990s, when the law was still in draft form, somewhere around one third of China's villages held elections and conducted them as the law stipulates. While passed in 1987 in draft form, it was turned into an official law in 1998, which means that all villages are now required to conduct elections. Whether they do and how well they implement the law remain questions for empirical research.

Despite continuing problems in implementation, the passage of the Organic Law has opened the door to significant political change. There is evidence that in some villages, particularly as villagers experience multiple rounds of elections and realize that their vote actually carries some weight, peasants enthusiastically participate to elect officials who have real decision-making power.[41] Party candidates have been rejected or voted out of office.

What is unusual about this freedom is that the impetus for village elections emanates from the central state. The passage of the Organic Law was pushed from above, not the result of bottom-up political action. The logic behind such a step by the regime, while perverse, makes political sense. Legislating competitive village elections is a step toward political change; some might say it is a political concession. Yet the reason why the regime has pursued such a policy may have nothing to do with its wanting to promote democracy as an end, but everything to do with the elections as a means to solve problems for the regime. The decision to allow village elections was a policy choice, a trade-off between the potential of increased peasant instability and amending existing political institutions. The price is that the higher levels give up their right to select the head of village government and allow instead democratic selection by the villagers themselves.[42]

The decision was a difficult one to make. Considerable debate and delay occurred before the policy was passed. Proponents of the policy won because elections could be sold as the most viable means for quelling peasant unrest and increasing regime legitimacy. Village elections became a safety valve designed to let peasants vent their dissatisfaction, but one meant to point the responsibility for continued poverty and poor village leadership away from the central authorities. Note that it was the poor villages that were originally targeted in the implementation of this policy. The regime was most concerned that elections occur in those places dubbed the "paralyzed villages."[43]

Most recently, the regime shows signs that it may even be ready to inch forward to complete the democratic process in the selection of village leaders. On a limited and experimental basis, the regime has consented to a more democratic selection of party secretaries, who are not subject to democratic election under the Organic Law. Through the use of a two-ballot system villagers have a say in the selection of candidates for the party secretary while the party members select the winner.[44] There are also signs that the regime may be ready to allow elections to spread to the higher levels, although these are still being controlled and monitored carefully. Experiments have been going on in selected townships, in which the population has been allowed to elect township government heads.[45] Variants of village elections are now being tried in the urban areas in the residents committees, although early research suggests that these elections are much less competitive and involve more state and party intervention.

A regime such as China's must weigh the costs of legislating new laws and institutions designed to protect peasants from cadre abuse and corruption versus the risk of further peasant discontent and potential uprisings. So far the state has managed to legislate new laws that allow the regime to openly take the peasants' side and support their demands but that at the same time do not jeopardize its own position. For example, requiring that information about village finances, quotas, taxes, and fees be openly displayed on village blackboards prevents or at least reduces abuse by village officials.[46] Similarly, the state has ordered that peasants be issued cards that clearly state how much tax they should pay to the township and to the village.

In the absence of political campaigns that characterized the Mao period, the state has turned to democratic methods—such as village elections and cadre accountability—not only to ameliorate peasant discontent, but also as a relatively low-cost way to help stem cadre corruption and improve local government. Giving peasants the right to dismiss their leaders protects the reputation of the Party itself. It redirects blame to the villagers themselves for choosing poorly. If these methods can solve some of the problems and lead poor villagers out of poverty, the state will gain legitimacy. While risky in the short term, over the longer run, such policies may force party members to be better leaders and solidify the Party's control at the local levels.

Contrary to what one might expect, positive views have been expressed in China about peasant visits and even marches to higher levels of government. The practice of petitioning to higher-level authorities [*shangfang*] has been pronounced a powerful method to push along the proper implementation of the Organic Law, a necessary means to deal with those cadres who have failed to take seriously and correctly implement democratic village elections.[47] The importance of receiving such complaints and no doubt of ensuring that no incidents stem from those reporting problems is reflected in the stationing of someone 24 hours a day at the Ministry of Civil Affairs to deal with emergencies related to the petitioners.

≺ V ≻

### *Risk-Mediating Factors for the Regime*

If we accept the explanation that the state is allowing increased realms of freedom to develop, we then must assess why it is doing so. Such actions, and the political unrest, threaten the system. The regime is opening itself up to increased risks, but a number of factors moderate the seriousness of the situation for the regime.

First, most of the incidents of unrest seem to be isolated cases. In sharp contrast to the Falun Gong, which the regime has cracked down hard on, there seems to be little if any network in place capable of coordinating either the workers or the peasants. The protesters seldom expand their activities outside their local area or factory, although there are exceptions, as earlier examples suggest. So far there are no signs that other groups who have grievances against the regime are attempting to coordinate larger-scale collective resistance. Political dissidents and intellectuals do not appear to be involved in these disturbances.[48]

Second, it must be highlighted that because of the variation that exists in the level of economic development, the occurrence of problems is largely limited to certain types of localities. For example, rural protests occur mostly in the poor areas of the countryside, not the rich industrialized areas along the coast. China is not faced with a situation in which peasants everywhere or workers everywhere are rising up in protest and taking to the streets. Among the SOEs there are sectors that are actually doing well. Not all factories or all workers are suffering. As Yongshun Cai has shown, there is tremendous variation in the situations faced by laid-off workers and in their political actions.[49]

Third, to be a laid-off worker in China is not the same as being pushed out into the streets to become homeless, as occurred in some cases in Eastern Europe, or as occurs with some unemployed in the United States. Unlike unemployed in capitalist systems, laid-off workers in China are still entitled to keep whatever benefits their factories provide. For those who were in the large state-owned factories, these are likely to include some sort of housing. The degree to which retention of benefits mediates discontent cannot be overemphasized. A development to watch is whether this practice continues as more pressure is put on factories to cut costs. At what point will all the benefits of the unit system be cut?

Fourth, and perhaps most important, the threat to the central state is mediated by the fact that in both rural and urban areas a common target of the protests is *local* officials. Local cadres, not the central state, are blamed for the problems that the peasants are suffering. The state can take the side of the peasants and not only punish corrupt cadres but legislate new regulations to better protect peasants in the future. The center can claim to be protector rather than culprit. In the urban areas, such arguments are harder to make because it is clear that the layoffs are the result of the centrally mandated SOE reform. Yet, as in rural areas, some of the angriest protests have been aimed at local officials such as corrupt factory managers. The state can point to its welfare policies and services for the laid-off workers. In addition to setting up the three-step safety net described earlier, the central state has created special offices, such as those in the Ministry of Civil Affairs, to help workers get retooled and find new employment, and to oversee welfare payments. Exposing corrupt or inept cadres can help the state's case. The exposure does not absolve the central authorities of responsibility, but again it redirects blame away from the state.

Blaming local authorities and poor implementation likewise allows workers and peasants a legitimate excuse to openly call for change without being accused of trying to overthrow the regime or its top leaders. Putting the blame on local officials helps explain why the regime is willing to allow more of this expression than we might otherwise expect. The citizens are being solicited to help the regime clean up the corruption that exists at the lower levels. This is an instance where the regime can allow and may even benefit from greater citizen participation.

Fifth, the regional inequalities that emerged with the economic reforms aid the regime's claims that many of the problems lie with local officials. The tremendous variation in types of economies and corresponding levels of income allows the central authorities to defend the overall thrust of its reforms and to blame problems on those local officials who fail to carry out state policies successfully. If it is widely perceived that the reform policies have resulted in successful economic development and wealth in other areas, just not in theirs, then those peasants in poor areas who are discontented are unlikely to oppose reform, even if they currently have not fully benefited from the fruits of reform.

The ambiguous feelings that the poor most likely have toward the regime are reflected in the growth in migration and the large floating population that one finds in cities and in the richer parts of the countryside. The conditions that these migrants endure in the cities certainly can elicit our sympathy.[50] But whether such conditions will lead to potentially violent discontent is questionable. As similar phenomena in other countries have shown, shantytowns do not necessarily lead to increased political activism.[51] The Chinese state may be viewed as rigid and unyielding in not abolishing the household registration [*hukou*] system that separates rural migrants from legal city dwellers, which in turn denies migrants social services and education for their children. But one also could argue that the state has in practice acceded to at least some of the migrants' demands, allowing them to remain in the cities most of the time. Except for the sporadic assaults on large communities such as Zhejiangcun in Beijing and the cosmetic migrant sweeps for big international events, authorities have allowed these migrants to slide into niches within the urban areas, to fill unwanted jobs. They earn more money than they would have been able to obtain had they stayed in their home localities or had there not been reform. An argument can be made that both the migrants and the political system have worked out ad hoc measures for allowing these not-quite-legal residents into the cities. The migrants are allowed to make the best of admittedly poor conditions to take advantage of the higher incomes in the cities and get what part of the wealth they can. This method of income redistribution may mediate the discontent that might otherwise erupt from the inequalities between the rich and the poor regions and may help close the gap. We need to look not just at what is happening in the cities where the migrants work, but also at what is happening in their home villages where the money is being re-mitted.[52]

In assessing the potential for discontent and unrest, it should be remembered that the plight of these rural migrants, regardless of how poor they are or how bad their living conditions are in the cities, is significantly different from those in other developing countries. In China, all peasant migrants have the security of knowing that they have a safety net. They may not like it, but they can always go home, where each has been allocated land to farm. One likely reason why the state has not abolished the land allocation attached to rural household registration is the regime's concern about the political consequences of sending migrants home when the urban economy is unable to support these extra laborers.[53]

≺ VI ≻

*A Glass Half Empty or Half Full?*

Is the political change in China a story of a glass half empty or half full? A convincing picture could be presented either way, depending on the aspect of political change and the level of the system one examines. Problems abound. The realms of freedom should not be overstated. China is far from being a democracy. The increased power of the National People's Congress may be due more to personalities than to institutional strengthening. Poor implementation and poorly trained legal personnel, including judges, limit the rule of law. Key posts within the bureaucracy remain subject to the Party-controlled *nomenklatura* approval system. Village elections were extended to all villages only in the late 1990s and are still likely to be poorly implemented in more than a few villages. Moreover, these elections exclude the post of village party secretary—who in many instances is the key decision-maker in a village. The two-ballot system begins to address this problem but the policy remains experimental and limited in implementation. Political action, especially collective action, must remain within certain bounds.

Yet, it is important to recognize that while there is continued hesitation toward political reform by the regime, the problems and periodic crackdowns obscure the much more accommodating stance that the regime is taking toward the many forms of overt, sometimes violent, articulation of grievances by hundreds, even thousands, of people in different localities. This is not to say that the regime has been submissive or completely accepting of the disturbances—the state continues to use its considerable coercive powers whenever it feels threatened.

China is still Leninist and wants to keep one-party control, and change must be compatible, first and foremost, with stability in a rapidly changing economic environment. But there is considerable room for selective realms of freedom to exist within a political system that refuses to grant greater political freedom. China has rejected the big bang approach for political change as it did for economic reform in favor of "groping for stones to cross the river." This has resulted in change that is significant, but often comes slowly and under the cover of existing institutions that have lost much of their original character. In some cases, the regime takes more radical and overt steps toward political change, such as the village organic law, when it is deemed necessary. But even then, the regime can use this outwardly radical political reform to serve its own ends and power—namely to reduce discontent and obtain better government, especially in the heretofore poor areas. The larger goal is to increase the legitimacy of the Party. It is unclear whether these reforms will be sufficient, but that is a separate issue.[54]

While those hoping for a more democratic China may bristle that popular election is being used by a communist regime for instrumental purposes, the end result is still one in which peasants finally have the right to elect at least one of their most important leaders. This is a new realm of freedom in practice regardless of the state's intent in passing this policy. If the recent experiments continue, free elections may extend also to party leaders within the village, and may even inch their way up to the townships. While less exciting than radical political change on a national level, elections at the grassroots levels first may result in more stable democratic politics in the longer run when and if elections extend all the way up the system. The accumulation of gradual reforms may eventually result in a changed political system much as the many changes to what was still officially a centrally planned economy pushed China to be a market-oriented economy, even though it still has Chinese characteristics. For China's leaders, the merit of such a go-slow policy is bolstered by the negative example of what happened both economically and politically in Eastern Europe, and particularly what happened in Russia. This example has no doubt dampened the spirit of those who might otherwise be calling for a quicker pace of political reform—among them the intellectuals, who up until this time have not tried to connect with any of the rural or urban incidents of political unrest. In a polity and economy in transition such as China, while current realms of freedom are wholly satisfactory to neither the Communist one-Party state nor its citizens, each side seems willing to make compromises as a realistic interim solution while furthering its own interests.

Whether China will have the luxury of a go-slow approach in the years to come is a different question. Will circumstances change in the coming years as more and more peasants migrate and as more and more workers are laid off? Will those who currently are operating in isolation begin to have networks? These are questions that cannot be answered but they also cannot be ruled out.

Whether the glass will contain more or less with regard to political reform will depend on China's continued willingness and ability to adapt its political institutions to the new realities that have evolved as the system has moved from a strict planned economy and control over its population. Can China continue to use more democratic rule, such as village elections, to its advantage in solving problems while still maintaining control? China suc-

ceeded to a large extent in its economic reforms by adapting existing Maoist institutions to the needs of a market context. In the
process, it radically changed the economic system. The regime is
likely to be much more selective concerning where political
change is allowed to take place. Nonetheless, those studying political change should be alert to significant political change occurring under the guise of a still Leninist system.

# Worship, Teachings, and State Power in China and Taiwan

ROBERT P. WELLER

A LEXIS DE TOCQUEVILLE wrote that "in the United States religion exercises but little influence upon the laws and upon the details of public opinion; but it directs the customs of the community, and, by regulating domestic life, it regulates the state."[1] In contrast, comparative surveys of values routinely show China as one of the least religious countries in the world.[2] Such surveys are, however, misleading because of the mismatch between Western ideas of religion and Chinese realities. Both organized religion and popular forms of worship are in fact growing rapidly in much of China, whatever people may say to poll-taking sociologists. Falun Gong and Christianity, which currently get the most press coverage in the West, are only the tip of the iceberg.

Very few of the most important recent religious developments in China have any stated political goals, democratic or otherwise. They survive instead by studiously avoiding politics. Nevertheless, religion has the potential to play an important indirect role through its ability to foster community ties and the kinds of social relations that will be important to the success of any future political transformation, roughly in the way that Tocqueville suggested for the United States. Partly by avoiding explicit politics, religion in China places limits on state power.

This conclusion rests partially on the recent history of Taiwan, which also went through a period of very rapid religious growth, beginning in the 1970s—just around the time that foreign social scientists had declared the imminent demise of traditional religion. Taiwan's various religious developments also avoided all politics—there was little alternative under the authoritarian rule of Chiang Kai-shek. Yet they were part of the reason for the success of democratization there, and they continue to play a very large role in Taiwan's new civil society. As well as looking at the role of religion in Taiwan's political transformation, this chapter explores the potential for similar developments in the People's Republic of China (PRC), as realms of religious freedom have expanded there since the end of the Cultural Revolution.

≺ I ≻

*On Definitions*

One problem in examining the role of religion in civil society is how to establish the cross-cultural relevance of our key analytical terms. Our entire social and political vocabulary of "freedom," "civil society," and even basic terms like "religion" and "society" did not exist in Chinese until the late nineteenth and early twentieth centuries. All of them entered Chinese through translations of Japanese works, which had coined them as translations for Western philosophical concepts. Even in the West, most of these words took on their modern connotations only during the Enlightenment. There is thus some danger in focusing on whether China has a civil society or even a religion: the question can easily deteriorate into the assumption that everything significant must simply reiterate the specific history of Western European philosophers. A brief examination of these terms—civil society and religion—may broaden the discussion in a way that will clarify the unique dynamics of the Chinese case.

There is still no single, accepted Chinese translation for "civil society." The main contenders are *minjian shehui* [popular society, most used in Taiwan], *shimin shehui* [bourgeois, in the sense of urban, society], and *gongmin shehui* [citizen's society]. As the term has evolved in English, it has several important features.[3] First, civil society groups are voluntary. Membership is not based on ascriptive ties of kith or kin, but on the free choice of autonomous individuals. Civil society thus exists as an intermediate world between the family and the state. Second, civil society groups must show a basic tolerance to other groups. Recognizing the right to disagree differentiates civil society groups from uncivil societies like the Ku Klux Klan. Finally, even though much of the recent literature on civil society has been concerned with its opposition to the state, such groups must also recognize the legitimacy of the state and its rules. The state, in turn, must guarantee a legal open space in which these groups can operate.

This emphasis on autonomous individuals making choices within a set of formalized rules does not fit well with Chinese religion. The fault, however, lies as much in Enlightenment and modernist assumptions about civil society as in Chinese religious culture. A relatively new literature on civil society outside the West has begun to suggest that there may be alternate models of civility based on less modern-looking ties of kinship, religion, and community.[4] In contrast to the formal and voluntary organizations we normally concentrate on, this literature points us instead toward an "informal political sector" that may be just as important in the success of political change. If Chinese religion proves to be important, it will be as part of this informal political sector of local ties and personal connections.

"Religion" itself is the other problematic term.[5] Religion, by Locke's time, included the key ideas of belief in a supreme power, ordered worship, and a code of ethics.[6] As the concept moved into China, where various twentieth-century governments framed their policies around it, these ideas remained important, along with sacred texts and a trained clergy. Christianity fit the definition well enough, as did clerical Buddhism or Daoism. The practice of the great majority of Chinese, however, was condemned as superstition [*mixin*, another word strongly influenced by Western thought] by both Republican and Communist governments. This mismatch between Western-influenced definitions of religion and Chinese practice is one reason why polls in China find so many people who claim to have no religion, even though we can see people worshiping throughout many areas of the country.

China, of course, already had its own developed vocabulary for discussing the social world, and it helps clarify the religious dynamics that still exist. The key terms covering the range of what we now loosely call religion in China were *bai* [worship] and *jiao* [teaching]. "Worship" described how someone interacted with gods or ancestors [*baishen* or *bai zuxian*], but also included interactions with secular superiors, like *baiqin* [to visit the parents of a wife or friend] or *baifang* [to pay a courtesy call on a superior].[7]

"Teachings" implied a social structure of teachers and students, often built around a textual base. The term covered Buddhism, Daoism, and sects like the White Lotus. Most Chinese worshiped without following any specific teaching. Neither term—worship or teaching—drew the clear line between sacred and secular realms that the Western idea of religion assumes. Broadening our usual concept of religion to encompass the range of these indigenous terms has the advantage of focusing attention on how religious practice shapes daily life apart from any prior assumptions about its separation from secular spheres like politics, or from its ties to formal structures like priestly hierarchies.

≺ II ≻

*Self and Society in Popular Worship*

Most Chinese worship is inherently local, both in the social relations it creates and in the sense of self it fosters. Every rural hamlet and many urban neighborhoods in Taiwan, for instance, have their own temples to the local Earth God [Tudi Gong *miao* or *shetan*]. The neighborhoods themselves build and maintain these shrines, and each local household in turn takes responsibility for making daily offerings there. Small temples like these were the first to be rebuilt in China in the 1980s, as part of the significant increase in local freedoms that followed on the economic reforms.[8] These shrines have now reappeared in many villages over a large area from Guangxi through Fujian. The god images in these temples are usually dressed as local gentry, and often appear as husband and wife, unlike the case in other kinds of temples. Like the gentry of old, Earth Gods are patrons who need to be treated with respect, and who provide security from outside threats like ghosts. In many parts of south China and Taiwan, villages also mark their spiritual and physical boundaries with five "forts" for guardian spirit soldiers.

Other kinds of deities mark off larger communities. Communities all over China featured one or more large temples that served multiple villages. They often were centered in market towns. Their deities, represented by wooden images, marked their turf by making the rounds of their villages on major festival days, and by

parading around in processions that consciously recollected imperial magistrates touring their counties. Community contributions
built and supported these temples, which often intermixed with
the most local levels of politics. Some had the ability to tax
households to raise funds for rituals or reconstruction, and many
in Taiwan served as the power base for a political faction. Committees of local leaders ran temples and arranged for rituals and
processions.

Parts of this symbol system refer to the national polity rather
than just localities. This broader reference to the national level
happens, for instance, when gods emulate local magistrates (or
perhaps the magistrates emulate local gods) by living in temples
that resemble magistrates' offices, or receive petitions (by burning
them in temple courtyards) modeled after imperial legal documents. The imperial government encouraged these trends by
granting official titles to some deities.[9] From the Song Dynasty to
the present, community temples and local elites also played at
this by petitioning for titles for their local gods (in imperial times),
or by pointing out the national significance of their god.[10] The current result is that some major community temples are devoted to
national deities, others honor purely local figures, and all of them
carry at least some of the trappings of imperial officialdom.

Claims of national identity, however, generally remained secondary to local identity. The Song Dynasty had already seen significant growth in temples to purely local deities, especially as the
elites cemented local bonds in the face of a weakening state.[11] This
trend has continued. Modern attempts to claim national authority
also tend to be undercut by local loyalties.

The managers of the temple to the Patriarch of the Clear
Stream [Qingshui Zushi Gong] in Sanhsia, Taiwan, for example,
circulated an origin story about their deity in which he stars as a
Song Dynasty loyalist against the invaders from the north. This
story was a transparent attempt to flatter Taiwan's Guomindang
(GMD) government, which saw itself in a similar role against the
Communists. It was not, however, circulated by people outside
the temple management. Stories of the Patriarch performing local
miracles were far more salient. People credited him with helping
them get into college, avoid nasty military assignments, or create
a successful business. Above all there are tales of how he had

helped local soldiers survive their service in the Japanese army during World War II. He typically appeared to soldiers from Sanhsia serving in Southeast Asia to warn of incipient attacks. He did not help the Japanese this way, nor did he even help Taiwanese from other parts of the island. This situation is common across China, as people have long reinterpreted even well-known national deities like Mazu to meet their local priorities, even at the cost of national interest.[12]

Community temples are not parts of large hierarchies, in spite of the implications of the imperial metaphor. Quite unlike the Catholic Church or the Chinese government, these temples are the financial, social, and symbolic creations of their local communities. They typically have no resident priests that would tie them into broader clerical hierarchies, and answer to no authorities beyond the community. Both Taiwan and the People's Republic have temple registration requirements, but both are enforced spottily now, and neither claims any authority over the religious details of the temples.

When temples link up, the connections are almost always economic and historical, but not directly tied to official political authority. The most frequent relationship among temples is called "incense division" [*fenxiang*], which typically occurs when emigrants to a new area bring some incense ash from their old temple to found a new daughter temple. They will return through periodic pilgrimages to renew the tie. Many temples in Taiwan have such ties with old temples in Fujian Province. Taiwanese have gone streaming back to these mother temples in the opening up of the last few years, partly to enhance their (and their temple's) prestige at home, partly to open the way for economic investment in China, and partly to express their own devotion. This broadest level of religious organization typically helps shape expanded social communities formed through historical ties.

Worship of ancestors also roots people locally. Ancestral tablets themselves can be copied and moved, but lineage halls are rooted to localities, and so are burial sites. The ritual cycle marks these localities clearly. Children living far away return home for the lunar new year; descendants of a common ancestor come together for major lineage hall rituals; and the annual grave cleaning ritual [Qingming Jie] can come close to tracing out the lineage on the ground as descendants begin the day at the grave of their earliest ancestor and gradually work their way down the kinship diagram from grave to grave. Grave cleaning was the first form of public worship to be observed throughout China after the Cultural Revolution.

Geomancy—the idea that natural energies can be focused through graves and houses to benefit the living—further cemented the importance of particular places. Graves were important for the geomantic benefits they offered nearby descendants, as well as giving the opportunity to honor ancestors. The link to a place thus involved cosmic forces as much as loyalty to ancestors. These strong ties to locality help explain why some Chinese refer to themselves as coming from a certain place even generations after their ancestors moved away. They also help explain why elites in imperial China (unlike Europe) often retained ties to their native villages and returned to live there after civil service careers.

Popular worship embedded people in social worlds as well as localities. One aspect of this social world was hierarchical. Ancestor worship, as one would expect in a place where Confucius was so important, marked generation, gender, and age seniority in all its rituals. Families made offerings to ancestors and aged parents or grandparents in strict generational order at the lunar new year, and descendants marked their exact relationship with the deceased through mourning dress at funerals. God temples also established hierarchies among the gods themselves and between gods and humans. This embrace of hierarchy occurred in the shared symbolism from imperial bureaucracy, the granting (or claiming) of ever more glorious imperial titles to gods, and the physical prostration of human supplicant to god. The Chinese term for worship, *bai*, captures this dynamic by referring equally to acts of hierarchical respect for spirits and for living superiors.

Chinese popular worship also shapes a world of horizontal social relationships. Lineages and local temple communities, for example, offer potential social resources that people can mobilize to raise capital or garner political support. These ties are not just reiterations of hierarchy, but also shapers of new social relationships. Events like funerals bring together wide ranges of kin, and weddings create new groups of ties between families. Sworn brotherhoods, which always have a religious dimension, cement horizontal ties among peers. Incense division networks also maintained useful social connections, which are currently easy to see as Taiwanese revive these old connections as routes to investment in China.

Popular worship thus interacts with local forms of power in complex ways, not all of which are directly relevant to issues of state control. Worship is part of the entire array of village and neighborhood social life and can both reinforce and challenge power relations between parents and children, men and women, landowners and laborers, and all the rest of the range of local ties. There is some danger in simplifying this complexity by saying that popular worship creates horizontal community ties. Nevertheless, from the point of view of state control—especially above the level of village and township—this creation of localized and socially embedded identities through popular worship, with all its internal power dynamics, is vitally important.

These identities and ties shape the "customs of the community," as Tocqueville suggested, but they also create the potential for direct social action. We already have a significant literature pointing to the importance of kin networks for entrepreneurs in all Chinese societies.[13] Temple networks have been just as important, because they are among the only community-level ties that existed beyond the political system. When local militias were set up at the end of the Qing Dynasty, for instance, they were often based in community temples. In another case, the five most powerful lineages in the New Territories united through one of their ancestral halls in 1899 to fight the British takeover.[14] Faced with a similar problem, Sanhsia in Taiwan organized resistance to the Japanese takeover in 1895 through the main community temple to the Patriarch of the Clear Stream.[15]

As an example, the broader civil influence of religion in modern times can be seen in Taiwan's large and influential environmental movement. Taiwan's transition away from martial law in July 1987 was a watershed for national environmental organizations, as it was for civil groups of all kinds. Several major environmental organizations were formed at about that time. While these national groups sometimes become involved in local protests, especially in very high profile cases, their influence is only indirect for the great majority of cases. Local organizers instigate and lead most environmental protest in response to what they consider threats to local health. They use any local ties available to help organize—religious ties, kinship and personal networks, and local political factions. Only some cases manage to mobilize temples, but they have been powerful where they have been brought in.

Given the intimate symbolic and organizational ties of major community temples to local authority, it is no surprise that relatively wealthy, politically conservative community leaders control most of them. It is thus often difficult to acquire their support for protests. Yet when temples can be won over, they offer the movement a powerful moral sanction in local terms, alongside a ready-made organizational network and a stockpile of funds. Indeed, both sides may try to mobilize religion. When Formosa Plastics decided to build Taiwan's sixth naphtha cracker (a large and often polluting kind of refinery) in Yunlin, Y. C. Wang [Wang Yong-qing]—CEO and one of the wealthiest men in Taiwan—called on each of the major local temples and offered a generous donation. Apparently as a result, none of them became involved in local protests.[16]

Earlier protests against Taiwan's fifth naphtha cracker, however, made very effective use of religion. This plant was to be built in a neighborhood of Kaohsiung City by China Petrochemicals, in a large refining complex already there.[17] Protesters had blockaded the west side gate to the compound soon after the new plant was proposed in 1987. The blockade continued through the next two years, supplemented by occasional blockades of the main gate after alarming incidents—once after one of the leaders was beaten and robbed by a drunk China Petrochemical employee, and again after extraordinary emissions from the main refinery.

Cai Chaopeng, one of the main leaders of the movement, was a religious specialist with an intimate understanding of the potential power of religion. Cai had run a fortune-telling business before the protests and had wide experience with planchette writing and other forms of Taiwanese religion. More recently he has taken lay Buddhist vows and is involved with a local Buddhist environmental group. Liu Yongling, another top leader, responded in an interview that they had asked one of their major local gods—Shen Nong, the god of agriculture—for support at the very beginning.

They used the simplest method of divination, throwing two curved pieces of bamboo root [*poe*], which can come up "yes," "no," or "laughing." Defying the odds, it came up "yes" nine times in a row. When the GMD tried it, he said, the result was always "no." Probably more critically, Cai managed to garner financial backing from this temple in August 1987—it offered the equivalent of nearly US $100,000 to the self-help committee, as life insurance for anyone killed in defense of the community.

The most creative use of local religious practice came in December 1987. As Cai Chaopeng and Liu Yongling told it, the protesters had left a handful of people to keep watch over the banner that represented their blockade of China Petrochemical. Plainclothes police came by late at night, bringing alcoholic gifts. When the sentries finally passed out, the police removed the banner, symbolically ending the blockade. Expecting trouble the next day, a thousand riot police were out in force to prevent a renewal of the blockade. When the protest organizers discovered this in the morning, they used the temple public address system to call people together. Religion provided an ideal mechanism to reestablish the blockade, because religious parades, unlike other forms of public demonstration, usually receive rubber-stamp official permission.

As part of their show of religious force, the group mobilized the temple's traditional martial arts performing group, a Songjiang Zhen, to support them while they set up a spirit altar at the gate. Such performing groups involve dozens of young martial arts enthusiasts, armed with spears and swords, who perform traditional routines at important festivals. They wear operatic costumes and makeup, and their steps are ritualized. Nevertheless, the weapons are real, the performers can fight, and the element of real physical threat was obvious to everyone. The police backed down, and in the end the protesters agreed to take the spirit altar down in return for the right to leave their banner (and the blockade) up.

The final crucial religious intercession occurred on May 5, 1990. This was the eve of a local referendum on building the plant. Everyone expected a victory for China Petrochemical; 81 percent of the people polled nationally supported building the plant. The forces most adamantly opposed to construction gathered 50 to 100 people to worship the God of Agriculture and ask his preference in

the referendum. Again they threw *poe,* and again they got a powerful response of eleven straight agreements with the most radical
position against construction. As word of this minor miracle got
out, a crowd began to build, finally developing to perhaps a thousand people. Most of them made incense offerings to the temple,
and the contents of the incense pot eventually burst into a large
fire. This phenomenon is called *hoat lo* [manifesting the incense
pot, Mandarin *fa lu*], and people consider it a powerful acknowl-
edgment of the deity's approval.

Further enhancing the power of the event, the goddess Guanyin
suddenly possessed an older woman. Putting her fingers into the
lotus mudra, the goddess/woman began chanting that the neighborhood would be doomed if the plant were built. Such spirit possession is not at all unusual in Taiwan and provides a powerful
possibility for mobilizing religious power, since the normally conservative authorities who manage temples cannot control what
their god says through a medium. After the fact, many people
credited this single event with the results of the next day—people
voted to oppose the naphtha cracker without compromise. In the
end, the government ignored the referendum and approved construction, but the long protest did succeed in pushing the company to set up a foundation (with assets equivalent to about US
$60 million) to benefit the neighborhood, and to promise extensive
investment in pollution control.

As protectors of community welfare, and often as symbols of
the interests of community over nation, local deities provide easy
cultural opportunities for social movements. Popular worship, in
addition, offers an established social network that can be mobilized. Indeed, temples and political factions together provide the
main lines through which leaders can normally mobilize local
people. They are too communal and locally based to be classic
civil society organizations, but they provide exactly the kinds of
informal political sector ties that can become important in the
construction of a new civil society under conditions like Taiwan's
lifting of martial law in 1987.

In contrast, national environmental organizations in both Taiwan and China look much more like "modern" civil associations.
They are legally registered organizations based on voluntary commitment to universalistic goals. As a result, they have never been

able to mobilize the power of local religion. Typical of modernizing elites anywhere, the leaders of these groups generally feel a
great distance from tradition-bound local religious practice, especially in the forms most effective in actual movements—possessed
mediums, flaming incense pots, powerful divinations. Just as important, they reject the localism inherent in the use of religion.
The gods of local temples are said above all to protect their immediate human communities, and they worry about the environment
only when it threatens their people. This position does not mesh
well with the universalist values of the elites. While popular worship has helped build a civil society in Taiwan, it remains tied to
purely local interests.

Western scholars, like environmental elites in Taiwan, have
tended to ignore communal, particularistic, and informal ties like
those of Chinese popular worship when looking for significant
political activity. Yet such ties empirically have had, and will continue to have, an important civic potential. Paul Katz has suggested that the introduced concept of *shehui* [from Meiji-era Japanese *shakai*], society, is less salient for understanding civil activity in China than the older meaning of the term *shehui*, the
community created around the shrine to the god of the locality.[18]
Limiting our vision only to the most modern-looking sectors of
society runs the danger of blinding us to some of its most powerful
social forces. Popular worship in Taiwan, and again now in many
parts of the People's Republic, fosters the kinds of community ties
that ultimately influence politics.

<    III    >

*Universalist Teachings*

People in late imperial times took part in popular worship by virtue of their places in local communities and kinship groups. Following an organized "teaching," however, was an act of personal
commitment. Becoming a Buddhist or Daoist, for example, usually meant learning particular texts, taking part in special rituals,
and committing oneself to a certain view of the world. It also usually involved becoming a personal follower of one or several teachers or priests. In most cases people did not see doing so as an al-

ternative to popular worship; following a teaching was a separate category of behavior.

The voluntary nature of these groups meant that people were organized more as congregations than geographic communities. Followers of a particular temple or teacher often came from scattered areas and formed a new kind of achieved community through a shared commitment to the teaching. This process bears a certain resemblance to the way Max Weber described Protestant sects creating generalized trust, because followers knew that fellow sectarians shared a similar set of values, even if they were strangers.[19] The belief systems themselves had no necessary resemblance to Protestantism, though, nor did such structures always fit under the Western rubric of religion. Organizationally, such groups need not have looked very different from other ways of passing on learning, like martial arts traditions. Their essentially voluntary nature, however, made them resemble civil society organizations more than the ascribed communities of popular worship.

The various kinds of teachings also offered explicit and universalizing views of the world, again providing at least a superficial resemblance to many modern civil society groups. Rather than a contextualized practice based on the act of offering incense, teachings placed their rituals into a larger philosophical framework backed up by long textual traditions. They generally claimed a universal validity far beyond the localized stories of community gods. The ideas of nirvana or the *dao* make a very different kind of claim about the world than tales of how the local god saved soldiers from a bombing raid.

Clerical Buddhism and Daoism continue to be viable options, having survived land reforms that undercut their finances and then the repression of the Cultural Revolution years. Both also have lay followers who practice meditation or read core texts. Measured by numbers of adherents, however, several other kinds of teachings demand attention, including especially Christianity, pietistic sects, and new forms of lay-oriented Buddhism.[20] Two examples are the Compassion Relief Merit Association [Ciji Gongde Hui], a new Buddhist movement that has spread around the world from Taiwan, and Falun Gong, a spiritual exercise program from China that also has spread.

Compassion Relief began in 1966 on Taiwan's poor east coast.[21] The founder was a nun named Zhengyan, who still provides charismatic leadership for the group. Beginning in a small temple near Hualian, she aspired to create a this-worldly Buddhism centered on charity, and above all on providing medical care for the poor. As the group tells it, her main inspirations were the sight of a miscarriage of an aboriginal woman who could not afford the hospital registration fee, an argument with some Catholic nuns about Buddhism's failure to care for society, and the earlier example of the monk Yinshun, who had tried and failed to create a movement for "humanistic Buddhism" in the 1950s.[22] Yinshun himself had ordained Zhengyan.

The group began with thirty housewives and five disciples of Zhengyan. The housewives contributed a few pennies a day, and the clergy made baby shoes for a little additional income. From these very modest beginnings, the group gradually grew through the 1970s. In 1979, Zhengyan announced plans to build a state-of-the-art hospital in Hualian, which was completed in 1986. In the process the group burst onto the national scene, gaining both political support and a surge in membership. By the early 1990s (after which they stopped releasing figures), they claimed about four million members (making them the largest civil association in Taiwan) and had branches in dozens of countries.

This extraordinarily rapid expansion beginning in the 1980s had several interlinked causes. Taiwan's lifting of martial law in 1987 freed all kinds of social organizations to grow outside the corporatist framework; Compassion Relief became the largest such organization. The 1980s were also the decade when Taiwan joined the ranks of the wealthier countries of the world. The late 1980s in particular were a period when a lot of wealth was chasing very few investment opportunities. People had money they could afford to contribute, and philanthropy appealed as a moral alternative to the perceived greed and selfishness of Taiwan's market economy.[23]

The organization continues to thrive. It is building a second hospital and runs a medical school, a nursing school, a television station, and a university. Its charitable budget surpassed the welfare budget of Taipei during the 1990s. Members have also expanded their work into other charitable areas and have often sent emergency help abroad. They further enhanced their reputation through their speedy and effective response to Taiwan's devastating earthquake of 1999, in contrast to how, in most people's perceptions, the government reacted.

Although the top leaders are nuns, this is essentially a lay movement that does not push people toward monastic vows. Followers make contributions, and the biggest donors are rewarded with special uniforms and titles as "commissioners." Zhengyan's main emphasis, however, is on action rather than donation. She urges followers to volunteer their time to Compassion Relief activities like visiting the sick, identifying and delivering relief to needy families, or organizing recycling programs. Followers also attend regular meetings, which provide some entertainment, testimonials about how activists' lives have changed, and often sermons from Zhengyan, either in person or by videotape. Sutra recitation plays only a small role, and the movement overall has little concern with Buddhist philosophy. Its appeal instead lies in the effort to change the world through charity.

The other remarkable feature of Compassion Relief is its gender balance—it is about 70 percent women, and the top leaders are women. The appeal to women is complex.[24] On the one hand, the movement has a very conservative gender message, based upon values traditionally seen as feminine. Participants are supposed to be kind, generous, and nurturing. One of the most popular songs in the group is called "Mother," and the ideas of Compassion Relief as a mother to its followers, and of the followers as mothers to the world, pervade the group. Many followers join feeling dissatisfied with their lives at home. Wealthy enough to have domestic help and conservative enough not to work, many of these women complain about meaningless lives and loveless marriages. The advice they receive, even for problems with drunken or abusive husbands, is typically to show more love and forbearance, and to know that they will eventually be loved in return.

This maternal stereotype has, however, been pulled out beyond the walls of family that previously hemmed it in. Women are no longer simply the "inside people" [neiren], a traditional term for wives. By merging with the Bodhisattva ideal of saving all beings, traditional feminine values of nurturing motherhood make a crucial transition to the realm of metaphor. Followers leave the confines of literal motherhood in the house, but expand the nurturing woman onto a global field. These women feed the poor, care for the sick, and organize disaster relief around the world. The gender message may be conservative, but the women's global impact rivals anything their husbands accomplish in their businesses.

Compassion Relief comes much closer to standard definitions of a civil association than to the localist traditions of Chinese popular worship. It is fully voluntary, based on shared interests and beliefs rather than ties of locality and kinship. Its values are universalistic rather than based in local society. And while it relies on charismatic leadership, it also exists within a formally defined legal realm, with an internal structure that is becoming increasingly rationalized. These differences do not, however, necessarily make Compassion Relief more important than popular worship in the consolidation of Taiwan's democracy.

China also has some massive organizations mobilized around a teaching. The increase in popular worship in China since the 1980s is not a national movement in the sense of having any organizational existence that transcends the essentially local roots of the vast majority of temples. To a lesser extent Christianity also is local, partly because the underground life of the house church movement makes larger organization very difficult, and partly because the fissile nature of Protestantism encourages localization.[25]

*Qigong* movements have been far more successful in creating national followings and organizations during this period.[26] Like geomancy or Chinese medicine, qigong centers on manipulation of cosmic energies [*qi*], which are characterized by qualities of yin and yang, the five phases [*wuxing*], and more arcane distinctions. Qigong adjusts and harmonizes the flow of these energies in the body through physical exercises. Advanced adepts sometimes claim supernormal skills, like the ability to levitate, bend metal bars, or cure by laying on hands. Qi-based practices remain robust in the PRC and have not been discouraged the way religion and especially "superstition" have. In fact, the government's early embrace of Chinese traditional medicine has helped consolidate the position of these ideas.

A qigong craze began in the 1980s, the same period when local temples began their resurgence. Groups gathered in public spaces around teachers for early morning exercise practices. As reputations increased, a few masters gathered enormous crowds in sports arenas, and some styles of qigong achieved national prominence, generally under the charismatic leadership of one such master. By the early 1990s some of these movements could claim millions of followers, and the government began to worry about the scale. While morning exercises continued, the largest mass meetings were stopped. Government psychiatrists also conveniently discovered "qigong deviation," a psychiatric ailment that stemmed from a disharmonious flow of qi. It was caused by poor practice or by practice of an improper form of qigong.[27]

Falun Gong, which is at base another form of qigong, was introduced to the public in 1992, at the height of the craze. The primary differences between Falun Gong and other forms of qigong were the idea of the *falun* [law wheel] and generally superficial borrowings from Buddhism and Daoism. The law wheel, from which the movement took its name, revolves constantly in the bellies of followers, forcing the qi into a continual and beneficial rotation through the body. This action allegedly allows for much faster progress toward health and supernormal powers than is possible through other forms of qigong. This wheel can be installed only by the leader, Li Hongzhi, in person or through his videos or appointed representatives.

The religious borrowings begin with many references to Li's early training by Daoist and Buddhist adepts (not backed up by any evidence outside his hagiographies) and the claim that he was born on the anniversary of the Buddha's birth (although his birth certificate shows a different date). They also include the moral system that Falun Gong promotes, based on the three primary values of truthfulness [zhen], benevolence [shan], and forbearance [ren]. Some of the physical movements of the exercises imitate postures of the Buddha, although there appears to be no deeper reference to Buddhist ideas. Li Hongzhi's use of Buddhist terms is generally idiosyncratic. This is true for the law wheel itself, which is a reference to the Buddhist idea of a dharma wheel, but in a completely different context. Li similarly reinterprets karma as a black substance that builds up in the body and causes disease after bad behavior—an idea only loosely related to its Buddhist original.

To an extent, Falun Gong appealed to people in China who

were experiencing problems. In particular, people who had been forced into early retirement or laid off from jobs in government or state-owned factories made up a significant portion of the following.[28] These had been the elites of the old socialist system, who now felt abandoned by the move to a market economy. They were not so much thrown into poverty (many had spouses who remained employed) as deprived of status and respect. Falun Gong for them provided an alternate community in which they could earn a new kind of respect. This dynamic is common in many religious groups, and has been documented, for example, in Taiwanese pietistic sects.[29] Both Falun Gong and Compassion Relief thus appeal to people who feel alienated by a changing social world—often women with unfulfilled family lives in the case of Compassion Relief, and people without medical insurance and sometimes jobs in the case of Falun Gong.

Most followers, whether or not they were newly laid off, initially joined Falun Gong for the promised health benefits. These have always been a major appeal of qigong movements. In part, this appeal was a reaction to the increasing commodification of medical care, which has made visits to the doctor prohibitively expensive for many people. In part, however, it also represents a redefinition of body and self in relation to the larger social and physical universe. For much of its history, the People's Republic had tried to define a new kind of selfless self—austere, disciplined, egalitarian, and dedicated to the common good of all the people (as represented by the state). This is the image of self embodied by Lei Feng, the hero of countless PRC propaganda tales. It was reinforced in every area, from dress—long-lasting, unostentatious clothing—to socialist realist sculpture.[30] The state still promotes this image sporadically, but the possibility of new self-images opened up again, along with much else, in the 1980s. The socially localized self of popular worship was one of the alternatives that stepped in. Qigong offered another kind of alternative, less rooted in social relations, where the individual body became attuned to the energies of the wider universe.

This placement of the individual in a larger energy universe also contrasts with geomancy, even though both have roots in qi theory.[31] Geomancy in practice is always rooted in the local social, temporal, and physical environment. Geomancers site houses and graves according to the specific characteristics of their clients, the time, and the geography of the site. Qigong emphasizes instead the direct interaction of the bodily microcosm with a universal macrocosm. It shows a fundamental universalism by allowing people to transcend the social and physical characteristics that geomancy and popular worship reinforce. Falun Gong increases this appeal to universalism further with its constant reference to general Buddhist principles.

Like many groups with charismatic leadership, Falun Gong was relatively amorphous once it grew beyond the bounds of Li's personal control. Members would try to bring in new followers, forming small cells of their own, and most people would not know who stood farther up the hierarchy.

Sale of books and videos generated an enormous income for the group. Initial lessons were free, as was typical for most forms of qigong, but followers would soon be expected to invest in high-priced publications and were also told that they could not share.[32] Looking at movement directives makes clear that this income source was a strong temptation for lower-level leaders and created pressures within the movement. A number of directives reserve the rights to publish books to Li himself, and others forbid lower leaders from making any statements in Li's name, unless specifically instructed.

Falun Gong thus has an inherent tension between the centrifugal tendencies of the cellular structure with its relative independence of local leaders, and the centralizing force of Li's charisma. Li tries to consolidate control through directives to the group, by the claims to special powers and knowledge in his writings, and even in his personal style. Some of his videos, for example, show him standing alone against a flamboyant sunrise—the sort of image we used to see of the Great Helmsman, Mao Zedong, during the Cultural Revolution. This kind of tension typifies many charismatic groups. The usual answer is to try to rationalize authority through clear bureaucratic structures of power.[33] This has been impossible for Falun Gong, however, because it had been forced semi-underground for a number of years even before the full-scale repression began in 1999. Instead, the group has had to promote Li's charisma ever more powerfully.

Groups like Compassion Relief or Falun Gong appear more like "civil society" than popular worship. They foster ties of trust through the new social communities they create, and they can mobilize those ties for social action. They are voluntary associations based on individual choice, rather than aspects of a particularistic world of local society and kinship. Their divorce from the local ties of popular worship has allowed both organizations (and others like them) to grow huge, encompassing millions of people in dozens of countries. Both also have belief systems that claim to be universal, but that clearly draw on long Chinese roots, allowing them to enter into an interesting interaction with globalizing models that emanate from Europe and North America. They meet the challenge of universalist claims from the West with universalisms and globalizations of their own, but stemming from indigenous resources. They are local responses, in a sense, to the specific challenges of Christianity, and more generally to the ideological slot for "religion" that modernist states (including both Taiwan and the People's Republic) demand. Popular worship instead is too locally grounded to serve this purpose.

Large, voluntary, globalizing associations like these are of course not necessarily better than the scattered localisms of popular worship for democratic transitions or even just building a public sphere. We already have seen how effectively the social tendrils of popular worship can feed into local social movements in Taiwan, and how they are parts of rebuilding community life in the People's Republic. They can help to create a public sphere exactly because of the localist and particularist roots of these practices.

The large, more modern-looking associations can organize on a far larger scale and on issues that appeal more globally. For these very reasons, however, they are also far more vulnerable to state control. The new Buddhists in Taiwan, for example, rarely take on the really controversial issues, like nuclear power, that local movements with religious ties can tackle.[34] Falun Gong, whose only real political agenda was to be left alone, has been almost completely crushed within China, exactly because its scale made it vulnerable in a way that the much more massive, but local and scattered, popular worship is not.

## ⋞ IV ⋟

### The Comparative Role of the State

These cases suggest a significant role for Chinese religious practices in creating independent civil institutions that have important, if indirect, political effects. In both China and Taiwan they fostered a realm of social connections independent from central authority. These connections were thoroughly intertwined with other local forms of power, as when local elites used local temples as militia bases in the nineteenth century, or Formosa Plastics gained temple support for its refinery construction through large donations. Nevertheless, local religious practice offered a robust pool of social relations that could have important political implications under the changed circumstances of the late twentieth century.

Forms of civil association created through religious worship and teachings survived even under authoritarian regimes that intended to leave very little free social space. In Taiwan, they helped allow the successful transition to democracy reach deep into the population quickly and effectively. However, such institutions do not inevitably lead to democratic transitions. Religion laid a groundwork for the transition in Taiwan, but it was intimately tied to state policy during the authoritarian period in ways that effectively kept it from being a direct cause of change on its own. Much the same appears to be true of religion in China today.

Typically modernist in its understanding of religion and attitudes toward "superstition," the Republican government had never been fond of Chinese popular worship, always deriding and sometimes repressing it from the very beginning of the GMD rule on the mainland.[35] The GMD never attempted to squelch it thoroughly in Taiwan after taking control in 1945, but nevertheless put intermittent pressure on several areas of popular practice. Spirit mediumship was periodically denounced as superstition, and some mediums were arrested for extortion. The central government also regularly complained about the amount of money "wasted" on rituals. Newspapers greeted important annual festivals from the 1950s to the 1980s with calls to be frugal and cut down on wasteful and unsanitary rituals. These campaigns had little overall effect.[36]

Beyond this one partial victory, however, it was hard to see the effect of government disapproval on popular worship. As Taiwan become a wealthier society in the late 1970s and 1980s, many new temples were built and many old ones were rebuilt on larger and more elaborate scales. Spending on rituals continues to be lavish, and popular worship in general has boomed along with the economy. The flexible, local, and relatively uninstitutionalized nature of popular worship makes it difficult for the government to control it firmly. People always seem able to find ways to adapt.

Furthermore, as modernist states, both the GMD and Communist regimes have given up the ability to manipulate popular worship from within the system. Constitutionally irreligious and ideologically contemptuous of popular worship, these states lost the power of the old imperial government to try to control worship from within, through the official state cult, promotion of certain deities, and regulation of ritual. This put lower-echelon state functionaries in the difficult position of having to mediate the contradictions between local practice and national policy. That job is especially delicate when local officials often share popular attitudes more than elite ideologies.[37]

Local officials caught in this bind would sometimes carry out the letter of the law without worrying too much about its spirit. They could do so by simply ignoring actual practice as long as it remained out of sight, or by allowing the practices to continue in disguise. For example, the Japanese colonial government in Taiwan (another modernist state) had banned the portion of the annual ghost festival that involved riotous attacks on raised platforms of offerings, with young toughs playing the part of starving ghosts, climbing over each other to grab the goodies. It reappeared almost immediately, however, as an athletic climbing competition between villages. The same young men competed for the same rewards, but could now claim they were improving their physical stamina as an act of imperial patriotism. This fairly transparent disguise was accepted.

In a later version of the same strategy, the Chiang Kai-shek government tried hard during the 1950s to get people to stop offering specially fattened pigs on the birthdays of their local gods. They branded the practice as both wasteful and unhealthy. People in Sanhsia responded by announcing that the winners of an agricultural competition to raise the fattest pigs (again showing their loyalty to government priorities) would be rewarded by being permitted to display their pigs in the temple plaza on the god's birthday. The old ritual thus remained fundamentally unchanged, but just received a new gloss.[38]

The relatively amorphous nature of popular worship allows it to serve as a reservoir of alternate values and alternate social relations, even under a culturally controlling authoritarian regime like Chiang Kai-shek's Taiwan. Local officials often have to accede to these local customs, except during truly extreme cases like the Cultural Revolution. Township-level political factions in Taiwan are in fact often based in temples, which helps explain a distinct lack of local enthusiasm for government campaigns against local worship. There are also reports that village election campaigns now in China again sometimes mobilize support from local temples, further pressuring local officials.

Local officials can also misjudge the situation. Too tough a position on local religion may lead to local resistance, as Dean documents for deity festivals in 1990s Fujian.[39] Local worship can also cause problems for local officials when they attract too much attention from the higher government levels. Recent repression of religion in Wenzhou, for instance, apparently took place when central government officials came to the city to praise its economy but also complained that local officials had ignored the upswelling of local religion for years. Some temples and graves were destroyed, but in other cases superficial disguise sufficed—some graves were simply painted green to blend in with the background.[40]

More institutionalized teachings fit modernist understandings of religion better. By definition, though, more institutionalized groups lack the flexibility of popular worship in the face of repression and control. They have texts that limit their range of interpretation and priests trained in long lines of various orthodoxies. In addition, they generally work on larger scales than the largely local organization of popular worship. These features bring them more quickly under official scrutiny. The result in Taiwan was that the government either repressed larger religious associations (most notably pietistic sects like the Way of Unity [Yiguan Dao], but also Rev. Sun Myung Moon's Unification Church and others) or brought them under careful corporatist control through official organizations like the Buddhist Association of the Republic of China (BAROC).

Taiwanese Buddhists provide a clear example.[41] Under the Japanese colonial government, the most important temples had developed close ties to the government and affiliations with Japanese sects of Buddhism—partly out of compulsion, and partly in an attempt to maintain control over land, ordination, and other resources. After the Japanese defeat in 1945 and the Communist victory in China in 1949, many important priests came to Taiwan. The BAROC itself was moved there and became the official intermediary between the government and the Buddhist institutions of the island. The leading Japanese-era temples lost their prominent positions almost immediately, partly as an aspect of the GMD reaction against all things Japanese, and partly because the powerful mainland priests had no ties to these temples. Dissenting voices, like Yinshun's call for a humanistic Buddhism in the 1950s (which would become so important 40 years later), were silenced. BAROC lobbied for its own interests, of course, but only within the confines of its unspoken corporatist bargain with the government—a monopoly over institutional Buddhism in exchange for loyalty and obedience.

Compassion Relief, which was founded at the height of this period, remained small and isolated on the east coast until it began to build its first hospital in the 1980s. By this time Chiang Kai-shek had been dead for several years, and a gradual loosening of cultural policy had begun.[42] By allowing and even encouraging Compassion Relief to build the hospital, the government signaled an important relaxation in the previous corporatist monopoly of BAROC. Compassion Relief succeeded in this very ambitious project, however, only because it developed close ties to the highest level of government.[43] As with any large organization at the time, success required very close cooperation with the government, and any kind of oppositional political stance was out of the question. Unlike the scattered and localized practice of popular worship, groups like this could not avoid the gaze of the central government.

Groups that would not or could not accept this bargain with the state suffered a harsh fate. Pietistic sects, which were the most important indigenous religious growth area in the 1970s, lived a life underground. These groups varied, but typically worshiped a creator goddess called the Eternal Venerable Mother [Wusheng Laomu], expected the arrival of the new Buddha Maitreya to mark the beginning of a new era, and communicated with various syncretic deities through spirit writing. They had a long history in China and had a family resemblance to some rebellious movements like the White Lotus. In practice, these groups preached very conservative messages in Taiwan. Gods would descend, for instance, and tell people to be loyal to the government and obedient to their parents. Yet the combination of the historical problems some of these groups had posed, the millenarian potential of their ideas, and their simple ability to mobilize huge numbers of followers (probably hundreds of thousands in a few cases) made these groups unacceptable to the government. The largest group (the Way of Unity) was outlawed until the general loosening up of the late 1980s, and most of the other groups maintained the lowest profile they could.[44]

The 1970s thus saw popular worship thriving at the local level, while pietistic sects had been forced into a cellular organization and tried to keep out of sight. Formally organized, national religious associations existed only in close cooperation with the state. Popular religion fared better only because it remained small and relatively informally organized. The general result was two tiers of religion—a modern-looking national sector under tight corporatist control, and a traditional-looking popular sector that remained locally rooted. Neither level was in a position to foment political change, although both offered the potential for a self-organized society under a new type of regime.

All of this changed in Taiwan in the late 1980s, especially after the lifting of martial law in 1987. The Way of Unity was legalized, opening the door to a more formalized and wider organization. Buddhist groups could come out from under the umbrella of their corporatist organization. Compassion Relief, Buddha Light Mountain [Foguang Shan], and Dharma Drum Mountain [Fagu Shan] each claimed millions of followers within a few years, and many smaller Buddhist organizations sprang up. BAROC, meanwhile, became a lame duck. Popular worship continued to thrive but suddenly was embraced by politicians instead of being barely tolerated. Temple visits became important parts of campaigns, with some candidates even reviving old rituals, like beheading chickens, to emphasize their vows.[45] Politicians recognized how much social capital was tied up in popular worship, and so were quick to take advantage of it as the political clouds lifted and as populist appeals became more important in winning elections.

The PRC has also changed radically over much the same time period, but in a very different way. China has moved away from the totalitarian excess of the Cultural Revolution, which intended to leave no room for formal religious teachings or popular worship. Its success was not complete—the major political campaigns forced most religious activities underground, but they reappeared with the lighter monitoring in between campaigns. Elizabeth Perry has shown how a number of sectarian religious movements in China (including the Way of Unity) actually became important in the midst of the Cultural Revolution.[46]

In the decades since the Cultural Revolution ended in 1976, however, China has increasingly opened up personal space for people, including free space for religious practice, as long as they keep away from politics. The government still brands popular worship as superstition, but tends to leave it alone as long as it stays small and local. Larger religious teachings come under the larger corporatist umbrella that China has developed to deal with social organizations of all sorts. In theory, at least, each sector will be represented by a single organization. There are thus separate associations for Protestants, Catholics, Buddhists, Daoists, and Muslims, all with very close ties to the state. A separate association represents the various qigong movements.

Much like that of earlier Taiwan, this system in practice leaves a lot of room at the grassroots for groups that are part of no large, formal association. All over China we find a revitalized popular worship, a house church movement that refuses the authority of the state-sponsored Christian (including Catholic) institutions, secret societies, and other shreds and patches of localized religious practice. We still have only very thin ethnographic studies, but there are a few clear patterns.[47] Localized worship has come back most strongly in rural areas, in the southern and northwestern parts of China, on small scales (Earth Gods before large community gods, private spirit medium sessions before large public rituals), and especially among women.[48] The pattern is clear: distance from political power in China correlates with religious resurgence.[49] For instance, women are taking over as spirit mediums even in areas where that had once been a mostly male calling.[50] Men feel they have too much at stake to risk such quintessentially "superstitious" behavior, but women have a better chance of being ignored by the local bureaucracy, at least beyond the realm of the birth control campaign.

Organization on a larger scale, however, is a different story, just as it was in Taiwan. Organizations that want to grow beyond the local level are either coopted into the corporatist structure or eventually repressed.[51] Falun Gong is an obvious example. The group initially accepted membership in the Chinese Qigong Association, but Li Hongzhi's claims to control a vastly superior system, so much better that it could not really be considered qigong at all, ultimately led to his separation from the corporatist umbrella in 1996. This declaration of independence could only strike the government as incendiary. Repression of the group stepped up almost immediately, and Li moved to the United States the next year.

Falun Gong's growing size and ability to mobilize people led to the government's using various forms of repression in several provincial cities (most notably Tianjin) and finally to the major national crackdown that began in July 1999. In October the government passed a law banning "heretic cult organizations" [xiejiao], which became the main legal tool in prosecuting members of Falun Gong and subsequently in repressing, albeit somewhat more gently, some other qigong and religious associations. This law explicitly considered these crimes more serious if the "heretic cults" crossed provincial borders—and thereby made explicit the implied policy of allowing much more personal freedom at local levels but insisting on tight control of anything at larger scales. While a small hard core of Falun Gong continues to demonstrate, and thus to invite ever harsher police repression, the movement as a whole has been crushed within China.

Corporatist policy toward religion in both Taiwan and the People's Republic thus promoted a split. At one end lie localist, informal groups often based on ties of kinship and community, which did well in both places in spite of general government disapproval. At the other end are larger groups that appear more "modern" and more "religious" by the standards of both the PRC and GMD-era Taiwan. They are formally organized, with roots in voluntary and individual decisions to accept a particular teaching. Unlike the localized groups of popular worshipers, these large associations also typically espouse universalist values. The government of China today is particularly concerned to coopt, control, or repress these large groups—as was that of Taiwan twenty years ago.

The resulting split in both cases involved a kind of irony. The groups most concerned with promoting morality and most organized along modern lines are the ones the government worries about above all. The Way of Unity in Taiwan, after all, was promoting filial piety and patriotism in Confucian language the government itself favored. Falun Gong's universal values of truth, benevolence, and forbearance were also hardly threatening. Popular worship, however, with its less modern-looking social base and localist values, has thrived. Although it too offers a kind of piecemeal morality, it can also glorify amoral or immoral characters—among them the matricidal official who became an important local deity in 1840s Guangxi, and the fee-for-service ghosts who would grant any request, no matter how corrupt, in 1980s Taiwan.[52]

In Taiwan, both those localist traditions and new forms of large associations have thrived since martial law was lifted, while the older corporatist institutions have faded. Neither popular worship nor religious institutions played a crucial role in forcing the transition to democracy, but they have been central to democracy's success there. Corporatist control had been successful in preventing religion at any level from actively fomenting political change. Yet it never prevented religious worship and teachings from creating a reservoir of values and social relations that lay outside authoritarian control, especially at the most local levels. These resources were crucial in Taiwan's success, and the same potential lies in the reborn religious activity of the People's Republic.

<V>

*Conclusion: An Alternate Civility?*

Religion has allowed Chinese and Taiwanese under authoritarian control to retain active reservoirs of values and social relations relatively insulated from government control.[53] Large religious institutions—like China's Falun Gong or Taiwan's Way of Unity—have generally contributed less to this retention than has local popular worship with its base in particularistic ties of kin and community. The larger institutions either entered into intimate relations with the government or were forced underground. Large, independent, universalizing religious institutions thrived in Taiwan only after martial law was lifted, and they were built in part on the thick social ties that already existed thanks to popular worship and other local forms of civil association. The disaggregated and flexible nature of popular worship made it both more difficult to repress and more likely to remain beneath the active attention of these governments.

Of course, neither local worship nor large belief-based associations were the primary forces that moved Taiwan to democratize, nor are they likely to play that role in China. The evidence from China and Taiwan does not really support Tocqueville's strong claim about religion, that "by regulating domestic life, it regulates the state." Instead, it suggests a softer version of his thesis—that Chinese popular worship provides one of the major building blocks of local society, and it therefore can play a central role in the realization and consolidation of any democratic opening. Chinese popular worship is not, of course, the usual stuff of civil society theory. In general its values are localist and not universalist, its social basis is particularistic and not voluntary or individualistic, and its organization is informal and not based on clear rules. Popular worship seems, in short, just too premodern for theories that tie civil society clearly to modernity.

In fact, however, there is nothing remarkably premodern here—the problem lies more in theories of modernity than in Chinese religious practice. The very lack of institutionalization in popular worship has allowed it to adjust easily to all kinds of changes. Its rapid growth as the economy has boomed in both China and Taiwan is further evidence of just how compatible it is with modernity. On the other hand the more "modern" looking religious institutions, with their universalist ideologies and rationalized organizations, have played a more minor role. The kind of authoritarian corporatism that Taiwan once practiced and that China is today emulating has been quite successful in keeping such groups under control. Local religion provided a crucial seedbed that allowed an independent society to grow once martial law was lifted in Taiwan. The People's Republic appears to be following a similar path.

<>

REFERENCE MATTER

# Notes

INTRODUCTION

1. J. H. Hexter, "The Birth of Modern Freedom," *Times Literary Supplement*, Jan. 21, 1983, 51.

2. Addendum, letter, J. H. Hexter to Peter W. Stanley, Ford Foundation, Feb. 13, 1989.

3. Ibid.

4. Ma Chenguang, "Human Rights a World Ideal," *China Daily*, Oct. 21, 1998, 1, reporting on the first international conference on human rights hosted by China.

5. Hexter, "Birth." See J. H. Hexter, ed., *Parliament and Liberty from the Reign of Elizabeth to the English Civil War* (Stanford, 1992).

6. Robert H. Taylor, ed., *The Idea of Freedom in Asia and Africa* (Stanford, 2002).

7. Klaus Mühlhahn, "China, the West and the Question of Human Rights: A Historical Perspective," in *asien, afrika, lateinamerika* 24, 3 (1996): 287–303.

8. *China Daily*, Oct. 21, 1998, 1.

9. See Louis Henkin, "The Human Rights Idea in Contemporary China: A Comparative Perspective," in R. Randle Edwards et al., eds., *Human Rights in Contemporary China* (New York, 1986), 7–39.

10. For a stimulating discussion of human rights as universally and historically defined see Xiaoqun Xu, "Human Rights and the Discourse on Universality: A Chinese Historical Perspective," in Lynda S. Bell et al., eds., *Negotiating Culture and Human Rights* (New York, 2001), 217–41.

11. See Stephen C. Angle and Marina Svensson, eds., *The Chinese Human Rights Reader: Documents and Commentary* (Armonk, NY, 2001).

12. Andrew J. Nathan, "Redefinitions of Freedom in China," in Taylor, ed., *The Idea of Freedom*.

13. John E. Schrecker, *The Chinese Revolution in Historical Perspective* (New York, 1991), 43.

14. See William C. Kirby, "China Unincorporated: Company Law and Business Enterprise in Twentieth Century China," *The Journal of Asian Studies* 54, no. 1 (Feb. 1995): 45.

15. See chap. 4 below.

16. Ibid.

17. See chap. 6 below.

18. Jean Chesneaux, *The Chinese Labor Movement, 1919–1927* (Stanford, 1968).

19. Deborah A. Kaple, *Dream of a Red Factory: The Legacy of High Stalinism in China* (New York, 1994).

20. Ben Fowkes, *The Rise and Fall of Communism in Eastern Europe*, 2d ed. (London, 1995), 52.

21. Alexander Eckstein, *China's Economic Development: The Interplay of Scarcity and Ideology* (Ann Arbor, MI, 1975), 263.

22. On the more artistic aspects of this custom see Dorothy Ko, *Every Step a Lotus: Shoes for Bound Feet* (Berkeley, 2001).

23. Gail Hershatter, *Dangerous Pleasures: Prostitution and Modernity in Twentieth-century Shanghai* (Berkeley, 1997).

24. Xiaoqun Xu, "Human Rights," 227.

25. Ralph N. Clough, *Island China* (Cambridge, MA, 1978).

26. See Wen-hsin Yeh, ed., *Becoming Chinese: Passages to Modernity and Beyond* (Berkeley, 2000).

CHAPTER 1

1. Hannah Arendt, *The Life of the Mind*, vol. 2, *Willing* (New York, 1978), 216.

2. See W. J. F. Jenner's challenging essay on "China and Freedom" in David Kelly and Anthony Reid, eds., *Asian Freedoms—The Idea of Freedom in East and Southeast Asia* (Cambridge, 1998), 65–92. The subheadings in Jenner's essay are: "The Primacy of Authority," "Respectable Subjects," "Bureaucratic Absolutism," "Religion Dwarfed," "Localism Stifled," "Commerce Encircled," and "Unfreedom of Expression."

3. Ibid., 88.

4. Ci Jiwei, "The Right, the Good, and the Place of Rights in Confucianism," forthcoming in a volume being edited by Tu Weiming and Wm. Theodore de Bary.

5. Henry Sidgwick, *The Methods of Ethics* (Indianapolis, 1981, repr. of the 1907 ed.), 105–6.

6. Ci, "The Right, the Good, and the Place of Rights in Confucianism," typescript, 18.

7. Ibid., 12.

8. Ibid.

9. Ibid., 13–14.

10. Ibid., 14.

11. Ibid., 15.

12. Ibid.

13. Ibid., 30.

14. Ibid.

15. The Chinese character shows a person standing alongside the num-

ber "two," suggesting mutuality, a person together with others, a person in society.

16. *Analects* 5: 12, 12: 2.

17. Mencius' discussion of the case of the sage king Shun's marrying without informing his parents (*Mencius* 4A26) is but one example among many.

18. As, for example, in his exchange with King Hui of Liang in *Mencius* 1A1.

19. David Hume, *An Inquiry Concerning the Principles of Morals,* "Why Utility Pleases," pt. 2, Charles W. Hendel, ed. (Indianapolis, 1957), 51.

20. Ibid., 47, n. 1.

21. Mencius, I believe, would also have shared Hume's view that "The notion of morals implies some sentiment common to all mankind, which recommends the same object to general approbation and makes every man, or most men, agree in the same opinion or decision containing it. It also implies some sentiment so universal and comprehensive as to extend to all mankind, and render the actions and conduct, even of the persons the most remote, an object of applause or censure, according as they agree or disagree with that rule of right which is established. These two requisite circumstances belong alone to the sentiment of humanity here insisted on." Hume, *An Inquiry Concerning the Principles of Morals,* "Conclusion," pt. 1, 93.

22. Ci, "The Right, the Good, and the Place of Rights in Confucianism."

23. Ibid.

24. For example, *Analects* 2: 17: "The Master said, 'You (a name for the disciple Zilu), shall I teach you about knowing? To regard knowing it as knowing it, to regard not knowing it as not knowing it—this is knowing.'" Trans. E. Bruce Brooks and A. Taeko Brooks in *The Original Analects— The Sayings of Confucius and His Successors* (New York, 1998), 112.

25. Trans. Brooks and Brooks in *The Original Analects,* 106. Brooks and Brooks relocate this saying from Book 9 of the *Analects* to Book 13.

26. Brooks and Brooks comment (ibid.), "This affirmation, that even a humble fellow's will is inalienable, is the strongest statement so far of what a modern reader might call individual rights."

27. Hannah Arendt, "What Is Freedom?" in *Between Past and Future— Eight Exercises in Political Thought* (New York, 1977), 149.

28. See, for example, *Analects* 4: 10 and *Mencius* 5A9 and 5B1.

29. An exception might be the discussion between Gaozi and Mencius of the relation between words, the mind, the *qi* and the will [*zhi*] in *Mencius* 2A2. Even here, this brief exchange is surrounded by accounts of the different kinds of valor of specific individuals.

30. David Keightley, "Theology and the Writing of History," in *Journal of East Asian Archaeology* 1 (1999): 1–4. In his earlier work Keightley reported that he had discovered only a few instances recorded on the oracle

bones or shells in which a diviner had openly declined, when it came to recording the actual outcome of events following a king's prognostications, to corroborate that the king's interpretation of the cracks had proved correct. His more recent work, based on further study of the bone and shell inscriptions, indicates that this expression of independence on the part of diviners was more common than had originally been apparent, despite the danger that it might have involved for the diviners.

31. *Mencius* 5A5.

32. *Zuo zhuan*, Duke Xiang, 25th year. In Burton Watson, trans., *The Tso chuan—Selections from China's Oldest Narrative History* (New York, 1989), 147.

33. The case of the great Han historian Sima Qian (145?–86? B.C.E.) is, of course, another example.

34. *Classic of Documents*, "Yinzheng" [The Punitive Expedition of Yin], in James Legge, trans., *The Chinese Classics* (Oxford, 1893–95; Hong Kong, 1979), 3: 164–65.

35. Adapted from Watson, trans., *The Tso chuan*, xv-xvi. There is a similar passage in the *Guoyu* [Discourses of the States], trans. by Watson in *The Tso chuan*, xvii.

36. See, for example, *Mencius* 1A1, 1A3, and 1A5.

37. See, for example, *Mencius* 1A7, 1B6, 1B8, 1B11, and 5B9.

38. That is, that the founder of the Shang dynasty disposed of the proverbially "bad last" ruler of the preceding Xia dynasty and that the founder of the Zhou in turn similarly dispensed with the "bad last" ruler of the Shang.

39. Tang's ousting of Jie is recorded in the *Classic of Documents*, "The Announcement of Zhonghui" (in Legge, trans., *The Chinese Classics*, 3: 177–83) and "The Announcement of Tang" (ibid., 184–90); King Wu's removal of Zhou, in "The Great Declaration" (ibid., 281–97) and "The Successful Completion of the War" (ibid., 306–17).

40. *Xunzi*, chap. 13; Harvard-Yenching Sinological Index series, *A Concordance to Hsün Tzu*, Supplement no. 22, p. 50, lines 12–16. Trans. John Knoblock in *Xunzi—A Translation and Study of the Complete Works* 2 (Stanford, 1990): 199–200. See also the poem in "Working Songs," in chap. 25: "Let me a foundation lay,/ Listen carefully to My Words!/ Stupid yet willful, his affairs are not ordered./ When the ruler allows suspicion to overcome him,/ none of his assembled ministers remonstrate,/ so disaster is certain to befall him."

41. Most of these powers of the state are discussed in varying degrees of detail by Jenner in "China and Freedom," 65–92. I have derived this list from his comprehensive yet succinct account.

42. For a brilliant account of the expression of dissent in poetry and painting during the Song and the ways in which a number of Song poets and painters drew on Du Fu, see Alfreda Murck, *Poetry and Painting in Song China—The Subtle Art of Dissent* (Cambridge, MA, 2000).

43. See Alan T. Wood, *Limits to Autocracy—From Sung Neo-Confucianism to a Doctrine of Political Rights* (Honolulu, 1995).

44. For having written poems critical of Wang Anshi's New Policies, Su Shi was arrested in 1079 and tried in what became known as the Crow Terrace Poetry Case. Convicted of "great irreverence" toward the emperor, he might under Song law have been punished by execution. However, his sentence was commuted to exile in Huangzhou in central China—an exile that lasted four years. After returning to the capital and high official positions during the Yuan-yu period (1086–93), Su was once again exiled—this time to Guangdong—in 1094 as a result of his differences with the party supporting the New Policies. In 1097 he was banished to the even more remote island of Hainan, being recalled only in 1100—too late, as he took ill and died in 1101. For a fascinating account of Su's poetry as a vehicle of dissent, see Murck, *Poetry and Painting in Song China*, esp. chaps. 2 and 6.

45. According to Frederick W. Mote's biography of Fang, "The stories of how Zhu Di commanded Fang, first in polite terms to draft the rescript announcing his succession, how Fang berated him as a criminal and a usurper, how the usurper then tortured him physically and psychologically, but to no avail, have become legend. In the ruthless purge of Jianwen supporters [supporters of the preceding emperor whom Zhu Di ousted], the execution of Fang Xiaoru and his brother, then all his kin, all his associates, his students, friends, neighbors and all persons even loosely connected with him . . . stands out for the ferocity and thoroughness with which this vindictive act of intimidation was accomplished . . . During the Yungle period the penalty for possessing even a scrap of Fang's writings was death . . . and although the suppression relaxed somewhat after that, the ban on his works was not lifted for a century. Yet he became the popular hero of his age, a venerated martyr, and among Confucian ethical philosophers thereafter, his uncompromising stand in defiance of the usurpation had profound impact as a moral example." *Dictionary of Ming Biography*, ed. L. Carrington Goodrich and Chaoying Fang (New York, 1976), 1: 431–32.

46. According to Chao-ying Fang's biography of Hai: "For almost a year [alone in the capital] he brooded over the erratic conduct of the emperor Zhu Hou-cong, with disapproval and despair. Finally (November 1565) he submitted a memorial criticizing him for his failure as sovereign, father, and husband, and for his inattention to the public business in the previous twenty years. This, he said, resulted in the prevalence of injustice, corruption, military weakness, heavy taxation, and destitution among the common people . . . He found fault with the emperor for his vanity, as shown by his search for longevity, for his senseless involvement of the court in Daoist prayer ceremonies, and for his eccentric ways of constructing buildings on the palace grounds . . . The emperor is said to have been deeply disturbed by the memorial, throwing it to the floor and then picking it up to read

again. There is also the story that he called Hai a beast and ordered guards dispatched to Hai's home to prevent his slipping away, but was calmed by a eunuch who said that a man like Hai would never go into hiding, for he had already purchased a coffin and made funeral arrangements before submitting the memorial." *Dictionary of Ming Biography* 1: 474–79.

47. Jenner, "China and Freedom," 76.

48. See the discussion of the term *ru* in Brooks and Brooks, trans., *The Original Analects* under 6: 13 (p. 34).

49. See *Analects* 8: 2, 8: 10, 17: 7 (in some texts 17: 8), 17: 23, 17: 24.

50. I.e., Confucius.

51. *Mencius* 2A2.

52. *Xunzi*, chap. 23. Harvard-Yenching Institute Sinological Index Series, *A Concordance to Hsün Tzu*, Supplement no. 22, p. 90, lines 82–84. Trans. John Knoblock in *Xunzi—A Translation and Study of the Complete Works* 3 (Stanford, 1994), 161. Valor of the "middle order" is scrupulous but unheroic, "attaching primary importance to purity of self and personal integrity, but considering material wealth trivial." Valor of an inferior order tends "to think unimportant one's own character but to place great store on material wealth; to remain complacent in the face of calamity and remain negligent and inattentive." That is, displays of valor run the gamut from supreme moral confidence at the highest level to a kind of earnest moral primness at the middle level to a complete moral vacancy at the inferior level. See also the discussion of valor in "Of Honor and Grace," in *A Concordance to Hsün Tzu*, p. 9, lines 16–20; Knoblock, trans., *Xunzi* 1: 188.

53. Trans. Brooks and Brooks, *The Original Analects*, 48.

54. *Mencius* 5A7 and 5B1.

55. *Mencius* 7B34.

56. *Analects* 15: 8.

57. *Mencius* 6A10, emphasis added.

58. *Xunzi*. Harvard-Yenching Institute Sinological Index Series, *A Concordance to Hsün Tzu*, Supplement no. 22, p. 3, lines 49–50; Knoblock, trans., *Xunzi* 1: 142.

59. Knoblock, trans., *Xunzi* 1: 142, n. 78.

60. Boris Pasternak, in *Dr. Zhivago*, has the priest Nikolai Nikolaievich say, "How many things in the world deserve our loyalty? Very few indeed. I think one should be loyal to immortality, which is another word for life, a stronger word for it." *Dr. Zhivago*, trans. Max Hayward and Manya Harari (New York, 1958), 9.

61. Arendt, "What Is Freedom?," 146.

62. With some Daoists—for example, Zhuangzi—freedom does seem to have been associated with estrangement from the world. But Daoist-style retreat from the world was rejected by Confucians from earliest times as virtually a negation of one's humanity. See, for example, *Analects* 18: 6 and 18: 7.

63. This point is beautifully made by Alfreda Murck in *Poetry and Painting in Song China.*

64. David Hawkes, trans., *Ch'u Tz'u: The Songs of the South* (Boston, 1962), 71. Quoted in Murck, *Poetry and Painting in Song China*, 82.

## CHAPTER 2

1. Consider what is said about the Ming in Charles O. Hucker, *The Censorial System of Ming China* (Stanford, 1966), 42.

2. Notably the so-called Donation of Constantine, a document purportedly by Constantine giving the See of Rome primacy over Antioch Constantinople, Alexandria, and Jerusalem and various other powers. In fact it was fabricated much later. See entry in *Oxford Dictionary of the Christian Church*, F. L. Cross, ed. (Oxford, 1957).

3. It is said that when Harold was in Normandy prior to the Conquest he took an oath to be William's man and assist him in obtaining the throne of England. See Frank Stenton, *Anglo-Saxon England* (Oxford, 1946), 569–76. It seems probable that Edward had previously designated William as his successor; ibid. at 532, 33, 37.

4. For the Domesday Survey see Stenton, *Anglo-Saxon England* 608–9, 644–49. For Magna Carta, see Austin Lane Poole, *From Domesday Book to Magna Carta* (Oxford, 1953), 476–77.

5. This is, or became, of course the English feudal system. See Stenton, *Anglo-Saxon England*, 672–75.

6. See the discussion of the way education in the Inns of Court prevented the common law from being supplanted by civil (Roman) law in William Holdsworth, *History of English Law* (London, 1924), 4: 268–72.

7. 77 Eng. Rep. (K.B. 1607). The case is discussed in J. R. Tanner, *Constitutional Documents of the Reign of James I* (Cambridge, 1930), 173–77.

8. For example, colonial lawyers, including Adams and Jefferson, received much of their legal education from reading Coke. They hated it. See Katherine Drinker Bowen, *The Lion and the Throne* (Boston, 1957), 513–14.

9. Notably in Mansfield's decision in Somerset v. Stewart, 98 Eng. Rep. (K.B. 1772). Somerset, a slave in Jamaica and Virginia, became free by coming to England.

10. Brown v. Board of Education, 347 U.S. 483 (1994). The origins of Brown and its subsequent history are dealt with at length in Richard Kluger, *Simple Justice* (New York, 1976).

11. Southern Pacific Co. v. Jensen, 244 U.S. 205, 222 (1917).

12. See Oliver W. Holmes, Jr., "The Path of the Law," in S. J. Burton, ed., *The Path of the Law and Its Influence* (Cambridge, 2000), 333, 336 (repr. of *Harv. L. Rev.* 10[1897]: 457, 461).

13. Marshall's decision in The Case of Marbury v. Madison, 5 U.S. (1 Cranch) 137 (1805) is usually cited as the authority for this position.

14. Alexis de Tocqueville, *Democracy in America*, trans. Henry Reeve, rev. by Francis Bowen, Phillips Bradley, ed. (New York, 1945), 1: 280.

15. See George A. Berman et al., *Cases and Materials on European Community Law* (St. Paul, MN, 1993), 142–49. See also Paul Craig and Grainne de Burca, *EU Law, Text Cases and Materials*, 2d ed. (Oxford, 1998), 299–303.

16. See Mauro Cappelletti, *Judicial Review in the Contemporary World* (Indianapolis, 1971).

17. Sun studied in Honolulu as a youth and spent much time in Hong Kong, the continental United States, and London. See Harold Z. Shiffrin, *Sun Yat-sen and the Origins of the Chinese Revolutions* (Berkeley, 1968), 10–40.

18. The Chinese constitution of 1982—still in force with some amendments—provides for a central government that is essentially tripartite. The National People's Congress "exercise[s] the legislative power of the state." (Art. 58) There is a president who, in effect, is the chief executive. "The people's courts in the People's Republic of China are the judicial organs of the state." (Art. 123) There is also what amounts to a Bill of Rights called The Rights and Duties of Citizens (Arts. 33–56) though it does not have much relation to our Bill of Rights. Of course the Chinese Constitution is different from that of the United States, even on paper, but the source of its structure is clear.

19. See Derk Bodde and Clarence Morriss, *Law in Imperial China* (Cambridge, MA, 1967), 63.

20. For a discussion of the way in which one office—the Grand Council—operated without much imperial interference (despite the necessity of the emperor's approval for all its actions) see Beatrice Bartlett, *Monarchs and Ministers. The Grand Council in mid-Ch'ing China 1723–1820* (Berkeley, 1991), 269–78. See also Professor Bartlett's exchange with Professor Norman Kutcher in *Journal of Asian Studies* 58 (1999): 449–52.

21. See Art. 409 of the Qing code, An Official Who Decreases Penalties (erroneously). This article punishes magistrates who intentionally award a penalty that is too high or too low, or if torture was improperly used. If there was simply a mistake (as opposed to an intentional act) the penalty was reduced. The text of the Code referred to here is the translation in William C. Jones, *The Great Qing Code* (Oxford, 1994).

22. The decision of the District Magistrate in any case that awarded more than bambooing was only a recommended sentence. It had to be reviewed before being executed. See Bodde and Morriss, *Law in Imperial China*, 113–43.

23. Ibid. See also Hucker, *The Censorial System of Ming China*.

24. See chap. 1.

25. Great Qing Code, Art. 93.

26. Ibid., Art. 275.

27. Quoted in Neil Genzlinger, "If Land Is Called Sacred, Bitter Disputes Can Erupt," *New York Times*, Aug. 14, 2001, sec. B5.

28. For a general discussion see Kung-chuan Hsiao, *Rural China, Imperial Control in the Nineteenth Century* (Seattle, WA, 1960), 1–10.

29. See Sybille van der Sprenkel, *Legal Institutions in Manchu China* (London, 1962, repr. 1966), 89–96. See also chap. 3.

30. Qing Code, Art. 78, Establishing a Son of the Official Wife [as One's Successor] Contrary to Law.

31. Qing Code, Art. 87, Establishing Separate Household Registration and Dividing [the Family] Property.

32. See van der Sprenkel, *Legal Institutions*, 80–89.

33. Ibid., 97–111.

34. Qing Code, Art. 95.

35. Ibid., Art. 101.1.

36. Substatute 1 to Art. 334 provides that no complaints from the people that involved minor matters of the household, marriage, and land would be accepted from the first day of the fourth month through the thirtieth day of the seventh month because that is the time when farmers are busiest. Complaints involving serious matters of breaking the law were to be handled as usual. A translation into English may be found in Mark Alee, *Law and Local Society in Late Imperial China* (Stanford, 1994), 11. By implication, complaints about wrongful acts involving family, marriage, and land that are not dealt with in the Code may be dealt with by the magistrate. There are no rules governing such matters in the Code, or, so far as I know, in any other official document.

37. See Philip Huang, *Civil Justice in China* (Stanford, 1996). Terms like civil, commercial, criminal, or administrative law did not exist in traditional China. Nothing like the imperial codes existed in the West. In my view, using Western terminology to study Chinese law makes about as much sense as using the terminology of Latin grammar—tense, mood, verb, noun, adjective—to describe and understand the Chinese language.

38. At least during the Qing. There was apparently a law examination during the Tang although few sat for it. See Wallace Johnson, trans., *The T'ang Code* (Princeton, NJ, 1979), 1: 5.

39. The legal secretaries are described in Bodde and Morriss, *Law in Imperial China*, 5, and in Tung-tsn Ch'ü, *Local Government in China Under the Ching* (Cambridge, MA, 1962, repr. Stanford, 1969), 97–101. The so-called legal treatises would not be recognized by westerners as being much more than descriptions of rules. It is not only Anglo-American lawyers who have noticed this. Lt. Philastre, a French officer who translated the Vietnamese code, was especially sharp. He wrote that "none of these collections [treatises], to my knowledge at least, contains an analysis of the whole of Chinese law or has tried to deduce from it any theory whatsoever. Each commentator picks over the law, phrase by phrase, and tries to bring out some comparison, to find some unforeseen circumstances, and most of all, to justify the provision of the law. Alongside certain remarks which show a great exactitude in criticism, there are often platitudes and wretched inanities." P.-L.-F. Philastre, trans., *Le Code*

*Annamite*, 2d ed. (Paris, 1909, Taiwan repr., 1967), 114. See Jones, *The Qing Code*, 2–4.

40. Tung-tsu Ch'ü, *Local Government in China*, 11.

41. For a discussion of the compilation of administrative regulations and "precedents" see Van der Sprenkel, *Legal Institutions*, 56–58. As an example of an administrative precedent for the route to be used in transferring troops from Sichuan to Taiwan see Thomas Metzger, *The Internal Organization of Ch'ing Bureaucracy* (Cambridge, MA, 1973), 192–93.

42. See chap. 1.

43. See Jonathan Spence, *The Search for Modern China* (New York, 1990, 1991), 112–14, 165–93.

44. See John K. Fairbank et al., *East Asia the Modern Transformation* (Boston, 1965), 613–26. See also Jonathan Spence, *The Gate of Heavenly Peace* (New York, 1981), 1–85.

45. See Jean Escarra, *Le Droit Chinois*, trans. Gertrude R. Browne (Seattle, WA, repr. Cambridge, MA, 1961), 152–81.

46. They are perhaps most conveniently available in English in James C. Lin et al., trans. and eds., *Major Laws of the Republic of China on Taiwan*, 2 vols. (Taipei, 1991).

47. Article 17 of The Common Program of the Chinese People's Political Consultative Congress (1949), trans. in *Fundamental Legal Documents of Communist China*, Albert E. Blaustein, ed. (S. Hackensack, NJ, 1962), 34.

48. See William C. Jones, "The Constitution of the People's Republic of China," *Washington University L. Q.*, 1985, 707.

49. References, including, in some cases, translation into English, can be found in China Law Reference Service (Hong Kong), hereafter *China Law*. Thus Civil Law, *China Law* 1420/86.04.12; Civil Procedure Law, *China Law* 1420/91.04.09; Criminal Law, *China Law*, 1430/97.03.14; Criminal Procedure Law, *China Law* 1430/96.03.17; Administrative Litigation Law, *China Law* 1100/89.04.04; Company Law, *China Law*, 2330/93.12.29.

50. See chap. 10.

51. See Karby Leggett, "Enemy of the State," *Wall Street Journal*, Nov. 23, 2001, A1.

52. See Michael Schoenhals, "The Central Case Examination Group," *China Quarterly* 145 (1996): 86. Schoenhals describes the way in which the Central Case Examination Group, a very high body, directed the treatment, including torture and its form, of high level cadres during the Cultural Revolution even when the violence seemed to be the spontaneous actions of the masses.

53. For the most important laws and regulations, see The Labor Law (1994); Regulations Governing the Settlement of Labor Disputes in Enterprises (1993, issued by the State Council); Trial Measures of Insurance for Industrial Injury of Employees in Enterprises (1996, issued by the Ministry of Labor).

54. See Sections 34 and 45 of Measures for Resolution of Traffic Accidents (1991, issued by the State Council), Section 1 of Circular of the Supreme People's Court and the Ministry of Public Security on Certain Issues Concerning the Handling Cases of Road Traffic Accident (Dec. 1, 1992).

55. For administrative handling of malpractice cases, see Measures for Handling Medical Malpractices (1987, issued by the State Council), and Explanations on Certain Issues Relating the Measures for Handling Medical Malpractices (May 10, 1988, issued by the Ministry of Public Health).

56. See particularly The Protection Law (secs. 34, 39, 50) (1993); Provisions Concerning Responsibilities of Repair, Replacement and Refund of Payment on Certain Products, issued jointly by State Economic and Trade Commission, State Bureau of Quality and Technology Supervision, State Bureau for Management of Industry and Commerce and other ministries in 1995; Provisions on the Punishment for Defrauding Consumers, issued by the State Bureau for Management of Industry and Commerce in 1996, as well as local measures such as Measures of Beijing City for Implementing Consumer Protection Law issued in 1995 and revised in 1997, Rules of Shanxi Province on Consumer Protection (1996), etc.

57. In the United States, Workmen's Compensation laws.

CHAPTER 3

1. Douglass C. North, "The Paradox of the West," in R. W. Davis, ed., *The Origins of Modern Freedom in the West* (Stanford, 1995), 7–8.

2. Douglass C. North and Robert Paul Thomas, *The Rise of the Western World* (Cambridge, 1973), 91.

3. For a detailed study of the Qing tax system and the reforms undertaken during the early eighteenth century, see Madeleine Zelin, *The Magistrate's Tael, Rationalizing Fiscal Reform in the Ch'ing Period* (Berkeley, 1984).

4. There is considerable controversy over periodization in Chinese history. For the purposes of this chapter early modern refers to the late Ming onwards, during which time one can identify a continuous process of growth of population, volume of trade, and output of agricultural and manufactured goods within a context of diminishing government controls and increasing privatization of factors of production. Some scholars would argue that modern growth in China can be traced only to the last several decades of market-oriented reform under the PRC.

5. Ho Ping-ti, *Studies on the Population of China, 1368–1953* (Cambridge, MA, 1959), 136–37.

6. Madeleine Zelin, "Government Policy Toward Reclamation and Hidden Land during the Yongzheng period," unpublished manuscript, 1. According to Lee and Wong, about 10 million Chinese migrated to open new or abandoned lands in China during the seventeenth and eighteenth centuries. Cited in Kenneth Pomeranz, *The Great Divergence, China,*

*Europe and the Making of the Modern World Economy* (Princeton, NJ, 2000), 84–86.

7. See James Millward, *Beyond the Pass: Economy, Ethnicity and Empire in Qing Central Asia, 1759–1864* (Stanford, 1998), for a brilliant discussion of the role that Han merchants played in the economic colonization of northwestern territories and the reliance of the Qing state on merchant sojourners for the support of their military presence in the region.

8. Millward, *Beyond the Pass*, 322–23.

9. Susan Mann has shown that in most areas of China women did not work outside the home until the nineteenth century, when community norms played an important role in determining which places supplied women workers for newly created factory jobs. Susan Mann, "Women's Work in the Ningbo Area, 1900–1936," in Thomas G. Rawski and Lillian M. Li, eds., *Chinese History in Economic Perspective* (Berkeley, 1992), 243–70.

10. Wu Chengming and Xu Dixin, eds., *Zhongguo ziben zhuyi di mengya* [China's sprouts of capitalism] (Beijing, 1985), 112–15.

11. Mi Chu Wiens, "Lord and Peasant, the Sixteenth to the Eighteenth Century," in *Modern China* 6.1 (Jan. 1980): 29.

12. Huang Pei, *Autocracy at Work, a Study of the Yung-cheng Period, 1722–1735* (Bloomington, IN, 1974), 226–36.

13. See Richard Lufrano, "Manuals and Petitions: Commercial Problem-Solving in Late Imperial China" (Ph.D. disser., Columbia Univ., 1987).

14. By interpenetration I do not mean that political elites controlled commercial activity by means of monopolies and the exercise of political power. Rather, in China commercial activity was engaged in at all levels of society, from farmers who worked as part-time peddlers, to scholars and officials who invested in economic enterprises either deliberately or as members of lineage estates. As Myron Cohen and others have shown, even farmers were engaged in buying and selling shares in temple and other forms of shareholding organizations. See Myron Cohen, "Writs of Passage in Late Imperial China: One Rural Community's Documentation of Practical Understandings," in Madeleine Zelin et al., eds., *Contract and Property Rights in Early Modern China* (Stanford, forthcoming).

15. The sale of degrees may also have influenced the decisions, particularly of local officials, although no systematic study has been made of public policy and merchant influence in the late Qing.

16. Although the Qing are famous for a number of attacks on tax evaders among the elite, most notably the 1661 Jiangnan tax case, far more important were the policies established during the Yongzheng reign to establish reliable tax rates through structural reform of the tax system. This policy also included measures to restrict arbitrary taxation of merchants. Zelin, *Magistrate's Tael*, passim.

17. Evelyn Rawski, *Education and Popular Literacy in Ch'ing China* (Ann Arbor, MI, 1979), 140.

18. Dorothy Ko, *Teachers of the Inner Chambers: Women and Culture in Seventeenth-Century China* (Stanford, 1994).

19. These include morality books [*shanshu*], sacred scrolls [*baojuan*], and ledgers of merit and demerit [*gongguo ge*]. See Tadao Sakai, "Confucianism and Popular Educational Works," in William T. deBary, ed., *Self and Society in Ming Thought* (New York, 1970), 341–62.

20. Richard John Lufrano, *Honorable Merchants: Commerce and Self-Cultivation in Late Imperial China* (Honolulu, 1997), 17.

21. Early Qing attempts to revive manorial farming in the form of enclosures in support of Manchu bannermen failed and most of the land attached to these estates was broken up and sold by the late eighteenth century.

22. Such farms made up a small proportion of total acreage in China and appear to have been found largely in north China. See Endymion Wilkinson, ed. and trans., *Landlord and Labor in Late Imperial China: Case Studies from Shandong* (Cambridge, MA, 1978); and Philip C. C. Huang, *The Peasant Economy and Social Change in North China* (Stanford, 1985).

23. According to Ray Huang, in some parts of the delta government land amounted to as much as 70 percent of all arable land in the mid-Ming. Ray Huang, *Taxation and Governmental Finance in Sixteenth Century Ming China* (Cambridge, 1974), 99.

24. Ibid., 104–8.

25. These lands can be distinguished from land previously in private hands by their tax designation as *gengming* or altered designation lands.

26. Liang Zhiping has determined that even banner land and state-owned official land [*guandi*] and military colony land [*tuntian*] could be alienated by the clever use of instruments used in the private land market. For example, in Chang'an xian, Shaanxi, it was customary for commoners to build on official land. They would then sell the property to someone with a written contract stating that the property was a mortgage that could never be redeemed [*laodang bushu*]. Doing so gave permanent title to the buyer as if it were sold, but it avoided breaking the law that said you could not sell official land. In Jehol perpetual lease [*yongyuan changzu*] contracts were used to enable people to buy banner land. Liang Zhiping, *Qingdai xiguanfa: shehui yu guojia* [Customary Law in the Qing Period: Society and the State] (Beijing, 1996), 59.

27. Zelin, *Magistrate's Tael*, 221–63.

28. Ibid., 245. Chao Kang's work using land registers for the Ming and Qing periods demonstrates that in some regions by the Qing individual plots were quite small, landlords were slow to accumulate land, and the size of landlord estates rarely exceeded several hundred mou. Chao Kang, *Man and Land in Chinese History: An Economic Analysis* (Stanford, 1986), 96–101, 115–28.

29. Philip Huang, *The Peasant Family and Rural Development in the Yangzi Delta, 1350–1988* (Stanford, 1990), 107.

30. Zigong shi dang'an guan et al., eds., *Zigong yanye qiyue dang'an xuanji* [A collection of salt industry contracts from Zigong] (Beijing, 1985).

31. Jing Junjian provides an excellent summary of the economic statutes in the Qing code. On *dian* see Jing's "Legislation Related to the Civil Economy of the Qing Dynasty," in Philip Huang and Kathryn Bernhardt, eds., *Civil Law in Qing and Republican China* (Stanford, 1994), 69–71.

32. Feng Shaoting, "Supplemental Payment in Urban Property Contracts in mid- to late-Qing Shanghai," in Zelin et al., eds., *Contract and Property Rights*.

33. For a comprehensive treatment of Chinese laws of property succession, inheritance, and transfer by will see Kathryn Bernhardt, *Women and Property in China, 960–1949* (Stanford, 1999); and David Wakefield, *Fenjia, Household Division and Inheritance in Qing and Republican China* (Honolulu, 1998).

34. While the law also stipulated that widows be succeeded by their closest nephew of the next generation, both Ming and Qing law allowed a widow to name an alternate nephew as heir if she could not get along with the senior nephew. Bernhardt, *Women and Property*, 63–65.

35. Ibid., 41.

36. Wakefield, *Fenjia*, 115–16.

37. Ibid., 71.

38. See Lillian Li, *China's Silk Trade: Traditional Industry in the Modern World, 1842–1937* (Cambridge, MA, 1981), 38–56.

39. Zelin, *Magistrate's Tael*, 103–4.

40. S. T. Leong, "The P'eng-Min: The Ch'ing Administration and Internal Migration," paper presented at the Fifth National Conference of the Asian Studies Association of Australia, Adelaide, May 18, 1984, pp. 4–5.

41. Anne Osborne, "Highlands and Lowlands: Economic and Ecological Interactions in the Lower Yangzi Region under the Qing," in Mark Elvin and Liu Ts'ui-jung, eds., *Sediments of Time* (Cambridge, 1998), 204.

42. Yan Ruyi, *Sansheng bianfang beilan, juan 9, shanhuo*, 1822.

43. Robert Gardella, "The Antebellum Canton Tea Trade: Recent Perspectives," *The American Neptune* 48.4 (Fall 1988): 269.

44. Mark Elvin, *The Pattern of the Chinese Past* (Stanford, 1973), 278. According to interviews with elderly salt workers at the Furong salt yard in Sichuan, by 1820 there were four daily labor markets at the salt yard. These interviews are quoted in Wu and Xu, eds., *Zhongguo ziben zhuyi di mengya*, 619–20.

45. For example, Evelyn Rawski cites a Ming period sample contract for the hiring of a village teacher. Rawski, *Education and Popular Literacy*, 26.

46. Of course labor mobility does not speak to the conditions encountered while in employment. While Chinese workers may have had greater opportunity to abandon unsatisfactory employment than their counterparts in other parts of the world, they still faced appalling working conditions and often found their access to work controlled by intermediate entrepreneurs such as secret societies and labor contractors. Workers could

also find their access to certain jobs blocked by powerful guilds that reserved certain occupations for natives of particular places, and labor recruitment in some trades continued to be based on place of origin down to the twentieth century.

47. Gilbert Rozman, *Urban Networks in Ch'ing China and Tokugawa Japan* (Princeton, NJ, 1973), 110.

48. See Susan Mann, *Local Merchants and the Chinese Bureaucracy* (Stanford, 1987).

49. G. William Skinner, ed., *The City in Late Imperial China* (Stanford, 1977), 275–351; and William Rowe, *Hankow: Commerce and Society in a Chinese City, 1796–1889* (Stanford, 1984), 1–10.

50. Xue Yunsheng, *Duli cunyi* [Doubts remaining after reading the substatutes], ed. Huang Jingjia, repr. (Taibei, 1970), 407–12, statutes 153 and 154. Subsequent references to statutes and sub statutes are based on the reference numbers used by Xue.

51. Jing, "Legislation Related to the Civil Economy of the Qing Dynasty," 72–81. Evidence that the state took its responsibilities seriously in debt-related cases abounds in the archives of magistrates courts. By the early twentieth century credit issues arising among merchants were also often handled through the mediation offices of chambers of commerce. See Madeleine Zelin, "Merchant Dispute Mediation in Zigong," in Huang and Bernhardt, eds., *Civil Law in Qing and Republican China*, 255–63.

52. Based on Qing statutory tax quotas and Wang Yeh-chien's estimates of surcharge collection in 1753. Wang Yeh-chien, *Land Taxation in Imperial China, 1750–1911* (Cambridge, MA, 1973), 72.

53. Zelin, *Magistrate's Tael*, 210–11.

54. Madeleine Zelin, "The Structure of the Chinese Economy during the Qing Period," in Kenneth Lieberthal et al., eds., *Perspectives on Modern China, Four Anniversaries* (Armonk, NY, 1991), 33.

55. Wu Chengming, "Lun Qingdai qianqi wuoguo guonei shichang" [A discussion of our country's internal market during the early Qing period], *Lishi yanjiu* 1 (1983): 103.

56. Dwight Perkins, *Agricultural Development in China, 1368–1968* (Chicago, 1969), 115.

57. See Loren Brandt, *Commercialization and Agricultural Development, Central and Eastern China, 1870–1937* (Cambridge, 1989).

58. For an excellent treatment of the increasing bureaucratization and regulation of merchants in late nineteenth and twentieth century China see the second half of Mann, *Local Merchants and the Chinese Bureaucracy*. See also Joseph Fewsmith on state corporatism in relation to merchants. Joseph Fewsmith, *Party, State, and Local Elites in Republican China: Merchant Organizations and Politics in Shanghai, 1890–1930* (Honolulu, 1985).

59. The closing of Chinese maritime trade during the 1660s and 70s was a response to the military threat posed by Ming-loyalist rebels based on

Taiwan. It is often forgotten that prior to the restriction of Western traders to Guangzhou (Canton) in 1767, foreign merchants had free access to China's coastal ports.

60. For a more detailed discussion of this issue, see Zelin, "Some Thoughts on Rights of Property in Pre-War China" in Zelin et al., eds., *Contract and Property Rights*.

61. Bernhardt, *Women and Property*, 44.

62. The only allusion to this in statutory law can be found in statute 93, substatutes 1 and 4. These, however, refer only to the prosecution of sons and grandsons who dispose of ancestral grave land or temple property without authority. The dynastic statutes are surprisingly silent on the matter of the unit of ownership. However, an examination of court cases makes it clear that unauthorized disposal of communal property, be it undivided household property or incorporated communal property, was a not uncommon source of legal disputes. For descriptions of such cases see Zelin, "Managing Multiple Ownership at the Zigong Salt Yard" in Zelin et al., eds., *Contract and Property Rights*.

63. Wakefield, *Fengjia*, 56.

64. See Madeleine Zelin, "Capital Accumulation and Investment Strategies in Early Modern China: The Case of the Furong Salt Yard," in *Late Imperial China*, June 1988, 79–122; and Myron Cohen, "Writs of Passage in Late Imperial China: One Rural Community's Documentation of Practical Understandings," in Zelin et al., eds., *Contract and Property Rights*.

65. This principle was incorporated in Article 954 of the Republican Civil Code. See Madeleine Zelin, "Merchant Dispute Mediation in Twentieth-Century Zigong, Sichuan," in Bernhardt and Huang, eds., *Civil Law in Qing and Republican China*, 271–73.

66. For official applications of this argument see examples in the unpublished collection of secret palace memorials at the National Palace Museum in Taibei, Taiwan. For example, a memorial by Yue Zhaolong dated Yongzheng 10,1,28 cites the inherent laziness of aborigines and their unwillingness to work beyond their subsistence needs. See also Oertai's memorial dated Yongzheng 5,3,12 which depicts aborigines as primitive people with no knowledge of the sophisticated farming techniques available to the Chinese. Conversely, it was also common for land grabbers who failed to cultivate their stake to lose their rights by virtue of failure to improve. Guo Songyi, "Qingchu fengjian guojia kenhuang zhengce fenxi" [An analysis of the land reclamation policies of the early Qing feudal state], *Qingshi luncong* 2 (1980): 117.

67. Myron Cohen, "The Role of Contract in Traditional Chinese Social Organization," *VIIIth Congress of Anthropological and Ethnological Sciences*, 1968, 132. Wakefield notes that by the Qing for a *fenjia dan* or an *yizhu* to be valid it had to be a written agreement. Wakefield, *Fengjia*, 58.

68. While cases could be adjudicated at the court of the county yamen, these courts did not make up a network in which the decisions of one

court were known to, or influenced by the decisions of other courts. Any consistency that is demonstrated in cases from one court to another was the result of adherence to the Qing Code and a high degree of uniformity in customary practice which may be understand as customary law.

69. While the rate of survival of company records such as ledgers and account books from the pre-Communist period is disappointing, large numbers of contracts have been preserved. The reason is twofold. On the one hand, contracts as one of the most important sources of evidence in a civil dispute were often appended to plaints stored in county and chamber of commerce archives. Equally important may have been the cumulative nature of contracts in China, whereby the terms of one contract often built on material contained in its predecessor contract. As a result, families carefully saved all their contracts, even when new agreements appear to have superseded old ones.

70. Man Bun Kwan, "Chinese Business History in the People's Republic of China, A Review," in Robert Gardella et al., eds., *Chinese Business History, Interpretive Trends and Priorities for the Future*, special issue, *Chinese Studies in History* 31.3–4 (Spring–Summer, 1998).

71. In 1934 the Zigong salt yard furnace merchants association ruled that prior to the time a well reached optimal production a partnership did not yet exist between the owners of the well site and the investors in the drilling of a well. Zigong Municipal Archives 17–1–682–6~7.

72. For a discussion of Qing land disputes, see Madeleine Zelin, "The Rights of Tenants in Mid-Qing Sichuan: A Study of Land-Related Lawsuits in the Baxian Archives," *Journal of Asian Studies* 45.3 (May 1986). For a discussion of merchant dispute mediation see Zelin, "Merchant Dispute Mediation," 249–308.

73. See Zelin, "Capital Accumulation"; Zelin, "Managing Multiple Ownership at the Zigong Salt Yard."

74. See for example Zelin, "Structure of the Chinese Economy" in Lieberthal et al., eds., *Perspectives on Modern China*; R. Bin Wong, *China Transformed, Historical Change and the Limits of European Experience* (Ithaca, NY, 1997); and Pomeranz, *The Great Divergence*.

75. Nathan Rosenberg and L. E. Birdzell, Jr., *How the West Grew Rich. The Economic Transformation of the Industrial World* (New York, 1986), 53.

76. For an excellent treatment of this central-local tension see Harrison Stewart Miller, "State vs. Society in Late Imperial China, 1572–1644" (Ph.D. disser., Columbia Univ., 2001).

77. Millward, *Beyond the Pass*, 121–22. This did not apply in most murder cases.

### CHAPTER 4

1. See the scholarly compilation of authors linking law and liberty in Friedrich Hayek, *Law, Legislation, and Liberty, 1. Rules and Order* (London, 1973), 61; I refer more directly to the quotation in n. 13 of chap. 2.

2. This conception was classically formulated by Montesquieu in his *L'esprit des lois*; Karl A. Wittfogel did a modern anti-totalitarian adaptation in *Oriental Despotism. A Comparative Study of Total Power* (New Haven, CT, 1957), particularly chap. 4.

3. See John Rawls, *A Theory of Justice* (Oxford, 1973), 235.

4. George T. Staunton, *Ta Tsing Leu Lee; Being The Fundamental Laws and a Selection From the Supplementary Statutes of the Penal Code of China* (London, 1810; reed. Taipei, 1966), "Translator's Preface," xi.

5. Rawls, *Theory*, 237 and 241.

6. Many examples of this kind of literature are described in Pierre-Étienne Will, ed., *Official Handbooks and Anthologies of China: A Descriptive and Critical Bibliography* (forthcoming).

7. See Jérôme Bourgon, "Uncivil dialogue. Law and Custom Were Not to Merge into Civil Law Under the Qing," *Late Imperial China* 23.1 (June 2002): 50–90.

8. See the modern edition by Huang Jingjia: Xue Yunsheng, *Duli cunyi* (Taibei, 1971), 5 vols.

9. See David C. Buxbaum, "Some Aspects of Civil Procedure and Practice at the Trial Level in Tanshui and Hsinchu from 1789 to 1895," *Journal of Asian Studies* 30.2 (1971): 255–79; Madeleine Zelin, "The Rights of Tenants in Mid-Qing Sichuan: A Study of Land-Related Lawsuits in the Baxian Archives," *Journal of Asian Studies* 45.3 (1986): 499–526; Philip C. C. Huang, *Civil Justice in China. Representation and Practice in the Qing* (Stanford, 1996).

10. I just summarize here the accurate remarks in Mark A. Allee, *Law and Local Society in Late Imperial China. Northern Taiwan in the Nineteenth Century* (Stanford, 1994), 226–28. See also his introductory remarks, p. 4: "What I will refer to throughout as civil cases were, to the Chinese courts, merely 'minor matters' that were handled with procedures that differed only slightly from those used in criminal cases. A single legal system handled all cases (except those involving bureaucrats charged with administrative malfeasance). However, even though the procedures of 'civil' adjudication were usually not significantly different from those of 'criminal' trials, it will occasionally be convenient for the purposes of our discussion to make the distinction."

11. Huang, *Civil Justice*, 218.

12. See Wang Huizu, *Zuozhi yaoyan* [Good recipes for assistants in local government], in *Wang Longzhuang Xiansheng yishu* [Works left by Mr. Wang Longzhuang] (Huizu, 1785), 16b; this paragraph is headed "Reading the Books" and gives a judgment on a case of illicit sexual intercourse as an example of a fair judgment after the Classics.

13. Huang, *Civil Justice*, 209. Such cases were settled by inferring notions as *qingli*: sympathy for the people's feeling about their own situation [*renqing*], appreciated thanks to the judge's common sense [*daoli*].

14. Ibid., 6.

15. See sub-statute no. 93-4, in *Duli cunyi*, 277.

16. See Jing Junjian, "Legislation Related to the Civil Economy in the Qing Dynasty," in Kathryn Bernhardt and Philip C. C. Huang, eds., *Civil Law in Qing and Republican China* (Stanford, 1994), 42–84, 45–47.

17. Ibid., 50; some of these penal sections are enumerated as follows: "Robbery," "Robbery in broad daylight," "Extortion of property," "Procurement of government or private property by fraud," "Conspiracy to commit theft," "Entering the house of another at night without proper cause."

18. See statute 76.

19. See statutes 87, 88.

20. See statute 90, al. 4.

21. For Africa, see Terence Ranger, "The Invention of Tradition in Colonial Africa," in Eric Hobsbawm and Terence Ranger, *The Invention of Tradition* (Cambridge, 1983); on Asia, see the lingering debates about the *Adatrecht* [customary law] of Indonesia, related in Clifford Geertz, *Local Knowledge. Further Essays in Interpretive Anthropology* (New York, 1983), chap. 8.

22. On Singapore, see Maurice Freedman, *The Study of Chinese Society* (Stanford, 1979), 95; on Hong Kong, see "The New Territories Land Ordinance No. 3," 1905; "The New Territories Ordinance," 1910, in *Chinese Law and Customs in Hong Kong* (Hong Kong, 1948).

23. Douglas R. Reynolds, *China, 1898–1912. The Xinzheng Revolution and Japan* (Cambridge, MA, 1993), chap. 6.

24. See the definition of *xiguan* in "Jia Yi zhuan" [biography of Jia Yi], *Qian Han shu* [History of the Former Han]; often repeated and commented, as in "Liu Fu *zhuan*," *Songshi* [History of the Song Dynasty] 12: 247. This amounts to a variation of *Lunyu* [Confucius' Analects], 17.2: "By nature [*xing*], men are nearly alike; by practice [*xi*], they get to be wide apart."

25. See Hozumi Nobushige, *Kanshû to hôritsu* [Custom and law] (Tokyo, 1878). The Japanese book gathers studies written primarily in English.

26. See the useful insights on the German Historical School in comparative perspectives, in Robert Jacob, "La coutume, les moeurs et le rite. Regards croisés sur les catégories occidentales de la norme non écrite," in Jérôme Bourgon, ed., *La coutume et la norme en Chine et au Japon*, *Extrême-Occident* 23 (Oct. 2001): 143–64.

27. Huang Zunxian, *Riben guo zhi* [Monograph on the Empire of Japan] (Shanghai, 1901), chap. 32.

28. Liang Qichao, "Zhongguo falixue fada shi lun" [Historical essay on the evolution of the Chinese jurisprudence], in *Yinbing shi wenji* [Works from the Ice Drinker's Studio] 5: 42; and *Lun Zhongguo chengwen fa bianzhi zhi yange deshi* [On the assets and shortcomings in the evolution of the Chinese written law], in ibid. 6: 4 and 45.

29. See Andrew J. Nathan, "Redefinitions of Freedom in China," in Robert Taylor, ed., *The Idea of Freedom in Asia and Africa* (Stanford, 2002).

30. On the Meiji customary law project, its diffusion in the Japanese colonial empire, and its influence on the Chinese, see Jérôme Bourgon, "Le
droit coutumier comme phénomène d'acculturation bureaucratique au Japon et en Chine," in Bourgon, ed., *La coutume et la norme*, 125–42.

31. See *Taiwan shiho furoku sankôsho* [The private law of Taiwan,
with documents appended] (Kyoto, 1910), 13 vols.

32. See for instance Chen Fu-mei [Chang] and Ramon Myers, "Customary Law and Economic Growth of China During the Ch'ing Period,"
pt. 1, *Ch'ing-shih wen-t'i* 3,2 (Nov. 1976): 1–32; pt. 2, ibid. 3,10 (Dec.
1978): 4–27; David C. Buxbaum, "Contracts in China During the Qing
Dynasty: Key to Civil Law," *Journal of Oriental Studies* 31.2 (1993): 195–
236; and Allee, *Law and Local Society*, 252–53.

33. See Wang Tay-Sheng, "Legal Reform in Taiwan under the Japanese
Colonial Rule (1895–1945): The Reception of Western Law" (Ph.D. thesis,
Univ. of Wash., 1992), 330–31.

34. I found two of them, dating from 1911 and 1915: these are the Wuqing manuscript in four fascicles, and the *Taopi gongdu*. See the complete
references in notes 45 and 55.

35. See Xiuding falü guan [Bureau for Revising and drafting the legisla-
tion], *Diaocha minshi xiguan zhangcheng shi tiao* [Regulation in ten articles about the enquiry on customs in civil matters].

36. See Reynolds, *China 1898–1912*, 184–85.

37. This continuity in the legal personnel of the empire and the Republic Bureau of codification is stressed by Philip C. C. Huang, *Code, Custom, and Legal Practice in China. The Qing and the Republic Compared*
(Stanford, 2001), 50.

38. See *Diaocha minshi xiguan wenti* [Questionnaire on the customs
on civil matters] (Beijing, 1907).

39. Admittedly, some sections witness a concern for the Chinese tradition: for instance, the "succession to the ancestors worship" counts thirteen questions, when "succession to property," more orthodox in regard to
Western civil law, counts only twelve questions.

40. "Any person who has a right, such that all the power to use, to reap
the fruit, and to dispose of [a thing] falls to this one and only person, this is
what is called 'right of property.'" (my translation) *Diaocha minshi xiguan wenti*, 3a.

41. See Sucheta Mazumdar, "Rights in People, Rights in Land: Concepts of Customary Property in Late Imperial China," in Bourgon, ed., *La
coutume et la norme*, 89–107.

42. *Wuqing xian, Fazhi ke: minshi fengsu, difang shengshi, minshi
shangshi, susong xiguan diaocha shu* [Wuqing district, Legal section: Book
of Reports on Customs on the Situation Among People, the Morals and
Habits, the Gentry and Scholars of the Place, the Civil, Commercial, and
Judicial Matters]; MS conserved at the "rare books" section of the Beijing
University library, undated, 4 fols.

43. Second fascicle, art. 2 of the *Wuquan* section [Rights on the things]. The manuscript bears no page number.

44. The most important particularity was that the tenant could sublet his right to till the land, and was not allowed to build a house or a grave, except on the margins of the land.

45. The tenant had a real right on the land, in counterpart of a sum amounting to a part of the market value of the land, of which a part was paid yearly, with the addition of a rent in kind. If the main owner sold the land, he owed a third of the price to the tenant, who can be therefore considered as a minor owner. The latter was allowed to build a dwelling or grave on the land.

46. See *Fujian shengli* [Provincial regulations of Fujian] (rep. Taibei, 1964), 3: 442–46; and comments in Melissa Macauley, *Social Power and Legal Culture. Litigation Masters in Late Imperial China* (Stanford, 1999), 228–41.

47. See Huang, *Code, Custom and Legal Practice*, 102–18.

48. *Minshang shi xiguan diaocha baogao lu* [Reports of the surveys on customs in civil and commercial matters] (Beijing, 1930).

49. Ibid., 735.

50. Jean Escarra, *Loi et coutume en Chine* (Paris, 1931), 20. For a recent confirmation of the low quality of this collection, see Huang, *Code, Custom and Legal Practice*, 9.

51. I refer more particularly to the first fascicle of the Wuqing survey.

52. See Liu Ruji, *Taopi gongdu* [Public Archives of the Tile Molder] (Anhui yinshuaju, 1911), vol. 12, "Fazhi ke" [Legal section].

53. See Pierre-Étienne Will, "The 1744 Annual Audits of Magistrate Activity and their Fate," *Late Imperial China* 18.2 (Dec. 1997): 1–50; and William T. Rowe, "Ancestors Rites and Political Authority in Late Imperial China. Chen Hongmou in Jiangxi," in *Modern China* 24.4 (Oct. 1998): 378–407.

54. For instance, items like "fixing moving populations" (1.a), "promoting the most profitable activities of the place" (3.a), "distinguishing false accusations from the real ones" (2.b), "tracking the infanticide of baby girls" (2.d), "investigating the frequency of suicides" (6.b), were also included in Qing provincial compilations, though in a less orderly way.

55. Liu Ruji, *Taopi gongdu* 12: 47 (reply of the Gentry of Qimeng district). Another reply protested that "Men of this district are not so selfish and treacherous that they would falsely invoke duties, to exercise their skill in competing rights and conflicting interests," ibid., 31.

56. Ibid., 94.

57. Ibid. Proportion of schooled children in the total population would have been as low as 7 percent for boys and 1 percent for girls in Wuyuan district.

58. See Béatrice David, "L'action de l'État chinois contre les 'mauvaises coutumes' matrimoniales. La natolocalité chez lez Zheyuanren du Guangxi," in Bourgon, ed., *La coutume et la norme*, 63–85.

59. Norbert Elias, *The Civilizing Process: Sociogenetic and Psychogenetic Investigations* (rep. Oxford, 2000).

60. Michel Foucault, *Discipline and Punish: Birth of the Prison* (New York, 1995). It might be necessary to recall that Foucault does not construe discipline as restricted to prison, but as a multifarious process permeating the whole social life.

61. See the introductory remarks in M. H. Van der Valk, *Interpretations of the Supreme Court at Peking. Years 1915 and 1916* (rep. Taipei, 1968; 1st ed. Shanghai, 1948), 1–52.

62. Dong Kang was distinguished by Shen Jiaben in 1900, when he was a young official of the Shaanxi department at the Board of Punishments. He was sent for some months to Japan for a survey on the prison system. He became an outstanding figure of the Commission for drafting the legislation in the last years of the Qing, then again in the same Commission under Yuan Shikai's presidency. He headed the Supreme Court from 1914 to 1918, and in 1921–22.

63. See Dali yuan [Supreme Court] 1923, *Dali yuan panli yaozhi huilan* [Collection of the essentials of the Supreme Court jurisprudence] (Beijing, 1923). English trans. Tcheng F. T., *The Chinese Supreme Court Decisions* (Peking, 1923); French trans. Jean Escarra, *Recueil des sommaires de la jurisprudence de la Cour Suprême de la République de Chine en matière civile et commerciale* (Beijing, 1924). As can be seen in the 1936 edition of the Civil Code, decisions of these years laid down the foundations of civil jurisprudence, which the later decisions completed without significant change of inspiration.

64. See decisions 64–1913; 901–1914; 122–1915; 1103–1915; 2354–1915.

65. Dec. 1276–1915; 1422–1917; 1438–1918.

66. See dec. 1156–1917 stating this principle; and, among many decisions related: 70–1914; 154–1916; 869–1916.

67. See dec. 845–1914; no. 1257.1915; 792.1916.

68. Wu Jingxiong, ed., *Zhonghua Minguo Liufa liyou panjie huibian* [The collection of the Six Codes of the Chinese Republic, with motives, judgments and interpretations of the Supreme Court] (Shanghai, 1936), vols. 1–2: *Minfa* [Civil laws].

69. See Kathryn Bernhardt, *Women and Property in China 960–1949* (Stanford, 1999), 177.

70. See Kathryn Bernhardt, "Women and the Law: Divorce in the Republican Period," in Bernhardt and Huang, eds., *Civil law*, 211.

71. See Bernhardt, *Women and Property*, 152–60.

72. Dec. 297–1921.

73. Dec. 411–1921; 697–1922.

74. Bernhardt, *Women and Property*, 154.

75. See Bernhardt, "Women and the Law," 188.

76. Huang, *Code, Custom, and Legal Practice*, 56.

CHAPTER 5

1. Quoted in John Fitzgerald, *Awakening China: Politics, Culture, and Class in the Nationalist Revolution* (Stanford, 1996), 257. See also ibid., 259; C. Martin Wilbur, *Sun Yat-sen, Frustrated Patriot* (New York, 1976), 278.

2. After the inauguration he visited Sun's Memorial Hall in Taipei, paying respects to Sun's statue in a large hall, on the walls of which are inscribed Sun's last will.

3. In Ssu-yu Teng and John K. Fairbank, *China's Response to the West: A Documentary Survey, 1839–1923* (Cambridge, MA, 1954), 228.

4. Karl Gerth, "Nationalizing Consumption, Consuming Nationalism: the National Products Movement in China, 1905–1937" (Ph.D. disser., Harvard Univ., 2000), 142. Further on fashion see Fitzgerald, *Awakening China*, 23–25, 55–57, 64.

5. John Fincher, "Provincialism and National Revolution," in Mary C. Wright, ed., *China in Revolution: The First Phase, 1900–1913* (New Haven, CT, 1968), 210.

6. See Westel Woodbury Willoughby, *Constitutional Government in China: Present Conditions and Prospects* (Washington, DC, 1922). Willoughby was an American political scientist and an adviser to the Chinese government.

7. Ch'ien Tuan-sheng, *Government and Politics of China, 1912–1949* (Stanford, [1950] 1970), 70.

8. Hu Shi, "Xianzheng wenti" [The question of constitutional government], *Duli pinglun* [The Independent Critic] no. 1 (May 22, 1932): 5–7.

9. Paulo Frank, "Constitutionalism in the Chinese Republic," unpub. ms., chap. 2, 59.

10. Lloyd E. Eastman, *The Abortive Revolution: China under Nationalist Rule, 1927–1937* (Cambridge, MA, 1974), 170.

11. Quoted in Eastman, *Abortive Revolution*, 171.

12. Hua-yu Li, "The Political Stalinization of China: The Establishment of One-Party Constitutionalism, 1948–1954," *Journal of Cold War Studies* 3.2 (Spring 2001): 40. Li cites Liu's translator in Moscow, Shi Zhe: see Shi Zhe, *Zai lishi junren shenbian* [Alongside the giants of history] (Beijing, 1991), 408.

13. William C. Kirby, "China's Republican Century," Keynote Address, International Conference on "The Role of the Republican Period in Twentieth Century China: Reflections and Reconsiderations," Venice, June 30-July 3, 1999.

14. Ch'ien Tuan-sheng, *Government and Politics of China*, 390.

15. Kuo Heng-yü, *Die Komintern und die chinesische Revolution* (Paderborn, 1979), 284.

16. Arif Dirlik, *The Origins of Chinese Communism* (Berkeley, 1989), 153. The opening and now partial publication of the Comintern archives in Moscow have demonstrated anew the massive influence of the Soviet

Union on China's domestic political landscape in the 1920s. See *Die Komintern und die national-revolutionäre Bewegung in China: Dokumente, Band 1: 1920–1925* (Paderborn, 1996); *Band 2: 1926–27, Teil 1 und 2* (1997).

17. Hans J. van de Ven, *From Friend to Comrade: The Founding of the Chinese Communist Party, 1920–1927* (Berkeley, 1991), 56.

18. Hung-mao Tien, *Government and Politics in Kuomintang China, 1927–1937* (Stanford, 1972), 18.

19. Su Shaozhi, paper presented to the conference "Construction of the Party-State and State Socialism in China," The Colorado College, 1993.

20. Broadly see Ch'ien Tuan-sheng, *Government and Politics of China.*

21. See Wen-Hsin Yeh, *The Alienated Academy: Culture and Politics in Republican China, 1919–1937* (Cambridge, MA, 1990), 174.

22. Xiaoquan Xu, "Human Rights," 230; see id., *Chinese Professionals and the Republican State* (New York, 2001), 121–28.

23. Fitzgerald, *Awakening China,* 257.

24. For an excellent discussion of factions in the GMD Party-State see Tien, *Government and Politics in Kuomintang China,* 45–72. On the dynamics of factionalism and the "patrimonial quality" of Chinese politics in the PRC of the 1980s see Kenneth Lieberthal and Michel Oksenberg, *Policy Making in China: Leaders, Structures, and Policies* (Princeton, NJ, 1988), 58–62.

25. Quoted in Eastman, *Abortive Revolution,* 308–9.

26. Sun Yat-sen, *The International Development of China* (New York, 1922), 191–92.

27. The term "developmental state" is appropriated from Chalmers Johnson's study of Japanese industrial policy of the same and later periods. See Johnson, *MITI and the Japanese Miracle: The Growth of Industrial Policy, 1925–1975* (Stanford, 1982), 17ff. On the aspirations of modern states to "the administrative ordering of nature and society" in the era of "high modernism," see James C. Scott, *Seeing Like a State: How Certain Schemes to Improve the Human Condition Have Failed* (New Haven, CT, 1998), 88 and 87–102, *passim.*

28. Lin Jiayou, "Shilun Sun Zhongshan zhenxing Zhongguo shangyede jingji sixiang ji qi yanbian" [The evolution of Sun Yat-sen's economic thought regarding the revitalization of China's commerce], in *Minguo Yanjiu* [Republican Research] 1, 1 (1994): 37.

29. Linsun Cheng, *Banking in Modern China* (Cambridge, 2003).

30. See Frederic Wakeman, Jr., *Policing Shanghai, 1927–1937* (Berkeley, 1995).

31. Mao Tse-tung [Mao Zedong], "On Coalition Government," *Selected Works* (Beijing, 1961–64), 3: 282–85, quoted in Suzanne Pepper, *Civil War in China: The Political Struggle, 1945–1949* (Berkeley, 1978), 220.

32. See Arlen Meliksetov, "'New Democracy' and China's Search for Socio-economic Development Routes (1949–1953)," in *Far Eastern Affairs* 1996, 1: 75–92, esp. 82–83; Bo Yibo, *Ruogan zhongde juece yu shijian de*

*huigu* [A review of some important policies and events], vol. 1, 1949–1956 (Beijing, 1991), 234–42.

33. Cited in Hua-yu Li, "Political Stalinization," 33.

34. On the plight of smaller opposition parties see Roger Jeans, ed., *Roads Not Taken* (Boulder, CO, 1992).

35. For a stimulating comparison between the Party-States that argues for a "single-state, two regime" model, see Robert E. Bedeski, *State-Building in Modern China: The Kuomintang in the Prewar Period* (Berkeley, 1981). For the textbook description see Kenneth Lieberthal, *Governing China: From Revolution Through Reform* (New York, 1995), 77.

36. Bedeski, *State-Building*, 20.

37. Konstantin Schevelyoff, paper presented to the conference "Construction of the Party-State and State Socialism in China," The Colorado College, 1993.

38. This is not to say that there was not criticism. Mao's "mistakes" were discussed by the CCP itself in its 1981 Resolution on Questions in Party History. But archives on Mao's rule remain largely closed and Chinese historians are limited in what they can write on his era: William C. Kirby, "Reflections on Official Histories of Twentieth Century China," paper presented to the International Conference on Modern Chinese Historiography and Historical Thinking, University of Heidelberg, May 2001.

39. Chiang quoted in Hsiao-shih Cheng, *Party-Military Relations in the PRC and Taiwan: Paradoxes of Control* (Boulder, CO, 1990), 136, cited in Steve Tseng, ed., *In the Shadow of China: Political Developments in Taiwan Since 1949* (London, 1993), 65.

40. Steve Tsang, "Transforming a Party-State into a Democracy," in Steve Tsang and Hung-mao Tien, eds., *Democratization in Taiwan: Implications for China* (Hong Kong, 1998), 5; Jay Taylor, *The Generalissimo's Son* (Cambridge, MA, 1999).

41. Interview of May, 1994, quoted in Linda Chao and Ramon H. Myers, *The First Chinese Democracy: Political Life in the Republic of China on Taiwan* (Baltimore, 1998), 292. On Lee Teng-hui as *ducai*, see 273. Ultimately Lee would seek to lead his followers out of the Guomindang itself, an act for which the former president and party chairman would be expelled from the GMD in September 2001.

42. Letter, Chen Yi to Chen Lifu, May 10, 1944, in *Minguo Dang'an* [Republican Archives] 1989, no. 3: 20–21.

43. On degrees of Leninism in the post-1950 GMD see Steve Tsang, "Chiang Kai-shek and the Kuomintang's Policy to Reconquer the Chinese Mainland, 1949–1958," in Tsang, *In the Shadow of China*, 67.

44. Investigation and studies of "2–28" include *Er-er-ba shijian ziliao xuanji* [Selected materials of the 2–28 Incident] (Taibei, 1992); *Nanjing di'er lishi dang'an guan guancang Taiwan er-er-ba shijian dang'an shiliao* [Historical materials regarding the Taiwan 2–28 Incident in the holdings of the Second Historical Archive, Nanjing] (Taibei, 1992); *Er-er-ba shjian yanjiu baogao* [Report on the 2–28 Incident], ed. Xingzhengyuan yanjiu er-

er-ba shijian xiaozu (Taibei, 1994); and Lai Tse-han et al., *A Tragic Beginning: The Taiwan Uprising of February 28, 1947* (Stanford, 1991).

45. Joseph R. Allen, "Taipei City Park: Public Space and Cultural Power," paper presented to the Taiwan Studies Workshop, Harvard University, May 2001.

46. Quoted in Pepper, *Civil War in China*, 227.

47. See chap. 10 below. See also Kevin J. O'Brien, "Villagers, Elections, and Citizenship in Contemporary China," *Modern China* 27.4 (Oct. 2001): 407–35.

48. See Lieberthal and Oksenberg, *Policy Making in China*, 137–38.

49. On the *danwei* in large private enterprises of the Republican period see Wen-hsin Yeh, "The Republican Origins of the *Danwei*: The Case of Shanghai's Bank of China," in Xiaobo Lü and Elizabeth Perry, eds., *Danwei: The Changing Chinese Workplace in Historical and Comparative Perspective* (Armonk, NY, 1997), 60–90.

50. See William Kirby, "Continuity and Change in Modern China: Chinese Economic Planning on the Mainland and on Taiwan, 1943–1958," *Australian Journal of Chinese Affairs* 24 (July 1990): 121–41.

51. See Thomas B. Gold, *State and Society in the Taiwan Miracle* (Armonk, NY, 1986), 76–77.

52. See William C. Kirby, "China Unincorporated: Company Law and Business Enterprise in Twentieth-Century China," *Journal of Asian Studies* 54.1 (Feb. 1995): 57–58.

53. Jean C. Oi, "Fiscal Reform and the Economic Foundations of Local State Corporatism in China," in *World Politics* 45.1 (1992): 100.

54. See Edward S. Steinfeld, *Forging Reform in China: The Fate of State-Owned Industry* (Cambridge, 1998).

55. David Shambaugh, "Building the Party-State in China, 1949–1965: Bringing the Soldier Back In," in Timothy Cheek and Tony Saich, eds., *New Perspectives on State Socialism in China* (Armonk, NY, 1997), 125–50.

56. Lieberthal, *Governing China*, 204.

57. With its wealth and local political machines, the GMD still retained huge advantages over the DPP in electoral politics. See Shelley Rigger, *From Opposition to Power: Taiwan's Democratic Progressive Party* (Boulder CO, 2001), 216–17.

58. See Joseph Fewsmith, *China Since Tiananmen: The Politics of Transition* (Cambridge, 2001). See also Wang Hui, *China's New Order: Society, Politics, and Economy in Transition* (Cambridge, MA, 2003).

59. Fewsmith, *China*, 229.

## CHAPTER 6

1. Michel Foucault, *Madness and Civilization: A History of Insanity in the Age of Reason* (New York, 1965); and *Discipline and Punish: The Birth of the Prison* (New York, 1977).

2. See especially the work of Nobel laureate Douglass C. North, *Struc-*

*ture and Change in Economic History* (New York, 1981); and *Institutions, Institutional Change and Economic Performance* (New York, 1990).

3. Paul Pierson, "Increasing Returns, Path Dependence, and the Study of Politics," *American Political Science Review* 94.2 (June 2000): 251–67.

4. Kathleen Thelen, "Historical Institutionalism in Comparative Politics," *Annual Review of Political Science* 2 (1999): 369–404.

5. Karl Marx, "The Civil War in France," in Karl Marx and Frederick Engels, *Selected Works* (New York, 1968), 256.

6. Marx, "The Civil War," 291.

7. Rex A. Wade, *Red Guards and Workers' Militias in the Russian Revolution* (Stanford, 1984), 3–4.

8. Wade, *Red Guards*, 37–41, 207.

9. *Erqi dabagong ziliao xuanbian* [Documentary collection on the great strike of February Seventh] (Beijing, 1983).

10. Shanghai Municipal Archives (SMA), ed., *Wusa yundong* [The May Thirtieth Movement] (Shanghai, 1991), 1: 92; *North China Herald*, Oct. 3, 1925, 14.

11. SMA, ed., *Wusa yundong* 1: 8; 2: 7.

12. Michael Tsin, *Nation, Governance and Modernity in China* (Stanford, 1999), 157.

13. Ibid., 158–67.

14. Central Archives and SMA, eds., *Shanghai geming lishi wenjian huiji* [Documentary compilation on Shanghai revolutionary history] (1986), bk. 2, vol. 4: 407. This 17-volume collection of the archives of the Communist Party in Shanghai from 1925 through 1927, published for internal circulation only, includes detailed transcripts of party meetings as well as documents produced by the local party and its affiliated organizations.

15. Ibid., 68.

16. Ibid., 159, 172.

17. Wu Hao [Zhou Enlai], "Shiyue geming" [The October Revolution], in *Shaonian* [Youth], no. 5 (Dec. 1, 1922).

18. *Shanghai geming*, bk. 2, vol. 5: 5.

19. Ibid., bk. 1, vol. 2: 152, 180.

20. Ibid., 3–4, 181–82.

21. *Liangong (bu), gongchan guoji yu zhongguo guomin geming yundong, 1926–1927* [The Soviet Communists (Bolsheviks), Comintern, and the Chinese national revolutionary movement, 1926–1927], trans. (from Russian) by Chinese Communist Party Central Party History Research Office (Beijing, 1998), vol. 4: 139–44.

22. *Shanghai geming*, bk. 2, vol. 5: 589.

23. Ibid., bk. 1, vol. 2: 234.

24. On March 5, 1927, in a top secret communication to the Comintern from Shanghai, Chen Duxiu requested a blueprint for establishment of a people's representative assembly. *Lianggong*, 148.

25. *Shanghai geming*, bk. 2, vol. 5: 592–93.

26. Ibid., bk. 1, vol. 2: 257–58.

27. Ibid., 274.

28. Zhu Hua, *Shanghai yibainian* [A century in Shanghai] (Shanghai, 1999), 158; *Shanghai geming*, bk. 2, vol. 6: 32.

29. *Shanghai geming*, bk. 2, vol. 4: 172, and vol. 6: 45, 126, 132; Frederic Wakeman, Jr., *Policing Modern Shanghai* (Berkeley, 1995), 138. On Gu's later defection and demise, see Wakeman, *Policing*, 151–60; Wu Jimin, *Zhou Enlai yu Shanghai miemen xuean* [Zhou Enlai and the bloody case of wiping out a family in Shanghai] (Taibei, 1998); Yu Ming, "Gu Shunzhang shijian yu Wu Hao qishi" [The Gu Shunzhang affair and the Wu Hao expose], in Jin Zhong, ed., *Hongchao zaixiang: Zhou Enlai renge jiepou* [Prime Minister of a Red Dynasty: Dissecting the Personality of Zhou Enlai] (Hong Kong, 1998), 223–29.

30. *Shanghai geming*, bk. 2, vol. 6: 160.

31. Ibid., 269.

32. Ibid., 347.

33. "Lao gongren huiyi Shanghai gongren sanci wuzhuang qiyi" [Elderly workers remember the Shanghai three workers' armed uprisings], *Shanghai wenshi ziliao* [Shanghai Historical Materials] (1978), no. 1. When the third uprising began, guns from the Zhabei defense league were used in the Communists' attack on the north train station. Shanghai Party History Research Office, *Zhou Enlai zai Shanghai* (Shanghai, 1998), 11.

34. Zhang Weizhen, "Shanghai zaoqi gongyun douzheng huiyi" [Memoir of struggles in the early Shanghai labor movement], *Shanghai wenshi ziliao xuanji* [Compilation of Shanghai Historical Materials], no. 88 (1998): 37; *Shanghai geming*, bk. 2, vol. 6: 407. The policy was subsequently modified to permit only "good" pickets to join the party; similarly, only "good" branches were to open their meetings to the populace at large (*Shanghai geming*, bk. 2, vol. 6: 445).

35. Harold R. Isaacs, *The Tragedy of the Chinese Revolution*, rev. ed. (Stanford, 1951).

36. Sun Yat-sen had explicitly declared, in his lecture on people's livelihood, that "in China, where industry is not yet developed, class war and the dictatorship of the proletariat are unnecessary." Sun Yat-sen, *San Min Chu I: The Three Principles of the People* (Shanghai, 1929), 440–41.

37. Number Two Historical Archives, Nanjing, document no. 627–667 (1927).

38. Ibid.

39. Guomindang Party History Archives, Taipei, document no. 7499 (June 21, 1927).

40. Number Two Historical Archives, no. 627–667 (1927).

41. Ibid.

42. Ibid.

43. Guomindang Party History Archives, Taipei, no. 7506. (July 24, 1927, petition from the Shanghai French Tramway Company.)

44. SMA, document no. D6–8–125.

45. SMA, nos. D6–8–559; D6–8–480.

46. SMA, no. Q6–31–58.

47. SMA, no. Q7–4.

48. *Shanghai diyi mianfangzhichang gongren yundongshi* [History of the Labor Movement in the Shanghai Number One Cotton Spinning and Weaving Mill] (Beijing, 1997), 97–99.

49. SMA, no. Q6–31–88.

50. SMA, nos. Q6–31–145; C1–2–5219; Q6–31–161.

51. *Shanghai diyi mianfangzhichang*, 116.

52. Ibid., 117–19.

53. SMA, nos. Q6–31–19; Q7–2; Q7–307.

54. SMA, nos. Q7–293; Q6–6–1065.

55. SMA, nos. Q6–31–135; Q6–31–45; Q6–31–538; Q6–31–230.

56. SMA, no. Q6–31–139.

57. Recruitment among young men increased greatly at this time, aided by the promise that Corps service exempted one from military conscription. SMA, no. Q6–31–265.

58. SMA, nos. Q6–31–132; Q6–31–133; Q6–31–566. Although the identification booklets for Industry Defense Corps members were stamped "secret" on front, the wearing of uniforms undermined any pretense at secrecy. SMA, no. Q6–31–529.

59. SMA, nos. Q6–31–230; Q6–31–529; Q6–31–261.

60. SMA, no. Q6–31–132.

61. SMA, nos. Q6–31–34; Q6–31–299.

62. SMA, nos. Q6–31–38; Q6–31–59; Q6–31–143.

63. At the Shanghai Number One Cotton Mill, for example, 800 of the more than 1,000 factory pickets active at this time later received meritorious service awards for their role in ferreting out enemy agents. *Shanghai diyi mianfangzhichang*, 163–77.

64. Shanghai Historical Materials Committee, ed., *Guanghui licheng* [Glorious milestone] (Shanghai, 1996), 255.

65. SMA, no. C1–1–32; Zhang Jinping, "Baiwan zhigong touru baowei dashanghai de zhandou" [A million workers join the battle to defend greater Shanghai], *Jingbei dashanghai* (Shanghai, 1994), 176–78.

66. For example, a group of GMD cadres from the Workers' Welfare Committee, wearing counterfeit "New Fourth Army Southeast District Special Deputy" armbands, apparently tried to assume control of factories in the Tilanqiao district. A raid by the PPPC uncovered more than 50 types of fake armbands in the possession of enemy agents. Zhang Jinping, "Baiwan zhigong," 178.

67. SMA, nos. C1–1–16; C1–2–163; Li Jiaqi, ed., *Shanghai gongyunzhi* [Shanghai labor movement gazetteer] (Shanghai, 1997), 430. One particularly pernicious rumor held that PLA soldiers had killed or injured more than 80 workers at the Shenxin Number Nine Cotton Mill (the site of a major strike the year before). The Shenxin factory was besieged with phone calls, inquiring about the alleged bloodbath, prompting its union to

dispatch representatives to other factories around the city to dispel the misunderstanding (Zhang Jinping, "Baiwan zhigong," 181).

68. Thanks to this initiative, more than 270 alleged enemy agents were rounded up in the wee hours of the morning on June 29; more than 70 were factory workers. SMA, no. C1–1–16; Zhang Jinping, "Baiwan zhigong," 180.

69. Beijing Municipal Archives, document nos. 101–1–2, 101–1–230.

70. SMA, no. C1–2–163.

71. SMA, no. B120–1–69. On that day seventeen US-made bombers piloted by Guomindang military personnel flew four sorties over the city, targeting power companies. According to official Chinese statistics, the assault resulted in more than five hundred fatalities, more than six hundred injuries, and more than 50 thousand refugees.

72. Zhang Jinping, "Baiwan zhigong," 182.

73. Ibid., 183–84.

74. SMA, no. C1–2–170.

75. SMA, nos. C1–2–167, C1–2–168, C1–2–490.

76. SMA, no. C1–2–167; Zhang Jinping, "Baiwan zhigong," 184.

77. Zhang Jinping, "Baiwan zhigong," 184.

78. Li Jiaqi, ed., *Shanghai gongyunzhi*, 432.

79. SMA, nos. C1–2–488; C1–2–682.

80. *Tewu puohuai gongchang de zuixing* [Criminal activities of factory sabotage by secret agents] (Shanghai, 1951), 13–14, 24, 29, 33, 40–41, 52–53.

81. Zhang Jinping, "Baiwan zhigong," 187–88; SMA, no. C1–1–60.

82. SMA, no. C1–1–54.

83. SMA, no. C1–1–72.

84. SMA, no. C1–2–458.

85. SMA, no. C1–2–458. Between January 11 and February 22, 1951, among the 3,341 counterrevolutionaries registered at privately owned factories in Shanghai were 1,643 former Industry Defense Corps members. SMA, nos. C1–2–483; Q6–31–265.

86. SMA, no. B127–1–1186.

87. SMA, nos. C1–2–487; Q6–31–265; Li Jiaqi, ed., *Shanghai gongyunzhi*, 432.

88. At the Guangzhong dye factory, the registration revealed that fourteen workers had served as "backbones" in the Industry Defense Corps. Of these, twelve had been dealt with in the Suppression of Counterrevolutionaries Campaign; two had been shot and ten sentenced to prison terms. One other had already died and the remaining backbone, who had just been discovered, was to be expelled. Nevertheless, the 50 ordinary members of the Industry Defense Corps, many of whom had switched over to the PPPC in the spring of 1949 and some of whom had subsequently joined the Communist Youth League or Communist Party, were permitted to remain in place. SMA, no. Q6–31–566.

89. SMA, no. C1–2–680.

90. SMA, no. C1–2–680.

91. Li Jiaqi, ed., *Shanghai gongyunzhi*, 432; SMA, C1–2–646.

92. Despite fierce contemporary debates over the meaning of the Second Amendment's provision that "A well regulated Militia being necessary to the security of a free State, the right of the people to keep and bear Arms shall not be infringed," it is clear that the Founders' intention was not to increase violent crime rates! Michael A. Bellesiles, *Arming America: The Origins of a National Gun Culture* (New York, 2000); Robert J. Spitzer, *The Right to Bear Arms: Rights and Liberties under the Law* (Santa Barbara, CA, 2001).

93. Joyce Lee Malcolm, *To Keep and Bear Arms: The Origins of an Anglo-American Right* (Cambridge, MA, 1994), 24–26.

94. Elizabeth J. Perry, "From Paris to the Paris of the East—and Back: Workers as Citizens in Modern Shanghai," in Merle Goldman and Elizabeth J. Perry, eds., *Changing Meanings of Citizenship in Modern China* (Cambridge, MA, 2002), 133–56.

95. Li Jiaqi, ed., *Shanghai gongyunzhi*, 433; *Yangpu quzhi* [Yangpu district gazetteer] (Shanghai, 1995), 683; *Zhabei quzhi* [Zhabei district gazetteer] (Shanghai, 1998), 675; *Renmin ribao*, June 10, 1989.

96. Zhang Yongkang, *Zhongguo gongren jieji de diwei he zuoyong* [The status and role of the Chinese working class] (Beijing, 1991), 241.

97. Ibid., 244.

98. Andrew G. Walder and Gong Xiaoxia, "Workers in the Tiananmen Protests: The Politics of the Beijing Workers' Autonomous Federation," *Australian Journal of Chinese Affairs* 29 (Jan. 1993): 1–30.

99. *Foreign Broadcast Information Service*, May 18, 1989, 49.

100. *Beijing Ribao* [Beijing Daily], June 4, 1989.

101. Valerie Bunce, *Subversive Institutions: The Design and the Destruction of Socialism and the State* (New York, 1999), 26.

CHAPTER 7

1. On Confucian beliefs and moral autonomy see chap. 1.

2. David S. Nivison, "Protest Against Conventions and Conventions of Protest," in Arthur F. Wright, ed., *The Confucian Persuasion* (Stanford, 1960).

3. Paul S. Ropp, *Dissent in Early Modern China: Ru-lin wai-shih and Ch'ing Social Realism* (Ann Arbor, MI, 1981), 224–25.

4. Robert Hegel, *The Novel in Seventeenth-Century China* (New York, 1981); David Der-wei Wang, *Fin-de-Siecle Splendor: Repressed Modernities in Late Qing Fiction, 1849–1911* (Stanford, 1997).

5. Frederic Wakeman, Jr., "The Price of Autonomy: Intellectuals in Ming and Qing Politics," *Daedalus*, Spring 1972.

6. Philip A. Kuhn, *Origins of the Modern Chinese State* (Stanford, 2002), 36–37.

7. Peter Bol, *This Culture of Ours: Intellectual Transitions in T'ang*

*and Sung China* (Stanford, 1992); Ray Huang, *1587: A Year of No Significance* (New Haven, CT, 1981); Mary Wright, *The Last Stand of Chinese Conservatism* (Stanford, 1962 and 1957).

8. Bol, *This Culture of Ours.*

9. Andrew J. Nathan, *Chinese Democracy* (Berkeley, 1985), 45–66.

10. Benjamin Schwartz, *In Search of Wealth and Power: Yen Fu and the West* (Cambridge, MA, 1964); Joseph R. Levenson, *Liang Ch'i-ch'ao and the Mind of Modern China* (Cambridge, MA, 1953).

11. Kuhn, *Origins of the Modern Chinese State*, 121–30.

12. Benjamin Elman, *A Cultural History of Civil Examination in Late Imperial China* (Berkeley, 2000).

13. Joseph Levenson, *Confucian China and Its Modern Fate: A Trilogy* (Berkeley, 1958, 1964, 1965), 2: 4.

14. Henrietta Harrison, *The Making of the Republican Citizen: Political Ceremonies and Symbols in China, 1911–1929* (Oxford, 2000).

15. Andrew Nathan and Leo Lee, "The Beginnings of Mass Culture: Journalism and Fiction in the Late Ch'ing and Beyond," in David Johnson et al., eds., *Popular Culture in Late Imperial China* (Berkeley, 1985).

16. Perry Link, *Mandarin Ducks and Butterflies* (Berkeley, 1981); Gail Hershatter, *Dangerous Pleasures* (Berkeley, 1997); Jeffrey Kinkley, *Chinese Justice, the Fiction* (Stanford, 2000); John Christopher Hamm, "The Sword, the Book, and the Nation: Jin Yong's Martial Arts Fiction" (Ph.D. disser., Univ. of Calif., 1999); Carlton Benson, "From Teahouse to Radio: Storytelling and the Commercialization of Culture in 1930s Shanghai" (Ph.D. disser., Univ. of Calif., 1996).

17. Sun Yat-sen, *Prescriptions for Saving China: Selected Writings of Sun Yat-sen* (Stanford, 1994), 3–18.

18. Schwartz, *In Search of Wealth and Power*, 77–78.

19. Lu Xun, "Wusheng de Zhongguo" [Silent China], *Lu Xun quanji* [Complete Works of Lu Xun] (Beijing, 1973), 4: 22–28.

20. Lu Xun, "Geming kafei dian" [Revolutionary Café], ibid., 4: 125–27.

21. Lu Xun, *Nahan* [Call to Arms], preface, *Lu Xun quanji* 1: 272–73.

22. Lu Xun, *Yecao* [Wild Grass], preface, *Lu Xun quanji* 1: 463–64.

23. Leo Lee, *Voices from the Iron House: A Study of Lu Xun* (Bloomington, IN, 1987).

24. Merle Goldman, *Literary Dissent in Communist China* (Cambridge, MA, 1961).

25. Jerome Grieder, *Hu Shih and the Chinese Renaissance: Liberalism in the Chinese Revolution, 1917–1937* (Cambridge, MA, 1970).

26. Zhang Zhongdong, *Hu Shih wu lun* [Five Disquisitions] (Taibei, 1987).

27. Hu Shi, "Renquan yu yuefa" [Human Rights and Constitutional Law], in Liang Shiqiu et al., eds., *Renquan lunji* [Essays on Human Rights] (Shanghai, 1930), 1.

28. Zhang Zhongdong, "Cong *Nuli* dao *Xinyue* de zhengzhi yanlun" [Political Speech and Writing from *Endeavor* to *Crescent Moon*], in *Hu Shih wu lun*, 53–55.

29. Liang Shiqiu et al., eds., *Renquan lunji.*

30. Wen-hsin Yeh, *The Alienated Academy: Culture and Politics in Republican China* (Cambridge, MA, 1990), chap. 5.

31. Hu Shi, "Xin Wenhua yundong yu Guomindang" [New Culture Movement and the Nationalist Party], in Liang et al., eds., *Renquan lunji,* 119–43.

32. Hu Shi, pref. in ibid., 1–2.

33. Parks Coble, *Facing Japan: Chinese Politics and Japanese Imperialism, 1931–1937* (Cambridge, MA, 1991).

34. John Israel and Donald W. Klein, *Rebels and Bureaucrats: China's December 9ers* (Berkeley, 1976); John Israel, *Student Nationalism in China, 1927–1937* (Stanford, 1966).

35. Wen-hsin Yeh, "Zou Taofen and Progressive Journalism," in Frederic Wakeman and Wen-hsin Yeh, eds., *Shanghai Sojourners* (Berkeley, 1992), 186–238.

36. A coup carried out by two generals against Chiang. The cause was rooted in strong disagreements over Nationalist military policies toward the Japanese on the one hand and the Chinese Communists on the other.

37. John Israel, *Lianda: A Chinese University in War and Revolution* (Stanford, 1998), 13–60.

38. Frederic Wakeman, *Spymaster* (Berkeley, 2002).

39. Wu Han, *You sengbo dao huangquan* [From Monk to Emperor] (Chongqing, 1944).

40. Wu Han, "*Jingpingmei* de zhuzuo shidai ji qi shehui beijing" [The Historical and Social Background for the Composition of the *Golden Plum*] *Du shi zhaji* [Notes on Reading] (repr. Beijing, 1955), 1–38.

41. Merle Goldman, *Chinese Intellectuals: Advise and Dissent* (Cambridge, MA, 1981).

42. For a profile of Mao as a philosopher king, see Li Rui, *The Early Revolutionary Activities of Comrade Mao Tse-tung,* trans. Anthony Sariti (White Plains, NY, 1977). Also Stuart R. Schram, *The Political Thought of Mao Tse-tung,* rev. ed. (New York, 1969); Merle Goldman and Leo Ou-fan Lee, eds., *An Intellectual History of Modern China* (New York, 2002), 395–498.

43. See chap. 5 above.

44. Perry Link, *The Uses of Literature: Life in the Socialist Chinese Literary System* (Princeton, NJ, 2000).

45. Merle Goldman has argued that the Communist Party's ability to mount ideological campaigns was much aided by factional discord within the ranks of Chinese intellectuals; that dissent was closely connected with discord that stemmed from pre-Communist personal rivalries along divisions in social connections, educational background, cultural styles, and political patronage. See Goldman, *Literary Dissent in Communist China* (Cambridge, MA, 1961). On Hu Feng and Lu Ling, Kirk Denton has argued that their case was no mere replay of age-old Confucian factional rivalry; the writers were jailed because they were strong advocates of a

brand of Western literary theory that favored individualist subjectivism. See Denton, *The Problematic of Self in Modern Chinese Literature* (Stanford, 1998). On the literary system, see Link, *Uses of Literature*.

46. Suzanne Pepper, *Civil War in China: The Political Struggle, 1945–1949* (Berkeley, 1978).

47. Roderick MacFarquhar, *The Origins of the Cultural Revolution*, 3 vols. (New York, 1974–97); Dali Yang, *Calamity and Reform in China: State, Rural Society, and Institutional Change Since the Great Leap Famine* (Stanford, 1996); Jasper Becker, *Hungry Ghosts: China's Secret Famine* (London, 1996).

48. Clive Ansley, *The Heresy of Wu Han: "Hai Rui's Dismissal" and Its Role in China's Cultural Revolution* (Toronto, 1971). And also Su Shuangbi and Wang Hongzhi, *Wenge diyi yuanan* [Number One Injustice in Cultural Revolution] (Hong Kong, 2000), 51–62, 107–66, 235–53.

49. MacFarquhar, *The Origins of the Cultural Revolution*, esp. vol. 2. Su Shuangbi and Wang Hongzhi, *Wenge diyi yuanan*, 107–25.

50. Su and Wang, *Wenge diyi yuanan*, 125–47.

51. Geremie Barme, *In the Red: On Contemporary Chinese Culture* (New York, 1999), chap. 9. The quote is from p. 253.

52. Ibid., esp. 194–95, 200.

CHAPTER 8

We would like to thank Professors Morris Slavin of Youngstown State University and Steven I. Levine of the University of North Carolina at Chapel Hill for their generous assistance and very helpful comments.

1. See, for example, Hu Sheng et al., *Zhongguo gongchandang qishinian* [Seventy Years of the Chinese Communist Party] (Beijing, 1991); Maurice Meisner, *Mao's China and After. A History of the People's Republic*, 3d ed. (New York, 1999), 55–108; Jonathan D. Spence, *The Search for Modern China* (New York, 1990), 514–41; Arlen Meliksetov, ed., *Istoriya Kitaya* [History of China] (Moscow, 1998), 618–34.

2. See John King Fairbank and Merle Goldman, *China: A New History*, enlarged ed. (Cambridge, MA, 1998), 350. They, however, believe that the period of the New Democracy came to an end in 1954.

3. Spence, *The Search for Modern China*, 541.

4. See *Selected Works of Mao Tse-tung* 2 (Peking, 1967): 327, 330–31.

5. See ibid., 305–34, 339–84.

6. See ibid. 3 (Peking, 1967): 205–70.

7. See Chiang Kai-shek, *China's Destiny* (New York, 1947).

8. As for the Soviet archives, a portion of the documents has recently appeared in nine collections. See Sergei N. Goncharov et al., *Uncertain Partners: Stalin, Mao, and the Korean War* (Stanford, 1993), 229–91; Giuliano Procacci, ed., *The Cominform. Minutes of the Three Conferences 1947/1948/1949* (Milano, 1994); Sergei L. Tikhvinsky, "I. V. Stalin Correspondence with Mao Zedong in January 1949," *Novaya i noveishaya isto-*

*ria* [Modern and Contemporary History] 4–5 (1994): 132–40; *Cold War International History Project* (hereafter *CWIHP*) *Bulletin* 6–7 (Winter 1995/1996): 5–19, 27–119, 148–69, 208–31, 271; 8–9 (Winter 1996/1997): 223–36; 10 (March 1998): 131, 133, 149–82; Odd Arne Westad, ed., *Brothers in Arms. The Rise and Fall of the Sino-Soviet Alliance, 1945–1963* (Stanford, 1998), 295–390; David Wolff, "'One Finger's Worth of Historical Events': New Russian and Chinese Evidence on the Sino-Soviet Alliance and Split, 1948–1959," *CWIHP Working Paper* 30 (Aug. 2000): 33–74; Andrei M. Ledovsky, *SSSR i Stalin v sud'bakh Kitaya. Dokumenty i svidetel'stva uchastnika sobytii. 1937–1952* [The USSR and Stalin in the Fates of China. Documents and Testimonies of A Participant of the Events. 1937–52] (Moscow, 1999), 46–176. Many relevant documents from the Chinese archives have also recently been published. See, for example, *Mao Zedong wenji* [Collected Works of Mao Zedong], 8 vols. (Beijing, 1993–96); *Jianguo yilai Mao Zedong wengao* [Mao Zedong Manuscripts Since the Foundation of the PRC], 13 vols. (Beijing, 1987–98); Pang Xianzhi et al., *Mao Zedong nianpu, 1893–1949* [Biographical Chronology of Mao Zedong], 3 (Beijing, 1993); Liu Chongwen et al., *Liu Shaoqi nianpu, 1898–1969* [Biographical Chronology of Liu Shaoqi] 2 (Beijing, 1996); Li Qi et al., eds., *Zhou Enlai nianpu, 1949–1976* [Biographical Chronology of Zhou Enlai] 1, 2 (Beijing, 1997); Yang Kuisong, *Zouxiang polie: Mao Zedong yu Mosike de enenyuanyuan* [Toward the Split: Loves and Grievances in Relations Between Mao Zedong and Moscow] (Hong Kong, 1999); Chen Jian, *China's Road to the Korean War. The Making of the Sino-American Confrontation* (New York, 1994).

9. Molotov's memoirs are quite revealing on this issue. See Albert Resis, ed., *Molotov Remembers. Inside Kremlin Politics. Conversations with Felix Chuev* (Chicago, 1993).

10. Milovan Djilas, *Razgovory so Stalinym* [Conversations with Stalin] (Frankfurt am Main, 1970), 32. This phrase was translated incorrectly in the American edition of the Djilas's memoirs. See Milovan Djilas, *Conversations with Stalin* (New York, 1962), 33.

11. Djilas, *Conversations with Stalin*, 80.

12. Ibid., 73.

13. For instance, on March 2, 1967, during his unofficial conversation with Yuri V. Andropov, secretary of the Soviet Party Central Committee, Wang Ming contended that in January 1943 he sent a detailed telegram to Stalin about "anti-Leninist," "Trotskyite" activity of Mao Zedong. See Russian State Archives of Social and Political History (hereafter RGASPI in Russian abbreviation), 495/225/6–2/6.

14. See Peter P. Vladimirov, *Osobyi Raion Kitaya 1942–1945* [Special District of China] (Moscow, 1975).

15. "Memoirs of Nikita Sergeevich Khrushchev," *Voprosy istorii* [Questions of History] 11–12 (1993): 68. An American translator of Khru-shchev's memoirs erroneously translated this expression as "a margarine Marxist." See Strobe Talbott, ed., *Khrushchev Remembers* (Toronto, 1971), 512.

16. As expressed in his *History of the Communist Party of the Soviet Union (Bolsheviks): Short Course* (Moscow, 1938).

17. N. S. Khrushchev, *Vospominaniya. Izbranniye fragmenty* [Memoirs. Selected Fragments] (Moscow, 1997), 341.

18. See Yugoslavian and Bulgarian records of Stalin's mentioning of this fact at a secret Soviet-Bulgarian-Yugoslavian meeting on February 10, 1948 in Moscow, published in *CWIHP Bulletin* 10: 131 and 133. Also see Vladimir Dedijer, *Tito Speaks* (London, 1953), 331; "Minutes, Mao's Conversation with a Yugoslavian Communist Union Delegation, Beijing, [undated] September, 1956," *CWIHP Bulletin* 6–7: 149; Shi Zhe, *Zai lishi juren shenbian* [Beside Historical Giants] (Beijing, 1995), 308. In his talk to the Bulgarian and Yugoslavian delegations at that time Stalin also admitted that the Soviets were wrong and the Chinese were right in their assessments of the perspectives of the future Civil War. In July 1949, during his meeting with Liu Shaoqi Stalin again noted that the Russians made some errors in the questions of the Chinese revolution. See Record of Kang Sheng's speech at a meeting of the CPSU and CCP delegations on July 13, 1963 printed in *CWIHP Bulletin* 10: 182. Also see *Problemy Dalnego Vostoka* [Far Eastern Affairs] 1 (1989): 141.

19. That Stalin in 1945 had some short-lived doubts in the CCP victory does not, of course, mean that he was in sharp opposition to the Communist revolution in China, as some historians think.

20. During the Chinese Civil War the Soviet embassy regularly received Politburo directives not to interfere in the conflict. See Ledovsky, *SSSR i Stalin v sud'bakh Kitaya*, 48–49. Even after the Communist takeover of the Chinese capital Nanjing, Moscow still pursued this policy, ordering the embassy to follow the Guomindang government down to Guangzhou.

21. "Minutes, Mao's Conversation with a Yugoslavian Communist Union Delegation," 151.

22. Cited in Ledovsky, *SSSR i Stalin v sud'bakh Kitaya*, 53.

23. It already became clear to some insiders at the Seventh CCP Congress. See Vladimirov, *Osobyi Raion Kitaya*, 424–37. Also see John W. Garver, *Chinese-Soviet Relations, 1937–1945: The Diplomacy of Chinese Nationalism* (New York, 1988), 261.

24. Cited in Ledovsky, *SSSR i Stalin v sud'bakh Kitaya*, 56; and Westad, *Brothers in Arms*, 298.

25. Cited in Ledovsky, *SSSR i Stalin v sud'bakh Kitaya*, 53; and Westad, *Brothers in Arms*, 298–99. The Ledovsky version of the document slightly differs from that of Westad.

26. Westad, *Brothers in Arms*, 299.

27. Ibid., 300.

28. *Mao Zedong wenji* [Collected Works of Mao Zedong] 5 (Beijing, 1996): 140–41, 145.

29. Cited in Yang Kuisong, "Why Mao Zedong abandoned New Democracy: On the Influence of the Russian Model," *Jindaishi yanjiu* [Study of Modern History] 4 (1997): 177.

30. See Pang et al., *Mao Zedong nianpu*, 449; Goncharov et al., *Uncertain Partners*, 40; Anastas I. Mikoyan, *Tak bylo. Razmyshleniya o minuvshem* [It Was So. Thoughts about the Bygone Years] (Moscow, 1999), 528–29.

31. Cited in Zhou Enlai, "Presentation at the All-China Financial and Economic Meeting," Archives of the Foreign Policy of the Russian Federation (hereafter AVP RF), 0100/46/374/121/9.

32. Ibid.

33. See *Selected Works of Mao Tse-tung* 4 (Peking, 1967).

34. See ibid., 411–24.

35. See RGASPI, 558/11/329/9–17, 29–38; *CWIHP Bulletin* 6–7: 5–19.

36. *CWIHP Bulletin* 6–7: 5, 6.

37. The Soviet social scientists of the time were active in the discussion of this subject. George B. Ehrenburg summarized the result of these discussions. See G. B. Ehrenburg, "On the Nature and Specifics of Popular Democracy in China," in L. V. Simonovskaia and M. F. Yuriev, eds., *Sbornik statei po istorii stron Dal'nego Vostoka* [Collection of Papers on the History of the Far Eastern Countries] (Moscow, 1952).

38. Shi, *Zai lishi juren shenbian*, 446–47.

39. See RGASPI, 558/11/329/9–17; *CWIHP Bulletin* 6–7: 5–7.

40. See I. F. Kurdiukov et al., eds., *Sovetsko-kitaiskiye otnosheniya, 1917–1957. Sbornik dokumentov* [Sino-Soviet Relations, 1917–1957. Collection of Documents] (Moscow, 1959), 196–203.

41. See RGASPI, 558/11/329/37; *CWIHP Bulletin* 6–7: 9.

42. See G. Ganshin and T. Zazerskaia, "Ukhaby na doroge 'bratskoi druzhby': Iz istorii sovetsko-kitaiskikh otnosheniii" [Bumps on the Road of 'Brotherly Friendship': On the History of the Sino-Soviet Relations], *Problemy Dalnego Vostoka* 6 (1994): 67–72; Shu Guang Zhang, "Sino-Soviet Economic Cooperation," in Westad, *Brothers in Arms*, 198.

43. See RGASPI, 558/11/329/34–35; *CWIHP Bulletin* 6–7: 8–9. Also see Mao Zedong's telegram to Liu Shaoqi of Jan. 25, 1950, on the Sino-Soviet talks and the drafting of the documents, translated in *CWIHP Bulletin* 8–9: 235.

44. See Khrushchev, *Vospominaniya*, 342, 344.

45. Mao recalled it during his Nov. 19, 1957, talk with the Soviet Minister of Foreign Affairs at the time, Andrei A. Gromyko, in Moscow. He then concluded: "Stalin was suspicious of us [and] he put a question mark above [sic!] us." Cited in Boris T. Kulik, *Sovetsko-kitaiskii raskol: Prichiny i posledstviya* [The Soviet-Chinese Split: Reasons and Consequences] (Moscow, 2000), 31, 32; Oleg B. Rakhmanin, "Mutual Relations Between I. V. Stalin and Mao Zedong Through the Eyes of a Witness," *Novoya i Noveishaya Istoriya* 1 (1998): 85.

46. See RGASPI, 558/11/329/17; *CWIHP Bulletin* 6–7: 7.

47. See "Record of Conversation, Mao Zedong and Soviet Ambassador to Beijing Pavel Yudin, July 22, 1958," in Westad, *Brothers in Arms*, 350.

48. "Mao Zedong on the Comintern and Stalin's China Policy," *Prob-

*lemy Dal'nego Vostoka* 5 (1994): 107; "Minutes, Mao's Conversation with a Yugoslavian Communist Union Delegation," 148–49; Kulik, *Sovetsko-kitaiskii raskol*, 95. Mao would repeat it in his conversation with Yudin, on July 22, 1958. The Chinese Minister of Foreign Affairs Chen Yi would also express the same considerations (see Wested, *Brothers in Arms*, 201, 350). In this connection Mao's entry into the Korean War to some extent looks like a demonstration of loyalty to Mao's Kremlin's boss.

49. Cited in Boris N. Vereshchagin, *V starom i novom Kitaye. Iz vospominanii diplomata* [In the Old and New China. From Recollections of a Diplomat] (Moscow, 1999), 75.

50. "Mao Zedong on the Comintern and Stalin's China Policy," 106–7. For an English translation see Westad, *Brothers in Arms*, 340.

51. See, for example, "Mao Zedong on the Comintern and Stalin's China Policy," 105, 109; Westad, *Brothers in Arms*, 338–39, 340, 348, 350, 354–55; Li Zhisui, *The Private Life of Chairman Mao: The Memoirs of Mao's Personal Physician* (New York, 1994), 117; Vereshchagin, *V starom i novom Kitaye*, 123.

52. See K. I. Koval, "I. V. Stalin's Moscow Negotiations with Zhou En-lai of 1953 and N. S. Khrushchev's Beijing Negotiations with Mao Zedong of 1954," *Novaya i Noveishaya Istoritya* 5 (1989): 104–7.

53. Koval, to be true, makes a mistake in dating these negotiations. Zhou's visit to Moscow in early 1953 is not confirmed by other sources.

54. Cited in Koval, "I. V. Stalin's Moscow Negotiations," 106. On Stalin's limited aid to China also see Westad, *Brothers in Arms*, 145, 197–200, 257.

55. See M. L. Titarenko et al., eds., *Istoriya Kommunisticheskoi partii Kitaya* [A History of the Chinese Communist Party] 2 (Moscow, 1987): 130.

56. See Kurdiukov, *Sovetsko-kitaiskiye otnosheniya*, 223. Mao asked Stalin to shorten the period of delivery of industrial equipment and military arms that had to be billed toward the loans from five to three or four years, but Stalin ruled it out. See RGASPI, 558/11/329/36; *CWIHP Bulletin* 6–7: 9.

57. See Ledovsky, *SSSR i Stalin v sud'bakh Kitaya*, 78.

58. Mao Zedong's telegram to CCP CC, Jan. 4, 1950, translated in *CWIHP Bulletin* 8–9: 229.

59. See Zhang, "Sino-Soviet Economic Cooperation," 197.

60. See RGASPI, 558/11/329/81; *CWIHP Bulletin* 6–7: 15–16; Kurdiukov, *Sovetsko-kitaiskiye otnosheniya*, 285; Chen Zhiling, "Li Fuchun," in Hu Hua, ed., *Zhonggongdang renwu zhuan* [Biographies of CCP Activists] 44 (Xian, 1990): 67. In this regard the Russian historian Boris T. Kulik's assertion that Stalin allegedly agreed to comply with all requests of Zhou Enlai, including his "call for construction of 151 [?] industrial enterprises in China," does not conform to historical facts. See Kulik, *Sovetsko-kitaiskii raskol*, 95.

61. See Koval, "I. V. Stalin's Moscow Negotiations," 107; Chen, "Li Fuchun," 62–63.

62. Most Western estimates, to be sure, give a figure of 12 percent per annum growth rate in the Soviet Union during its first five-year plan, but it is doubtful that Stalin believed Western statistics. See Meisner, *Mao's China and After*, 127.

63. See RGASPI, 558/11/329/75, 85; *CWIHP Bulletin* 6–7: 14, 16. Also see Li, *Zhou Enlai nianpu* 1: 258.

64. Li Fuchun conveyed the contents of his talks with Saburov to Zhou Enlai and Chen Yun. See Kulik, *Sovetsko-kitaiskii raskol*, 126; Chen, "Li Fuchun," 63.

65. See Li, *Zhou Enlai nianpu* 1: 284–85; Kulik, *Sovetsko-kitaiskii raskol*, 126.

66. See Li Fu-ch'un [Li Fuchun], "Report on the First Five-Year Plan, 1953–1957, July 5–6, 1955," in Robert R. Bowie and John K. Fairbank, eds., *Communist China 1955–1959: Policy Documents with Analysis* (Cambridge, MA, 1962), 53, 61.

67. See Hu Sheng, ed., *Kratkaya istoriya KPK (1921–1991)* [Short History of the CCP] (Beijing, 1993), 530.

68. For a summary of Liu's report see Liu, *Liu Shaoqi nianpu*, 304–5.

69. Cited in "Diary of the Soviet Ambassador to China V. V. Kuznetsov. Records of the Talk with Liu Shaoqi, November 9, 1953," AVP RF, 0100/46/12/362/185.

70. See Jerome Cooper, "Lawyers in China and the Rule of Law," *International Journal of the Legal Profession* 4, 1 (1999): 71–89.

71. Interview with K. V. Shevelev, Senior Research Fellow of the Institute of Far Eastern Studies of the Russian Academy of Sciences, at Moscow, Russia, Aug. 20, 2000. Shevelev, who met with Kovalev frequently, was informed about it by Kovalev himself. Kovalev made an open statement about Stalin's "betrayal" of Gao in 1991 in the Russian journal *Problemy Dal'nego Vostoka*, but at that time failed to specify what kind of information was contained in Gao's reports, which Stalin handed to Mao Zedong. I. V. Kovalev, "Stalin's Dialogue with Mao Zedong," *Problemy Dal'nego Vostoka* 6 (1991): 91. The fact that Stalin gave some secret information he had received from Gao Gang to Mao Zedong is confirmed by Khrushchev and Bo Yibo. See Strobe Talbott, ed., *Khrushchev Remembers. The Last Testament* (Boston, 1974), 243–44; Bo Yibo, *Ruogan zhongda juece yu shijian de huigu* [Review of Several Important Policies and Events] 1 (Beijing, 1991): 40–41. Khrushchev and Bo, however, believed that Gao's information was contained in Kovalev's report to Stalin. The Kremlin leader also gave this report to Mao. (The editor of Khrushchev's memoirs erroneously attributed Kovalev's report to Alexander S. Panyushkin, who at the time was actually the Soviet Ambassador to the United States.) Khrushchev also said that Gao accused not only Liu Shaoqi, but also Zhou Enlai of being allegedly "the most vocal opponents" of the Soviet Union and the Bolshevik Party.

72. "Mao Zedong on the Comintern and Stalin's China Policy," 106. For an English translation see Westad, *Brothers in Arms*, 340.

73. See Kovalev, "Stalin's Dialogue with Mao Zedong," 89.

74. At that time the Soviet Union was composed of sixteen republics. In 1956, the Karelo-Finn Republic would become an autonomous region of the Russian Federation, as it had been prior to 1940.

75. See Kovalev, "Stalin's Dialogue with Mao Zedong," 89; Bo, *Ruogan zhongda juece yu shijian de huigu*, 37.

76. Peter S. Deriabin, Joseph Culver Evans, *Inside Stalin's Kremlin: An Eyewitness Account of Brutality, Duplicity, and Intrigue* (Washington, 1998), 110, 229–30.

77. See *Liu Shaoqi xuanji* [Selected Works of Liu Shaoqi] 1 (Beijing, 1981); *Zhou Enlai xuanji* [Selected Works of Zhou Enlai] 1, 2 (Beijing, 1980).

78. See *Obrazovaniye Kitaiskoi Narodnoi Respubliki. Dokumenty i materialy* [The Formation of the People's Republic of China: Documents and Materials] (Moscow, 1950), 30–49.

79. See N. G. Sudarikov, ed., *Konstitutsiya i osnovnyie zakonodatel'nyie akty Kitaiskoi Narodnoi Respubliki* [Constitution and Main Laws of the People's Republic of China] (Moscow, 1955), 381–92.

80. See ibid., 475–81. Also see chap. 9 below.

81. See in detail Arlen V. Meliksetov, "'New Democracy' and China's Search for Socio-economic Development Routes (1949–1953)," *Far Eastern Affairs* 1 (1996): 79–82.

82. See *Selected Works of Mao Tse-tung* 5 (Peking, 1977): 71; Michael I. Sladkovsky, ed., *Informatsionnyi byulleten. Seriya A: "Kul'turnaya revolyutsiya" v Kitaye. Dokumenty i materialy (perevod s kitaiskogo). Vypusk pervyi: "Hongweibing" Press on Liu Shaoqi* [Bulletin of Information. Series A: The "Cultural Revolution" in China. Documents and Materials (Translated from Chinese), 1: "Hongweibing" Press on Liu Shaoqi] (Moscow, 1968): 73–74.

83. Bo, *Ruogan zhongda juece yu shijian de huigu*, 234–35. Also see *Selected Works of Mao Tse-tung* 5: 108–9.

84. See Andrei M. Ledovsky, *Delo Gao Gana—Rao Shushi* (Moscow, 1990), 99; Bo, *Ruogan zhongda juece yu shijian de huigu*, 242; *Selected Works of Mao Tse-tung* 5: 93–94, 101–11; AVP RF, 0100/46/374/121/8–19.

85. See Li, *Zhou Enlai nianpu* 1: 289–90.

86. See Kurdiukov, *Sovetsko-kitaiskiye otnosheniya*, 284; Li, *Zhou Enlai nianpu* 1: 290.

87. See Kurdiukov, *Sovetsko-kitaiskiye otnosheniya*, 284–85; Li, *Zhou Enlai nianpu* 1: 289–90.

88. See Khrushchev, *Vospominaniya*, 333; Jerrold L. Schecter and Vyacheslav V. Luchkov, eds., *Khrushchev Remembers. The Glasnost Tapes* (Boston, 1990), 142.

89. He Ganzhi, *Istoriya sovremennoi revoliutsii v Kitaye* [History of the Modern Revolution in China] (Moscow, 1959), 682.

90. See *Jianguo yilai Mao Zedong wengao* 4: 548.

91. See Li, "Report on the First Five-Year Plan," 43–91.

92. Record of conversation, Yudin and Zhou Enlai, Oct. 10, 1954, cited in Westad, *Brothers in Arms*, 16.

93. See Koval, "I. V. Stalin's Moscow Negotiations," 108–13.

94. D. T. Shepilov, "Memoirs," *Voprosy istorii* 10 (1998): 25.

95. Cited in Koval, "I. V. Stalin's Moscow Negotiations," 113.

96. The Soviets would have to return their share to the Chinese by January 1, 1955, and the Chinese would have to compensate them in goods.

97. See information of Soviet military historians, introduced in Westad, *Brothers in Arms*, 16, 39. For detailed personal accounts of Khrushchev's visit see Talbott, *Khrushchev Remembers. The Last Testament*, 245–50; D. T. Shepilov, "Memoirs," *Voprosy istorii* 9: 18–31; 10: 3–30; Koval, "I. V. Stalin's Moscow Negotiations," 113–18; Shi Zhe, *Feng yu gu—Shi Zhe huiyilu* [Peak and Valley: Shi Zhe's Memoirs] (Beijing, 1992), 106–15.

98. Cited in Chen Jian and Yang Kuisong, "Chinese Politics and the Collapse of the Sino-Soviet Alliance," in Westad, *Brothers in Arms*, 285.

99. See Shi, *Feng yu gu*, 101–15; Li Yueran, *Waijiao wutai shang de xin Zhongguo lingxue* [New China's Leaders on the Diplomatic Scene] (Beijing, 1989), 52–53.

100. See Talbott, *Khrushchev Remembers*, 516–17; Khrushchev, *Vospominaniya*, 336, 356–57. For an account of Mao's request to receive an atom bomb and a submarine fleet see Shepilov, "Memoirs," *Voprosy istorii* 10: 28–29.

101. See "Memo, PRC Foreign Ministry to the USSR Embassy in Beijing, March 13, 1957," *CWIHP Bulletin* 6–7: 160; Meisner, *Mao's China and After*, 113; Bo, *Ruogan zhongda juece yu shijian de huigu*, 295–96.

102. See *The China Quarterly* 1 (Jan.–Mar. 1960): 38.

103. See Meisner, *Mao's China and After*, 113. Shepilov contends that over 11,000 Chinese students and more than 8,000 workers and technicians studied in the USSR. See Shepilov, "Memoirs," 26.

104. Cited in "Diary of the Soviet Ambassador to China V. V. Kuznetsov," 184–85.

105. See V. G. Gel'bras, *Sotsial'no-ekonomicheskaia struktura KNP: 50–60-ye gg.* [Socio-Economic Structure of the PRC: the 1950s–1960s] (Moscow, 1980), 60.

106. See *Selected Works of Mao Tse-tung* 5: 131–40.

107. See L. P. Deliusin, ed., *Agrarniye preobrazovaniya v Narodnom Kitaye* [Agrarian Reforms in People's China] (Moscow, 1955), 361–86.

108. See Jiang Boying et al., "Deng Zihui," in Hu Hua, ed., *Zhonggongdang renwu zhuan* [Biographies of CCP Activists] 7 (Xian, 1990): 369–70. For a detailed account of Deng Zihui's opposition to Mao see Frederick C. Teiwes and Warren Sun, eds., *The Politics of Agricultural Cooperation in China: Mao, Deng Zihui, and the "High Tide" of 1955* (Armonk, NY, 1993).

109. See *Selected Works of Mao Tse-tung* 5: 186–87. According to Soviet estimates of the time, the Chinese Communists dismantled some 200,000 cooperatives. See Meliksetov, *Istoriya Kitaya*, 640. This number corresponds to the figure appearing in some Red Guard *dazibao* [big-character posters] criticizing Liu Shaoqi during the Cultural Revolution for his previous anti-cooperative activity. See Sladkovsky, *Informatsionnyi byulleten*, 111.

110. See *Selected Works of Mao Tse-tung* 5: 187.

111. Ibid., 199; *Jianguo yilai Mao Zedong wengao* 5: 251.

112. He would continue to expound these ideas and on December 6, 1955, would claim that "Chinese peasants are better than English and American workers. That is why we can construct Socialism according to principle 'much more, much better, and much faster', not looking back at the Soviet Union all the time." See O. Borisov [O. B. Rakhmanin] and M. Titarenko, eds., *Vystupleniya Mao Ze-duna, ranee ne publikovavshiesya v kitaiskoi pechati* [Mao Zedong's Speeches that Have Not Been Previously Published in Chinese Press] 1 (Moscow, 1975), 54–55. While formulating this principle for the first time, Mao, however, did not attribute a meaning of the new Party's general line to it. He still considered the Soviet model totally appropriate, arguing just for the more rapid pace of its implementation.

113. "Minutes, Mao's Conversation with a Yugoslavian Communist Union Delegation," 151. Translators of the minutes made a mistake in the translation of the title of Stalin's article.

114. See Westad, *Brothers in Arms*, 17.

115. See Jiang, "Deng Zihui," 371.

116. Calculated from *Zhongguo gongchandang lishi jiangyi* [Lectures on History of the Chinese Communist Party] 2 (Changchun, 1981): 590–91.

117. The Chinese, to be sure, protested this contention. See "Memo, PRC Foreign Ministry to the USSR Embassy in Beijing," 159–60.

118. Nikita S. Khrushchev, *The Crimes of the Stalin Era. Special Report to the 20th Congress of the Communist Party of the Soviet Union* (New York, 1956).

119. "Mao Zedong on the Comintern and Stalin's China Policy," 107, 108. For an English translation see Westad, *Brothers in Arms*, 341, 342.

120. For Chen Boda's authorship of the article see *Jianguo yilai Mao Zedong wengao* 6: 59.

121. For Mao's corrections of the article see ibid., 59–67. The meetings had taken place from March 17 through April 4. See Wu Liangxi, *Yi Mao zhuxi* [Recalling Chairman Mao] (Beijing, 1994), 2–7.

122. Later, on April 28, 1956, in his concluding remarks at the enlarged meeting of the Politburo, Mao Zedong conceded that "we are not going to tell . . . the masses" about "[all] bad things that Stalin and the III International have done." See Borisov and Titarenko, *Vystupleniya Mao Ze-duna*, 93.

123. See "On the Historical Experience of the Dictatorship of the Proletariat," *Renmin ribao*, Apr. 5, 1956.

124. Cited in Chen and Yang, "Chinese Politics and the Collapse of the Sino-Soviet Alliance," 263.

125. *Selected Works of Mao Tse-tung* 5: 284.

126. See Stuart R. Schram, ed., *Chairman Mao Talks to the People: Talks and Letters: 1956–1971* (New York, 1974), 61–83.

127. See *Selected Works of Mao Tse-tung* 5: 303, 304, 305, 306.

128. See Li Ping, *Kaiguo zongli Zhou Enlai* [The First Premier Zhou Enlai] (Beijing, 1994), 356. See also Chen and Yang, "Chinese Politics and the Collapse of the Sino-Soviet Alliance," 287.

129. See *Jianguo yilai Mao Zedong wengao* 6: 105.

130. It, nevertheless, very quickly became known outside China. Members of a Yugoslavian Communist Union Delegation, for instance, mentioned "On the Ten Great Relationships" in their conversation with Mao Zedong in September 1956. See "Minutes, Mao's Conversation with a Yugoslavian Communist Union Delegation," 151.

131. See A. S. Perevertailo et al., eds., *Ocherki istorii Kitaya v noveisheye vremya* [Essays on History of China in Modern Times] (Moscow, 1959), 576.

132. See ibid., 573.

133. See Xiao Xiaoqin and Wang Youqiao, eds., *Zhonghua renmin gongheguo sishi nian* [Forty Years of the People's Republic of China] (Beijing, 1990), 109.

134. See *Selected Works of Mao Tse-tung* 5: 312–23; *Eighth National Congress of the Communist Party of China* 1: *Documents* (Peking, 1956), 5–11.

135. *Jianguo yilai Mao Zedong wengao* 6: 148.

136. "Record of Conversation, Mao Zedong and Soviet Ambassador to Beijing Pavel Yudin, July 22, 1958," 349. Mikoyan delivered a speech on September 17.

137. *Eighth National Congress of the Communist Party of China*, 137.

138. Ibid., 200.

139. See *Jianguo yilai Mao Zedong wengao* 6: 165.

140. "Minutes, Mao's Conversation with a Yugoslavian Communist Union Delegation," 151.

141. See Liu, *Liu Shaoqi nianpu*, 378; Li, *Zhou Enlai nianpu* 2: 4–14; *CWIHP Bulletin* 6–7: 153–54; Khrushchev, *Vospominaniya*, 358–61.

142. See *Renmin ribao* and *Hongqi* [Red Banner] Editorial Boards, *Vozniknoveniye i razvitiye raznoglasii mezhdu rukovodstvom KPSS i nami. Po povodu otkrytogo pis'ma TsK KPSS* [The Origin and Development of Divergences Between the CPSU Leadership and Us. On the Open Letter of the CPSU CC] (Beijing, 1963), 12; "Records of Meeting of the CPSU and CCP Delegations, Moscow, July 5–20, 1963," in Westad, *Brothers in Arms*, 378.

143. See "Records of Meeting of the CPSU and CCP Delegations, Mos-

cow, July 5–20, 1963," 378. He would continue to talk with Yudin on the Stalin issue between late 1956 and 1958.

144. See N. S. Khrushchev, *Report of the Central Committee, CPSU to the XXth Congress of the Communist Party of the Soviet Union* (New York, 1956), 37–39. It is noteworthy that beforehand Mao had not opposed this thesis. He did not argue against Liu Shaoqi's contention in his draft of the "Political Report" to the Eighth Congress that "the Twentieth Congress of the Communist Party of the Soviet Union . . . made an outstanding contribution to the easing of international tension and to the struggle for world peace and human progress." See *Jianguo yilai Mao Zedong wengao* 6: 138. Having been slightly corrected, this statement came into the final text of Liu's Report. The polemic about a "peaceful transition" was clearly artificial: nobody could predict the future. Nevertheless, the Soviets and the Chinese would continue to develop it until the end of the 1970s.

145. *Selected Works of Mao Tse-tung* 5: 341.

146. Ibid., 332–37, 342, 347–48.

147. See Bo, *Ruogan zhongda juece yu shijian de huigu*, 555–59.

148. See ibid., 556–57; *Zhou Enlai xuanji* 2: 229–38. For a detailed analysis see K. V. Shevelev, *Formirovaniye sotsial'no-ekonomicheskoi politiki rukovodstva KPK v 1949–1956 gg.* [The Formation of the Socioeconomic Policy of the CCP Leadership in 1949–1956] (forthcoming).

149. See Shevelev, *Formirovaniye sotsial'no-ekonomicheskoi politiki.*

150. See *Jianguo yilai Mao Zedong wengao* 6: 285.

151. "More on the Historical Experience of the Dictatorship of the Proletariat," *Renmin ribao*, Dec. 29, 1956.

152. Kurdiukov, *Sovetsko-kitaiskiye otnosheniya*, 329.

153. See *Selected Works of Mao Tse-tung* 5: 354–55, 356, 364–66, 380; Borisov and Titarenko, *Vystupleniya Mao Ze-duna*, 117–18, 119, 124, 126–28, 138, 139; Chen and Yang, "Chinese Politics and the Collapse of the Sino-Soviet Alliance," 266.

154. See *Selected Works of Mao Tse-tung* 5: 408–14. This slogan had first been shaped by Mao as early as December 1955, at a Politburo meeting, but at the time it was not realized due to the opposition of the Party apparatus and the suspicion of the intellectuals. For a detail analysis of the campaign see Roderick MacFarquhar, *The Hundred Flowers Campaign and the Chinese Intellectuals* (New York, 1974).

155. See Meliksetov, *Istoriya Kitaya*, 649.

156. Li, *Kaiguo zongli Zhou Enlai*, 362–63. Chen Jian and Yang Kuisong were the first to make this sensational information of Li Ping available for English-language readers.

157. *Selected Works of Mao Tse-tung* 5: 491.

158. See Borisov and Titarenko, *Vystupleniya Mao Ze-duna* 2: 102–25.

159. Ibid., 116.

160. Cited in Li, *Kaiguo zongli Zhou Enlai*, 360–61.

CHAPTER 9

Earlier versions of this chapter formed parts of the Clarke Lecture at Cornell University; the inaugural lecture for Smith College's new major in East Asian Studies; and presentations given at the University of Pennsylvania, Yale, and Harvard. The authors gratefully acknowledge the research assistance of Chen Xiaoping, Yu Hairong, and Zang Dongsheng and the bibliographic help of Zang Dongsheng. We owe a special debt of gratitude to William C. Kirby, Richard W. Davis, and the Center for the History of Freedom at Washington University for their roles in the conference at which this chapter was first presented, and to the Harvard Law School for financial support.

1. Liu Junning, "Classical Liberalism Catches on in China," *Journal of Democracy* 11 (July 2000): 48–59. To be sure, Liu is speaking here most fundamentally of economic liberalism. For a sampling of work by American observers viewing China through a comparable prism, see James Dorn, *China in the New Millennium: Market Reforms and Social Development* (Washington, DC, 1998). One of the fuller expositions of ideas of freedom in China is David Kelly and Anthony Reid, eds., *Asian Freedoms: The Idea of Freedom in East and Southeast Asia* (Cambridge, 1998).

2. See, for example, the essays by Pei Minxin and David Zweig in Elizabeth J. Perry and Mark Selden, eds., *Chinese Society: Change, Conflict and Resistance* (London, 2000).

3. At first blush, the suggestion that the first three decades of the PRC may have been marked by particularism may seem odd, given the state's efforts during that period at fostering uniformity (in remuneration, culture, attire). What is meant here is the state's according of differential treatment to citizens on the basis of their class background, so that the treatment of two individuals having divergent pedigrees might vary sharply—as distinct from the notion that all citizens are equal under law. See Jerome A. Cohen, *The Criminal Process in the People's Republic of China 1949–1963: An Introduction* (Cambridge, MA, 1968). Particularism, of course, was a prominent feature of imperial Chinese law. See William C. Jones, Intro., *The Great Qing Code* (Oxford, 1994).

4. This vision of law exerts a powerful influence in the approach the World Bank, the Ford Foundation, the United States government, and a range of other actors have taken toward development in China. See William P. Alford, "The More Law, the More . . . ? Taking the Measure of Legal Reform in the People's Republic of China," published at the website of the Stanford University Center for Research on Economic Development and Policy Reform (2000); and William P. Alford, "Exporting the 'Pursuit of Happiness'," *Harvard Law Review* 113 (May 2000): 1677–1713.

5. On the influence, at least in the legal arena, of the idea that we have reached an "end of history," see Alford, "Exporting the 'Pursuit of Happiness.'"

6. The revised Law was promulgated via a Decision of the Standing

Committee on the National People's Congress. "Quanguo Renmin Daibiao Dahui Changweihui Guanyu Xiugai (Zhonghua Renmin Gongheguo Hunyin Fa) de Jueding" [The Decision of the Standing Committee of the National People's Congress Regarding the Amendment (of the Marriage Law of the People's Republic of China)]. This Decision is reprinted in Peng Peiyun, ed., *Zhonghua Renmin Gongheguo Hunyinfa Shijie* [An Explanation of the Marriage Law of the People's Republic of China] (Beijing, 2001), 245–51.

7. One recent report suggests that there are 128 million illiterate women in China, 110 million of whom reside in the countryside. Xinhua [New China News Agency], "China Helps Women Escape Illiteracy," Emerging Markets Datafile, May 14, 1999.

8. The National Audit Bureau of the PRC estimated that more than the equivalent of $15 billion US in public funds was lost to corruption in 1999, although some would place the estimate many times higher. The noted economist Hu Angang, for instance, estimates that during the decade of the 1990s, China lost between 13.2 and 16.8 percent of its GDP (or roughly 150 billion dollars) to various forms of malfeasance and misfesance. Hu Angang, *Zhongguo: Tiaozhan Fubai* [China: Fighting Against Corruption] (Hangzhou, 2000), 34–66. See also Anthony Kuhn, "Corrupt Officials' 'Escape Route' Alarms China," *Los Angeles Times*, Apr. 22, 2001; James Kynge, "Banker's Fall Throws Spotlight on China's Missing Billions," *Financial Times*, Jan. 16, 2002, at 4.

9. The *Taiping* Heavenly Kingdom, at least as a theoretical matter, advocated a breaking down of traditional Chinese practices that subordinated women.

10. Reformers associated with the May Fourth movement saw an elevation of the status of women as a critical step in the broader recasting of Chinese society for which they called. See Chow Tse-tung, *The May Fourth Movement: Intellectual Revolution in Modern China* (Cambridge, MA, 1960).

11. Neil J. Diamant, "Re-examining the Impact of the 1950 Marriage Law: State Improvisation, Local Initiative, and Rural Family Change," *China Quarterly* 171 (2000): 171–98.

12. This law may rightly be seen as one of history's more momentous efforts at social engineering—designed, as it was, to address the residue of legal and other constraints on the freedom of women with respect to the marital relationship and beyond. See Diamant, "Re-examining the Impact."

13. See Diamant, "Re-examining the Impact."

14. Lu Feng, "The Work Unit: A Unique Form of Social Organisation," in *Chinese Social Sciences* 1 (1989): 71, trans. in Michael Dutton, *Streetlife China* (New York, 1996), 55–60.

15. The size and nature of the floating population are treated in Dorothy Solinger, *Contesting Citizenship in Urban China: Peasants, Migrants, the State and the Logic of the Market* (Berkeley, 1999).

16. Such data are recorded in the United Nations Development Pro-

gramme, *The China Human Development Report* (New York, 1999). For a thoughtful account of gains during this period, see Heather Xiaoquan Zhang, "Understanding Changes in Women's Status in the Context of Recent Rural Reform," in Jackie West et al., eds., *Women of China: Economic and Social Transformation* (New York, 1999).

17. The state of women's studies in the PRC is the topic of Wang Zheng, "Research on Women in Contemporary China," in Gail Hershatter et al., *Guide to Women's Studies in China* (Berkeley, 1998).

18. See, for example, Kate Xiao Zhou, "Market Development and the Rural Women's Revolution in Contemporary China," in Dorn, *China in the New Millennium*.

19. There is, to be sure, very substantial disagreement among Chinese scholars as to what constitutes a high divorce rate, what the most significant causes of divorce are, or even how to calculate divorce rates (that is, whether one should look to the number of divorces relative to new marriages or relative to the population as a whole), although all agree that the incidence of divorce has been increasing steadily since the 1970s, with approximately 178,000 divorces recorded in 1978, 850,000 in 1992, 1,050,000 in 1995 and 1,200,000 in 2000. So it is, for instance, that advocates of greater restrictions on divorce contend that divorce is a serious problem in China by pointing out that between 1990 and 2000, divorces increased by 51 percent and marriages fell by 10.8 percent (Xinhua [New China News Agency], "PRC Marriage Law Amendment Said to Reflect Democracy," May 11, 2001) while their opponents say that at least relative to the United States and Western Europe, divorce is not common in China. Complicating efforts to make sense of these arguments is the inherent unreliability of many of the statistics upon which they are based. The ease with which divorce has been granted has varied enormously during the history of the PRC, with, for instance, the state encouraging divorce between 1950 and 1953 in an effort to free women from what were viewed as oppressive relationships, but by the mid-1950s, believing that this problem had been addressed, discouraging further divorces for fear of their impact on social stability. There also appears to be considerable geographic variation at any given time as to the ease of divorce. Major cities such as Beijing and Shanghai are seen as places in which one could relatively readily secure a divorce compared to rural areas in which social stigma, cadre and familial pressure, the low educational and economic status of women (vis-à-vis their urban counterparts), and the fact that not all marriages may have initially been formally registered with the state as is required by law may have made their impact felt. Compounding all this further is the sheer difficulty now for rural officials (some of whom may have relatively little training in such matters) of tracking the status of marriages at a time when millions of families are divided by China's vast internal migration and in a situation in which regionalization is a growing problem in the courts and public administration (meaning that data is not always effectively shared across political boundaries).

Useful treatments of divorce rates include Xu Anqi, "Zhongguo Lihun Xianzhuan, Tedian Ji Qi Qushi" [The Current Situation, Characteristics and Trends of Divorce in China], *Shanghai Shehui Kexue Yuan Xueshi Zazhi* [The Scholarly Journal of the Shanghai Academy of Social Science] 2 (1994): 156–65; Xu Anqi and Ye Wenzhen, *Zhongguo Hunyin Zhiliang Yanjiu* [Studies on Chinese Marital Quality] (Beijing, 1999); Huang Ling-bao, "Lihun Xianxiang yu Lifa" [The Phenomenon and Legislation of Divorce], in Yang Dawen and Wu Changzhen, eds., *Zouxiang Ershiyi Shiji de Zhongguo Hunyin Jiating* [Toward the Twenty-first Century for Chinese Marriage and Family] (Changchun, 1995), 82–94; Tian Lan, "Wo Guo Gaige Dachao Zhong zhi Lihunlu Shangsheng" [The Increasing Divorce Rate in Our Reform] in Yang and Wu, eds., *Zouxiang Ershiyi Shiji*, 94–204; Wang Xingjuan, "Hunyin 'Chongji Bo'" [A 'Lashing Wave' at Marriage], *Hunyin yu Jiating* [Marriage and Family] 1 (1997): 46–47; Xiao Yongge, "Jiuliu Nian: Lihun Dageming" [1996: Divorce Revolution], *Xingwei Kexue* [Behavorial Science] 2 (1996): 2–4; and Ming Tsui, "Divorce, Women's Status, and the Communist State in China," *Asian Thought and Society*, May 2001, 103–25.

20. Mayfair Mei-hui Yang, "From Gender Erasure to Gender Difference: State Feminism, Consumer Sexuality, and Women's Public Sphere in China," in Mayfair Mei-hui Yang, ed., *Spaces of Their Own: Women's Public Sphere in Transitional China.* (Minneapolis, 1999).

21. The resurgence of prostitution is discussed in Peter Goodman, "Sex Trade Thrives in China: Localities Exploiting a Growing Business," *Washington Post*, Jan. 4, 2003, at A1. The earlier history of prostitution is the subject of Gail Hershatter, *Dangerous Pleasures: Prostitution and Modernity in Twentieth Century Shanghai* (Stanford, 1997).

22. Human Rights in China, Asia Monitor Resource Centre, *China Labour Bulletin*, and Hong Kong Christian Industrial Committee, *Report on the Implementation of CEDAW in the People's Republic of China* (New York, 1998); Harriet Evans, *Women and Sexuality in China: Female Sexuality and Gender since 1949* (New York, 1997).

23. Human Rights in China, *China Labour*. A much-cited survey conducted by the All China Women's Federation suggests that domestic violence occurs in some 30 percent of Chinese families. Xinhua [New China News Agency] English Language Service, "PRC Lawmaker: Items Against 'Family Violence' Urged in Marriage Law Amendment," Apr. 26, 2001. The problem of spousal violence involves persons with "high and low educational attainment and professionals as well as workers." Helen Zia, "China: The Other Half of the Sky" (Global Frontlines: China. www.fvpf.org/global/gf_china.html, 1999).

24. Sing Lee and Arthur Kleinman, "Suicide as Resistance in Chinese Society," in Perry and Selden, eds., *Chinese Society*, 224.

25. Guojia Jiguan, Nuxing Nan Jin, *Zhongguo Funü Bao* [China Women's News], Jan. 8, 1996, 1. Indeed, even well-known national law schools have been among those discriminating against women. See Wang Zhen-

min, "Zhao Sheng Zige yu Fazhi Shuiping" [Qualifications for the Recruitment of Students and the Standards of the Rule of Law], *Fazhi Ribao* [The Legal System Daily], Oct. 28, 1997, 7. Efforts by a center affiliated with another leading law school to address such issues are considered in The Centre for Women's Law Studies and Legal Services of Peking University, *Theory and Practice of Protection of Women's Rights and Interests in Contemporary China—Investigation and Study on the Enforcement of the UN Convention on the Elimination of All Forms of Discrimination Against Women in China* (Beijing, 2001).

26. Margaret Y. K. Woo, "Chinese Women Workers: The Delicate Balance Between Protection and Equality," in Christine K. Gilmartin et al., eds., *Engendering China: Women, Culture and the State* (Cambridge, MA, 1994).

27. "Xia Gang dui Nanu Liangxing de Butong Yingxiang" [The Loss of One's Job Is a Different Phenomena for Men and Women], *Zhongguo Funü Bao* [China Women's News], May 28, 1998, 3. Zhou Jian, "Xia Gangle, Jia zai Fengyu Zhong" [The Loss of One's Job, The Trials and Tribulations in the Family], *Zhongguo Funü Bao* [China Women's News] Jan. 5, 1997, 1.

Some have noted that women are fairly active in initiating divorce. See Tsui, "Divorce." These suggestions warrant careful scrutiny, in part because of the overall difficulties described earlier with respect to statistics in this area and in part because even the best available data do not indicate how many women may be initiating divorce in response to domestic violence or spousal abandonment. At least one author has intimated that some women wishing to divorce have been deterred by a fear that they would lose their housing. "Evolution of the Marriage Law," *Beijing Review*, Mar. 2001.

28. Zhou, "Xia Gang."

29. Miao Xiuqiu, "Funu Weiquan Renzhong Daoyuan" [Women Have to Shoulder a Heavy Burden to Preserve Their Rights], *Zhongguo Funü Bao* [China Women's News] July 22, 1996, 2. Data from Heilongjiang province suggests that, during the mid-1990s, after divorce up to 80 percent of rural women were losing the land on which they had been living and working.

30. Some of the efforts of Chinese authorities are chronicled in a 1994 white paper. See Information Office, State Council of the People's Republic of China, "The Situation of Women," reported by *Xinhua*, Beijing, June 3, 1994. English version available at British Broadcasting Company, June 11, 1994.

31. See, for instance, the writings of Li Xiaojiang such as *Tiaozhan yu Huiying: Xin Shiqi Funü Yanjiu Jiangxue Lu* [Challenge and Response: A Record of Lectures on Women's Studies for a New Era] (Zhengzhou, 1996).

32. "Zhonghua Renmin Gongheguo Funu Quanyi Baozhang Fa" [The Law of the People's Republic of China for the Protection of the Rights and Interests of Women], published in *Renmin Ribao* [The People's Daily] Apr. 10, 1992, 3.

33. For an intriguing study of Chinese inheritance law see Frances H.

Foster, "Linking Support and Inheritance: A New Model from China," *Wisconsin Law Review* (1999): 1199–1258.

34. Thoughtful discussions of such measures include Michael Palmer, "The Re-emergence of Family Law in Post-Mao China: Marriage, Divorce and Reproduction," *China Quarterly* 145 (Mar. 1995): 110; Ronald C. Keith, "Legislating Women's and Children's 'Rights and Interests' in the PRC," *China Quarterly* 149 (Mar. 1997): 29–55; and Margaret Y. K. Woo, "Law and the Gendered Citizen" (1999 draft).

To be sure, the argument might be made that however well-intentioned, some of these measures may not have advanced the interests of women. Labor law measures, for instance, that were meant to be protective of women (in the sense of sheltering them from dangerous employment) may unwittingly have worked to reinforce limitations on women securing certain high wage jobs, while there are serious questions about the impact of measures such as the 1994 Mothers and Infants Health Law [*Muying Baojian Fa*], which some observers suggest is essentially a eugenics statute.

35. Re-education through labor is an administrative sanction to be applied by the public security apparatus without reference to the courts whereby an individual may be subject to up to three years of detention in a labor camp (which term may be extended).

36. Wu Changzhen is also a member of the Executive Committee of the All China Women's Federation and Vice Chair of the Beijing Women's Federation. For a good example of her writing, see Wu Changzhen, "Guangdong Sheng Chonghun, Naqie, Pinju, Hunwailian Xianxiang Diaocha" [An Investigative Report on the Phenomena of Bigamy, Concubinage, Illicit Cohabitation, and Other Extramarital Affairs in Guangdong Province], *Minzhu yu Fazhi* [Democracy and Law] 17 (1997): 32–33.

37. See, for example, Wu Hong, "Dui Lihun Buneng Meiyou Xianzhi" [With Regard to Divorce, You Can Not Eschew Restrictions] in Li Yinhe and Ma Yinan, eds., *Hunyin Fa Xiugai Lunzheng* [Debates Over Revision of the Marriage Law] (Beijing, 1999), 113–14; Zhou Dongqing, "Yingdang Jiaqiang Lihun Xianzhi" [It Is Necessary to Strengthen the Restriction on Divorce] in Li and Ma, eds., *Hunyin*, 118–19; Ge Chenhong, "Lun Lihun Ziyou de Xiangduixing" [On the Relativity of the Freedom of Divorce] *Funü Yanjiu Luncong* [Collection of Women's Studies] 4 (1998): 10–11; Chen Mingxia and Xue Ninglan, "Guanyu Lihun Ziyou yu Wo Guo Caipan Lihun Biaozhun de Jidian Sikao" [Some Thoughts on the Freedom of Divorce and Our Nation's Statutory Standard for Divorce], *Funü Yanjiu Luncong* [Collection of Women's Studies] 4 (1998): 18–20.

38. Wu Hong, "Dui Lihun."

39. "Divorce: Freedom and Costs," *Women of China* 2001–2.

40. One member of the National People's Congress went so far as to suggest that 95 percent of officials in Guangdong found to have committed economic crimes had mistresses. Xinhua [New China News Agency], "PRC Marriage Law Amendments Attract High Level Attention," Oct. 28, 2000.

41. Zhu Suli, "Lengyan Kan Hunyin" [Looking at Marriage with a Cold Eye] in Li and Ma, *Hunyin*, 48. For an example of the type of sentiment against which Zhu was reacting see the remarks of Lu Heng in Hu Qihua, "'Til Death Us Do Part'—Not Any More," *China Daily*, Oct. 28, 2000 ("The increase in the divorce rate reflects the social progress made in China").

42. Xiao Xuehui, "Hunyinfa de Xiugai Yingyu Xiandai Wenming Fazhan Fangxiang Tongbu" [The Revision of the Marriage Law Should be Consistent with the Developing Trends of Modern Civilization], *Funü Yanjiu Luncong* [Collection of Women's Studies] 2 (1998): 8.

43. Li Yinhe, "Xiugai Hunyinfa Shi Yao Jingti Daotui" [Be Vigilant against Regression in the Revision of the Marriage Law], *Funü Yanjiu Luncong* [Collection of Women's Studies] 2 (1998): 4–5; Chen Xinxin, "Fandui Lihun Xianzhi" [Oppose Restrictions on Divorce] in Li and Ma, *Hunyin*, 176.

44. "He Weifang Zhuanfang" [An Exclusive Interview with He Weifang], *Sanlian Shenghuo Zhoukan* [Sanlian Life Weekly], Mar. 28, 2001 at www.sina.com.

45. Chen, "Fandui Lihun," 180–81.

46. Zhang Kun, "Opinions Split on Marriage Law," *China Daily*, Sept. 12, 2001.

47. Li Yinhe, "Xiugai Hunyingfa," 5.

48. Xu Anqi, "Baohu Lihun Ziyou" [Protect the Freedom of Divorce], *Nanfang Zhoumo* [Southern Weekend] Sept. 21, 2000, 2.

49. Li, "Tiaozhan."

50. Other issues of note included the treatment of so-called *de facto* marriages (those that had not been officially registered, particularly prior to the introduction in 1994 of revised rules for the registration of marriages), the idea of invalid marriages (such as those that might be the product of coercion rather than free will), and the treatment of marital property in the situation of debts to third parties.

51. Wang Xingjuan, "Hunyin 'Chongji Bo'," 46–47.

52. The Beijing University study is discussed at Xiao, "Hunyinfa." The latter figure, based on a study conducted in Wuxi, is reported in *Zhongguo Funü Bao* [Chinese Women's News], Sept. 23, 1996, 1.

53. This loophole appears to have been especially utilized by men whose first child was a daughter. This is an area in which comprehensive statistical data does not appear to be available. In one study, based on fieldwork done in Guangzhou and eleven neighboring cities, Wu Changzhen reports some 358 children born from 508 cases of bigamy between 1990 and 1992. Wu Changzhen, "Guangdong Sheng Chonghun." A more recent report from Nanhai in Hainan indicates that 188 children were born from 391 cases of bigamy between 1992 and 1995 and that many of these children had difficulty in securing education and other societal benefits as they lacked a *hukou*—a registered permanent residence. *Zhongguo Funü Bao* [Chinese Women's News], Dec. 2, 1999, 2.

54. To be sure, Mao Zedong took a somewhat more open stance on this issue in the initial version of his famed 1927 report on the Hunan peasantry and, as his former physician observed, in his personal life.

55. The narrowness of this definition may explain how, for instance, the number of criminal actions regarding bigamy has dropped in recent years even as the phenomenon of extramarital liaisons has grown. *Zhongguo Funü Bao* [Chinese Women's News], Dec. 3, 1999.

56. To be sure, advocates of this position expressed a range of views as to what might constitute constructive, as distinct from formal, bigamy. So it was, for instance, that some in the All China Women's Federation argued that bigamy should include married individuals who in another relationship also held themselves out as wed or who lived for more than six months with someone to whom they are not married (*Nanfang Zhoumo* [Southern Weekend] Sept. 21, 2000, 2), while others involved in these debates were willing to construe a shorter period of adultery as amounting to bigamy. In the alternative, it was rumored that the Guangdong All China Women's Federation advocated use of the administrative sanction reeducation through labor for persons committing adultery that did not constitute bigamy.

57. Ma Jijun, "Shilun Jianli Lihun zhi Sunhai Peichang Zhidu" [On the Establishment of the Divorce Compensation System], *Funü Yanjiu Luncong* [Collection of Women's Studies] 4 (1997): 7.

58. "An Insider Talks about the Key Issues," *Beijing Review*, Mar. 2001.

59. Ma Yinan reporting the views of the 1999 Annual Conference of China's Association of Marriage Law Studies, *Minzhu yu Fazhi* [Democracy and Legal System] 1 (2000): 13.

60. This draft is reproduced in Wang Shengming and Sun Lihai, eds., *Zhonghua Renmin Gonghehuo Hunyinfa Xiugai Lifa Ziliao Xuan* [A Selection of Materials from the Drafting of the Amendments to the Marriage Law of the People's Republic of China] (Beijing, 2001), 433–58.

61. "An Insider Talks."

62. Chen Wei, "Jianli Wo Guo Lihun Sunhai Peichang Zhidu Yanjiu" [Studies on the Establishment of the Divorce Compensation System], *Xiandai Faxue* [Modern Jurisprudence] 6 (1998): 6–9; Jiang Yue, "Fuqi You Xianghu Zhongshi de Yiwu" [Spouses Should Have a Duty to be Faithful to Each Other] in Li and Ma, eds., *Hunyin*, 271–75; Wang Geya, "Lun Lihun Sunhai Peichang Zhidu" [On the Divorce Compensation System] in Li and Ma, eds., *Hunyin*, 237; and Li Mingsheng, "Wo Kan Lihun Zhong de Sunhai Peichang Wenti" [My Views on the Issue of Divorce Compensation] in Li and Ma, eds., *Hunyin*, 241–44. It also would provide a basis for prenuptial agreements in a new, more property-conscious China. In the words of NPC delegate Wu Shuqing, "A contract that specifies the property before marriage will not only maintain purity of love, but also reduce the possibility of fighting over money when a marriage ends." Meng Yan, "Extramarital Affairs under Spotlight," *China Daily*, Dec. 26, 2000.

63. Based on an interview with Professor Long Yifei in Beijing, July 2000.

64. Lu Chunhua, "Lifa Chengfa 'disanzhe' shizaibixing" [It is Imperative to Use Law to Punish the 'Third Party'] in Li and Ma, eds., *Hunyin*,
282–83.

65. Zhou Xiaozheng, "'Peiouquan' Duanxiang" [Conclusive Thoughts
on a "Rights to Compensation"] in Li and Ma, eds., *Hunyin*, 289–90.

66. Ibid. Also see, Wang Jianxun, "Falu Daode Zhuyi Lifa Guan Pipan"
[A Criticism of the Legal Moralistic Approach to Legislation] in Li and
Ma, eds., *Hunyin*, 24. Interestingly, Wang draws on the famed Oxford legal
philosopher H. L. A. Hart's celebrated response to Lord Devlin to buttress
her claim that if society took too stringent an approach toward the regulation of sexuality, freedom more generally would be impaired.

67. Wu Xiaofang, "Hunyin Jiating fa: Caoan Chutaiqian de Yichi Tao-
lun" [A Discussion of the Drafting of the Law on Marriage and Family],
*Zhongguo Lushi* [Chinese Lawyer] 10 (1998): 10–11; Chen Xinxin, "Du
Hunwailian de Renshi Yinggai Quanmian, Keguan" [For an All Sided and
Objective Understanding of Extramarital Affairs] in Li and Ma, eds., *Hun-
yin*, 300; and Xiao Xuehui, "Lifa Buyingdang Chengfa 'Disanzhe'" [Legis-
lation Should Not Punish the 'Third Party'], ibid., 302; Li Dun, "Yingdang
Chengren Gonglingyu he Silingyu de Huafeng" [Recognizing the Differ-
ences Between the Public and Private Spheres], ibid., 80; and Pan Suiming,
"Du Xiugai Hunyinfa de Wuge Yiwen" [Five Questions for Revising the
Marriage Law], ibid., 104.

68. To make this distinction is not to suggest that the PRC's judiciary,
then or for that matter now, should be understood as non-political. It
should be noted that judicial action was not then (and is not now) required
for a divorce (which may be granted administratively).

69. Kay Ann Johnson, *Women, the Family and Peasant Revolution in
China* (Chicago, 1983), 213.

70. Tsui, "Divorce," 110.

71. Ibid. at 110.

72. Ha Jin, *Waiting* (New York, 1999).

73. Ibid. at 12.

74. Among these effects were the termination of otherwise viable marriages on political grounds (that is, divorces designed to spare one spouse
suffering on account of the "bad" political background of the other) and
the formation of marriages between urbanites sent down to the countryside and peasants that in some instances at the end of the Cultural Revolution came to be seen as preventing the former from returning to the cities from which they had come.

75. Yang Dawen, "Guanyu Wanshan Hunyin Jiating Lifa de Jianyi he
Shexiang" [Opinions and Suggestions on Completing Legislation on Marriage and the Family] in Wu and Yang, eds., *Zhouxiang Ershiyi Shiji*, 16–
17.

76. See, for example, Li Cheng and Wang Hongcai, "Lihun Lifa Xintan"
[A New Inquiry into Divorce Law Legislation], in Wu and Yang, eds.,
*Zhouxiang Ershiyi Shiji*, 72–78; and the following, all of which are in Li

and Ma, eds., *Hunyin*: Zhang Xianyu, "Hunyin Polie Yuanze Ying Cheng-wei Lihunde Fading Liyou" [The Principle of the Breakdown of the Marriage Should Be the Statutory Reason for Divorce], 131–36; Cao Shiquan, "Caipan Lihun Biaozhun de Pingjia yu Xuanze" [The Evaluation and Selection of a Standard in Judging Divorce], 144–46; Deng Hongbi, "'Hunyin Guanxi Polie' Zuowei Zhunyu Lihun de Fading Tiaojian" ['Breakdown of the Marital Relationship' as the Statutory Condition for Divorce], 148; and Tong Man, "Ganqing Polie Yuanze Zhiyi" [Questioning the Principle of the Breakdown of Emotion], 149–54; also Chen Mingxia and Xue Ninglan, "Guanyu Lihun Ziyou yu Wo Guo Caipan Lihun Biaozhun de Jidian Si-kao" [Some Thoughts on the Freedom of Divorce and Our Nation's Statutory Standard for Divorce], *Funü Yanjiu Luncong* [Collection of Women's Studies] 4 (1998): 20–23.

77. Xinhua English Language Service, "Expert Says More Chinese Concerned About Quality of Marriage," Mar. 9, 2001.

78. Yang Dawen, "Guanyu Wanshan Hunyin Lifa."

79. Xia Zhen, "'Ganqing polie' Zhuowei Panjue Lihun de Liyou Burong Zhiyi" ['Breakdown of Emotion' as Reason for Court's Decision Allows of No Doubts], in Li and Ma, eds., *Hunyin*, 162–67.

80. Li Zhongfang, "Jianchi Lihun Liyou de 'Ganqing Shou'" [Adhere to the 'Emotion Test' as a Reason for Divorce] in Li and Ma, eds., *Hunyin*, 168–71. Indeed, a survey conducted of 4,000 adults of both genders by the ACWF found that more than 73 percent wished to retain the "breakdown of emotion" standard. Cited in Feng Xiaoqing, "A Review of the Development of Marriage Law in the People's Republic of China," *University of Detroit Mercy Law Review* 79 (Spring 2002): 331–98.

81. In fairness, it should be noted, however, that other observers expressed the view that some women were putting off possible divorces, "waiting for the formal promulgation of the Draft Revision of the Marriage Law with an eye to getting more compensation." Lu Pipi, "New Marriage Law Sparks Concern," *Beijing Review*, Mar. 2001.

82. Xia, "'Ganqing Polie.'"

83. In the NPC's legislative plan, laws placed in the first tier are definitely to be taken up whereas those placed in the second tier will be, if time permits.

84. We use the term Party-State advisedly, recognizing that in today's China, the two are not as fully synonymous as was the case in earlier years and that, indeed, even the party itself now should not be understood as a monolith, at least prior to the formation of a party line (as the very debates that are the subject of this chapter illustrate). Nonetheless, to ignore, as many American scholars are wont to, the hovering omnipresence of the party in major state decisions, manifested in part through the *nomenkla-tura* system that limits candidates for important official positions to persons in the party or blessed by it, seems wishful at best.

85. There is, of course, something quite patronizing in the assumption that women are to voice their concerns chiefly through the All China

Women's Federation, given the great impact on women's lives and society more broadly of economic, political, and other matters that might not be seen as "women's issues" (and so, are the responsibility of agencies not likely to be especially responsive to the Federation). It should be noted that opinion as to the issues addressed in this chapter was not necessarily uniform across the different levels of the Federation (particularly prior to the articulation of the Federation's final official position).

86. For a further discussion of the PRC legislative process, see William P. Alford and Benjamin L. Liebman, "Clean Air, Clear Processes? The Struggle Over Air Pollution Law in the People's Republic of China," *Hastings Law Journal* 52 (2001): 703–48.

87. Peng Peiyun's previous positions included heading up China's family planning authority.

88. Given that the National People's Congress convenes in plenary session only once a year, for approximately two weeks, the principal body for the promulgation of new legislation is the NPC's Standing Committee. Comprising approximately 160 members, the Standing Committee meets regularly throughout the year.

89. Xinhua [New China News Agency], "Li Peng Chairs NPC Discussion of Marriage Law Amendments," Dec. 25, 2000.

90. It is interesting that the NPC leadership decided against having the NPC plenary session approve a new Marriage Law and instead had the Standing Committee incorporate the changes ultimately made in the 1980 Marriage Law in a decision [*jueding*] amending the earlier Law. The PRC's Constitution specifies that "basic" laws are to be promulgated by the full NPC, even as it authorizes the Standing Committee to issue and amend laws (with the distinction between basic and other laws not being spelled out in the Constitution, but presumably having to do with the former being laws of fundamental importance). Some prior amendments of basic laws, such as the criminal and criminal procedure laws, were promulgated by the NPC's plenary session. The decision to route the Marriage Law revisions through the Standing Committee, rather than treat it as a new law, may have been intended as a way of suggesting that although some 33 changes were made, the fundamental character of the earlier Law has been retained.

91. Some during the Standing Committee's debates expressed the view that treating anything short of officially registered second marriages as constituting bigamy might run into particular difficulties in minority areas, some of which were marked by a high prevalence of unregistered "common law" marriages and less of a commitment to monogamy.

92. Indeed, few key terms in this Law are defined, whether because of the political difficulty of reaching agreement on their meaning, a desire to allow those applying the law more room for local variation, a concern about keeping the law simple and therefore accessible to the masses, or the quality of the drafting process. See note 99 below.

93. The revised Marriage Law at Article 45 does authorize victims to

commence private prosecutions and the procuracy to initiate public prosecutions against persons committing the "crimes of bigamy, domestic violence [which, as indicated at . . . is not specifically identified as a crime in the criminal law] or family maltreatment, and abandonment of family members." It should be noted that although there was broader agreement regarding domestic violence than the standard for divorce, here, too, some divergence was expressed concerning, for example, such issues as whether provisions regarding such abuse were better suited to the criminal law, as opposed to the marriage law, and whether it should encompass marital rape.

94. Article 39.

95. Article 40.

96. See Articles 37, 39, 40, 41, 42, and 46.

97. The four incorporated in the Law are bigamy and cohabitation; domestic violence or maltreatment, leading to abandonment; incorrigible "bad habits" such as gambling and the taking of drugs; and a two-year separation because of marital disharmony. This list is also appreciably shorter than those in the "experts'" draft of a revised law and in the January 2001 draft law circulated by the Standing Committee—each of which included adultery.

98. Wu, "Revision of the Marriage Law."

99. Xinhua [New China News Agency], "Li Peng Chairs NPC's Session on Draft Civil Code," Dec. 23, 2002.

100. On December 25, 2001, the Supreme People's Court issued its first interpretation of the revised Marriage Law. That interpretation, *inter alia*, provides further definition of terms such as domestic violence and cohabitation (which it indicates is not to be equated with bigamy), specifies that Article 46 is intended to make possible compensation for both material and emotional harm, and offers further detail as to the registration of marriages. *Guanyu Shiyong Zhonghua Renmin Gongheguo Hunyingfa Ruogan Wenti de Jieshi* [An Interpretation of Certain Questions with Respect to the Application of the Marriage Law of the People's Republic of China]. Posted at the chinalawinfo.com/new law. Dec. 27, 2001.

101. In China, the publicity accorded a case often can be quite revealing, at least as to points that the authorities would like to see emphasized. This holds true for official publications, such as the Gazette of the Supreme People's Court which may publish lower level cases it thinks might provide useful models or underscore messages that the political authorities wish to accentuate. It was even the case for the popular media which, though freer than twenty years ago, both continue to receive guidance as to acceptable areas of coverage and may be rebuked for going too far (as was the *Nanfang Zhoumo*, a number of key staffers of which were recently discharged for this very reason).

102. The parrot purportedly mimicked the husband's warm words to his lover—and did so with a good Sichuan accent to boot. Gethin Chamberlain, "Who's Not a Clever Boy Then," *Scottish Daily Record*, June 21, 2001.

103. In making this point, we are aware of the arguments of Richard Epstein and others who contend that the market may offer better solutions to problems of employment discrimination than state action. Richard A. Epstein, *Simple Rules for a Complex World* (Cambridge, MA, 1995). This has yet to occur in China, whether because of the distorting impact of corporatism on the Chinese market or limitations in the argument more generally.

104. These arguments are considered in Alford, "The More Laws, the More"; and William P. Alford, "Of Lawyers Lost and Found: Searching for Legal Professionalism in the People's Republic of China," *East Asian Law and Development: Universal Norms and Local Culture*, Arthur Rosett et al., eds. (London, 2002).

105. The state's general emphasis on formal processes did not, however, carry over to the newly addressed area of domestic violence with respect to which the amended Law pushes persons believing themselves victimized first to utilize relevant neighborhood, village, or workplace committees before invoking public protection. Notwithstanding the limitations in official processes pointed out in this chapter, the distancing of women from the police does not seem advantageous from the view point of cutting down domestic violence.

106. The frequency of counsel in different kinds of cases is recorded in judicial administration year books. Such data is discussed in William P. Alford, "Lawyers in China" (unpub. ms., 1998).

107. In fairness, part of the appeal of this argument lies in the extent to which Chinese life was previously politicized. See Alford, "The More Laws."

108. Xiao Ming, "Should the Law Punish Extramarital Love," *Forum on Women*, Jan. 2001 (quoting Ding Lu of the All China Women's Federation).

109. For an excellent study of the role that women may yet have to play in political and societal transformation in China, see Robert P. Weller, *Alternative Civilities: Democracy and Culture in China and Taiwan* (Boulder, CO, 1999).

110. Looked at positively, the assignment of this responsibility to the Federation may yet help it adapt itself to these new circumstances.

111. For instance, approximately one half of the Standing Committee's members are said to represent particular parts of the country while the remainder have an interest group constituency-based portfolio; but all were, essentially, appointed centrally and the large majority (60 to 80 percent by some counts) are said to reside permanently in Beijing. Alford and Liebman, "Clean Air," 742.

112. This echoes the more general, yawning divide between prosperous urban regions and the Chinese interior discussed by scholars such as Wang Shaoguang. See, for example, Wang Shaoguang, "Openness and Inequality: Can China Compensate the Losers of its WTO Deal" (unpublished paper, August 2001).

113. Nancy Cott, *Public Vows: A History of Marriage and the Nation* (Cambridge, 2002).

114. Michael Sandel, *Democracy's Discontents: America's Search for a Public Philosophy* (Cambridge, 1996).

115. Martha Minow, "Forming Underneath Everything That Grows: Toward a History of Family Law," *Wisconsin Law Review* 1985, 4: 819–98.

## CHAPTER 10

1. See John P. Burns, "The People's Republic at 50: National Political Reform," in *The China Quarterly* 159 (Sept. 1999): 580–94; Murray Scot Tanner, "The National People's Congress," in Merle Goldman and Roderick MacFarquhar, eds., *The Paradox of China's Post-Mao Reforms* (Cambridge, MA, 1999), 100–128; and Murray Scot Tanner, "The Erosion of Communist Party Control over Lawmaking in China," *China Quarterly* 138 (June 1994): 381–403.

2. See Minxin Pei, "Citizens v. Mandarins: Administrative Litigation in China," *China Quarterly* 152 (Dec. 1997): 832–62; Pittman Potter, "The Chinese Legal System: Continuing Commitment to the Primacy of State Power," *China Quarterly* 159: 673–83; and Stanley Lubman, *Bird in a Cage: Legal Reform in China after Mao* (Stanford, 1999).

3. See Tianjian Shi, *Political Participation in Beijing* (Cambridge, MA, 1997); also see his more recent "Mass Political Behavior in Beijing," in Goldman and MacFarquhar, eds., *The Paradox of Post-Mao Reforms*, 145–69.

4. For the Mao period see Jean Oi, *State and Peasant in Contemporary China: The Political Economy of Village Government* (Berkeley, 1989), esp. chaps 6 and 7.

5. See Li Lianjiang and Kevin O'Brien, "Villagers and Popular Resistance in Contemporary China," *Modern China* 22, no. 1 (1996): 28–61; Kevin O'Brien and Li Lianjiang, "The Politics of Lodging Complaints in Rural China," *China Quarterly* 143 (Sept. 1995): 756–83; and Kevin O'Brien, "Rightful Resistance," *World Politics* 49, no. 1 (Oct. 1996): 31–55.

6. David Zweig, "The 'Externalities of Development': Can New Political Institutions Manage Rural Conflict?" in Elizabeth J. Perry and Mark Selden, eds., *Chinese Society: Change, Conflict, and Resistance* (London, 2000), 127.

7. See Thomas Bernstein, "Instability in Rural China," in David Shambaugh, ed., *Is China Unstable? Assessing the Factors* (Washington, DC, 1998); and Thomas Bernstein and Xiaobo Lu, *Taxation without Representation in Contemporary Rural China* (Cambridge, 2003.)

8. Bernstein, "Instability in Rural China," 98.

9. Ibid.

10. See Andrew Walder, *Communist Neo-Traditionalism: Work and Authority in Chinese Industry* (Berkeley, 1986).

11. Not all of these are new. Urban residents always could complain to officials in government bureaus, and there were strikes even during the Maoist period. See Ching Kwan Lee for a study of changes in worker political action over time, "Pathways of Labor Insurgency," in Perry and Selden, eds., *Chinese Society*, 41–60.

12. See Cai Yongshun, "The Silence of the Dislocated: Chinese Laid-off Employees in the Reform Period" (Ph.D. disser., Stanford Univ., 2001); also see Dorothy J. Solinger, "The Potential for Urban Unrest: Will the Fencers Stay on the Piste?," in Shambaugh, ed., *Is China Unstable?* 79–91; and Ching Kwan Lee, "Pathways of Labor Insurgency."

13. See, for example, Walder, *Communist Neo-Traditionalism: Work and Authority in Chinese Industry*.

14. Reported in Yongshu Cai, "The Resistance of Chinese Laid-Off Workers in the Reform Period," *China Quarterly* 170 (June 2000): 327–44.

15. *Datoushi* [A Comprehensive Perspective] (Beijing, 1998), cited in Cai, "Resistance of Laid-Off Workers."

16. Solinger, "The Potential for Urban Unrest."

17. Lee, "Pathways of Labor Insurgency."

18. Cai, "Resistance of Laid-Off Workers."

19. Solinger, "The Potential for Urban Unrest."

20. This occurred in Sichuan. See Cai, "Resistance of Laid-Off Workers."

21. See, for example, volumes such as David Shambaugh, ed., *Is China Unstable?* (Armonk, NY, 2000).

22. See Jean Oi, *Rural China Takes Off: Institutional Foundations of Economic Reform* (Berkeley, 1999).

23. See Yongshun Cai, "Between State and Peasant: Local Cadres and Statistical Reporting in Rural China," *China Quarterly* 163 (Sept. 2000): 783–805.

24. See Oi, *State and Peasant in Contemporary China*.

25. For further details on these problems see Jean Oi, "Two Decades of Rural Reform in China: An Overview and Assessment," *China Quarterly* 159: 616–28.

26. One and a half million retired workers failed to receive their pensions in 1997. On pensioners, see William Hurst and Kevin J. O'Brien, "China's Contentious Pensioners," paper presented at the Annual Meeting of the American Political Science Association, Aug. 30-Sept. 2, 2001, San Francisco, CA.

27. See Cai, "The Silence of the Dislocated."

28. This point is developed in ibid.

29. See Oi, *State and Peasant*.

30. There usually were not sufficient numbers of party members in a team to form a party branch.

31. For an elaboration and documentation of this system see Oi, *State and Peasant*.

32. For a discussion of team leaders as gatekeepers of their team members' economic as well as political well being see ibid.

33. The village head is officially called the chairman of the village committee.

34. The situation is dramatically different in the rich, industrialized villages where cadres still control numerous resources on which peasants depend. See Oi, *Rural China Takes Off*.

35. See Li and O'Brien, "Villagers and Popular Resistance in Contemporary China."

36. See Shaoguang Wang, "The Rise of the Regions: Fiscal Reform and the Decline of Central-State Capacity in China," in Andrew G. Walder, ed., *The Waning of the Communist State: Economic Origins of Political Decline in China and Hungary* (Berkeley, 1995), 87–113.

37. See Bernstein, "Instability in Rural China."

38. A recent report stated that in Shenyang where there are many laid-off workers, demonstrations have become so common that city authorities announce their locations in advance to prevent traffic congestion. See "Old-Line Communists at Odds With Party in China," *New York Times*, July 2, 2000, 3.

39. Thomas Bernstein, "Financial Burdens, State Capacity, Rural Instability and Village Elections," unpub. ms., 1999.

40. This *feigaishui* system was to be put into effect in 2001, but it was then put on hold because of problems it would cause in the shortfall in revenues in many rural areas. It is now being tried in a portion of the provinces.

41. The degree to which elected officials wield effective power varies significantly. See Jean C. Oi and Scott Rozelle, "Elections and Power: The Locus of Decision-Making in Chinese Villages," *China Quarterly* 162 (June 2000): 513–39.

42. I elaborate this argument in "Economic Development, Stability and Democratic Self-governance," in Maurice Brousseau et al., eds., *China Review 1996* (Hong Kong, 1997), 125–44.

43. See Oi and Rozelle, "Elections and Power."

44. Lianjiang Li, "The Two-Ballot System in Shanxi Province: Subjecting Village Party Secretaries to a Popular Vote," *China Journal* 42 (July 1999): 103–18.

45. But there have been reports that such elections are illegal and banned. Ministry of Civil Affairs officials say that the experiments with township elections continue, but remain low key and are not allowed to be publicized.

46. See O'Brien and Li, "The Politics of Lodging Complaints in Rural China."

47. Li Qiuxue, "Cunmin shangfang yu cunweihui xuanju" [Villager petitions to the upper levels and village elections], unpub. paper presented at Zhongguo nongcun cunmin weiyuanhui xuanju xueshu yanjiuhui, Wuhan, Oct. 14–16, 2000.

48. See Merle Goldman, "Politically-engaged Intellectuals in the 1990s," *China Quarterly* 159: 700–11.

49. See Cai, "The Silence of the Dislocated."

50. See Dorothy Solinger, *Contesting Citizenship in Urban China: Peasant Migrants, the State, and the Logic of the Market* (Berkeley, 1999).

51. See, for example, Joan M. Nelson, *Access to Power: Politics and the Urban Poor in Developing Nations* (Princeton, NJ, 1979).

52. Some work suggests that substantial amounts of money are being sent home. Elisabeth J. Croll and Huang Ping, "Migration For and Against Agriculture in Eight Chinese Villages," *China Quarterly* 149 (Mar. 1997): 128–46. Also Yuen-Fong Woon, "Labor Migration in the 1990s," *Modern China* 25, no. 4 (July 2000): 475–512.

53. See Oi, "Two Decades of Rural Reform: An Overview and Assessment."

54. See Zweig, "The 'Externalities of Development.'"

CHAPTER 11

1. Alexis de Tocqueville, *Democracy in America* (New York, 1945), 314–15.

2. One study, for example, uses such data to show that, of 43 countries studied, Chinese are least likely to rank religion very important in their lives, least likely to express belief in God, and least likely to consider religious faith important to teach children. Ronald Inglehart et al., *Human Values and Beliefs: A Cross-Cultural Sourcebook* (Ann Arbor, MI, 1998), 5-9, 5-175, 5-234.

3. See Adam B. Seligman, *The Idea of Civil Society* (New York, 1992). On China, see Robert P. Weller, *Alternate Civilities: Democracy and Culture in China and Taiwan* (Boulder, CO, 1999).

4. For examples, see Robert W. Hefner, "A Muslim Civil Society? Indonesian Reflections on the Conditions of Its Possibility," in Robert W. Hefner, ed., *Democratic Civility: The History and Cross-Cultural Possibility of a Modern Ideal* (New Brunswick, NJ, 1998), 285–321; Charles Lindholm, "Justice and Tyranny: Law and the State in the Middle East," *Journal of the Royal Asiatic Society* ser. 3, 9 (1999): 375–88; A. Richard Norton, ed., *Civil Society in the Middle East* (Leiden, 1995); Jenny B. White, "Civic Culture and Islam in Urban Turkey," in Chris Hann and Elizabeth Dunn, eds., *Civil Society: Challenging Western Notions* (London, 1996), 143–54.

5. The issue first struck me when I was interviewing an old woman in rural Taiwan. I asked about her religion [Hokkien dialect *congkao*] and was met with a blank stare—she did not know the term. After some explanation, she announced that she had no religion, she just offered incense [Hokkien *gian hiu*] every day.

6. Talal Asad, *Genealogies of Religion: Discipline and Reasons of Power in Christianity and Islam* (Baltimore, 1993), 40–43.

7. One could argue for the more genteel *li* instead of *bai*. *Li* is a better Confucian term, but like *bai*, includes a wide range of sacred and secular

ritualized behavior—good manners, diplomacy, sacrifices at state cult altars, and so on.

8. The rapid increase in local worship across many (but not all) parts of China is another side to the increased realms of freedom discussed in chapter 10 in this volume.

9. See James L. Watson, "Standardizing the Gods: The Promotion of T'ien Hou ('Empress of Heaven') Along the South China Coast, 960–1960," in David Johnson et al., eds., *Popular Culture in Late Imperial China* (Berkeley, 1985), 292–324; Prasenjit Duara, "Superscribing Symbols: The Myth of Guandi, Chinese God of War," *Journal of Asian Studies* 47 (1988): 778–95.

10. See, for example, Valerie Hansen, *Changing Gods in Medieval China, 1127–1276* (Princeton, NJ, 1990).

11. Robert Hymes, *Way and Byway: Taoism, Local Religion, and Models of Divinity in Sung and Modern China* (Berkeley, 2002).

12. Watson, "Standardizing the Gods."

13. E.g. Susan McEwen, "Markets, Modernization, and Individualism in Three Chinese Societies" (Ph.D. disser., Boston Univ., 1994); Gary G. Hamilton, "Culture and Organization in Taiwan's Market Economy," in Robert W. Hefner, ed., *Market Cultures: Society and Morality in the New Asian Capitalisms* (Boulder, CO, 1998), 41–77.

14. Hugh D. R. Baker, "The Five Great Clans of the New Territories," *Journal of the Hong Kong Branch of the Royal Asiatic Society* 6 (1966): 38–39.

15. Very little of this kind of event has returned in the People's Republic so far, but temples have resisted the government to put on their own rituals. There is a well-documented example in Kenneth Dean, *Taoist Ritual and Popular Cults of Southeast China* (Princeton, NJ, 1993), 103–14.

16. This information is based on interviews conducted near the site, August 1993.

17. This summary is based on newspaper reports for the period, interviews with some local residents, and interviews with Cai Chaopeng and Liu Yongling, two of the top leaders of the protest, in July 1992.

18. Paul R. Katz, "Local Elites and Sacred Sites in Hsin-Chuang: The Growth of the Ti-Tsang An During the Japanese Occupation," paper presented at the Third International Conference on Sinology (Taipei, June 29–July 1, 2000), 31.

19. Max Weber, "The Protestant Sects and the Spirit of Capitalism," in H. H. Gerth and C. Wright Mills, eds., *From Max Weber: Essays in Sociology* (New York, 1946), 302–22.

20. Christianity may account for as much as 4 to 5 percent of the population in China, as it does in Taiwan. The large numbers of underground Christians in China, however, make a good estimate impossible. The pietistic sects are also widespread in China, but almost entirely underground. In Taiwan, where they have been legalized, the largest sect claims about a

million adherents. These groups tend to focus on spirit-writing sessions and often highlight Maitreya (the Buddha of the next age) and a goddess called the Eternal Venerable Mother [Wusheng Laomu]. The new Buddhists are based in Taiwan, with many followers in overseas Chinese communities but not in China.

21. See Hwei-syin Lu, "Women's Self-Growth Groups and Empowerment of the 'Uterine Family' in Taiwan," *Bulletin of the Institute of Ethnology, Academia Sinica* 71 (1991): 29–62; Hwei-syin Lu, "Taiwan Fuojiao 'Ciji Gongdehui' de Daode Yiyi [The Moral Significance of Taiwan Buddhist 'Ciji Merit Association']," paper presented at the International Conference on Chinese Buddhist Thought and Culture, Shanxi University, July 12–18, 1992; Chien-yu Julia Huang and Robert P. Weller, "Merit and Mothering: Women and Social Welfare in Taiwanese Buddhism," *Journal of Asian Studies* 57 (1998): 379–96; Wei'an Zhang, "Fuojiao Ciji Gongde Hui Yu Ziyuan Huishou [The Buddhist Compassion Merit Society and Recycling]," paper presented at the Workshop on Culture, Media and Society in Contemporary Taiwan, Harvard Univ., June 12, 1996.

22. For more detail on Yinshun, see Charles Brewer Jones, *Buddhism in Taiwan: Religion and the State, 1660–1990* (Honolulu, 1999).

23. For an expansion of this argument, see Huang and Weller, "Merit and Mothering."

24. See Hwei-Syin Lu, "Gender and Buddhism in Contemporary Taiwan: A Case Study of Tzu Chi Foundation," *Proceedings of the National Science Council, ROC (C)* 8, no. 4 (Oct. 1998): 539–50; Huang and Weller, "Merit and Mothering."

25. For a good example of the process in Latin America, see David Martin, *Tongues of Fire: The Explosion of Protestantism in Latin America* (Oxford, 1990).

26. See Nancy Chen, "Urban Spaces and Experiences of *Qigong*," in Deborah Davis, ed., *Urban Spaces: Autonomy and Community in Post-Mao China* (New York, 1995); Robert P. Weller, *Resistance, Chaos and Control in China: Taiping Rebels, Taiwanese Ghosts and Tiananmen* (London, 1994), 16–17.

27. For more on qigong deviation, see Nancy N. Chen, "Deviation and the State: Psychiatry and Popular Practice in Contemporary Urban China," paper presented at the Association for Asian Studies annual meeting, Washington, D.C., Apr. 3, 1992.

28. Numbers, as usual with this group, are impossible to estimate. Li Jiansheng, an anthropologist who worked in Tianjin (an important Falun Gong center), estimated that about a third of the followers in one neighborhood there fell into this category (personal communication).

29. See David K. Jordan and Daniel L. Overmyer, *The Flying Phoenix: Aspects of Chinese Sectarianism in Taiwan* (Princeton, NJ, 1986). Christian missions are also often initially successful with marginalized groups.

30. It was also an image that the state systematically undercut with special privileges for cadres.

31. Geomancy has also been increasing in the PRC over the past two decades. See Ole Bruun, "The *Fengshui* Resurgence in China: Conflicting Cosmologies Between State and Peasantry," *China Journal* 36 (1996): 47–65.

32. This is according to followers interviewed after they had emigrated.

33. Compassion Relief has self-consciously been rationalizing its organization for about a decade. See Chien-yu Julia Huang, "Recapturing Charisma: Emotion and Rationalization in a Globalizing Buddhist Movement from Taiwan" (Ph.D. disser., Boston Univ., 2001).

34. As a parallel, big businesses in Taiwan or Hong Kong were also not particularly active in the push for democratization. Small firms, which did not have the close governmental ties of the big firms, were far more active. See Alvin Y. So, "Hong Kong's Problematic Democratic Transition: Power Dependency or Business Hegemony?" *Journal of Asian Studies* 59 (2000): 359–81; Hsin-Huang Michael Hsiao, "Formation and Transformation of Taiwan's State-Business Relations: A Critical Analysis," *Bulletin of the Institute of Ethnology, Academia Sinica* 74 (1993): 1–31.

35. For the early Republican period, see Prasenjit Duara, "Knowledge and Power in the Discourse of Modernity: The Campaigns Against Popular Religion in Early Twentieth-Century China," *Journal of Asian Studies* 50 (1991): 67–83.

36. The only major exception was the movement to consolidate rotating rituals (like the annual ghost festival) onto a single day, which was largely successful.

37. I have had several county-level cadres in the PRC, for instance, pull me aside to explain that they are good Communists and educated men (and therefore not at all superstitious), but that they have had uncanny experiences with spirit mediums.

38. For more detail on these cases, see Robert P. Weller, *Unities and Diversities in Chinese Religion* (Seattle, WA, 1987).

39. Dean, *Taoist Ritual and Popular Cults of Southeast China.*

40. This case is documented in some detail in Mayfair Mei-hui Yang, "Spatial Struggles: State Disenchantment and Popular Re-Appropriation of Space in Rural Southeast China," paper presented at the Workshop on Civilizing Discourses and the Politics of Culture in Twentieth-Century China, Fairbank Center, Harvard University, May 12–13, 2001.

41. The most useful study in English on this is Jones, *Buddhism in Taiwan,* which is the source for much of the information in this paragraph.

42. See Edwin A. Winckler, "Cultural Policy on Postwar Taiwan," in Stevan Harrell and Chün-chieh Huang, eds., *Cultural Change in Postwar Taiwan* (Boulder, CO, 1994).

43. See Huang, "Recapturing Charisma," 157–62.

44. One group, the Cihui Tang, managed to register with the official Daoist association and operated more openly and on a larger scale than the others.

45. See Paul R. Katz, "Chicken-Beheading Rituals and Dispute Resolution in Taiwan During the Japanese Occupation," paper presented at the Association for Asian Studies annual meeting, San Diego, Mar. 11, 2000.

46. Elizabeth J. Perry, "'To Rebel Is Justified': Cultural Revolution Influences on Contemporary Chinese Protest," paper presented at the Program in Agrarian Studies, Yale University, Nov. 17, 1995.

47. The most important exception has been work done on Daoism and popular worship in Fujian. See, for instance, Dean, *Taoist Ritual and Popular Cults of Southeast China.*

48. For more detail on this, see Weller, *Alternate Civilities,* 84–100.

49. This is parallel to the imperial situation discussed in chapter 7 in this volume, in which distance from the state (through exile) opens up new ways to inscribe meaning, even as it allows the government to control difference.

50. See Jun Jing, "Female Autonomy and Female Shamans in Northwest China," paper presented at the annual meeting of the American Anthropological Association, Atlanta, 1994.

51. This is comparable to discussion in chapter 10 of how resistance will be tolerated on small scales in China today, but not if it grows larger.

52. Robert P. Weller, "Matricidal Magistrates and Gambling Gods: Weak States and Strong Spirits in China," *Australian Journal of Chinese Affairs* 33 (1995): 107–24.

53. This is comparable to the high level of economic freedom coupled with a lack of political freedom during the Qing Dynasty; see chap. 3.

≺ ≻

# Index

In this index an "f" after a number indicates a separate reference on the next page, and an "ff" indicates separate references on the next two pages. A continuous discussion over two or more pages is indicated by a span of page numbers, e.g., "57–59." *Passim* is used for a cluster of references in close but not consecutive sequence.